Fighting Terrorism and Drugs

This book breaks new empirical, theoretical, and methodological ground.

Empirically, it offers a unique compendium of international police cooperation in general, and the fight against terrorism and drugs in particular. The analytical focus is on the preferences of large European countries: Britain, France, Germany, and Italy. These countries are examined as members of the international system, and not only as EU Member States.

Theoretically, the book asks a crucial question. What makes large European countries willing to engage in international police cooperation, despite the fact that such cooperation erodes their monopoly of the legitimate use of force? The author finds that their governments are primarily driven by a belief that international policing will contribute to the solution of practical problems, while institutional factors and concerns with national sovereignty play a secondary role.

Methodologically, the book adopts the pragmatic research technique of abduction as a tool for mapping an entire policy field. It looks at international police cooperation from a truly international perspective, examining 48 case studies in a comparative mood and spanning a time period from the 1960s to the present day.

The book will be of interest to students and scholars of international relations, foreign policy analysis, historical political sociology, terrorism, criminology, international law, European integration, and research methodology.

Jörg Friedrichs is Lecturer in Politics at the University of Oxford, UK. He wrote this book as a Research Associate at International University Bremen, Germany, and as a Max Weber Fellow at the European University Institute in Florence, Italy.

Routledge Advances in International Relations and Global Politics

1 **Foreign Policy and Discourse Analysis**
France, Britain and Europe
Henrik Larsen

2 **Agency, Structure and International Politics**
From ontology to empirical enquiry
Gil Friedman and Harvey Starr

3 **The Political Economy of Regional Cooperation in the Middle East**
Ali Carkoğlu, Mine Eder and Kemal Kirişci

4 **Peace Maintenance**
The evolution of international political authority
Jarat Chopra

5 **International Relations and Historical Sociology**
Breaking down boundaries
Stephen Hobden

6 **Equivalence in Comparative Politics**
Edited by Jan W. van Deth

7 **The Politics of Central Banks**
Robert Elgie and Helen Thompson

8 **Politics and Globalisation**
Knowledge, ethics and agency
Martin Shaw

9 **History and International Relations**
Thomas W. Smith

10 **Idealism and Realism in International Relations**
Robert M. A. Crawford

11 **National and International Conflicts, 1945–1995**
New empirical and theoretical approaches
Frank Pfetsch and Christoph Rohloff

12 **Party Systems and Voter Alignments Revisited**
Edited by Lauri Karvonen and Stein Kuhnle

13 **Ethics, Justice and International Relations**
Constructing an international community
Peter Sutch

14 **Capturing Globalization**
Edited by James H Mittelman and Norani Othman

15 **Uncertain Europe**
Building a new European security order?
Edited by Martin A Smith and Graham Timmins

16 **Power, Postcolonialism and International Relations**
Reading race, gender and class
Edited by Geeta Chowdhry and Sheila Nair

17 **Constituting Human Rights**
Global civil society and the society of democratic states
Mervyn Frost

18 **US Economic Statecraft for Survival 1933–1991**
Of sanctions, embargoes and economic warfare
Alan P. Dobson

19 **The EU and NATO Enlargement**
Richard McAllister and Roland Dannreuther

20 **Spatializing International Politics**
Analysing activism on the internet
Jayne Rodgers

21 **Ethnonationalism in the Contemporary World**
Walker Connor and the study of Nationalism
Edited by Daniele Conversi

22 **Meaning and International Relations**
Edited by Peter Mandaville and Andrew Williams

23 **Political Loyalty and the Nation-State**
Edited by Michael Waller and Andrew Linklater

24 **Russian Foreign Policy and the CIS**
Theories, debates and actions
Nicole J. Jackson

25 **Asia and Europe**
Development and different dimensions of ASEM
Yeo Lay Hwee

26 **Global Instability and Strategic Crisis**
Neville Brown

27 **Africa in International Politics**
External involvement on the continent
Edited by Ian Taylor and Paul Williams

28 **Global Governmentality**
Governing international spaces
Edited by Wendy Larner and William Walters

29 **Political Learning and Citizenship Education Under Conflict**
The political socialization of Israeli and Palestinian youngsters
Orit Ichilov

30 **Gender and Civil Society**
Transcending boundaries
Edited by Jude Howell and Diane Mulligan

31 **State Crises, Globalisation and National Movements in North-East Africa**
The horn's dilemma
Edited by Asafa Jalata

32 **Diplomacy and Developing Nations**
Post-cold war foreign policy-making structures and processes
Edited by Justin Robertson and Maurice A. East

33 **Autonomy, Self-governance and Conflict Resolution**
Innovative approaches to institutional design in divided societies
Edited by Marc Weller and Stefan Wolff

34 **Mediating International Crises**
Jonathan Wilkenfeld, Kathleen J. Young, David M. Quinn and Victor Asal

35 **Postcolonial Politics, The Internet and Everyday Life**
Pacific traversals online
M. I. Franklin

36 **Reconstituting the Global Liberal Order**
Legitimacy and regulation
Kanishka Jayasuriya

37 **International Relations, Security and Jeremy Bentham**
Gunhild Hoogensen

38 **Interregionalism and International Relations**
Edited by Heiner Hänggi, Ralf Roloff and Jürgen Rüland

39 **The International Criminal Court**
A global civil society achievement
Marlies Glasius

40 **A Human Security Doctrine for Europe**
Project, principles, practicalities
Edited by Marlies Glasius and Mary Kaldor

41 **The History and Politics of UN Security Council Reform**
Dimitris Bourantonis

42 **Russia and NATO Since 1991**
From cold war through cold peace to partnership?
Martin A. Smith

43 **The Politics of Protection**
Sites of insecurity and political agency
Edited by Jef Huysmans, Andrew Dobson and Raia Prokhovnik

44 **International Relations in Europe**
Traditions, perspectives and destinations
Edited by Knud Erik Jørgensen and Tonny Brems Knudsen

45 **The Empire of Security and the Safety of the People**
Edited by William Bain

46 **Globalization and Religious Nationalism in India**
The search for ontological security
Catrina Kinnvall

47 **Culture and International Relations**
Narratives, natives and tourists
Julie Reeves

48 **Global Civil Society**
Contested futures
Edited by Gideon Baker and David Chandler

49 **Rethinking Ethical Foreign Policy**
Pitfalls, possibilities and paradoxes
Edited by David Chandler and Volker Heins

50 **International Cooperation and Arctic Governance**
Regime effectiveness and Northern region building
Edited by Olav Schram Stokke and Geir Hønneland

51 **Human Security**
Concepts and implications
Shahrbanou Tadjbakhsh and Anuradha Chenoy

52 **International Relations and Security in the Digital Age**
Edited by Johan Eriksson and Giampiero Giacomello

53 **State-Building**
Theory and practice
Edited by Aidan Hehir and Neil Robinson

54 **Violence and Non-Violence in Africa**
Edited by Pal Ahluwalia, Louise Bethlehem and Ruth Ginio

55 **Developing Countries and Global Trade Negotiations**
Edited by Larry Crump and S. Javed Maswood

56 **Civil Society, Religion and Global Governance**
Paradigms of power and persuasion
Edited by Helen James

57 **War, Peace and Hegemony in a Globalized World**
The changing balance of power in the 21st century
Edited by Chandra Chari

58 **Economic Globalisation as Religious War**
Tragic convergence
Michael McKinley

59 **Globalization, Prostitution and Sex-trafficking**
Corporeal politics
Elina Penttinen

60 **Peacebuilding**
Women in international perspective
Elisabeth Porter

61 **Ethics, Liberalism and Realism in International Relations**
Mark D. Gismondi

62 **Law and Legalization in Transnational Relations**
Edited by Christian Brütsch and Dirk Lehmkuhl

63 **Fighting Terrorism and Drugs**
Europe and international police cooperation
Jörg Friedrichs

Fighting Terrorism and Drugs

Europe and international police cooperation

Jörg Friedrichs

Routledge
Taylor & Francis Group
LONDON AND NEW YORK

First published 2008
by Routledge
2 Park Square, Milton Park, Abingdon, Oxon OX14 4RN

Simultaneously published in the USA and Canada
by Routledge
270 Madison Ave, New York, NY 10016

Routledge is an imprint of the Taylor & Francis Group, an informa business

Transferred to Digital Printing 2009

Typeset in Garamond by
Newgen Imaging Systems (P) Ltd, Chennai, India

British Library Cataloguing in Publication Data
A catalogue record for this book is available from the British Library

Library of Congress Cataloging in Publication Data
A catalog record for this book has been requested

ISBN10: 0-415-40892-X (hbk)
ISBN10: 0-415-54351-7 (pbk)
ISBN10: 0-203-93456-3 (ebk)

ISBN13: 978-0-415-40892-9 (hbk)
ISBN13: 978-0-415-54351-4 (pbk)
ISBN13: 978-0-203-93456-2 (ebk)

Look at the wood, look at the trees, and then do it all over.

Confucius (attributed)

Contents

Illustrations

Figures

Tables

Boxes

Preface

This book tries to break new empirical, theoretical, and methodological ground. Empirically, it offers a unique compendium of international police cooperation in general, and the fight against terrorism and drugs in particular, spanning a time period from the 1960s to the present day. The analytical focus is on British, French, German, and Italian state preferences. Theoretically, it asks a crucial question. What makes these large European countries willing to engage in international police cooperation, despite the fact that such cooperation may erode their monopoly of the legitimate use of force? As sources of state preferences, it considers interests, institutions, and ideas from the domestic, national, or international level, which can influence state preferences either positively or negatively. Methodologically, the book adopts the pragmatic research technique of abduction as a tool for mapping an entire policy field.

While there is much theoretically informed research on how states meet or fail their political objectives given specific preferences, the nature and origin of these preferences is often neglected. My research objective is to understand and explain state preferences in the specific policy field of international police cooperation. Instead of trying to test an abstract theoretical template (deduction), or 'simply' gathering and processing all relevant facts (induction), my strategy is to start at an intermediate level and to clarify which patterns of similarity and difference can be detected in the policy field under examination (abduction).

The book is the offspring of a research project on *The Internationalization of the Monopoly of the Legitimate Use of Force*. The project was part of a collaborative research centre on *Transformations of the State*, and received generous funding from the German Research Foundation (*Deutsche Forschungsgemeinschaft*). Between January 2003 and August 2006, the project was based at International University Bremen, Germany. From September 2006 to August 2007, a Max Weber Fellowship at the European University Institute in Florence gave me enough leisure to finish the manuscript and monitor the editorial process.

I am grateful to the project director, Markus Jachtenfuchs, as well as to International University Bremen and the European University Institute in Florence for providing a supportive and prosperous research environment. Special thanks are due to the research students participating in the project. Eva

Herschinger collected material and contributed case studies on France, while Christiane Kasack and Holger Stritzel did the same for Germany. The case studies on Britain and Italy (and some on Germany) are my own.

To create a common pool of empirical data, we mainly relied on the critical analysis of official sources. These ranged from archival data for the 1960s/1970s to press releases for the 1990s/2000s. We sometimes also used parliamentary debates, journal articles, news agencies, memoirs, and a limited number of background interviews with diplomats and decision makers. The objective was to arrive, through a critical assessment of the best sources available, at an accurate description and explanation of European state preferences on international policing.

Every member of the team had full access to the common pool of empirical data, but examined these with a different research question in mind. Since ours was an intensely collaborative research project, with regular meetings and a constant exchange of ideas, and with unified sets of analytical criteria to secure inter-coder reliability, especially in the empirical chapters of this book, the contribution of other participants is hardly separable from my own.

Many friends and colleagues have illuminated my views on both theoretical and substantive issues: Heiner Busch, Simon Dalferth, Axel Domeyer, Rosalba Fratini, Cornelius Friesendorf, Noemi Gal-Or, Bibi van Ginkel, Friedrich Kratochwil, Martin Kraus, Xymena Kurowska, Peter Mayer, Thorsten Müller, John Occhipinti, Vittorio Emanuele Parsi, Ferruccio Pastore, Gianfranco Poggi, Berthold Rittberger, Ursula Schröder, Pascal Vennesson, Wolfgang Wagner, Moritz Weiß, Silke Weinlich, Bernhard Zangl, Daniel Ziblatt, and Michael Zürn.

Helpful stimuli on methodology came from Andrew Bennett, Klaus Boehnke, and Margrit Schreier. It was extremely useful to participate, in the final stage of the manuscript, in the 2007 Institute for Qualitative Research Methods at Arizona State University. Discussants and other participants at scientific conferences also provided most valuable comments. Among others, they include Jan Beyers, Tanja Börzel, Alessandro Colombo, James Davis, Gunther Hellmann, Daniel Lambach, Berthold Rittberger, Stephan Stetter, and Niels van Willigen. Thanks are also due to the *Leiden Journal of International Law* for the permission to reprint parts of Chapter 3.

The book has greatly benefited from a number of informal background conversations. Contacts were provided by Heiner Busch, Gerhard Flach, Ferruccio Pastore, Virgilio Ilari, and James Sheptycki. On their advice, more than a dozen practitioners were approached at a variety of state bureaucracies: the Presidency of the Council and the Ministries of the Interior and Foreign Affairs, Rome; the Federal Ministry of Foreign Affairs, Berlin; the Federal Criminal Police Office, Wiesbaden; the National Criminal Intelligence Service, London; and the European Monitoring Centre for Drugs and Drug Addiction, Lisbon. I am extremely grateful to all of my interlocutors for the interesting information and insights obtained, although I feel that for reasons of confidentiality it would be inappropriate to disclose their individual names.

Over the years, many student assistants have contributed to the project. Substantive contributions were made by Axel Domeyer, Jordan Mihov, Maria Popova, Raphael Muturi, Mariya Shisheva, and Dana Silvina Trif. Others provided logistic support: Katsiaryna Barschynskaya, Ben Dryden, Leif Goerigk, Adham Hudaykulov, Kirils Jegorovs, Sophia Ojha, and Simona Spassova. Particular thanks are due to Dimitar Stoilov who created the supporting website, and to David Barnes who patiently proofread the entire manuscript and excogitated the quote by pseudo-Confucius that has become the motto of this book.

Last but absolutely not least, I want to thank my family, both on my own and on my wife's side, for their support. I would like to extend this to some closer friends: Rahel and Konrad Feilchenfeldt, Rosalba Fratini, Martin Kraus, Maite Lopez Suero, and Stefan and Christel Rautenberg. If there is something like a zest for life shining through the pages of this book, then this is primarily due to my beloved wife Kerstin and our little son Lukas Valentin.

1 Introduction

International policing is often invoked as the inevitable answer to global threats such as terrorism and drug trafficking. To the extent that terrorists and drug traffickers operate beyond national borders, states need to cooperate internationally to suppress the phenomenon. From a problem-solving perspective, states can hardly be justified in refusing to cooperate at an international level against terrorism and drugs. In fact, if we accept that global threats must be fought collectively for the struggle to succeed, then the failure of a state to cooperate can only be attributed to a fatal lack of awareness, if not outright complicity with the criminals.

From a different perspective, international police cooperation poses a real challenge to states.[1] The reason is that it impinges on the territorial monopoly of the legitimate use of force, which in the tradition of Max Weber is considered to be the defining characteristic of modern statehood. If this is true, then states should be expected to watch jealously over their monopoly of force. Insofar as policing is the epitome of this monopoly, states should be unlikely to accept any binding commitment to international police cooperation. Accordingly, there should be close limits to the willingness of states to engage in international policing.

On the one hand, states are motivated by an interest in fighting global threats such as international terrorism and drug trafficking; on the other hand, they are constrained by an interest in maintaining national sovereignty and the monopoly of force. Apart from this dilemma, states are also torn by other countervailing incentives. While there is a wide array of institutions to facilitate international police cooperation, existing institutions such as Europol can also make it more difficult for states to promote international policing in more encompassing frameworks, such as Interpol. Even normative ideas can either motivate a state to cooperate, as for example when there is moral outrage after a terrorist attack; or they can act as obstacles, as for example when a state prefers a permissive attitude to the idea of 'zero tolerance' for drugs.

International policing is of clear empirical, theoretical, and normative relevance. The empirical relevance is obvious, especially with regard to the fight against global threats such as terrorism and drugs. Nevertheless, 'want' and 'can' do not automatically derive from 'ought'. International policing is an unlikely area for harmonious cooperation due to its direct relationship with sovereignty and the monopoly of force. The conditions under which international police cooperation can take place are therefore also of theoretical relevance. Furthermore there are also normative reasons for concern, given that the monopoly of force has served as the foundation of national and international order for centuries. It is problematic, to say the least, if states allow that monopoly to be eroded with no clear alternative.

In short, the analytical objective of this book is to shed light on 'who wants what, when, why' with regard to international policing. How far, under which circumstances, and for what reasons are states willing, or unwilling, to internationalize their monopoly of force?

The focus is on the preferences of four large Western European states: the United Kingdom, France, the Federal Republic of Germany, and Italy. These countries are interesting because they tend to prefer an international crime-fighting approach to the more militaristic approach of the United States (Katzenstein 2003; Andreas and Nadelmann 2006). While there is still no European Leviathan in the making, the internationalization of the monopoly of force is uniquely advanced in Europe. Nevertheless, European countries sometimes share the 'instinct' of other modern states to preserve their monopoly of force as much as possible.

One thing needs to be established right from the start. Britain, France, Germany, and Italy have been selected because they constitute an interesting sample of comparable countries, and not simply because they are Member States of the European Union. They seek cooperation in any geographical and institutional framework, from the United Nations to bilateral forms of cooperation, and from the OECD to the Council of Europe. The EU is only one of these geographical and institutional frameworks, although it is true that in recent times it has attained a privileged status. The four countries selected are not treated as EU Members, but as members of the international system. Despite the selection of European countries, this book is not an exercise in EU studies, but rather a contribution to international relations in general.

In the remainder of this chapter, let me introduce state preferences and international police cooperation as the core concepts of the study and provide some preliminary methodological considerations. The first section derives a conceptual understanding of state preferences from the theoretical literature. The next two sections place the notion of international policing in the wider perspective of historical political sociology. The second section expounds Max Weber's understanding of the monopoly of force and introduces the idea of a 'chain of coercion.' The third section provides a historical sketch of the evolution of the monopoly of force and characterizes international policing as potentially leading to a transformation of modern statehood. The fourth section, finally, contains reflections on abduction as a pragmatic research strategy and prepares for the concrete application of this methodology in Chapter 2, and throughout the book.

State preferences

According to the title of a famous book, politics is about *Who Gets What, When, How* (Lasswell 1936). As this oft-quoted slogan suggests, the essence of politics is strategic interaction in order to obtain distributive outcomes. After seventy years, the view of politics as 'who gets what, when, how' still appeals to many political scientists. According to this view, the analytical focus of political science must be on bargaining and implementation, while the political preferences of the actors involved can be taken as given.

Against this, one might reasonably argue that an answer to the question of 'who gets what, when, how', even where it is possible, hardly leaves us satisfied. Logically, it begs the prior question of 'who wants what, when, why'. If we stop taking preferences as given, we immediately realize how much difference it makes whether the actors involved in a political issue want one thing rather than another. In fact, the analysis of strategic interaction and its distributive outcomes hardly makes any sense without a previous understanding of the preferences of the actors involved.

For example, it is certainly an interesting question to ask who carries the day in the fight against terrorism and drugs: European states with their predilection for a crime-fighting approach, or the United States with their penchant for a 'war on drugs' and a 'war on terror'. Arguably, however, the question of why European states differ from the US in their approach to terrorism and drugs is as interesting as the question of who succeeds in shaping the concrete terms of international cooperation and their practical outcomes.

Both in the general case of international politics and in the particular case of international policing, it is important to understand what states want, why, and under what circumstances they want it, and what this entails for international cooperation. Only if we learn to understand national preference formation, can we ever hope to properly understand international politics and its distributive outcomes. This is not to say that outcomes can be directly deduced from preferences. International politics follows the logic of collective action, which almost necessarily implies paradoxical effects and unintended consequences. Nevertheless, national preferences are logically and chronologically prior to social interactions, and they are therefore a precondition for the understanding of the international political process.

In general, preferences can be understood as either exogenous or endogenous to social interaction. For an exogenous understanding, take as an example the following definition: 'When we speak of a person having a preference, we mean that the person can connect choices by a relationship that indicates that the person likes one alternative better than, or just as much as, another' (Bueno de Mesquita 2001: 241). It is understood that all alternatives are fully available, and the person can choose freely among them. Accordingly the preferences are understood as independent from, or exogenous to, social interaction.

Social constructivists prefer an endogenous understanding of preferences. From this perspective preferences are a function of social intercourse, and they must be expected to change as intercourse unfolds (Gerber and Jackson 1993). Actors are seen as defining and redefining their preferences in a social environment, presumably following the 'logic of appropriateness' rather than the 'logic of consequences'.[2] Together with the fluctuations of social intercourse, preferences are expected to fluctuate (Adler 1997; Checkel 1998).[3] They are therefore understood as being dependent upon, or endogenous to, social interaction.

In this book, I adopt a third possibility between these extremes: positional preferences. Let us assume that the preferences of an actor are determined by 'the way it orders the possible outcomes of an interaction' (Frieden 1999: 42).[4] This implies a ranking among the anticipated results of social or political intercourse (see Clark 1998).[5] The possible outcomes are not commodities among which the actor can choose freely, since they depend on the strategic behaviour of other players. Thus understood, preferences are not exogenous because they always imply social interaction. However, preferences are not entirely endogenous either because they are a function of *anticipated* (and not *ongoing*) interaction.

The exogenous understanding of preferences may be adequate for situations in experimental psychology or microeconomic modelling; the endogenous understanding may be adequate for constellations of identity politics and groupthink; however, it is positional preferences that are most adequate in political science. In a political situation, the preferences of an actor are almost always dependent on the choices that are effectively available in a strategic context. Actors anticipate the preferences, power, and strategic behaviour of their fellow actors, and this in turn influences them in the way they formulate their own preferences.

If we apply this to international politics, state preferences can be defined as 'an ordered and weighted set of values placed on future substantive outcomes, often termed "states of the world", that might result from international political interaction' (Moravcsik 1998: 24). Since state preferences are related to the anticipated outcomes of political interaction, they can be conceptualized by an analytical two-step. In the first step, states formulate their preferences; in the second step, they bargain over substantive outcomes (Legro 1996: 119).[6]

When talking about state preferences (or national preferences), I usually mean the preferences of the state as a corporate or collective actor. Of course the state is not monolithic, and it is an abstraction to attribute preferences to it as if it were an individual person. Nevertheless governments often *do* have the ability, just as people, to connect choices by a relationship that indicates that they like one potential outcome of social interaction better than another (Scharpf 1997: 54–8). At least for large and important states it is reasonable to assume that, more often than not, their ideas about foreign policy objectives are sufficiently clear to justify talking about state preferences.

Empirically, state preferences can be understood as government preferences to the extent that a government represents a country in a meaningful way. In international relations this condition is usually met, for example when governments send executive representatives to the negotiation table and closely supervise their bargaining moves.[7] This is particularly true in policy fields that are closely controlled by the executive branch of the state, such as military cooperation or international police cooperation.

The monopoly of force

There is a wide consensus that the monopoly of the legitimate use of force – henceforth 'the monopoly of force' – is *the* defining characteristic of modern statehood (Grimm 2003: 1044–5).[8] As one scholar has put it, 'the state's function is policing. States have a common interest in monopolizing coercion within their territories' (Thomson 1995: 226–7).

The German sociologist Max Weber, in his famous lecture Politics as a Profession, defines the state as a human association that successfully claims the monopoly of legitimate physical violence in a given territory. The modern territorial state, which is understood by Weber as only one among many possible devices for people to rule over people, claims to be the only legitimate source of the right to use force (Weber 1992 [1919]: 5–13).

In his posthumous oeuvre, *Economy and Society* and *Staatssoziologie*, Weber left additional clarifications to his understanding of the modern state (Weber 1968 [1922]: Ch.1 §17, Ch.9 §1–2; 1956: §3). Overall, he distinguished three defining characteristics of modern statehood. The first two are territoriality and public administration. The third and decisive one is the monopoly of force. Weber remarks that it is usually sufficient for a state to use physical violence as a last resort – that is, only when other means of disciplining have failed. Insofar as such latent force is generally perceived as legitimate, it is the monopoly of the physical use of force that makes the modern state so extremely powerful.

This is not to deny that people rule over people by means of many institutions other than the state. It is easy to see, however, that the modern state is distinct from any of these. A Mafia organization uses force in a given territory, but it is neither accepted as legitimate nor managed through public administration. Trade unions are territorially organized and managed through administration, but they are not entitled by law to use force. In traditional societies the housefather is sometimes authorized to use coercion, but he has no territory

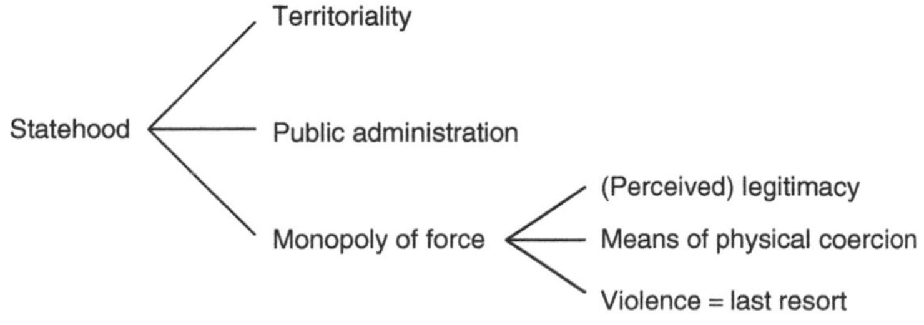

Figure 1.1 The monopoly of force according to Weber.

and does not manage his family through administration. Moreover, his right to use coercion is mostly residual insofar as it is located in a sphere that has been deliberately left unregulated by the law. The same can be said about the right of the citizens of some states to hold guns (Malcolm 2002).[9]

According to a Weberian (or ideal-typical) understanding of the monopoly of force, in the modern world only the state can exercise or delegate the legitimate 'right' to use force. This begs the question: what does it take for such an ideal-typical modern state to effectively control the monopoly of force? Let us recall that, according to Max Weber, the monopoly of force is the monopoly of the *legitimate* use of the *physical* means of coercion. To fully control the monopoly of force, it is not sufficient for a modern state to monopolize the physical means of coercion alone. A modern state and/or its citizens would also need to be in a position to define autonomously when the physical use of these resources is legitimate.

While this is certainly true, it begs another question. Even if there is a consensus that the use of force is legitimate in a particular case, it does not necessarily follow that any means to tackle the case is allowed. At least in the case of modern bureaucratic and constitutional states, there is no direct link from the legitimacy of force to its physical use. A modern state would also need to control the choice of the methods by which coercion shall be applied.

All this amounts to a 'chain of coercion' that reaches from the legitimization of force to the choice of appropriate methods, and from the choice of appropriate methods down to the physical use of force. Both in the field of military coercion and in the field of policing (see Figures 1.2 and 1.3), it is possible to draw such an ideal-typical chain with the actual use of force as the last resort.

In an abstract, ideal-typical world, the state is in a position to define, on normative grounds, the internal and external threats against which force shall be applied (discourse level). Furthermore, the state has the final word in determining what constitutes a legitimate and legal case for enforcement, whether by military means or by the police forces (legitimization level). Moreover, the state freely selects the methods, such as strategic bombing in the military field or torture in the field of policing, by which a legitimate case shall be translated into coercive action (methods level). The political trigger to send the military out, or the police in, is also entirely in the hands of that state (authorization level). Finally, the state tightly controls the actual operations of the soldiers and police forces on the ground (operational level). A state would need to control

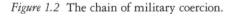

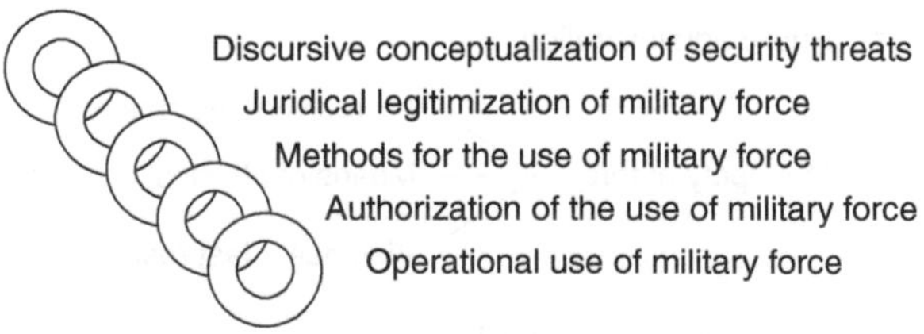

Figure 1.2 The chain of military coercion.

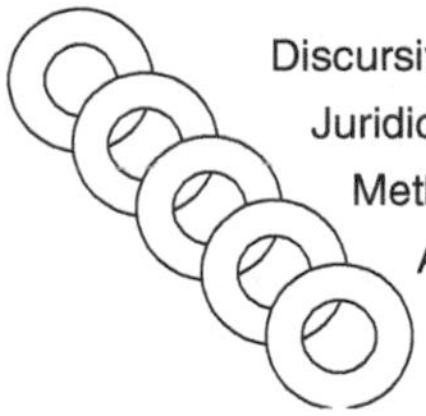

Figure 1.3 The chain of police coercion.

the entire chain of coercion, from top to bottom, in order to completely control the monopoly of the legitimate use of force.

Such a vision of total control sounds rather shocking, since an absolute monopoly of force would entail the ultimate institutionalization of power (Popiz 1992: 258–60). Fortunately for the citizen, the chain of coercion is 'only' a myth, or ideal type, which no state on earth has ever fully achieved.[10] For good or for ill, any move towards this ideal type is a step towards the further monopolization of force. Any step away from it, by contrast, should count as a step away from the monopoly of force, or towards the de-monopolization of force.

Historical trajectories

Although the monopoly of force and the chain of coercion are ideal conceptual types, they have concrete roots in history. To provide the necessary background, a digression on the formation and transformation of the monopoly of force is needed. The objective is to provide a rudimentary historical political sociology of this fundamental institution, sketching how the monopoly of force emerged from the middle ages to the early modern era; how it was split into a military branch of external security on the one hand, and a police branch of internal security on the other; how it evolved into its most mature form in the second half of the twentieth century; and whether and to what extent the world is today experiencing another transformation, namely an internationalization and/or privatization of the monopoly of force.[11]

Formation

Already before Max Weber, political philosophers had provided fictitious accounts of how the monopoly of force might have come about. To quote only the most famous of them: Thomas Hobbes postulated a contractual origin of the *Leviathan* whereby, to overcome the war of all against all and remove the fear of a violent death, the constituents endow their future king with the power to impose law and order by force (Hobbes 1998 [1651]).

Weber offers a historically more plausible account. He suggests that the monopoly of force is the product of functional necessities that imposed themselves upon primordial political units. To be successful in war-making, whether offensive or defensive, these units were compelled to concentrate the command, and at a later stage the control, of the means of coercion. While this in the short run improved their competitiveness in the power struggle with rival units, in the long run it necessarily led to the emergence of a coercive apparatus. Once in place, this coercive apparatus started to suppress the private use of violence. According to Weber this was also in the interest of economic stakeholders because the King's peace facilitated their commercial activities. Once the state monopoly of violent coercion had come to be considered legitimate by the subjects, and once there was a bureaucratic apparatus to administer the monopoly of force, the modern state was in place (Weber 1968 [1922]: Ch.9, §2).

Another dean of German sociology, Norbert Elias, developed a more elaborate and historically more accurate model of the monopolization process (2000 [1939]: 262–4, 268–77). The classic example is the centralization of political power in medieval and early modern France (ibid. pp. 277–362), but Elias goes so far as to say that the monopolization process operates like a 'clockwork' – every time, every place. Moreover, the model is said to apply not only to the monopolization of force but also to the monopolization of taxation, and to less important state monopolies such as the right to mint coinage. All state monopolies are seen as the result of a secular process of competitive selection and concentration.

These are clearly bold assertions, but there seems to be more than just a grain of truth in the idea of a 'King's mechanism'. To begin with, Elias uses a certain view of 'feudal anarchy' in the middle ages as a baseline for his own account. Before the beginning of the state-formation process, as it were, coercion tended to be used for whatever purpose a feudal lord deemed appropriate, and the distinction between the internal and the external, as well as the public and private use of violence was at best an intuitive one.

Between the ninth and the eleventh century, then, feudal lords started to decrease in number through an endless series of 'elimination contests'. This led to the emergence of consolidated territorial units ('states'), which continued the selection mechanism. During the process, larger and larger territorial units arose that ruled over more and more people, and accumulated increasingly large amounts of material resources under their control.[12]

However, there was a flipside to this concentration process. The more powerful the individual ruler became, the less he was able to control his territory and its population directly. The ruler became increasingly dependent upon an administrative apparatus, the members of which tended to become independent stakeholders in the game. At the end of the day, the ruler himself turned from the private 'owner' of 'his' state into its first civil servant.

In the next stage of the mechanism the governed themselves – first the bourgeoisie and later the unwashed masses – became involved in the exercise of rule. This helped to create what one may call the ethos of the civilized subject. From the beginning, the process of monopolization had created a mentality by which rule was increasingly experienced not only as inescapable but also as legitimate (Elias 2000 [1939]: 363–447). In the constitutional and democratic state, then, substantive parts of the population had learned to embrace the monopoly of force, as well as the monopoly of taxation, as a legitimate instrument of governance.

From medieval times to the nineteenth and twentieth century, there was a secular trend towards the monopolization of force in Europe. This entailed the centralization of force in the hands of territorial rulers and the dispossession of minor competitors. However, there was a paradoxical flipside to this trend. In parallel with the monopolization process, the need to administer a large territory led to a shift from the private administration of violence to the public management of coercion. Over time, the group of people with a stake in the political control of force was expanded to include first the bourgeoisie and later the wider citizenry.[13] To the extent that the legitimacy of force has come to be accepted by those subject to rule, physical violence is a last resort in the hands of those 'running' the state.

Differentiation

With the consolidation of territorial states, it became possible to distinguish the ideal of an internal 'zone of peace' where the private use of violence was illegitimate, from the dreadful reality of an external 'zone of war'. Between the sixteenth and the nineteenth century, this found its institutional expression in the functional and organizational differentiation between the military and the police. Initially, feudal henchmen made sure that order was preserved on their own soil. Later, Europe's rulers started to replace their feudal entourage with professional armies. Subsequently they discovered that, apart from extreme situations, the preservation of internal order follows a different logic from military warfare. In fact, a standing army is hardly adequate to deal with political adversaries or common criminals, let alone to crush civil unrest or to tackle generalized situations of lawlessness (Mann 1993: 403–12).

Although to a different degree, and despite different traditions related to differences in the state-building process, all European states started to introduce 'forces of order' as a complement to their military forces. This led to a functional distinction between the internal and external aspects of the monopoly of force (Knöbl 1998).[14] As a result, in the late-absolutist and early constitutional state of the nineteenth century two branches of the executive – the military and the police – were directly concerned with coercion (Poggi 1978: 108).[15]

The distinction between an internal 'zone of peace' and an external 'zone of war' had dramatic consequences for the use of violence by non-state actors. In the internal 'zone of peace', the use of force in private asymmetrical relationships was slowly de-legitimized. Most notably in the labour contract, the use of physical coercion started to become a taboo. To the extent that the modern state was recognized as the internal 'pacifier' and guardian of contractual 'freedom', an apparently non-violent capitalist market could emerge (Giddens 1985: 190–1; Rosenberg 1994; Teschke 2003). In the external 'zone of war', the indiscriminate use of violence was endemic and the elimination of non-state violence took much longer than in the internal 'zone of peace' (Thomson 1994). The emergence of the public/private dichotomy was thus intertwined with the emergence of the inside/outside dichotomy.

As a result of the process, the military and the police are the two organizational apparatuses that embody the external and internal aspects of the monopoly of force. Of course there are other bodies involved in the administration of force, such as customs authorities, secret services, or prison guards. Nevertheless, the military and the police are the only organizations dealing with the monopoly of force in general, and not only within a closely circumscribed area of competence. In metaphorical terms it is fair to say that the military represents the 'sword of the state', whereas the police are the 'arm of the law'.

If one applies Weber's criteria – perceived legitimacy of the monopoly of force and use of physical coercion as a last resort – then the democratic and constitutional welfare state of the second half of the twentieth century can justifiably be considered the culmination of modern statehood.[16] This is not to deny that there has been a dark side to the process. The history of the monopoly of force is a history of military conflict, which ultimately led to total warfare in the twentieth century. It is also the history of the 'policing state', which emerged in several waves and culminated in the regimes of Hitler and Stalin (Chapman 1970).

In the long-term view, however, and despite some grievous set-backs, the 'taming' of coercive power in the modern state is a secular achievement. This is not to deny that other social systems, such as education and the market, are also involved in disciplining the population. Nevertheless, it is fair to say that modern societies are internally pacified and only the state is specialized in last-resort control (Poggi 1990: 1–25). Moreover, the military and the police are under direct control of the public administration. In retrospect and to the later-born, the history of the monopoly of force is the history of the modern democratic and constitutional welfare state as crystallized in the second half of the twentieth century (Reinhard 2000).

Transformation

If we accept the Weberian understanding of the monopoly of force (see Figure 1.1) as a baseline against which to measure historical reality, there is a limited number of ways in which it can change. First, there can be a configurative change in the monopoly of force, namely through a loss of legitimacy and a concomitant need to move from last-resort control to the massive use of physical force. Second, the monopoly of force can become divorced from public administration. Commercial or societal actors can take over those functions which the state is not any longer able or willing to perform. Third, the monopoly of force can be de-coupled from territoriality. The locus of legitimate authority can move away from the state, namely towards the international or to the sub-state level.

Empirically, the first possibility is hardly observed.[17] At least as far as the OECD World is concerned, there is little evidence that the populations of

Western democracies are losing their belief that the state is legitimately entitled to use force.[18] The trend seems rather to point in the opposite direction. From the 1960s to the 1980s there was an anti-authoritarian contestation of the police monopoly of force, and in the military field there was a Cold-War pacifism challenging the right of the state to wage war. Both of these challenges receded over the 1990s and have largely been overcome in the 2000s. While civil libertarians and pacifists have gradually lost their grip over public opinion, the call for the military and the police forces to take a tough line against domestic and international threats is growing louder.[19]

The second possibility, too, is less warranted by empirical evidence than conventional wisdom would suggest. As far as the developing countries of the Third World are concerned, private violent actors have indeed become serious competitors to the state (Münkler 2005). In the developed world, by contrast, their activity remains strictly regulated by the law. While there are some tendencies in the direction of the privatization of force, one should be careful not to exaggerate these. This is despite the fact that, both in the military field and in the field of policing, there are private actors such as mercenary companies or private security providers (Coker 2001; Mandel 2002; Johnston and Shearing 2003; P.W. Singer 2003; Avant 2005; Wulf 2005; L. Johnston 2006).[20] These tendencies however are mostly concentrated at the lowest level of the chain of coercion. While they certainly do have repercussions at the methods level, the legitimization of force is hardly affected. However, it should be emphasized that this applies only to the OECD World. In the Third World, the privatization of force is much stronger.

The third possibility, that is, the internationalization of the monopoly of force, poses a more serious threat to the states of the OECD world. The main reason is that, while the privatization of force remains in the lower echelons of the chain of coercion, the internationalization of the monopoly of force trickles down from the legitimization level and has already affected all the other links in the chain, with the partial exception of the control of physical force at the operational level (Friedrichs 2006b). Within the OECD world, the internationalization of the monopoly of force seems to be most advanced in Europe. It seems to be less intense in Northern America, while in the Far East it is still in its infancy. In the Third World, states are mainly too weak to engage in sustained police cooperation.[21] Generally speaking, in the Global South the privatization of violence is more intense than the internationalization of force, while in the North it seems to be the other way round.

Given the institutional differentiation of the monopoly of force into a military and a police branch, there is a fourth possibility: a fusion of the two branches. After the 'war on drugs' in Latin America, and building on the Israeli experience in the fight against Palestinian insurgents, since 9/11 a similar tendency can be observed in the case of the US 'war against terrorism'. In the rest of the OECD world, however, states are generally careful to maintain the distinction between the military and the police. At the level of the European Union, this is reflected in the distinction between the second pillar of 'foreign and security policy' and 'security and defence policy' on the one hand, and the third pillar of 'justice and home affairs' and 'police and judicial cooperation' on the other. In certain countries of the Third World, there has never been a neat and systematic distinction between the military and the police.

The police and the military – as we have seen, these are the two organizations that embody the internal and the external aspects of the territorial monopoly of force. Potentially, international cooperation in either field can affect the very core of modern statehood. While there are already some pioneering studies on national preference formation in the military field (Moravcsik 1993b; Legro 1994; Knopf 1998; Finnemore 2003; Koenig-Archibugi 2004), the more neglected field of international police cooperation has been selected.[22] In short this study is concerned with the internationalization of the monopoly of force, but only insofar as the internal aspects of that monopoly are concerned.

Internationalization

At least in the developed world, the second part of the twentieth century was the 'golden age' of the monopoly of force (Jachtenfuchs 2005). The world was sliced up into formally independent states that were all, at least in theory, bureaucratically administered and, more or less successfully, claimed the monopoly of the legitimate use of force. The geopolitical environment of the Cold War did not allow for direct military conflict among the major powers, although wars by proxy took place under exceptional circumstances. Many states in the Third World were weak, but at least in theory they enjoyed sovereignty. Especially in the democratic welfare states, the incumbent political order had reached such a degree of consensus among its citizenry that the use of force against criminals and extremists was mostly considered legitimate. This in turn made it possible to limit the use of physical violence to a means of last resort.

Nevertheless, if we take a closer look, some first steps towards the internationalization of the monopoly of force took place already in the twentieth century. States accepted an increasing number of international agreements that limited their discretion in the use of the monopoly of force. At the legitimacy level of the chain of coercion, the *United Nations Charter* (1945) prohibited wars of aggression. At the methods level, the *Geneva Convention Relative to the Treatment of Prisoners in War* (1950) and the *United Nations Convention against Torture* (1985) also limited the discretion of states to apply force as they pleased. The control of the monopoly of force thereby became in part dependent on international norms, although the control of actual law enforcement operations was formally left untouched (Morgenthau 1963).

More recently, it seems that the world has been experiencing an increasing de-monopolization of force at all levels of the chain of coercion. Accordingly, there is no guarantee that the monopoly of force will continue to resemble the ideal type outlined by Max Weber. The reason is not so much the gradual loss of acceptance on the part of those who are subject to political rule. In the developing countries of the Third World, the real challenge to the state monopoly of force is the privatization of violence. In the industrialized West, the more important challenge to sovereignty is the ongoing internationalization of the monopoly of force.

Max Weber tied the monopoly of force to the modern state. In his vision, it was by necessity a territorial monopoly. As it internationalizes, it loses its connection with territoriality and thus is in a process of deep transformation. This book is concerned with one aspect of this transformation, namely the internationalization of police affairs. The examination concentrates on the 1960s/1970s and 1990s/2000s, and there is a focus on European state preferences. Despite this focus, the study should be seen in the wider context of the formation and transformation of the monopoly of force.

This book follows the exhortation that 'empirical research on issues concerning sovereignty should focus on the organization and use of violence', including a possible transformation of the monopoly of force (Thomson 1995: 230). We shall see that large Western European states are increasingly ready to delegate an important part of their policing powers to the international level, not only to the European Union but also to the United Nations and elsewhere. Although to somewhat different degrees, they seem to accept an internationalization of their monopoly of force and a concomitant loss of territorial control. What exactly do these countries want, and why do they want it? This is going to be my focus.

Research strategy

The method used in this book is a methodologically informed version of what the American pragmatist Charles Sanders Peirce used to call 'abduction' (Peirce 1998: vol. 5, §590–604; vol. 7, §218–22). So far, abduction has mostly been used as a free-floating signifier, sometimes attached to programmatic statements or research designs forswearing a positivist methodology (e.g. Ruggie 1998: 94; Finnemore 2003: 13). To end this unfortunate state of affairs and lead beyond fashionable concept dropping, the present chapter will try to lay the foundations for a more self-conscious use of abduction and formulate explicit guidelines for its use as a pragmatic research strategy for comparative case study research.

The task is not to provide the ultimate interpretation of what the dean of American pragmatism actually wanted to say (see Josephson 2000; Magnani 2001; Reichertz 2003). The task is rather to recommend abduction as a practical tool for social-scientific methodology, and to show how the design of this study is an application of the template. While theory testing is neither the only nor the most important objective of pragmatic research, the main task of abduction is to match research design with the problem at hand. Nevertheless, abduction can be easily made amenable to the construction of a plausible theory. This book for example is specifically designed to 'abduct' a sector-specific theory of national preference formation.

The typical situation for abduction is when you become aware of a certain class of phenomena that intrigues you for some reason, but for which you lack applicable theories. You simply trust, although you obviously do not know for certain, that the observed class of phenomena is not random. Therefore you start collecting pertinent observations and, at the same time, applying concepts from existing fields of your knowledge. Instead of trying to impose an abstract theoretical template (deduction), or simply gathering and processing all relevant facts (induction), you start reasoning at an intermediate level (abduction).

If the concepts selected do not help you to see the kind of orderly patterns you are looking for, you may either reject or refine them. Alternatively, you may redefine the boundaries of the class of phenomena under examination. Eventually, a procedure of mutual adjustment and 'educated guesswork' will lead to a framework of analysis (or set of propositions, or even theory) which will allow the researcher to grasp the class of phenomena as it evolves in the very process of research.

This is more or less what we do in our own social practice when confronted with complex challenges. Take as an example the way one learns to drive a car.[23] Almost everybody will agree that the decisive stage is getting acquainted with the practice of navigating through traffic. What the novice learns in driving lessons is helpful to a certain extent, but she will quickly find out that what really matters is driving as a social practice. What she really needs is useful frames for driving in certain classes of situations. Driving in Naples during the rush hour poses a different challenge to driving on a small country road in Nebraska. Trucks and buses move differently to mopeds and bicycles. Fellow drivers using the horn, talking on the cell-phone, or wearing melon hats must be treated with special care.

Traffic is clearly not random. As with any other social practice, it is full of contingent behavioural regularities and reasonably clear rules of behaviour. Nevertheless, we do not discover these regularities and rules of behaviour by anything even remotely resembling experimentation, deductive theory testing, or other standard social-scientific methodologies. The bottom line is that, in our own practice, most of us manage to deal with a lot of difficult challenges, and the way we do this is completely different from, and far more efficient than, the way knowledge is generated according to standard scientific methodologies. Science is often a poor emulator of what we are able to achieve in practice. Human practice is the ultimate miracle, and science would do well to mimic it at least in some respects.

If we agree that abduction is what we do in social practice when confronted with complex challenges; and if we agree, further, that abduction works better than what we usually do in social science; then it will be worthwhile exploring whether and to what extent it can improve the way we generate social-scientific knowledge.[24] One would expect the result to be quite different, on the one hand, from purely idiographic research and, on the other hand, from the search for scientific laws through deductive theory testing or inferential statistics.

Fortunately, there is no need to start from scratch. Abduction can build upon existing methods of comparative case study research.[25] Unfortunately,

Box 1.1 Seven pragmatic principles

1. The purpose of research, including personal motivation, must be stated in public.
2. Orientation in a relevant field is more important than causal theorizing.
3. Pragmatic research is constituted more by concepts than by theory.
4. Analytical distinctions should elicit patterns of similarity and difference.
5. Case sampling may follow a 'most important' or a 'most typical' case scenario.
6. Complexity can be reduced by appropriate formal tools.
7. Abduction is eventually compatible with causal theorizing.

though, comparative case study research is not always practiced in a very practical way. Its typical objective is causal inference rather than the efficient generation of useful knowledge. Even *Qualitative Comparative Analysis* and *Fuzzy-Set Social Science*, which are bold enough to abandon the quantitative template and drop the ideal of correlation analysis, nevertheless depend upon heavy epistemological assumptions about necessary and sufficient causation (Ragin 1987, 2000; cf. Mahoney and Goertz 2006).

As will become clear from the following discussion of seven pragmatic principles (Box 1.1), abduction provides an alternative to conventional methods of comparative case study research. Let us start with the purpose of research. A pragmatic researcher should be affirmative about the fact that the main purpose of research is the generation of useful knowledge with a particular research interest in mind. Whatever that interest is, it should be stated in public. It is simply not true that personal motivation 'should not appear in our scholarly writings' (King *et al.* 1994: 15). On the contrary, the interest of the researcher should always be stated as clearly as possible. It will then be up to the relevant evaluators and the peer community at large to establish whether and to what extent a specific research project serves a legitimate, useful, and relevant purpose. Truth in social science is not simply a property of the world. Truth claims are meaningful only in the context of our motivations and the questions we ask.

Causal inference is neither the only legitimate nor the most important purpose of pragmatic research. Usually, the goal of abduction is to enable orientation in a complex field of research. This consists of mapping a class of phenomena in order to increase cognitive understanding and/or practical manipulability. To reach this objective, it is mostly sufficient to detect patterns of similarity and difference that allow for the identification of a certain degree of order within an otherwise confusing field. To the extent that abduction helps make intelligible or malleable a field that previously escaped our cognitive or operational parameters, it has served its most important purpose. In some cases, it is possible to formulate a sort of 'grounded theory' (Glaser and Strauss 1967; Strauss and Corbin 1998). However, this is not always necessary. Given the contingent nature of the social world, contingent generalizations, rather than the quest for causal laws, are appropriate for the social sciences (Schedler 2007). While existing theories can help by informing the process of abduction, a pragmatic researcher will not agree that causal inference is a necessary condition for success.

Abduction is concept-driven rather than theory-driven. Concepts, rather than full-blown theories, allow the pragmatic researcher to constitute a meaningful field of research. The pragmatic researcher will reject a 'causal, ontological, and realist view of concepts' (Goertz 2005: 5; cf. Sartori 1970, 1984), and prefer a view that recognizes their constitutive, inter-subjective, and semantic nature (Davis 2005). Not only do concepts constitute our field of observation, but what we see in that field will in turn elucidate or modify our initial understanding of the concepts. Especially during the initial stages of the research process, it would be counterproductive to ban the adjustment of concepts. Instead, the pragmatic researcher will start by engaging in a careful reworking of concepts. The very process of research should then lead to increasing operational and denotative clarity. Rather than accepting the positivist view that the definition of concepts should be stipulated at the beginning of the research process and then be held constant, it is better to allow for the mutual adaptation of conceptual framework and empirical findings. Self-imposed conceptual blinkers are not useful, nor is it helpful to cast concepts into the Procrustean bed of a lexical definition. Human cognition happens in a hermeneutic circle, and we should welcome the kind of circularity in which our understanding of the whole is modified by our progressive understanding of its parts.

A field of research is constituted by a limited number of core concepts, maybe two or three. It is then divided, by further conceptual distinctions, into a variety of subfields or 'domains'. Whereas positivist research designs examine the causal impact of variables, abduction is concerned with the heuristic value of core concepts and conceptual distinctions. Core concepts and the field, as well as conceptual distinctions and domains, are two sides of the same coin. Usually, conceptual distinctions take the shape of overlapping categorizations. When useful, they elicit patterns of similarity and difference that increase our knowledge. If not, it will be better to try other distinctions. Since the objective of abduction is detecting patterns of similarity and difference, it should remain possible to readjust conceptual distinctions in the course of research, especially in the early stages of the process. Instead of causal inference, it will then be possible to examine whether and how different distinctions are important in structuring the field under examination. Since the objective is to map a class of phenomena, finding the most useful distinctions is an important achievement in itself.

The next issue is sampling strategies. Usually, pragmatic case sampling will follow a 'most important' or a 'most typical' case design. As we have seen, a field of research and its domains are constituted by a small number of core concepts and a larger number of conceptual distinctions. A pragmatic researcher will tend to select either the most important or the most typical cases in each domain. Either of these sampling strategies is reasonable, but to avoid unnecessary asymmetries it is convenient to choose one of them.[26] An important reason for choosing a 'most important' or a 'most typical' case design is that, in practice, the conceptual boundaries of a field or domain are always contested. Social-scientific concepts are hardly ever mirrored by a homogenous population of real-world manifestations with clearly defined boundaries. There are always borderline cases that are hard to subsume under the concept at hand. At best, a reasonable degree of consensus can be expected for the empirical prototypes or theoretical ideal types at the core of the case population (Davis 2005: 61–91). Especially at the beginning of a research programme, it is therefore practical to study those cases that are close to the core of a field or domain, regardless of its boundaries.[27]

Then there is the problem of controlling complexity and, closely related, cognitive and emotional biases. Social science can be understood, at least in part, as being geared towards the containment of complexity and biases. On the one hand, abduction offers a promising research strategy precisely because it helps to detect patterns of similarity and difference in a complex field of research. On the other hand, due to the practice of drawing distinctions there is also an inherent drift in abduction towards complexity. While some distinctions divide the field into domains, thereby determining case selection and preparing the ground for cross-case analysis, there will be other distinctions which structure the examination of cases and thereby specify the parameters for within-case analysis. Abduction typically involves a large number of cross-cutting distinctions that produce a large number of case studies for intra-case and inter-case comparison. This may easily lead to a degree of complexity beyond our cognitive capacities. There are limits beyond which it becomes difficult to keep track of the ramifications of our own research design, and it is precisely when we reach these limits that we are tempted to indulge in cognitive or emotional biases.

When a purely hermeneutic approach to data analysis is beyond our cognitive capacities, formal tools can help to make sure that patterns of similarity and difference remain detectable despite the complexity induced by cross-cutting conceptual distinctions. For example, complexity can be controlled by virtue of the following four instruments: structured-focused comparison, formal coding, synthetic indices, and descriptive statistics. While abduction is fundamentally based on a qualitative understanding of the cases, it is possible to set up a unified set of aspects that shall be covered in every narrative. This is typically done by the method of structured-focused comparison.[28] Formal coding will then involve the creation of a matrix containing the most pertinent information from each case study. Synthetic indices can be used to aggregate this information, while descriptive statistics can help to detect patterns of similarity and difference in the dataset. Once detected, it is fundamentally important always to (re)interpret the patterns in the light of qualitative evidence.

The latter point in particular warrants a few remarks. When using statistics, a pragmatic researcher will preferably use intuitive tools such as frequency counts or cross-tabulation, which make it easy to check statistical findings against the qualitative record. While there is no need for a taboo against using inferential statistics as long as it is done for heuristic purposes, one has to be extremely careful with the alchemy of statistical methods that smuggle unwarranted assumptions such as the homogeneity or independence of cases into the dataset, and thereby 'miraculously' lead to sweeping generalizations across and beyond the sample. Formal research tools can be helpful, but statistical sophistication is not a goal of pragmatic research. As we have seen on several accounts, the goal of abduction is far more straightforward: the detection of patterns of similarity and difference within a given field. The pragmatic researcher will therefore keep analytical procedures as simple and intuitive as possible.

While causal theory is not the main purpose of abduction, an intelligent pragmatic research design can allow for the formulation of a causal theoretical model. Abduction is certainly not geared towards the detection of covering laws.[29] Nevertheless, pragmatic research is amenable to the search for causal theory in a broader sense. This can be accomplished by means of the same tools that are used for abduction as a descriptive instrument. Imagine a dataset containing observed causal pathways. If the number of pathways in the dataset is sufficiently large, nothing prohibits observing, coding, and counting their frequency. Abduction can be used not only for mapping descriptive patterns of similarity and difference, but also patterns of similarity and difference in the explanation of the observations made. Abduction is therefore as suitable for mapping patterns of causality as for descriptive purposes.

In a nutshell, abduction can be seen as a comparative case study method. It starts with a research interest that relates to some relevant purpose. The specific field of research is constituted by a limited number of core concepts. A variety of distinctions are applied to divide the field into a number of domains. The most important or most typical cases in each domain are examined to establish whether and how each underlying distinction is important in structuring the field under examination. To that end, cross-case analysis is combined with within-case analysis. Despite a healthy dose of scepticism, formal methods can be helpful to control complexity, avoid biases, and analyse the data. The ultimate goal, however, is not methodological sophistication but orientation in a complex field. In addition to mapping a field descriptively, the development of a causal theory is also an option.

2 Essentials

This brief but essential chapter sets the analytic frame for understanding the rest of the book. Abduction, as argued, does not entail mechanistic concepts of causation, nor does it operate with the notion of dependent and independent variables. Instead, it points to the constitutive importance of concepts. Core concepts and conceptual distinctions are the basis for being able to detect patterns of similarity and difference, and thereby to 'map' a field of research.

The core concepts have already been presented in the last chapter: state preferences and international police cooperation. In combination, they constitute the field of research: state preferences on international policing. To structure the field and prepare the ground for the empirical analysis, the present chapter focuses on conceptual distinctions. The distinctions introduced in the first section serve for case design, those introduced in the second section for descriptive mapping, and those in the third section for the explanatory mapping of the field.

Case design

State preferences on international police cooperation can be expected to vary according to the following distinctions: country, threat, time, and level. In other words, they depend upon the specificities of a particular country; on the kind of threat posed by a certain type of criminality; on the characteristic features of a given period of time; and on the position of an issue along the chain of coercion (see pp. 6–7), which goes from the discursive conceptualization of deviant behaviour down to concrete operational law enforcement.

To flesh out these distinctions with specific content, the choice fell on the preferences of the four largest and most important West European countries: Britain, France, Germany, and Italy; on cooperation against the two most relevant types of international crime: terrorism and drugs; in the two most salient time periods: the 1960s/1970s and the 1990s/2000s; and on the three decisive levels of international cooperation: legitimization, methods, and authorization (see Figure 2.1).

The countries selected are Britain, France, Germany, and Italy. These are all comparable countries. Apart from all being western democracies, they are the

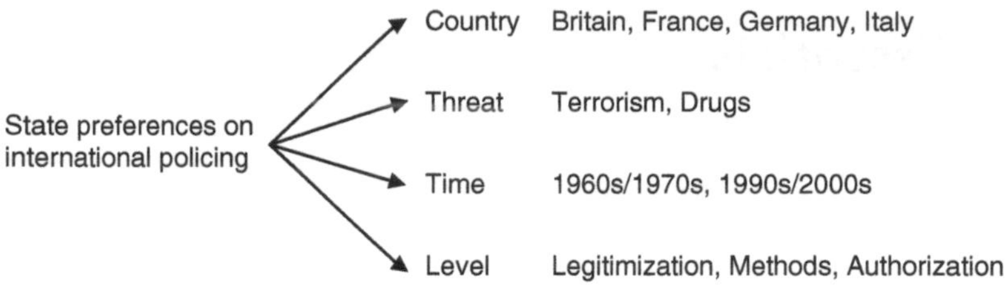

Figure 2.1 Distinctions for case sampling.

four largest EU Member States. Nevertheless comparison between them is not trivial, because their historical heritage and political systems are fairly different (centralized vs. federalist, common law vs. civil law, presidential vs. parliamentary). As already mentioned, I look at their preferences for or against international police cooperation not only in Europe but from a truly international perspective, including cooperation at the United Nations, at the transatlantic level, and elsewhere.

The most salient threats from international crime are posed by terrorism and drugs (F.E.C. Gregory 1991: 148). Since they both constitute a deep challenge to the state, terrorism and drugs are matters of 'high policing' (Brodeur 1983). This is of course not to deny that most people are more worried about trivial forms of crime such as petty fraud or street-corner violence. As far as international cooperation is concerned, however, states are more concerned with high policing. Terrorism and drugs can therefore be chosen as a proxy for international police cooperation. The paramount importance of terrorism is easily understandable. By justifying their deeds in the name of a political cause, terrorists raise an explicit challenge to the state monopoly of force.[1] The crucial relevance of drug enforcement is related to the fact that the trade in narcotics and psychotropic substances constitutes the world's largest illicit market (Fijnaut and Paoli 2004).[2]

The time periods under examination are the 1960s/1970s and the 1990s/2000s. The 1960s and 1970s were the formative years of the current international regimes on terrorism and drugs. Drugs became a matter of increased international concern already in the 1960s, while terrorism appeared on the international agenda mainly in the 1970s. A comparison between the 1960s/1970s and the 1990s/2000s is interesting because of the changed institutional setting: while in the former period the international fight against terrorism and drugs was still in its infancy, international policing has since become far more institutionalized.

Finally, state preferences are examined at three levels: legitimization, methods, and authorization. Without an armoury of permissible methods, the legitimization of crime fighting does not directly translate into the authorization of police action. Therefore, international policing should be examined at all three of these different levels. In an ideal-typical world, the chain of coercion has five levels (see Figures 1.2 and 1.3). Controlling the monopoly of force would mean controlling the entire chain of coercion from the discursive conceptualization of deviant behaviour down to operational law enforcement. For pragmatic reasons, however, the examination of state preferences can be limited to the inner three links of the chain.[3]

Taken together, these dimensions (country, threat, time, level) constitute a useful shopping basket of analytical categories. The choice of four countries, two threats, two time periods, and three levels leads to a matrix with 48 fields (4 × 2 × 2 × 3). To fill in the matrix, the next step is the selection of concrete cases where states have formulated preferences on cooperation against either threat, in either time period, and on each of the three levels of the chain of coercion. The strategy is to select only the most salient cases. To establish which cases are most salient, the tactic employed was reliance on the existing literature and, where necessary, on background interviews with scholars and decision makers. The result is a sample of 12 cases or 48 case studies, with each case being organized into four case studies (one per country).

The fight against terrorism

An overview of the empirical cases selected for international police cooperation against terrorism is provided in Table 2.1. Faithful to salience as the main selection criterion, each cell contains the case deemed most relevant for a given period of time and on a given level of abstraction. In 2003 and 2004, the sample was submitted for critique to scholars and decision makers in different European countries. Despite some disagreement over detail, the paramount relevance of all the cases selected was broadly confirmed.

Each row in the table corresponds to a chapter in Part I, with every chapter split into one section on the 1970s (left-hand column) and another on the 2000s (right-hand column).

Chapter 3 deals with the search for a comprehensive approach to the legitimization of the fight against international terrorism. In fact, for the legitimacy of this fight it is absolutely crucial for states to agree on a common problem definition. Insofar as there is a common understanding, the use of extraordinary sanctions is considered legitimate. By contrast, if there is no common problem definition, the predetermined breaking point of any antiterrorist coalition is disagreement about who is an 'evil' terrorist and who is

Table 2.1 Cases selected for the international fight against terrorism

	1970s	*2000s*
Legitimization	Comprehensive approach to international terrorism	Comprehensive convention on international terrorism
Methods	Special commando units and information exchange	Exchange of antiterrorist intelligence
Authorization	European Convention on the Suppression of Terrorism	European Arrest Warrant

a 'good' freedom fighter. Although states are in desperate need of agreement on a common understanding of international terrorism, the legal definition of the problem poses an eminently political challenge. The crux is that defining international terrorism is tantamount to determining the international public enemy. As Carl Schmitt has forcefully argued, the power to define the public enemy is the ultimate prerogative of the sovereign (Schmitt 1922; 1932). Transfer of this power to the international sphere would constitute a major political transformation (Friedrichs 2006a).

Ever since the early 1970s, the UN has been the most relevant international forum for the legitimization of the fight against terrorism. Already in 1972, the General Assembly started a debate about the necessity to agree on a legal definition of terrorism. That debate ended in disagreement in 1979, but in the 2000s there is again an attempt to agree on a comprehensive convention against terrorism that would include a legal definition. It is easy to see that such a convention would considerably limit the discretion of states to determine, autonomously and on a case-by-case basis, the international public enemy. It is therefore hardly surprising that the hegemonic powers (the US and the UK) are unhappy to see the item on the UN agenda. France and Germany, by contrast, cautiously support the draft comprehensive convention.

Chapter 4 discusses the most relevant antiterrorist methods. Since 1972, when terrorism was placed on the international agenda, states have been trying to find common ground on strategies for suppressing the phenomenon. In the 1970s, this was mainly a question of the use of special commando units, such as the SAS in Britain or the GSG-9 in Germany (Dobson and Payne 1982). At the same time, states tried to place the exchange of antiterrorist information on a more solid institutional basis. For example, the TREVI Group provided a forum for the horizontal exchange of information amongst European governments and their law enforcement agencies. Information was also exchanged through more informal channels, such as the Police Working Group on Terrorism (PWGOT). Secret services also played an important role (Bigo 1996).

In the 2000s, after the advent of suicide bombing, special commando units are no longer of much use and, instead, intelligence has become the single most important weapon in the fight against terrorism (Ball and Webster 2003). Instead of TREVI, the Member States of the European Union are now cooperating within the formal institutional framework of Europol. Nevertheless, other forums for the exchange of secret-service intelligence still play a crucial role. As is often the case, different states have a predilection for different institutional frameworks. Thus, France and Britain prefer informal channels such as personal contacts between secret-service agents, while only Germany is enthusiastic about formal cooperation at Europol.

Chapter 5 deals with the authorization level, where the exemption of political offenders from extradition was singled out in the 1970s as the most important impediment to effective international cooperation against terrorism. Under the political exemption clause, terrorists could claim the status of political offenders. Thereby, they were not only protected against extradition but sometimes even enjoyed political asylum. As a remedy, in 1977 the Member States of the Council of Europe agreed on the European Convention on the Suppression of Terrorism, which limited the political exemption clause with regard to terrorist offences. However, divergences in national preferences first watered down the text of the convention and later hampered its ratification and implementation. For an entire decade, France, in particular, persistently objected to the elimination of the political exemption clause (Gal-Or 1985).

After 9/11, this problem was solved among EU Member States by employing another device: the mutual recognition of court rulings. Since then, the so-called European Arrest Warrant has led to the practical abolition of the political exemption clause (Wagner 2003; Blekxtoon and Ballegooij 2005). But again, different national preferences jeopardized the implementation of the new legal instrument. Most notably, the Italian Government under Berlusconi was not happy with the long list of 32 serious offences to be prosecuted under the European Arrest Warrant, and therefore obstructed its ratification. In 2001 parts of the German Government also had serious problems with the Warrant, and in 2005 the Federal Constitutional Court forced the legislator to present a revised ratification law (Schorkopf 2006).

The fight against drugs

The fight against organized crime in general, and against drugs in particular, is the second most relevant field of police cooperation. In no other field is police cooperation so close and able to look back to such a long continuous history as in drug enforcement.[4] Table 2.2 provides an overview of the empirical cases on international police cooperation against drugs. Each row corresponds to a chapter in Part II, divided into two parts by time periods.

Chapter 6 is about international drug prohibition, which concerns meta-political authority. Drug prohibition is about deciding what – for example cocaine or tobacco – shall be regulated by the free market, and what shall be manipulated by political fiat (Thomson 1995: 222–3; cf. Andreas and Nadelmann 2006: 17–58). As in the case of terrorism, the United Nations is traditionally the most important source of legitimacy for drug prohibition. In the 1960s and early 1970s the drug prohibition regime reached a new momentum, mainly because it was being pushed forward by the United States.

Table 2.2 Cases selected for the international fight against drugs

	1960s/1970s	*1990s/2000s*
Legitimization	International drug prohibition	International drug prohibition
Methods	Diffusion of American drug enforcement techniques	Fighting criminal finance
Authorization	Joint efforts in the Nixon years	Cross-border investigation in Europe

This led to the passing of two important landmark agreements at the United Nations: the 1961 Single Convention on Narcotic Drugs, and the 1971 Convention on Psychotropic Substances (McAllister 2000).[5] Both conventions further limited the discretion of individual states to define the drug problem autonomously and thereby to determine on their own when it is legitimate to use force.

It is interesting to analyse the way European states responded to these developments. In the beginning, drugs were seen as a typical US problem. For a variety of reasons, most Western European states had only a limited interest in further criminalizing them. As European societies faced up to similar drug problems as the United States, a more vigorous attitude carried the day. Nevertheless, global drug prohibition continued to be contested. Around the mid-1990s, some European states (notably Britain and Germany) started emancipating themselves from the UN regime. While this has led to a partial re-nationalization of drug prohibition, there is also an emergent EU regime that may, at some future point in time, become a regional alternative to the global drug prohibition regime of the United Nations (Elvins 2003).

Chapter 7 is dedicated to drug enforcement methods. In the late 1960s and early 1970s, drug addiction as a mass-phenomenon caught European states by surprise. Since the US had longstanding experience with the problem, American agencies were at the vanguard in the propagation of drug enforcement methods. Throughout the 1970s, there was an unprecedented diffusion of these techniques to the rest of the world.[6] The new methods included, among other things, intrusive forms of surveillance, extensive undercover operations, and reduced charges or immunity from prosecution to known drug dealers in order to 'flip' them into becoming police informants. Although American-style techniques posed a challenge to the legal systems of Western European states, different countries reacted in different ways. Some states, such as France and Germany, tended to embrace the new investigative methods, whereas other countries, such as Italy, were somewhat less enthusiastic (Nadelmann 1993; Fijnaut and Marx 1995).[7]

Over time, this resulted in an armoury of aggressive drug enforcement techniques which, after the adoption of the 1988 United Nations Convention against Drug Trafficking, have been accepted by all European states. Since then, the cutting edge of international drug enforcement has shifted to the fight against criminal finance, where the idea is to deprive criminals of their profits by means of asset confiscation and measures against money laundering (Mitsilegas 2003; Masciandaro 2004). Although no state dared to openly challenge this idea, there were again different national preferences on international cooperation against criminal finance (with Britain being one of the most, and Germany one of the least enthusiastic supporters).[8]

Chapter 8, finally, deals with the political authorization of operational drug enforcement across borders. Whereas the global drug prohibition regime of the United Nations was rapidly advancing during the 1960s and 1970s, cross-border cooperation against drug trafficking was still in its infancy and had not yet developed beyond occasional raids on criminal gangs. This started to change with the Franco-American impasse over the so-called French connection, a huge drug trafficking ring based in Marseille. At first it took considerable political pressure from Washington to bully Paris into cooperation (Gévaudan 1985; Friesendorf 2007). In concomitance with the 'French connection' case, however, France and Germany started cooperating with other states – notably the United States – on a more systematic basis. Since then, cross-border investigations have become a fairly common practice among police officers (Busch 1999), and over the 1980s and 1990s this led to the creation of a dense network of bilateral and multilateral agreements to facilitate such operations.

The latest achievement in Europe is a multilateral legal umbrella for so-called Joint Investigation Teams, with the possible participation of Europol. In the absence of such a legal framework, police officers run the risk of legal prosecution themselves when embarking on unauthorized cross-border missions. Moreover, it is far from certain whether the evidence found on such missions can be used in court. Joint Investigation Teams are significant because, if the police choose to abandon the practice of more informal arrangements, they place practical police cooperation within a multilateral legal framework (Schalken and Pronk 2002; Plachta 2005). Nevertheless, different European countries have different preferences as to the desirability and practical applicability of the new instrument. In any case the use of Joint Investigation Teams is optional, and some European states such as Britain are not particularly keen to recommend it to their police forces.[9]

Descriptive mapping

The main part of this book consists of six chapters containing 12 cases with regard to specific policy issues (see Tables 2.1 and 2.2). Since each of these cases is examined across four countries, the full sample of case studies amounts to 48 (please note the terminological distinction between 'cases' and 'case studies'). For narrative purposes and for the sake of comparative analysis, each case study is further disaggregated into a variety of aspects. Figure 2.2 contains the analytical distinctions drawn for the descriptive mapping of state preferences.

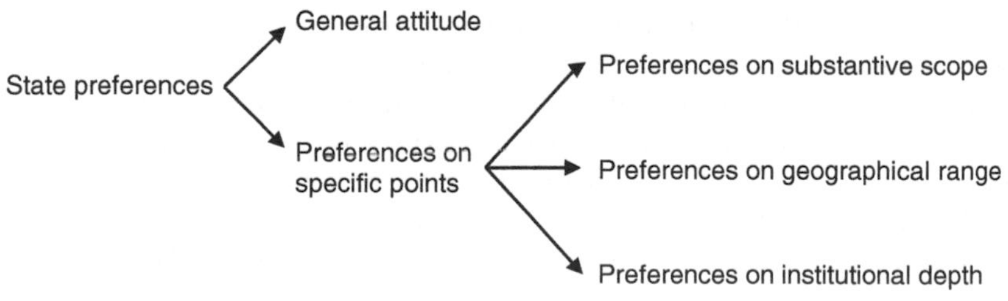

Figure 2.2 Distinctions for descriptive mapping.

A government does not usually simply support or oppose international cooperation on a given case, but has different preferences on different negotiable aspects of the policy issue at stake. Take as an example the general approach to fighting international terrorism. One state (say, Germany) may be willing to undertake binding multilateral commitments with as many states as possible, but only against international terrorism if narrowly conceived, namely Osama Bin Laden and his associates. Another country (say, the United States) may prefer informal coalitions of the willing with a limited number of partners, but to fight terrorism in a broader sense, including both rogue states and ordinary criminals alleged to support terrorist activities.

Which of the two countries is more willing to engage in international cooperation against terrorism? Although both countries in general have a positive attitude on cooperation, a precise answer to this question is not possible without drawing a categorical distinction between three different dimensions of national preferences on international cooperation.[10]

- Preferences on the *substantive scope* of cooperation, that is with regard to the question of how many issues are to be covered.
- Preferences on the *membership range* of cooperation, that is with regard to the number of countries that are to participate.
- Preferences on the *institutional depth* of cooperation, that is with regard to the degree of binding institutional commitment.

These distinctions provide a unified set of categorical questions, to be answered for every single case study on the basis of the primary and secondary sources available. Is a government willing to broaden the substantive scope of international cooperation? Does it intend to widen membership range? Does it want to deepen institutional commitment?

Finally, one has to add a fourth question that actually precedes the other three. Does a government support international cooperation in the first place? If this is not the case, policy preferences formulated on the first three questions can take on a different meaning, since they may be hypocritical.

The distinction between general attitude and preferences on substantive scope, membership range, and institutional depth (henceforth: 'mindset', 'scope', 'range', and 'depth') constitutes the narrative template for the qualitative chapters in Parts II and III of this volume where a structured and focussed description of state preferences is offered for each case study.

The questions on the general attitude and preferred membership range of a country are fairly straightforward. For the former, there are three possibilities: a state either supports international cooperation, or opposes it, or is indifferent. For the latter, it is easy to rank countries: a country prefers either a smaller or a larger group of states to participate in an international regime. For preferences on substantive scope and institutional depth, by contrast, it has been necessary to follow a more sophisticated procedure: namely to establish for every single case the three or four key topics related to substantive scope and institutional depth, and subsequently to establish whether a state had a positive, neutral, or negative attitude on these topics.

An obvious problem resides in the sheer complexity engendered by this procedure. To control this complexity and make it possible to detect patterns of similarity and difference, it is necessary to develop a standardized template for data gathering and analysis. State preferences have therefore been formally coded and entered into two index-based datasets (see Appendices 1 and 2 and <http://www.joerg-friedrichs.de/policingdata>). This procedure makes the collected data amenable to rigorous statistical analysis, the results of which are presented in Chapter 9.

As already mentioned, the first question is always whether or not a state supports international cooperation. If this is not the case, one must assume that its declared preferences on particular bargaining items are only rhetorical, if not downright hypocritical. Having taken that into consideration, state preferences on substantive scope, membership range, and institutional depth can be put on an ordinal scale of measurement, which makes them amenable to rigorous comparison. However, it is not sufficient to simply derive ordinal values from specific preferences on specific issues. The willingness of a country to cooperate with other countries is strong if, and only if, it goes beyond the status quo of cooperation already obtained in past rounds of international negotiations. Preferences should therefore always be measured against the degree of cooperation to which a state is committed at the moment when new preferences are formulated.

In line with these considerations, the willingness of a state to cooperate with other states in any particular case can be measured using a formal index. The index (Ξ) is derived from three sub-indices, which measure preferences on substantive scope (I1), membership range (I2), and institutional depth (I3). The sub-indices are in turn derived from six parameters, which cover specific preferences on scope (P2), range (P4) and depth (P6), combined with the question of whether a state strives for a relative advance in comparison to the status quo, namely greater scope (P3), range (P5) or depth (P7) of international cooperation than in the past. The six parameters are preceded by a forced-choice parameter, which measures whether a country supports international cooperation in the first place (P1).[11]

Box 2.1 contains the codebook for the determination of the index and its sub-indices.

Depending on whether a state takes an internationalist or a nationalist attitude, the parameters and indices will take positive or negative values. The indices and sub-indices are scaled to the interval [–1; 1].[12] They can be computed via a set of mathematical formulae, which are based on simple arithmetic averages (see Figure 2.3).

Box 2.1 Index for the description of state preferences

P1: Does the country believe that the problem should be dealt with internationally?
[Yes = 1; unclear = 0; no = –1]

I1: Preferences on substantive scope
P2: What is the substantive scope of the intended agreement?
[Sum of positive (=1), neutral (=0), or negative (=–1) preferences on four topics]
P3: Would the intended agreement restrict or expand the substantive scope of an existing international regime?
[Strongly restrict = –4; restrict = –2; status quo = 0; expand = 2; strongly expand = 4]

I2: Preferences on membership range
P4: What is the membership range of the intended agreement?
[Case-by-case = 0; in-between = 1; EU = 2; in-between = 3; universal = 4]
P5: Would the intended agreement restrict or expand the membership range of an existing international regime?
[–4; –3; –2; –1; 0; 1; 2; 3; 4] (Difference between status quo and intended regime)

I3: Preferences on institutional depth
P6: What is the institutional depth of the intended agreement?
[Sum of positive (=1), neutral (=0), or negative (=–1) preferences on four topics]
P7: Would the intended agreement restrict or expand the institutional depth of an existing international regime?
[Strongly restrict = –4; restrict = –2; status quo = 0; expand = 2; strongly expand = 4]

$$I_1 = \text{Minimum}\ [P1;0.125(P2+P3)]$$
$$I_2 = \text{Minimum}\ [P1;0.125(P4+P5)]$$
$$I_3 = \text{Minimum}\ [P1;0.125(P6+P7)]$$
$$\Xi = 0.33(I1+I2+I3)$$

Figure 2.3 Arithmetical formulae.

Explanatory mapping

The explanation of empirical evidence is the decisive complement to its thorough description. While there are an infinite number of idiosyncratic reasons for a state to support or eschew international cooperation, for analytical purposes it is appropriate to classify these reasons along a finite number of causal pathways. First, state preferences can be determined by three different sources: material interests, institutional frameworks, and normative ideas.[13] Second, they can originate from the three familiar levels of analysis: domestic, national, and international.[14] Third, this can have either a positive or a negative impact on the willingness of a state to cooperate with other states. Figure 2.4 contains a graphical overview of these distinctions.

The result is an inventory of 18 possible causal pathways (3 × 3 × 2). If the US Government supports free trade because this is what leading industrialists demand, then this is an example of the causal pathway 'domestic interests with a positive impact'. If London is opposed to the automatic extradition of criminal offenders to the United States because the death penalty is considered to be incompatible with the British constitution, then this is an example of 'national institutions with a negative impact'. If the German Chancellor Gerhard Schröder, caught up in the global outcry after 11 September, vowed unconditional solidarity to the US, this was an example of 'international ideas with a positive impact'.

To guarantee a maximum degree of analytical precision, it is important to make these distinctions as operational as possible. First and foremost, a state preference is determined by material interests, institutional frameworks, or normative ideas to the extent that decision makers are concerned with any of the following categorical questions:

- Would cooperation be beneficial or detrimental due to its consequences?
- Would cooperation be easy or difficult to reconcile with existing institutions?
- Would cooperation be right or wrong on moral or normative grounds?

The answers to these questions can usually be found in appropriate sources, such as official documents, files in public archives, press releases, or journalistic reporting. The researcher should be careful not to attribute intentions unrelated to, or even contradicted by, the documentary evidence. Like a good historian, he should try to provide an 'inference to the best explanation' from the available

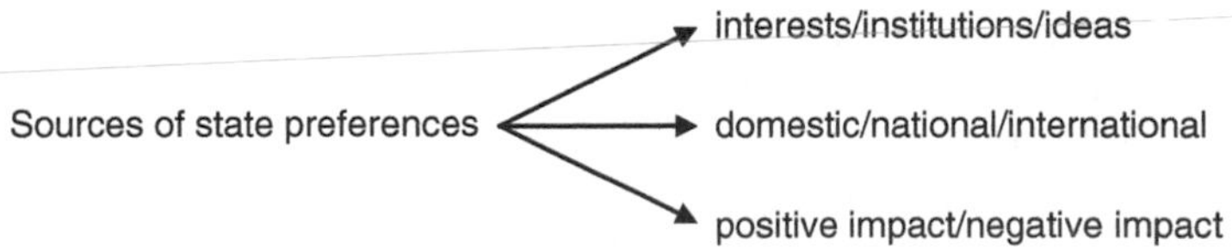

Figure 2.4 Distinctions for explanatory mapping.

sources. To the extent that a national preference is determined by the first question, a state is motivated by interests ('If we don't defeat drugs, our young generations will be endangered'). When the second question is in the foreground, institutional frameworks are the key determinant ('Due to our basic legal principles, we cannot accept entrapment as a drug enforcement technique'). Finally, normative ideas are the source of national preferences when the position of a state is determined by questions of right or wrong ('Drugs are a dangerous expression of moral decay, and we must fight this evil scourge').

As far as levels of analysis are concerned, 'national' is coded only in the following cases: (1) when a government is motivated by something it views as an interest of the nation as a whole, (2) when it is motivated by an institution with constitutional rank, or (3) when the normative idea underlying a government preference rests on a national consensus. In all other cases, explanations are attributed either to a domestic, viz. sub-national, or to an international frame of reference. Finally, it is important to note that in the present context the terms 'positive' and 'negative' must not be understood as value judgements. They simply indicate whether international cooperation is encouraged or discouraged by a given set of explanatory factors.

While an inventory of 18 causal pathways is sufficiently fine-grained to allow for considerable flexibility, critics may nevertheless debate the adequacy of the analytical framework. There are borderline cases where interests, institutions, and ideas are hard to distinguish. Some important items are absent from the list. For example, the category 'ideas' is limited to normative ideas and does not cover epistemic ideas. External shocks and landmark events such as 11 September, which arguably can have a deep impact on state preferences, are not explicitly mentioned. Furthermore, national preferences may also be determined by political culture. Different actor constellations such as expert communities, professional diplomats or nongovernmental organizations, are also absent from the list, and so on and so forth.

Against these and similar objections, I would argue that borderline cases can be kept to a minimum by the clear formulation of categorical questions. As far as epistemic ideas and events such as 11 September are concerned, they do not have an immediate causal impact. Only to the extent that they affect material interests, touch institutional frameworks, or upset normative ideas, do they influence the political process. A similar argument can be made about political culture and actor constellations. They do not have an immediate impact on national preference formation. Rather than operating as independent causal factors, they promote the material interests, favour the institutional frameworks, or transport the normative ideas determining state preferences. In short, the 18 causal pathways mentioned are the proximate causes that influence national preference formation. This is not to deny that there may be other, more remote causes. However, to put it in Aristotelian terms, this study is concerned with the efficient causes of state preferences rather than with their prime movers.

Overall, the distinctions suggested serve primarily as a template for the structured, focussed narratives provided in Parts II and III. In addition to that, nominal values are entered into a dataset (see Appendix 3 and <http://www.joerg-friedrichs.de/policingdata>), amenable to statistical analysis, the results of which are presented in Chapter 9.

Theoretical considerations

Before moving on to the empirical part of this study, where specific case studies are presented, let me introduce a number of theoretical considerations. Based on these considerations the book will offer a meaningful theoretical contribution, in addition to providing a useful descriptive and explanatory mapping of state preferences on international police cooperation.

To make this possible, the 18 causal pathways suggested in the last section are connected with causal expectations derived from existing explanatory approaches: liberal theory of international politics, liberal intergovern-mentalism, orthodox realism, normative approaches, institutional approaches, social institutionalism, and neoclassical functionalism.

Liberal theory of international politics

At present, Andrew Moravcsik's 'Liberal theory of international politics' (1997) is the most outspoken theory of national preference formation. According to this theory, state preferences are determined by the domestic level of analysis. Along with the distinction between interests, institutions, and ideas, there are three distinct variants of liberal theory.

- Commercial theory assumes that state preferences are the result of societal interests, mostly coming from pressure groups in the domestic arena.
- Republican theory focuses on the institutional mechanisms that determine which domestic preferences 'win out' in the process of preference aggregation.
- Ideational theory assumes that state preferences are the result of domestic normative ideas or social identities, rather than the outcome of interests or institutions.

Let us now relate the liberal theory of international politics to our inventory of 18 causal pathways. Since liberal theory, as a whole, is agnostic about the impact of domestic factors on the pursuit of international cooperation, it apparently refers to six of our 18 causal pathways: domestic factors – interests, institutions, ideas – with a positive or a negative impact on the willingness of a state to cooperate with other states.

Liberal intergovernmentalism

Moravcsik himself sympathizes with commercial theory, which is the most 'scientific' and elegant variant of liberal theory. According to commercial theory, state preferences are the result of pressures that come from society, that is, from the domestic arena of interest politics. These pressures are aggregated into state preferences and subsequently translated into national bargaining positions. At this point the stage of national preference formation is concluded and the second stage of the 'international cooperation two-step' (Legro 1996) kicks in, namely inter-state bargaining over substantive outcomes.

Sailing under the flag of liberal intergovernmentalism, commercial theory has been empirically applied to European integration 'from Messina to Maastricht' (Moravcsik 1998).[15] For example, French farmers in the 1950s and 1960s knew that they were competitive in Europe, but less so at the global level. They were aware that a common European market in agricultural products, combined with high protective barriers against the world market, would serve their interests. Since French farmers were better mobilized and more politically aware than other domestic stakeholder groups, as for example the consumers of agricultural goods, they succeeded in determining De Gaulle's bargaining position in the negotiations for the Common Market (Moravcsik 2000).[16]

Not only in this particular case but more in general, liberal intergovernmentalism holds that the most important domestic stakeholder groups exercise pressure on their government to further their particularistic interests. Via processes of domestic preference aggregation, the interplay of the demands raised by the most important stakeholder groups translates into national preferences, which will then determine the bargaining position of a country at the international negotiation table (for a germane account see Chase 2005).

The theory is particularly well-designed for economic cooperation and market integration, where domestic stakeholder groups can anticipate the effects of alternative political outcomes. It is an open empirical question whether and to what extent the theory can be applied to other policy fields, where it is more difficult for domestic stakeholder groups to anticipate the net gains and losses that would result from different political choices. Nevertheless, a priori there is no reason why state preferences should not be determined by domestic interests in other policy fields as well. Moravcsik himself is not entirely clear whether his theory is only suitable for the specific field of economic cooperation and market integration, or whether it should be considered universally applicable (1998: 4–5, 494–501).

Commercial theory corresponds with two causal pathways from our list: domestic interests with a positive, or negative, impact on the willingness of a state to cooperate.

Orthodox realism

Liberal theory is the most explicit general theory for the explanation of state preferences. While other theoretical approaches are not deliberately designed to account for national preferences, it is nevertheless possible to derive expectations from them.

For example, an orthodox realist would predict that states will usually be reluctant to cooperate with other states because of their concerns about national sovereignty (Morgenthau 1948). This is not to exclude the possibility that occasionally a state may have an overriding interest in international cooperation, but in an anarchical world one would expect that states should usually not be ready to undergo formally binding commitments (Waltz 1979). Correspondingly, the causal path 'national interests with a negative impact' should be extremely frequent.

More than in any other policy field, an orthodox realist would expect this in the field of 'high politics' where national sovereignty and state survival are most directly at stake. The most prominent example is great power politics in the military field (Mearsheimer 2001). International police cooperation is likely to be another interesting case in point.

A political sociologist in the tradition of Max Weber would predict that international police cooperation will be particularly difficult because policing is directly related to the monopoly of the legitimate use of force, which is understood as the defining characteristic of sovereign statehood. In a similar spirit, an orthodox realist would predict that the national interest in preserving sovereignty should be a frequent impediment to international police cooperation.[17]

Normative approaches

Normative approaches emphasize the fact that ideas can have an important effect on state preferences (Finnemore and Sikkink 1998). Most prominently, norm entrepreneurs at the domestic or transnational level are said to have a profound influence on governments (Risse *et al.* 1999; Finnemore 2003). However, there is no logical reason to exclude state preferences also being determined by the national level itself. At least in some situations, governments may pursue a moral agenda that reflects the broad normative consensus of the entire nation, or at least the political ideology of the ruling coalition representing that nation (Aspinwall 2002, 2007). To paraphrase a famous dictum by Alexander Wendt (1999: 92–138), normative approaches would lead one to expect that ideas should matter 'all the way down', from the international sphere, through the national level, down to the domestic arena.

There is no reason to assume, though, that normative ideas will always have a positive impact on state preferences. While the academic literature tends to view norms as an incentive for international cooperation, in reality a norm can just as well impede the willingness of a state to cooperate. Accordingly, any causal pathway containing normative ideas as the source of national preference formation is consistent with normative approaches. In other words: normative ideas can originate from the domestic, national, or international level, and they can have a positive or a negative impact on the willingness of a state to cooperate with other states. This amounts to six causal pathways of our nventory of 18 possible explanations.

Institutional approaches

Similarly, institutional approaches would predict that institutional effects play a predominant role in the determination of state preferences.[18] Historical institutionalism assumes that, depending on a variety of path dependencies and other historical contingencies, institutions at any level of analysis have an important positive or negative effect on state preferences on cooperation with other states (March and Olsen 1989; Pierson 2004). Any causal pathway in which an institution determines a national preference is therefore consistent with institutional approaches, no matter whether the institution is located at the domestic, national, or international level, and whether it has a positive or a negative effect. Altogether, this amounts to another six causal pathways from our menu of 18 possible explanations.

Social institutionalism

Sociological institutionalism is an interesting alternative to historical institutionalism, focusing on cultural and socialization effects (Alderson 2001; A.I. Johnston 2001).[19] There is a strong theoretical case that international institutions have a positive impact on the readiness of states to cooperate with each other (Wendt 1999). While there is less research on the effects of domestic and national institutions, it seems reasonable to assume that these 'parochial' institutions, at least on balance, should have a net negative effect on international cooperativeness (A.I. Johnston 2005: 1025–7; Zürn and Checkel 2005: 1047).[20] National and domestic institutions tend to socialize states into a compartmentalized world of organizational turfs that end at national borders, thereby making it harder for them to envisage international cooperation.

Since this is slightly different from what 'sociological institutionalism' in the tradition of the Stanford School would entail (Meyer *et al.* 1997), let us label this set of theoretical expectations 'social institutionalism'. According to this approach, international institutions can be expected to have a positive socialization effect on states, whereas national and domestic institutions would rather tend to prevent governments from international collaboration. In our terminology, this adds up to the following three causal pathways: international institutions with a positive effect, and national and domestic institutions with a negative effect.

Neoclassical functionalism

Functionalist scholars believe that individual states, as well as the international community as a whole, have a powerful interest in the solution of practical problems, and that this creates imperatives that make international cooperation more

Table 2.3 Causal expectations of existing explanatory approaches

Explanatory approach	*Causal expectations*
Liberal theory of international politics	Domestic interests/institutions/ideas (with positive/negative impact)
Liberal intergovernmentalism	Domestic interests (with positive/negative impact)
Orthodox realism	National interests (with negative impact)
Normative approaches	Domestic/national/international ideas (with positive/negative impact)
Institutional approaches	Domestic/national/international institutions (with positive/negative impact)
Social institutionalism	International institutions (with positive impact); national/domestic institutions (with negative impact)
Neoclassical functionalism	National/international interests (with positive impact); international institutions (with positive impact)

desirable to governments.[21] Presumably, over time this leads to 'positive feedback': there will be a growing institutional environment at the international level, and states will thereby be motivated to envisage even more international cooperation. In the long run, national elites are expected to gradually shift their loyalties to the international sphere (Mitrany 1943; Groom and Taylor 1975).

Let us call this theoretical approach 'neoclassical functionalism', in order to avoid confusion with 'neo-functionalism' as a theory of European integration. From this neoclassical functionalist standpoint, one would expect that national interests, international interests, and international institutions should have a positive effect on the willingness of a state to cooperate with other states. These three causal pathways should, according to neoclassical functionalism, explain the bulk of state preferences with regard to international cooperation.

Table 2.3 provides an overview of the causal pathways associated with the various explanatory approaches listed in this section.

Part I

The international fight against terrorism

As a special service to interested readers, this book is complemented by a supporting website: <http://www.joerg-friedrichs.de/policingdata>. If you want to follow the deep structure of my study, you are invited to consult this site in parallel to reading Chapters 3 to 8.

For aesthetic reasons, it is hardly possible to make the logic underlying structured-focussed comparison fully transparent without lapsing into an overly schematic and cumbersome style. The website offers a solution to this problem by providing the missing link between the qualitative narratives in Chapters 3 to 8 and the statistical data analysis in Chapter 9.

For each case, the website offers two tables – one descriptive, one explanatory – containing the empirical data in synoptic format. When you click on a cell, a popup window will open providing a qualitative comment on the value in question. The full datasets are also published in SPSS and Excel format in the 'Downloads' section.

If you select 'Archive' from the main menu, you will be redirected to another website containing most of the primary sources mentioned in the notes to the case studies on the 1960s and 1970s: material from national archives, protocols of parliamentary debates, newspaper articles, and official documents from international organizations.

3 The comprehensive approach

The predetermined breaking point for any antiterrorist coalition is disagreement about the proper delimitation of the phenomenon. Are the opponents of the US Army in Iraq terrorists, or are they insurgents? Is the PLO a terrorist organization, or is it a national liberation movement? Did the Apartheid system in South Africa, with its support for racist groups in neighbouring countries, engage in international terrorism?

Ever since decolonization, there has been disagreement as to whether international terrorism covers activities by national liberation movements, and certain acts of state-committed and state-sponsored political violence. In the 1970s, states such as Algeria, Libya, and Syria struggled to exempt national liberation movements from the definition of terrorism, and to include state terrorism instead. At least in part, this is still true after the terrorist attacks of 11 September 2001. For example, there is profound disagreement as to whether the violent activists in Palestine and Chechnya are terrorists or freedom fighters. In view of the international fight against terrorism this is unfortunate because, to fight terrorism effectively at the practical level, a common understanding of the problem is desperately needed. To secure the international coalition against terrorism, states would have to agree on who should legitimately be fought as an international terrorist.

In international as well as in domestic politics, the fight against terrorism tends to follow the 'politics of the latest outrage' (Wilkinson 2000: 197). Domestic laws and international conventions are generally discussed, and eventually agreed upon, only after major events. This pattern can be detected from the very first and inconclusive attempt to set up a comprehensive convention on international terrorism. That attempt was undertaken by the League of Nations between 1934 and 1937, after the assassination of King Alexander of Yugoslavia and the French Foreign Minister by a Croatian exile (Dubin 1991).

The same pattern could again be observed in the 1970s. After a series of terrorist attacks, most prominently on the Olympic village in Munich in September 1972, the quest for a common understanding of international terrorism took centre stage at the United Nations, in its General Assembly and its Legal Committee. It soon became apparent that due to profound political disagreements no consensus could be reached, and in 1979 the entire debate ended in failure. During the 1980s and 1990s, the problem was therefore left on one side, and a more pragmatic approach held sway. Over the last few decades, this approach has led to more than a dozen conventions against particular manifestations of international terrorism.

Nevertheless, in the absence of an overarching legal framework, these sector-specific conventions do not agglomerate into a coherent whole. While affording some help in dealing with international terrorism, they do not provide guidance on how to tackle the threat of new kinds of violence against innocent victims. It is therefore not surprising that, after a break of more than twenty years, the search for a common understanding of terrorism has again returned to the agenda of the United Nations (Ginkel 2003; Gioia 2004; Peterson 2004). The discussions had a difficult start in 2000. After the terrorist outrage of 11 September 2001, however, the debate became more intense. But although there has been considerable progress in recent years, no final agreement has yet been reached on a comprehensive convention on international terrorism (Gioia 2006; Hafner 2006).

But is a comprehensive convention at the United Nations at all necessary? While the UN could not agree on a comprehensive convention, the Member States of the EU were at least able to agree on minimum standards for the legal definition of the phenomenon. After a difficult start in the late 1970s and 1980s (Cardona 1993: 249), after 9/11 the EU finally acted on a proposal by the European Commission. In June 2002, the Council adopted a framework decision containing a summary definition of terrorism and obliging the Member States to prosecute certain acts as terrorist offences.[1] While this is an important step for the harmonization of criminal law in Europe, the EU definition of terrorism is only a small step towards a comprehensive international approach. Except for the United States and the United Kingdom, most states would agree that the United Nations is still the most important forum for the legitimization of the global fight against terrorism, and that regional arrangements alone cannot solve this problem.

Similarly, it is cold comfort that there are by now more than a dozen UN conventions against particular manifestations of terrorism such as skyjacking, assaults on diplomats, hostage-taking, and so forth. Despite the obvious usefulness of these instruments, they do not bring us significantly closer to a shared understanding of the problem. In most of these instruments the word 'terrorism' is not even used, let alone defined. As already stated, this is unfortunate because the lack of consensus about the contours of the phenomenon can undermine international coalitions. After more than 30 years, a comprehensive convention on international terrorism is still a desideratum (Friedrichs 2006a).[2]

Agreement impossible (1972–79)

Between 1972 and 1979, the world had to learn the hard way how difficult it is to agree on a common understanding of international terrorism.[3] In September

1972, when world public opinion was outraged by the terrorist attacks on the Olympic village in Munich, UN Secretary General Kurt Waldheim placed international terrorism on the agenda of the General Assembly. The initiative was welcomed by a majority of western countries including West Germany, Israel, and the United States, while most Arab and African countries had serious misgivings. Only a few days later, the United States submitted a draft *Convention for the Prevention and Punishment of Certain Acts of International Terrorism*.[4] The US draft was explicitly and deliberately limited to certain acts of international terrorism and did not suggest any legal definition of the phenomenon.

Nevertheless, the initiative faced stout opposition from the Non-Aligned Group, spearheaded by Algeria. Many Arab and African countries argued that it would be appropriate first to discuss the root causes of terrorism before suggesting repressive measures. Moreover the non-aligned countries, many of which were themselves the offspring of national liberation movements, suspected that the entire initiative was intended to outlaw their brethren fighting against colonialism and oppression. They maintained on the contrary that 'state terrorism' was actually the most harmful and deadly form of terrorism. These allegations were not very much to the point if one considers the letter of the US draft, which took a relatively moderate and pragmatic stance. But whether justified or not, the fierce opposition of the non-aligned phalanx ultimately scuttled the US draft in the General Assembly (Department of State 1973; Hoffacker 1975; E.H. Evans 1978).

Instead, at the instigation of Algeria and other Members of the Non-Aligned Group (and against the vote of the United States) the General Assembly adopted a resolution establishing an Ad Hoc Committee on International Terrorism.[5] Despite this tactical defeat, the United States and many other Western countries were ready to engage in the deliberations of the Ad Hoc Committee. As could have been expected however, the main problem was agreeing on a common understanding of international terrorism. At its first round of meetings in 1973, the Ad Hoc Committee did not reach any substantive consensus and could only restate 'the diversity of existing views on the various aspects of the subject submitted for consideration'.[6] Although the Ad Hoc Committee on International Terrorism was reconvened twice, in 1977 and 1979, it finally had to be suspended without any tangible results due to a blatant lack of political consensus.[7]

Disagreement started with the apparently innocuous question of if and when concrete measures should be taken against international terrorism. Many non-aligned countries held that first it was necessary to study the underlying causes of terrorism, and that only after understanding the legitimate reasons behind the grievances raised by international terrorists would it make sense to take practical steps. In this spirit, for example, the Algerian delegation not only pinpointed certain root causes of international terrorism, but also suggested that terrorism could sometimes be justified: 'Violence becomes terrorism, when situations which lead to violence are exacerbated'.[8] Terrorism was seen by the non-aligned countries as the inevitable consequence of fundamental freedoms being violated, and accordingly as a cause for political sympathy rather than moral retribution. Against these and similar arguments, the United States and other Western countries insisted that in their domestic legislation states did not wait for the underlying causes of crime to be identified before enacting penal laws against criminals.[9]

Similarly, it was contested whether international terrorism should be condemned regardless of motive, or whether certain causes such as national emancipation struggles could justify the political use of violent means. Again, on behalf of the Non-Aligned Group, the Algerian delegation was outspoken on the point: a distinction should be made between 'heinous terrorism' and 'terrorism that was political in origin and purpose'.[10] The Western response was somewhat ambiguous. On the one hand, most delegations paid lip service to the 'legitimate' claims of national liberation movements. On the other hand, they insisted that the end could never justify the means, and that violence against innocent people could not be condoned under any circumstances.[11]

In any case, the Non-Aligned Group was adamant on the inclusion of state terrorism in the Ad Hoc Committee's mandate. Acts of violence by colonial, racist, and alien regimes, they maintained, constituted 'the cruellest and most pernicious form' of international terrorism and therefore had to be given the highest priority during the deliberations.[12] Against this, Western states insisted that in international law there already existed appropriate provisions to restrain state violence, for example the Geneva conventions and the convention against genocide. While rejecting the inclusion of state-perpetrated terrorism, however, some Western states paradoxically demanded the inclusion of state-supported or state-sponsored terrorism. To cover up these and similar inconsistencies, some states (most prominently the United States and the United Kingdom) opposed a definition of terrorism as being counterproductive and called for practical measures instead.

In fact, the moral justification of political violence used by national liberation movements, and especially by the PLO, was in the real or perceived interest of many Third World regimes (Migliorino 1976, 1979a). These regimes therefore demanded the exemption of national liberation movements from the definition of international terrorism, and called for the inclusion of state terrorism instead; moreover, they asked that the causes of terrorism be analyzed before taking measures against it.

In the remainder of this section, we will consider the positions taken by the major European states. In September 1972, when the new item was placed on the agenda of the United Nations General Assembly, all Western countries summarily welcomed the initiative. However, after the non-aligned countries had started using the topic for propaganda purposes, their reactions differed. Was it reasonable to define international terrorism in the first place? Should a proper definition of terrorism include or exclude national liberation movements? Was state terrorism part of the phenomenon to be defined, or should it be subsumed under some other category? And last but not least: Was it necessary to study the underlying causes of terrorism before taking concrete measures?

Britain

At a previous attempt, in the 1930s at the League of Nations, to adopt a draft comprehensive convention on international terrorism, Britain had been unenthusiastic about, if not highly critical of, the legal project.[13] In the autumn of 1972, when a similar discussion unfolded at the United Nations, the United Kingdom was initially very interested.[14]

The main reason was that Britain had a national interest in a strong condemnation of international terrorism, since this might have helped to criminalize external support for the Irish Republican Army. As one official in the Foreign Office put it, the objective was to have 'a periodic stick with which to beat the Irish Government'.[15] Another objective was to demonstrate the 'lack of effective action by the Republic of Ireland against IRA cross-border terrorist activity'.[16] At least initially, Britain therefore warmly welcomed the UN debate on international terrorism.

Subsequently, it soon emerged that a comprehensive approach to international terrorism was a two-edged sword. First and foremost, Britain had a national interest in keeping the autonomy to determine its own enemies. The best way to achieve this was to cooperate with other states on a case-by-case basis rather than to insist on a comprehensive approach (Friedrichs 2006a). Moreover, Britain most definitely did not want to provoke international debate on the 'underlying causes' of terrorism in Northern Ireland.[17] Nor did it want to jeopardize its good relationships with the Arab world. In October 1972, the Egyptian Foreign Minister was reassured during a visit to London that Britain wanted terrorism to be dealt with as an international problem and not as a specifically Arab problem.[18] Thus, due to a number of overruling national interests, Britain became disenchanted with the UN debate. Moreover, there were clear normative limits to Britain's readiness to accept an exemption for national liberation movements: 'Freedom fighting with propaganda is one thing; with bombs another'.[19]

Britain's initial flirtation with the topic completely evaporated in 1973, when the non-aligned countries started using the debate for propaganda purposes. From then on, the United Kingdom worked for a 'decent burial' of the item.[20] The bottom-line of the official British bargaining position had always been that 'the main immediate objective should be to devise concrete, agreed measures to prevent senseless acts of violence which maimed or killed innocent victims'.[21] Accordingly, Britain opposed a legal definition of the phenomenon and preferred concrete measures against international terrorism. The study of underlying causes, important as it might be, should not be allowed to hamper the adoption of such measures. Moreover, Britain torpedoed all attempts by the Non-Aligned Group to exclude national liberation movements from the definition of international terrorism and to include state terrorism instead.[22]

The United Kingdom maintained this pragmatic approach, according to which it was better to devise sector-specific conventions against particular manifestations of international terrorism than to insist on the ambitious objective of a comprehensive approach, until the debate was ended in 1979. For obvious reasons, the United Kingdom had a national interest in practical cooperation with other states to fight its 'own' political enemies in Northern Ireland. Accordingly, London was keen to achieve concrete results as quickly as possible. Such a pragmatic position did not seem to require a comprehensive approach, whether at the global level in the United Nations or at the regional level in the Council of Europe.[23] From the British viewpoint, the quest for a comprehensive approach looked like a dangerous distraction from tackling the 'real' practical problems. Cooperation with other states on a case-by-case basis was seen as more practical and, at the same time, as the best way to preserve national autonomy in identifying the public enemy.

France

Contrary to the pragmatic view of the United Kingdom, France considered international terrorism to be a moral ill. Paris saw it therefore as its duty to help find an adequate political response to the problem. At the same time, France agreed with the non-aligned countries that the phenomenon of international terrorism should be legally defined.[24] In line with such considerations, in 1973 the French Ministry of Justice submitted a proposal for the definition of international terrorism. According to this proposal, international terrorism was

> a heinous act of barbarism committed in the territory of a third State by a foreigner against a person possessing a nationality other than that of the offender for the purpose of exerting pressure in a conflict not strictly internal in nature.[25]

Unlike its fellow Western democracies, France subscribed to the axiom that 'the phenomenon of terrorism could not be dealt with unless its causes were eliminated.'[26] Moreover, as we have just seen, France was convinced that a legal definition of terrorism was the best way to legitimize the international fight against terrorism. Despite several changes in Government, these two fundamental pillars were not significantly altered during the 1970s. As it seems, a moralizing approach to international terrorism was part of the French national consensus. At the same time, France did also have an interest in maintaining a large sphere of influence in its former colonies in the Third World, most notably in the Arab countries. An accommodating stance on international terrorism furthered this interest. Only on the exclusion of national liberation movements from the definition of terrorism was the French delegation to the United Nations somewhat more hesitant, although not entirely opposed to the idea.[27]

In any event, France shared the conviction of many states that the fight against terrorism needed the support of all countries, and had to be universal in order to be effective. Paris therefore believed that the interest of the international community would be best served by a universal agreement. Early on, France had suggested to the Secretary General that the agenda item 'terrorism' should be amended to 'international terrorism', adding a qualifying epithet and thereby assuaging the concerns of some African and Arab delegations.[28] Once the item of international terrorism had been included on the agenda of the 27th General Assembly, France did not see any reasonable alternative to the United Nations as the legitimate framework for a comprehensive approach to terrorism. On several occasions, France insisted that the UN, rather than the EEC or the Council of Europe, was the proper place to devise a comprehensive strategy.[29]

It was relatively safe for France to take such a conciliatory stance, since the Ad Hoc Committee was used as a talking shop by the newly independent countries of the Third World. This situation engendered so much disagreement that the debate was never going to reach the point where a serious commitment would have become necessary. It was therefore easy for France to lend moral support to the Ad Hoc Committee, even though Paris was not particularly satisfied with its work.[30] First, everyone should have an opportunity to present his ideas and opinions; then the debate should move on to study the underlying causes; subsequently there should be an attempt to formulate a definition of terrorism; 'after that, it would be much easier to consider measures to combat international terrorism'.[31] This attitude must have further contributed to the slow pace of the work in the Ad Hoc Committee, and France did not stress a need to speed up the process. All in all, one gets the impression that, while formally courting the favour of the non-aligned countries, in reality France was not entirely unhappy that the Ad Hoc Committee on International Terrorism had become a talking shop.

During the 1970s, France considered international terrorism to be less of a danger to French territory than a problem in the international sphere (Cerny 1981). It is difficult to assess the degree to which Paris would have been willing to accept an institutionally binding convention, but France would probably not have accepted measures that would seriously infringe upon its national sovereignty. From other cases in the 1970s, we know that France was generally greatly concerned about sovereignty.[32] In the particular case of terrorism, Paris would certainly have opposed a surrender of its freedom to determine the public enemy at its own discretion. However, due to a fundamental lack of consensus among the parties concerned, the debate never reached the point where it would have become necessary for France to declare itself explicitly on this point.

Italy

In the early 1970s, Italy was committed to a 'global peace strategy' for the Middle East. The idea was that the only way towards an enduring end to political violence in Palestine was a comprehensive approach that would take into account the legitimate political, social, and economic grievances of the Third World in general, and of the Palestinian people in particular. Since international terrorism had become part and parcel of the Palestinian conflict, a comprehensive approach to this problem resonated well with the normative outlook of Italian foreign policy.[33]

In line with this global peace strategy, Italy strove for a universal consensus on international terrorism as a necessary element in a fair and equal settlement to the Palestinian conflict. The Italian delegation at the United Nations called for a compromise that should meet with as wide an international approval as possible.[34] Moreover, Italian decision makers stressed that 'any action regarding the problem of terrorism can only be effective if it is undertaken on a global scale', thereby invoking the international interest in a solution to the problems connected with terrorism.[35] Initially, Italy even refused to deal with the problem of international terrorism at other forums, such as the Council of Europe.[36] If necessary, Rome preferred a weak regime with universal membership to a strong regime lacking the support of a great majority of states.

At the same time, Italy played the role of diplomatic bridge-builder (Migliorino 1979b). In November 1972, the US delegation at the United Nations found itself in an impasse due to the fierce resistance of the Non-Aligned Group, and strongly encouraged Italy to try and mediate between the opposing camps.[37] The role of bridge-builder was in the Italian national interest since successful mediation would have brought considerable credit with the American ally and diplomatic prestige to Italy. To achieve this end, Italy sponsored a compromise proposal which eventually failed in December 1972.[38] In line with this role, Italy abstained from ambitious demands and took a compromising stance on most substantive points.

But even if Italy saw itself as a mediator, it did not abstain from formulating explicit preferences. For example, Rome recognized the importance of studying the underlying causes of terrorism and emphasized that the right of any people to struggle for self-determination and dependence was inalienable, and should therefore not be affected by cooperative efforts aimed at eradicating international terrorism.[39] This was in line with the aforementioned 'global peace strategy', which saw the PLO and other national liberation movements as victims of a dreadful political situation rather than as international terrorists. But, on the other hand, Italy emphasized that atrocities could not be condoned, however politically motivated they might be, and that a study of the underlying causes of terrorism had to be without prejudice to the urgent consideration of concrete measures.[40] As far as possible, Italy also preferred to avoid the 'thorny problem' of finding a legal definition of international terrorism.[41]

At a later opportunity, Italy recommended that the phenomenon of 'state terrorism' should not be dealt with under the label of international terrorism but rather under the rubric of human rights violations.[42] Moreover, Italy started calling more energetically for concrete measures against international terrorism,[43] and after the kidnapping of the former Italian Prime Minister Aldo Moro in 1978 became even more pragmatic in demanding close international cooperation on practical issues.[44]

Given this pragmatic turn, however, it is quite surprising that Italy was now officially in favour of defining terrorism.[45] Nevertheless, this position need not be taken too seriously. The Ad Hoc Committee had failed to reach a consensus, and therefore there was no longer any risk in adopting all sorts of popular standpoints. For example, in 1981 senior Italian politician Giulio Andreotti (1981b: 552) continued to draw a distinction between terrorists and freedom fighters and in 1986, seven years after the demise of the Ad Hoc Committee, the Italian Minister of Defence gave an interview in which he called for the adoption of a comprehensive convention on international terrorism.[46]

Germany

In September 1972, Germany was heavily affected by the terrorist assault on the Olympic village in Munich. Since the country had been caught unprepared, and since it took some time for its Government to adopt an effective strategy, there seemed to be a national interest in legal action by the entire international community. Moreover, Germany was morally outraged at international terrorists taking innocent lives. This moral outrage was shared by many other states. Given the widespread international indignation after the Munich attack, an international legal approach to the problem of terrorism became even more appealing to the German Government.

At the time, however, the Federal Republic of Germany was not yet a Member of the United Nations. At an EEC meeting held in Frascati on 12 September 1972, the German Foreign Minister asked the nine fellow Member States to insist to the General Assembly on the necessity of an international convention against terrorism in all its forms.[47] During the next five months, Germany tried to lobby the other EEC states to take a coordinated position at the United Nations. In particular, a comprehensive convention on international terrorism was seen as a desirable goal. This does not however mean that Germany wanted a legal definition of terrorism. On the contrary, it was suggested that the very word 'terrorism' should be avoided.[48] Since Germany had a declared national interest in fighting terrorism through international collaboration, the country took a pragmatic stance and was keen on reaching results quickly.

When it finally joined the United Nations, in 1973, Germany formally disclosed its position: concrete measures against terrorism were more important than a study of its underlying causes; on the one hand, an antiterrorist convention should not affect the right of every nation to fight for self-determination and independence; on the other hand, however, 'nobody should be given the right to use violence indiscriminately and endanger innocent human lives'.[49] In fact, an internal document states that Germany's main concern was 'the protection of innocent private persons and the proscription of the use of violence by both non-state actors and by states'.[50] Due to the outrage after the Palestinian terrorist assault of September 1972, and maybe also due to a historically rooted feeling that political violence by the state can be worse than political violence by private citizens, the condemnation of terrorism by both national liberation movements and by states made moral sense to German decision makers.

Since Germany did not have any delegate on the Ad Hoc Committee on International Terrorism, the country kept a relatively low profile. Nevertheless, the Sixth Committee of the General Assembly was used to reiterate the German position.[51] At the beginning, Germany's objective was the conclusion of a comprehensive convention on international terrorism. Accordingly, Germany emphasized that 'the United Nations was the appropriate forum to deal with the issue, which concerned all mankind'.[52] As we have seen, Germany had a national interest in dealing with terrorism through a universal effort of the entire international community, as embodied by the UN. Moreover, since the United Nations was already dealing with terrorism when Germany joined the organization, it was natural to confirm the UN as the competent body.

Already in 1973, however, it turned out that the lowest common denominator at the UN was too low for a universal consensus to be reached. For tactical reasons, Germany therefore started to focus its activities on more exclusive multilateral forums. According to the German rationale, the EEC or the Council of Europe stood a higher chance of reaching a consensus because they had fewer participants. Even NATO was deemed more suitable to reach a political consensus on terrorism than the United Nations,

> Within the United Nations, views are so diametrically opposed that even a compromise solution seems unlikely. Accordingly, the fight against international terrorism should not be pursued further at the United Nations. Conversely, undertakings within European multilateral bodies, as well as NATO, are all the more important. Since the number of participants in these bodies is much lower than at the United Nations, there is more hope for concrete results. According to previous experience, it seems reasonable to proceed step by step, that is to select particular, narrowly circumscribed problems for the fight against international terrorism.[53]

From 1976, then, Germany focussed on its own political project: the *International Convention against the Taking of Hostages* (Lagoni 1977: 268–71).[54] According to a chief officer from the Ministry of Justice, Germany's initiative was a reaction to the failure of previous attempts to reach a comprehensive agreement (Corves 1978: 210). From this failure, Germany had concluded that concrete measures against certain manifestations of terrorism were better than endless discussions about its essence and underlying causes. In principle Germany would have welcomed a comprehensive convention on international terrorism, but in the absence of a viable consensus the German Government had increasingly come to prefer a more pragmatic and piecemeal approach.

Towards an agreement (2000–06)

As we have seen in the introduction to this chapter, a comprehensive convention on international terrorism would be a crucial step towards a shared understanding of the problem. Nevertheless, the debate from 1972 to 1979 was the last serious attempt to reach a common understanding for many years to come. There was an interruption of more than two decades, during the 1980s and 1990s, but since the year of 2000 there has been a new attempt to find a common understanding and, once again, the UN General Assembly is the institutional body where the debate is taking place.[55]

The formal preconditions were established between 1996 and 2000, on the basis of a General Assembly resolution and a draft convention submitted by India.[56] As in the 1970s, the General Assembly established an Ad Hoc Committee, supported by a Working Group. Among other tasks, the Committee was mandated to elaborate a comprehensive convention on international terrorism. Three years after the establishment of the Committee, in 1999, the General Assembly formally gave the starting signal for the Ad Hoc Committee to deal with the elaboration of a comprehensive convention.[57] After a revised draft had been submitted by India, in 2000, the diplomatic negotiations could finally start.[58] Since then, the Ad Hoc Committee and the Working Group have discussed the draft Comprehensive Convention on International Terrorism once a year.[59]

Already in 1999, the UN had adopted a convention on the financing of terrorism. This convention contains, for the first time, an embryonic definition (Gioia 2006: 10–13). Building on this precedent, the latest version of Article 2 of the draft Comprehensive Convention on International Terrorism contains a relatively broad definition of the term. According to this definition, certain serious offences against persons or heavy damage to property qualify as offences within the meaning of the Convention 'when the purpose of the conduct, by its nature or context, is to intimidate a population, or to compel a Government or an international organization to do or abstain from doing any act'.[60] Although the word 'terrorism' is used only in the title and in the preamble of the draft, the definition in Article 2 is clearly meant to be a definition of international terrorism.

Initially, the bargaining positions were quite similar to the familiar ones of the 1970s. Many Third World states insisted that terrorism be clearly distinguished from acts of legitimate self-defence by national liberation movements.[61] Most notably, the 56 Members of the Organization of the Islamic Conference (OIC) demanded the exemption of national liberation movements from the reach of the convention: 'People's struggle including armed struggle against foreign occupation, aggression, colonialism, and hegemony, aimed at liberation and self-determination in accordance with the principles of international law shall not be considered a terrorist crime'.[62] Predictably, such an exemption was bluntly rejected by a large majority of Western states.

Despite this apparent continuity, on closer examination it turns out that there has been a significant departure from the traditional view of Arab countries that state terrorism is the most deadly and harmful form of terrorism to be covered by a comprehensive convention. Of course this view was initially brought to the negotiation table and is still reiterated in certain contexts, especially with hindsight to Israel.[63] But the exclusion of state terrorism has now become negotiable under the condition that political violence by national liberation movements be exempted as well. Thus, in January 2002 the OIC Group rejected a proposal to exempt only the activities of armed forces and not also that of insurgents against these forces.[64]

This led to a fierce controversy over draft Article 18, of which two versions were on the table. The version of the Ad Hoc Committee's coordinator was very clear in exempting the 'activities of armed forces', but remained nebulous as to whether this would cover the activities of parties to an armed conflict other than the regular troops of a state. To avoid this kind of ambiguity, the OIC alternative version asserted that 'the parties during an armed conflict, including in situations of foreign occupation', were to be exempt from the provisions of the Convention.[65]

At least for situations of armed conflict and foreign occupation, this would mean the exemption of both state terrorism and national liberation movements from the reach of the comprehensive convention. The most obvious application of the exemption clause is the conflict in Israel/Palestine, where neither the activities of the Israeli state nor the activities of Palestinian insurgents could be branded as terrorism. Another possible application is the conflict in Iraq, where violent actors are fighting foreign occupation. Due to the uncompromising attitude of both sides, the two conflicting versions of Article 18 still remain the key problem to be solved.

In 2005, a consolidated draft was transmitted to the General Assembly, broadly following the coordinator's version, and renaming Article 18 as Article 20. The same draft did also add some conciliatory language to the preamble.[66] As could have been predicted, however, the OIC was not satisfied and the discussion started anew.[67]

While there is still no solution to the thorny problem of national liberation movements, an interesting development can be observed with regard to the traditional claim that before taking specific measures it is necessary to study the underlying causes of international terrorism. While an OIC resolution from 2000 still alluded to the 'underlying causes' argument,[68] and while Islamic states periodically repeat this argument and demand a high-level conference to discuss the problems connected with international terrorism, the question of the causes underlying the phenomenon no longer seems to pose a serious obstacle to the conclusion of a comprehensive convention.

Altogether, it seems that considerable progress has been made in comparison to the difficult situation in the 1970s. Nevertheless, the discussions illustrate once more how hard it is to agree on the conceptual boundaries of terrorism, let alone reach a legal definition of the term. In the first weeks after 11 September, a breakthrough seemed in sight. But although disagreement could quickly be limited to only one article (Article 18 on the exemption of state terrorism and/or national liberation movements), the attempt to reach a comprehensive convention was frustrated again by the mutually exclusive claims of certain Western states and certain Third World countries (Wiesbrock 2002).

It will again be interesting to compare the bargaining positions of the four major West European states. Despite the fact that, in recent decades, the Member States of the European Union have often been represented by the country holding the EU presidency, the best way of knowing the national position of a particular country is still to rely on the statements of its national delegates. For example, in 2003 Italy declared on behalf of the EU that '[t]he European Union believed that negotiations on the draft comprehensive convention on international terrorism on which agreement had been reached should not be reopened, and it reaffirmed its readiness to contribute to reaching a consensus on the outstanding issues'.[69] As we shall see, however, the Italian Government was at best a lukewarm supporter of the draft comprehensive convention.

While EU presidency statements are notoriously vague, Member States are of course free to formulate their own policy statements whenever they deem it appropriate. Indeed, the most important problem with EU presidency statements is that they tend to paper over substantive differences between individual bargaining positions and represent the lowest common denominator. It is therefore more enlightening individually to analyse the statements of the delegations of the most important Member States, rather than to accept at face value what is said on behalf of the European Union as a whole.

The main substantive points of contention are still the same as in the 1970s. Should international terrorism be legally defined? Must national liberation movements be included in, or excluded from, the definition of terrorism? Is it necessary to study the underlying causes of terrorism, or is it sufficient to take concrete measures?

Unlike in the 1970s, however, the West is not any more on the defensive against state-sponsored revolutionary movements in the Third World (Bremer 1993). Most countries now converge on the important point that 'state terrorism' should not be covered by the comprehensive convention. Another difference from the situation in the 1970s is that there is not much noise around the meetings of the Ad Hoc Committee and the Working Group. Most institutional aspects of the draft Convention are manipulated by legal experts. These experts have been successful in converting the question of institutional commitment into a technicality, so that states usually do not formulate explicit preferences on it. In some countries, such as France, where political decision makers seem to be less in favour of a comprehensive convention than legal experts, this has apparently led to a higher institutional commitment than would otherwise have been the case. In other countries, such as Germany, where political decision makers are more in favour of a comprehensive convention than legal experts, the effect has been the reverse.

To many countries the idea of an overarching comprehensive convention has been made more palatable by the fact that there already exists a legal *acquis* of more than twelve sector-specific conventions against particular aspects of international terrorism. Moreover, one should not forget that the United Nations has been struggling with a comprehensive approach to international terrorism ever since the 1970s. Even for countries with a moderately critical attitude, such as Italy, there does not seem to be any reasonable alternative to the universalistic framework of the United Nations.

Britain

Britain hardly supports the comprehensive convention on international terrorism and is explicitly opposed to a legal definition of the problem at the United Nations. At first glance this is surprising, since the United Kingdom is one of the few European countries where terrorism was legally defined before 9/11.[70] A more careful look, however, reveals that, as a close ally of the United States in the military 'coalition of the willing' against terrorism, Britain has a national interest in keeping its discretion to define the international public enemy on a case-by-case basis, rather than being dragged into a universal agreement.

In October 2001, the British permanent representative at the United Nations maintained that a legal definition of terrorism at the international level was superfluous and maybe even counterproductive,

> There is common ground amongst us all on what constitutes terrorism. What looks, smells and kills like terrorism is terrorism. (…) But there are also wars and armed struggles where actions can be characterized, for metaphorical and rhetorical force, as terrorist. This is a highly controversial and subjective area, on which, because of the legitimate spectrum of viewpoints within the United Nations membership, we will never reach full consensus. (…) Our job now is to confront and eradicate terrorism pure and simple: the use of violence without honour, discrimination or regard for human decency.[71]

By and large, it seems that the United Kingdom is pursuing the same pragmatic approach as in the 1970s. This is made easier by the fact that, after the terrorist attacks of 9/11, Britain, like the United States, has two alternative outlets for its initiatives against terrorism (Jonge Oudraat 2004). On the one hand is the General Assembly and its Sixth Committee. On the other hand, the United Kingdom has a permanent seat on the Security Council and its Counter Terrorism Committee (CTC). Between these two options, Britain clearly prefers the pragmatic approach of the Security Council to the legalist approach of the General Assembly. In 2003, the British delegation even remained absent from the meetings of the Ad Hoc Committee.[72]

As Sir Jeremy Greenstock, then chairman of the CTC, put it in early 2002, 'the General Assembly is 189 equal voices and votes, with no party discipline and no particular leadership, and it is chaos most of the time in terms of getting collective answers'.[73] This explains the predilection of the United Kingdom to use its permanent seat on the UNSC rather than its voice in the UNGA. During his term as chairman of the Counter Terrorism Committee, Greenstock used all his influence to keep the CTC as operational as possible and to prevent it from being dragged into debates on the legal definition of terrorism and its causes, and on the legitimacy of political violence by national liberation movements (Williams 2002; Mani 2004). In the General Assembly and its Sixth Committee, the United Kingdom hardly spoke at all on the comprehensive convention on international terrorism.[74]

All of a sudden, after the terrorist attacks on the subway system in London in July 2005, the United States and Britain apparently tried to break free of deadlock and joined the Secretary General in calling for an instant solution to the problem of defining terrorism.[75] The United Kingdom, in particular, started calling for a comprehensive convention on international terrorism, including an unequivocal definition and condemnation of the phenomenon.[76] For the definition, the plan was to condemn terrorism in all its manifestations, amounting to the 'deliberate and unlawful targeting and killing' of civilians, since this could not be 'justified or legitimized by any cause or grievance'.[77]

But does that mean that London and Washington reversed their negative attitude to the comprehensive convention in general, and to the definition of terrorism in particular? It is easy to see that the proposed definition was so broad that it basically would have constituted a carte blanche for determining the international public enemy on a case-by-case basis. For example, the definition suggested by the United Kingdom would have included attacks on Israeli civilians by Palestinian insurgents. Britain was not at all ready to compromise with the Muslim world on an exemption clause for national liberation movements. Accordingly, what seemed to be a revolution in the British bargaining position should rather be seen as a tactical move. Since there was no exemption for national liberation movements, it is hardly surprising that this ostensible attempt to reach a breakthrough at the UN's 60th anniversary meeting in September 2005 failed, due to the resistance of the Arab and Middle Eastern countries that were wary of the Palestinian liberation struggle being outlawed.[78] After the failure of this adventurous episode, Prime Minister Tony Blair's official spokesman argued that what mattered most was not a 'perfect' definition of terrorism but the practical measures taken to combat it.[79]

One may indeed doubt whether the initiative was at all intended to solve the problem of a consensus definition of international terrorism, or whether it was not rather meant to raise the stakes so high that the entire project of a comprehensive convention on international terrorism would fail. Given the negative stance of the United Kingdom (and the United States) on almost all other occasions, the latter hypothesis seems more plausible.

France

The French position, in contrast, was already distinguished before 9/11 by an emphasis on the desirability of a comprehensive convention.[80] French decision makers often stress that the entire international community is threatened by terrorism. As President Chirac said on 19 September 2001, the struggle against terrorism was the fight of the entire international community defending itself against murderers who were committing crimes that put freedom and human rights in jeopardy.[81] Accordingly, Paris maintains that a global and comprehensive approach to terrorism would be the most efficient way to meet international concerns. At the same time, the French Government perceives a strategic interest in preventing the hegemonic powers (namely the United States, but also the United Kingdom) from defining the international public enemy on a case-by-case basis. A comprehensive convention on international terrorism would further this objective.

This goes hand in hand with support for the United Nations. From the French standpoint, the fight against terrorism must be universal in order to be effective and therefore needs the support of all countries. Accordingly, it is in the interest of the international community to pursue a multilateral approach at the United Nations. France considers the UN, and especially the General Assembly, as the only institutional framework sufficiently inclusive to provide the fight against terrorism with the necessary legitimacy.[82] In other words, one should

> start by strengthening the mobilization of the international community as a whole. The United Nations can and must play a major role in this new drive. Because it is a world body, it must be at the centre of our efforts.[83]

But although the French support for the comprehensive convention is unequivocal, Paris often avoids controversial points. For example, it is almost certain that France would welcome a legal definition of international terrorism.[84] This is suggested by the fact that a legal definition might be helpful to limit the discretion of the US-led 'coalition of the willing' to determine the international public enemy on a case-by-case basis. Nevertheless, the problem of the definition of international terrorism has not been explicitly addressed. Similarly, France has remained silent on the question of whether political violence by national liberation movements should fall under a comprehensive convention.

Only on one point has Paris been outspoken. Apparently for normative reasons, French decision makers of all shades and colours stress the point that one must deal with the underlying causes of terrorism, such as injustice and poverty. They seem to see it as a moral duty to overcome these underlying causes and thereby to defeat terrorism. Take as an example the following statement by the French Foreign Minister:

> We are waging a merciless fight against terrorism. Let us at the same time address its roots. That means putting an end to situations that terrorists exploit; giving the world's excluded hope again; restoring dignity to those peoples deprived of it; and ensuring that dialogue and cooperation among civilizations, cultures and religions prevail, rather than conflict and intolerance.[85]

Similar statements are reiterated in various forms by high-ranking state officials on different occasions. In full continuity with the official French position of the 1970s, the concern with the underlying causes of terrorism is the typical *ceterum censeo* of French diplomats at discussions on international terrorism.[86]

Germany

Under the aegis of Chancellor Schröder and Foreign Minister Fischer, Germany was even more vigorous than France in its support for a comprehensive convention. In fact, Germany had pledged support for the Indian draft convention already before 11 September.[87] The same policy was later continued by the new Government of Merkel and Steinmeier. Terrorism is seen as an attack on internationally shared values such as human dignity, freedom, tolerance, and democracy. Accordingly, the German Government seems to believe that the international community has a moral duty to devise a comprehensive response to the problem. As Germany sees terrorism as attacking the very values the United Nations stands for, the UN is seen as the appropriate geographical and institutional forum to find a legal response to the challenge. From this standpoint, only the UN 'can give international legitimacy to the response to terrorism'.[88]

At the same time, Germany also emphasizes the instrumental interest of the state system in a comprehensive strategy against terrorism. Since Berlin is convinced that the fight against terrorism cannot be effective without a universal coalition, the United Nations is seen as 'uniquely suited to the task ahead'.[89] If one takes this at face value, there is no reasonable alternative to the United Nations as the most universal institutional and geographical framework.[90] As the German Foreign Minister pointed out in 2003: 'What we need is a system of global cooperative security. (…) It is the United Nations that provides us with the appropriate framework for that.'[91]

According to the German rationale, after 9/11 the existence of twelve sector-specific conventions is not sufficient any more. To ensure that effective action is taken against terrorism, all countries have an interest in a comprehensive convention. Berlin believes that the international community has a collective interest in fighting terrorism, and that this collective interest is best served if the United Nations conclude a comprehensive convention to fill the loopholes left by the 'piecemeal approach'.

Already in November 2001, the German Foreign Minister stressed the necessity of analysing 'the full range of causes and circumstances that permit such hatred and violence to grow'.[92] Problems of underdevelopment were held to be at the root of international terrorism, and their solution was seen as a key element in the fight against the phenomenon.[93] In January 2003, the Foreign Minister explicitly declared his conviction that, for a comprehensive strategy against terrorism to be successful, it had to be supported by the reconciliation of political conflicts in the Arab world, and by humanitarian and economic aid to those countries where terrorism was finding its breeding ground.[94]

Moreover, Germany would welcome a universally binding definition of terrorism.[95] This is presumably because Berlin wants to counteract the tendency of the United States to define terrorism on a case-by-case basis. For example, on the eve of the Iraq war of 2003, Germany was opposed to the United States unilaterally declaring that the regime of Saddam Hussein was related to terrorism. More generally, one may argue that Germany has a national interest in a restrictive legal definition of terrorism that will make it harder for the United States to identify terrorists at its own discretion.[96]

But even assuming that this is the 'objective' German national interest, Berlin is hardly aware of it. On the contrary, if it were up to the German Government, the Comprehensive Convention would cover national liberation movements. The reason provided on the website of the Foreign Ministry, both under Chancellor Schröder and under Chancellor Merkel, has clear moral overtones: 'There is no justification for terrorism. Only legitimate means shall be available for the pursuit of legitimate ends'.[97] Berlin cultivates a special relationship with Israel, and it would be embarrassing for Germany to be caught condoning political violence by Palestinian terrorists. Presumably for the same reason, Israeli violence against civilians is never condemned as terrorist crime.

Italy

Under the Berlusconi Government, Italy kept a relatively low profile on the comprehensive convention on international terrorism. Shortly after the outrage of 9/11, the Italian Foreign Minister declared that his country supported a swift conclusion of the negotiations for a comprehensive convention.[98] Roughly at the same time, Italy suggested a 'safeguard clause' to make the sector-specific conventions prevail whenever they were in contradiction with the comprehensive treaty (Barberini 2002: 203). As the Italian delegate pointed out in October 2001, the purpose of the comprehensive convention was to integrate the sector-specific approach with a general legal instrument that would allow the repression of any terrorist act, wherever and by whomever committed.[99]

Since 2002, the Italian delegates at the United Nations in New York, although generally sympathetic to the project, have hardly raised their voice in the debate. This self-restraint is in contrast not only to the outspoken language used by other European countries on the same topic, but also to Italy's own active role as a mediator in the 1970s. While it is possible that Italian diplomats were more active behind closed doors, one cannot reconstruct the details of the Italian position from official UN documents. Unfortunately, the situation is little better in statements by the Italian Government in the domestic context. While Foreign Minister Renato Ruggiero was quick to declare to the Italian House of Representatives the general support of his country for a comprehensive convention, preferences on more specific points were not disclosed.[100]

One is therefore forced to turn to more informal sources. According to one interlocutor at the Foreign Ministry in Rome, Italy initially followed the United States in opposing the Comprehensive Convention as drafted by India. In 2000, after the Indian draft had been rewritten with strong US involvement, Italy took a more positive attitude. In the aftermath of the terrorist attacks of 11 September 2001, however, the American position switched again to the negative. Due to Italy's national interest in good relationships with the United States, there can hardly be any strong commitment to the comprehensive convention as long as the American Government is opposed to it.[101]

Although Rome in principle does not reject the idea of defining terrorism, the same source in the Foreign Ministry reveals that Italy follows the position of its American ally in being sceptical about the comprehensive convention in general, and about the exemption of national liberation movements in particular. In broad lines, the logic runs like this: 'The Palestinians are the enemies of Israel; the United States is a friend of Israel; Italy is a friend of the US; therefore, Italy should not support an international agreement that would exempt the Palestinians from facing terrorist charges.' Still according to the same interlocutor in the Foreign Ministry, this is the reason why Rome tends to oppose a definition of international terrorism that would exclude political violence by national liberation movements such as the Palestine Liberation Organization or Hamas.

It seems, however, that Rome is not only influenced by the national interest in good relationships with the American ally, but also by the 'logic of appropriateness' generated by its membership in the European Union. In a framework decision of 21 September 2001, the EU Member States committed themselves to supporting the draft Comprehensive Convention on International Terrorism. Soon after, Foreign Minister Renato Ruggiero declared his support in the Italian House of Representatives.[102] Moreover, as a Member State of the European Union Italy was far from being adamant that national liberation movements had to be included in the definition of terrorism. In 2001, Italy did not oppose an EU compromise proposal suggesting that an explicit reference to the principle of national self-determination could be included in Article 18, now renamed as Article 20, of the draft Comprehensive Convention (Barberini 2002: 208).

4 Antiterrorist methods

It is not easy for liberal democracies to find an adequate response to terrorism. Because of their identity as constitutional states, they cannot physically eliminate or radically suppress their political enemies. Instead, they are compelled to develop an armoury of more subtle antiterrorist methods (E.H. Evans 1978; Wilkinson 1981, 2000). To minimize the risk to life and limb of the victims, and in part even to avoid unnecessary bloodshed amongst terrorists, they have established special commando units with the professional ability to intervene in terrorist attacks. To prevent such attacks from happening in the first place, and to capture the perpetrators when an attack has already occurred, they have also introduced sophisticated systems of surveillance. Other methods include negotiation techniques for hostage scenarios, aviation security, target hardening, the protection of diplomatic premises and, more recently, the fight against terrorist finance.

In the face of the common terrorist threat, most of these techniques were not developed in isolation but in close cooperation between those liberal democracies that were most concerned about terrorism. Since the early 1970s, when international terrorism raised its ugly head, states have been trying to find common ground on strategies to suppress the phenomenon. Already at the beginning of the 1980s, cooperation between police forces and secret services on the development of antiterrorist methods was more advanced than cooperation on the political and judicial aspects of the fight against terrorism (Dobson and Payne 1982: 26–7). It is fair to say that the development of efficient antiterrorist techniques was a collective endeavour in which all liberal democracies were involved, although to somewhat different degrees.

The present chapter deals with the international aspects of the most important antiterrorist methods. Initially, the main challenge was the establishment of special commando units such as the British SAS or the German GSG-9, and the international exchange of secret-service and police information on terrorists (Dobson and Payne 1982; Bigo 1996). In the 2000s, since the advent of suicide bombing, special commando units are no longer of much use and, instead, intelligence has become the single most important method in the fight against terrorism (Charters 1991: 227). Especially in the aftermath of 9/11, this has led to a tremendous intensification of surveillance (Ball and Webster 2003).

Nevertheless, it is still a challenge for states to ensure that antiterrorist intelligence is effectively exchanged between police agencies and secret services.[1]

Special commando units and information exchange (1972–80)

The starting signal for West European countries to improve their antiterrorist methods was the Palestinian assault on the Olympic village in Munich, on 5 September 1972. On that day, when Palestinian terrorists took nine Israeli athletes hostage, the Western world in general, and Germany in particular, experienced a humiliating disaster. In a shootout the following day, the German police showed themselves completely unprepared to deal with the situation. Their attempt to rescue the athletes ended with the tragic deaths of all the hostages and one German policeman (Reeve 2000).

To prepare for similar scenarios in the future, many European countries set up special commando units. Over the following years, these units became important hotbeds for the development of novel methods of fighting terrorism.[2] Since most countries were confronted with roughly the same challenges at the same time, cooperation burgeoned among the units. On the one hand, there was the opportunity for the units concerned to support each other and exchange 'best practices'. On the other, this cooperation was also a good way for states to show their mutual solidarity in the fight against terrorism.

One can get a flavour of this collaboration from the following statement by Charlie Beckwith, the commander of the US Delta Force:[3]

> Delta began an exchange program with the SAS. From a sergeant they sent, we learned quite a bit about booby traps. He'd spent time in Belfast. Then, too, GSG-9 looked us over, and we them. So too, the French Groupe d'Intervention de la Gendarmerie Nationale (GIGN), and the Israelis. Delta became a part of the free world's counterterrorist community. We learned and we taught.
>
> (Beckwith and Knox 1983: 171)

Nevertheless, not all countries were equally keen to support this kind of cooperation. Britain and Germany were happy to put their special commando units in touch with their foreign counterparts, so that they could learn from them or even teach them from their own experiences. France and Italy, by contrast, offered much less support for the exchange of 'best practices' among special commando units. This was even more evident with regard to operational collaboration, for example in the liberation of hostages. Britain and Germany were much more willing than France and Italy to support the participation of their special commando units in joint operations with their foreign counterparts.

Closely related, there was the more principled question of how to deal with terrorism in the first place. Was it better to take an uncompromising stance and fight terrorists relentlessly, or was it better to take a more flexible approach and negotiate in order to save human lives? There was a strong case that sometimes it was expedient to negotiate, especially in hostage-taking scenarios (Miller 1980). Nevertheless, in the 1970s there was an emergent international norm of non-negotiation. The observance, or disregard, of this so-called no-concessions principle is another indicator of the degree to which a country was committed to international cooperation on antiterrorist methods (Bell 1978: 78–93, 168–97; John 1991; Clutterbuck 1993). Only Britain generally took a hard-line, while Germany, France, and Italy were all ready to accommodate terrorist demands.

As far as the international exchange of information was concerned, it was easy to agree in principle that the arms-length exchange of human intelligence among secret services and police agencies was not sufficient. In practice, however, it was often difficult for states to accept the sharing of sensitive information. To begin with, there were concerns about national sovereignty. Moreover, 'all states jealously tend to guard their own national security data for fear that such intelligence will be compromised or even destroyed in the process of international exchange' (Chalk 1996: 119). Finally, there were significant differences in the human and material resources available to the police forces and secret services of different countries (Robertson 1994: 110–11).

Hence, different countries held different views as to the desirable scope of international cooperation. This can be seen, for example, from their attitude to concrete collaboration on the ground. While Britain and Germany pushed for the direct exchange of investigators on cross-border missions, other countries preferred to limit cooperation to information exchange via central bureaus and liaison officers. Similarly, while Britain and Italy did not yet possess significant computer networks, already in the 1970s Germany was busy constructing databases and providing electronic information to its neighbours. France, by contrast, was explicitly opposed to the idea of relying on computerized data and highlighted the value of personal contacts among professionals.

In the second half of the 1970s, there was a certain move towards the institutionalization of information exchange at the European level. After the failure of efforts to deal with terrorism at the United Nations, West European countries began approaching the problem of improved information exchange on a regional basis (Kerstetter 1978: 545). Britain and Germany in particular called for the establishment of intergovernmental forums for the exchange of secret information among the Member States of the European Community, and potentially also beyond. For example, after 1977 the TREVI Group provided an institutional forum for European law enforcement agencies to gather and exchange information.[4] After 1979, information was also exchanged through a more informal channel, the Police Working Group on Terrorism (PWGOT). In 1978, officials from the German, Italian, Austrian and Swiss secret services began meeting in the highly informal 'Vienna Club'. Once more, it seems that

Britain and Germany were more willing to support institutionalized cooperation than either France or Italy.

Germany

Already in September 1972, at a ministerial meeting of the European Community, the German Foreign Minister proposed studying the possibility of further cooperation against terrorism, including 'the exchange of information on terrorist activities, visa requirements and the supervision of aliens, and methods of combating terrorism'.[5]

In fact, Germany was one of the countries most severely hit by the problem. From 1972, it was targeted by international terrorist groups such as the Palestinian 'Black September'. Soon thereafter, German terrorist gangs such as the 'Red Army Faction' developed strong international links to Middle Eastern terrorism. Accordingly, the German Government perceived a national interest in cooperating with other states in order to improve antiterrorist methods. From 1972 on, international cooperation, including collaboration with the special commando units of other countries and the exchange of antiterrorist information, was an integral part of the German strategy against terrorism (Bundesminister des Innern 1978: 16–17; Katzenstein 1990: 53).

The readiness of the German Government for international cooperation was reinforced by domestic agencies such as the Federal Border Guard Group 9 (GSG-9), the Federal Criminal Police Office (BKA), and the Federal Office for the Protection of the Constitution (BfV).[6] All of these agencies were keen to find effective ways of fighting terrorism, and to further this end they promoted the widest possible international collaboration with their foreign counterparts. Fully in agreement with the leaders of the GSG-9 and the BKA, the German Government was convinced that international cooperation on cutting-edge methods was necessary to counter the terrorist threat more effectively.[7]

The failed rescue attempt after the terrorist attack of 5 September 1972 served in particular as a wake-up call for Germany to prepare for similar contingencies in the future. Only three days after the debacle, on 8 September 1972, the Minister of the Interior Hans-Dietrich Genscher decided on the establishment of a German special commando unit (Tophoven 1985: 91). Despite the decentralized structure of German policing, this decision was quickly endorsed by the Conference of Interior Ministers of the Federal Republic.[8] Subsequently, the German special commando unit *Grenzschutzgruppe 9* was set up under the command of Colonel Ulrich Wegener.

Systematic cooperation with the special commando units of other countries was encouraged by the German Minister of the Interior, who gave the commander of GSG-9 the explicit order to go abroad and study 'best practices'. Later, the Minister was to declare in an interview: 'I asked Mr. Wegener to look around the world for options. By this, we were pursuing the objective of exploiting the experience of existing units of this kind, thereby avoiding undesirable developments for ourselves'.[9] However, the exhortation of the Minister of the Interior was hardly necessary. In the words of Ulrich Wegener:

> From the beginning, I have attached great importance to international cooperation. Without the exchange of experience with friendly special units abroad, the fight against international terrorism is all up in the air. Everybody must be willing and ready to learn from his fellows.
>
> (Wegener, as quoted in Tophoven 1985: 82)

At an early stage, GSG-9 was therefore committed to collaboration with the special commando units of foreign countries. Although Germany was one of the first European countries to establish a special commando unit, and therefore necessarily had to enter unknown territory, GSG-9 was keen to learn from the experience of other countries.[10] In particular, it tried to learn from the tactics employed by the British SAS and the Israeli special forces, while recognizing that the experiences of the latter were not directly applicable to the German situation (Scholzen and Froese 2001: 10).

Once it had gained a certain professional standing, GSG-9 could shift from the role of disciple to that of teacher. From 1975, the unit organized an international commander meeting on a yearly basis. Later on, after the success of 1977, when it rescued an airplane in Mogadishu without a single casualty among the hostages, more than 50 countries asked for German cooperation. Some requested help with the creation of their own units, while others sent delegations to visit the headquarters of GSG-9 near Bonn. As a result, some countries such as the Netherlands, Somalia, Saudi Arabia, and Singapore modelled their special commando units on GSG-9. Other countries, including the United States, Switzerland, and Austria, benefited from German know-how. Close cooperation was also established with France, Israel, and the United Kingdom (Tophoven 1985: 74–84; Scholzen and Froese 2001: 24–5). GSG-9 even hosted an international Anti-Terror Workshop and organized a Combat Team Competition for 22 special commando units from a variety of countries.[11]

Apart from training, GSG-9 was also sent abroad on concrete operations. Already in 1976, it assisted the Dutch special commando unit in a dangerous hostage-taking situation. At the Mogadishu operation, in 1977, logistical help was accepted from the British SAS. The favour was reciprocated in 1980 during a hostage drama at the Iranian embassy in London, when Wegener assisted the British SAS in planning the raid on the Iraqi terrorists inside the building (Tophoven 1985: 84, 93).[12]

Still in the same year, Wegener also offered German assistance to the US Delta Force for the raid into Iran to liberate the diplomats held hostages at the US embassy in Tehran: 'Charlie, am prepared to put in Teheran German TV crew. STOP. Would you like your people on it? STOP'. The offer was eventually ignored because the Pentagon did not like the idea of accepting help from a foreign country. However, this was deeply regretted by the head of the US

Delta Force: '[Y]ou don't understand. He's my friend. He knows Delta; he's visited us. He knows how we operate and what we need. He'll help us.'[13]

While Germany was very cooperative as far as collaboration among special commando units was concerned, the opposite was true about the no-concessions principle. Bonn was not at first ready to accept the emergent international norm that no concessions should be made to terrorists. Instead, Germany pursued a flexible approach and frequently gave in to terrorist demands. In February 1972, for example, Palestinian terrorists abducted a German airplane flying from New Delhi to Frankfort, and received a ransom of 5 Million Dollars. In October 1972 terrorists hijacked another airplane between Beirut and Munich, and succeeded in extorting the release of their fellow terrorists who had perpetrated the Munich attack one month before (John 1991: 77–80).

Only between 1975 and 1977, did the German policy become hard-line. After the 1975 hostage drama at the German embassy in Stockholm, the last straw was the 'hot autumn' of 1977 when terrorists abducted the leading German industrialist Schleyer and hijacked a Lufthansa plane to Mogadishu. In these two crucial cases, the German Government finally decided under the leadership of Chancellor Helmut Schmidt that it would not comply with terrorist demands (Pridham 1981: 34–5). Nevertheless Bonn still maintained that, especially in hostage-taking scenarios when human lives were endangered, the decision on whether to negotiate or not was contingent on the circumstances at hand (Bundesregierung 1977: 148–9). Between 1979 and 1980, for example, the BKA had a mandate to cultivate relationships with the PLO in order to accommodate the Palestinians (Dietl 2004: 196–201; cf. Sobieck 1994: 55–7).

The German hesitation in adopting the no-concessions principle can be attributed to the moral value attached to the protection of human life. This attitude reflected a broad normative consensus in post-war Germany and was also supported by the federal constitution. Initially, Bonn was convinced that giving in to terrorist demands was the best way to protect the lives of innocent people. After it turned out that such an accommodative stance placed a perverse incentive on terrorists to hit even harder, the same rationale was used to argue for a hard-line approach. Or, in the words of the West German Ambassador to Israel, von Puttkamer: 'We have to act according to our law, which means to save the lives of our citizens. Saving human lives has priority'.[14]

As an alternative to paramilitary rescue operations or shameful accommodation, the German Government had a special predilection for the collection of antiterrorist information. In pursuit of this strategy, Bonn perceived a national interest in exchanging information with a wide array of West European countries. The objective was to use all available information in order to protect Germany from international terrorists, as well as from German terrorists hiding abroad. Accordingly, officials from the Federal Criminal Police Office and the Federal Office for the Protection of the Constitution met on a regular basis with their counterparts from other European countries in order to exchange information. From 1977, such exchange was facilitated by liaison offices, both at the BfV and at the BKA (Katzenstein 1990: 56; Anderson *et al.* 1995: 54; Busch 1995: 168, 311). Sometimes, the BKA also sent officers abroad for terrorist investigations.[15]

The head of the BKA, Horst Herold, especially, was convinced that thoroughly organized data was the key to success in national and international investigations. Hence, Germany was the first country to build up systematic databases and to provide computerized information to other countries (Busch *et al.* 1985: 115–46). Computerization started in 1972 with INPOL, and from 1975 the BKA developed the PIOS database to improve counterterrorist investigations.[16] This database, which was part of the more comprehensive INPOL system, contained a massive amount of information on potential terrorist suspects (Busch 1995: 174). To make the best possible use of such information, Germany was ready to provide data to other European countries, namely to the Member States of the European Community and to the other European Member States of Interpol (Wiesel 1985: 212). The achievement in creating an accessible database and providing fast and accurate information to other European police forces was highly appreciated and admired (Dobson and Payne 1982: 122).

Since Germany had a national interest in making the prevention of terrorist incidents more effective, Bonn systematically promoted the creation of institutional forums for the international exchange of antiterrorist information. These forums included TREVI, PWGOT, and the Vienna Club. Already in September 1972, at a ministerial meeting of the European Community, the German Foreign Minister had proposed improving the exchange of information on terrorist activities.[17] In 1974, the German Minister of the Interior prepared a similar proposal for a ministerial conference on internal security (Busch 1995: 306). It is thus fair to say that, along with Britain, Germany was among the founders of TREVI (Bundesminister des Innern 1978: 3–4, 16–17). In 1975, in an attempt to intensify international police collaboration in the heat of the second wave of West German terrorism, Bonn was also involved in the creation of the Vienna Club (Katzenstein 1990: 56). Finally, in 1979 Germany was among the initiators of the Police Working Group on Terrorism, which was intended as a further instrument for the improvement of European police cooperation against terrorism (Benyon *et al.* 1993: 278).

Britain

During the 1970s, Britain was also extremely supportive of international cooperation on antiterrorist methods. The British Government perceived a strong national interest in avoiding a 'British Munich', that is an attack on British soil similar to the 1972 terrorist assault on the Olympic village in Munich. International cooperation on antiterrorist methods was seen as an obvious means to further this end. In October 1972, the British Government therefore installed a Cabinet Working Group on Terrorist Activities to discuss innovations in the field of counterterrorism, including the armoury of antiterrorist methods in a variety of countries.[18]

Thereafter, Britain was at the forefront of international efforts to make antiterrorist methods more efficacious. International cooperation among special commando units and secret services was seen as an important means of avoiding Munich-style incidents. Accordingly, the British strategy was based on a thorough assessment of the international state of the art. If one considers that still in the 1960s terrorism had been largely absent from the international agenda, it is remarkable how thoroughly Britain developed an 'internationalist' attitude on this sensitive matter.

British collaboration on the improvement of antiterrorist methods was greatly facilitated by the fact that domestic institutions, such as the Special Air Service and the British secret services (MI5, MI6), were ready to face the challenge. This in turn was mainly due to the longstanding experience of these agencies with problems of counter-insurgency and domestic terrorism in Northern Ireland. In particular, the professionalism of the British special commando unit, the SAS, acquired through the colonial and Ulster experiences, made it easier and more attractive for Britain to join international efforts to improve antiterrorist methods (Wilkinson 1988: 33; Taillon 2001: 1–39).[19] Largely for similar reasons, the British secret services were also well-prepared to co-operate with their foreign counterparts in the exchange of relevant information.

While Prime Minister Edward Heath immediately endowed the SAS with the task of coping with the horrific scenario of a 'British Munich', Home Secretary Charles Douglas-Home harboured certain misgivings that this might lead to the escalation of civil unrest in Northern Ireland (Wilkinson 1974: 142; Dobson and Payne 1982: 11–12). For a while, this may have slowed down the pace of Britain establishing a special commando unit with a capability for deployment at home and abroad. In March 1973, the SAS was still under reorganization, and London even used these organizational adjustments as an excuse that the unit temporarily could not be sent abroad for training missions.[20] But be that as it may, in March 1974 a stout supporter of special commando units came (back) to power: Prime Minister Harold Wilson (Wilkinson 1974: 142–3). Since then, the SAS has trained many special commando units from a variety of countries, including Germany and the United States (Dobson and Payne 1982: 60–1).

In 1977, Britain organized a training course for senior British police officers called 'Exercise Europa', in combination with a counterterrorism conference for all chief police officers from the Member States of the European Community (Police College 1977; Dubois 1979: 36). At a more technical level, many countries copied the famous 'killing house' at Hereford, where marksmen were trained in close quarter battle, that is the perilous skill of shooting terrorists in the closed confines of a room without hitting the hostages to be rescued (Geraghty 1993: 414). The SAS, in turn, adopted from the German GSG-9 the principle of 'leading from the front' (Scholzen and Froese 2001: 25). All in all, it appears that

Britain was remarkably committed to both teaching the latest antiterrorist techniques to other countries, and learning them from other countries.

In a nutshell, Britain was very much ahead in the field of special commando operations due to the colonial and Ulster experience. This fostered the willingness of the SAS and its political patrons to commit the country to international cooperation, and to collaborate with as many countries as possible. In fact, the SAS developed excellent working relationships with its counterparts in virtually every part of the world.

There was apparently only one partial exception from this rule. Since the SAS was involved in protecting the rulers of some Arab States, its relationship with Israel was sometimes rather complicated and had to be conducted through the commander of the German GSG-9, Ulrich Wegener (Dobson and Payne 1982: 61). However, this does not mean that British cooperation on counterterrorism was not extended to Israel. For example, in 1972 London allowed Israeli divers to carry out underwater checks to detect explosives on the bottom of Israeli ships anchored in British ports.[21]

In general, London hardly posed any limits to international cooperation on antiterrorist methods. In 1977, with the explicit approval of the British Prime Minister, the SAS sent two men to participate in the legendary GSG-9 operation at Mogadishu and contributed a collection of flash-bang grenades to stun the terrorists in the decisive moments of the raid (Clutterbuck 1990: 122; Geraghty 1993: 422–4; Sievert 2004: 135, 145). In the same year, stun grenades were also provided to the Dutch in a dangerous hostage situation (Dobson and Payne 1982: 60–1).[22] In 1980, Britain accepted the help of the commander of the German GSG-9, Ulrich Wegener, in planning the successful raid against the occupied Iranian embassy in London (Tophoven 1985: 84).[23]

Britain was also one of the first Western countries to systematically observe the no-concessions principle. After some initial vacillation in the 'black September' of 1970, when the United Kingdom had released the Palestinian terrorist Leila Khaled to avoid major bloodshed among the passengers of three airplanes held capture in the Jordanian desert, Britain became almost adamant against terrorist blackmail (Snow and Phillips 1970; Clutterbuck 1975: 100–1; John 1991: 100–3).[24] This hard-line attitude culminated fifteen years later, when Margaret Thatcher was able to proudly declare,

> On behalf of Her Majesty's Government, we in Britain will not accede to the terrorists' demands. The law will be applied to them as to all other criminals. Prisoners will not be released. Statements in support of the terrorists' cause will not be made. If hijacked aircraft land here, they will not be allowed to take off. For in conceding terrorist demands, the long-term risks are even greater than the immediate dangers.[25]

The leading position of the United Kingdom was also reflected by its readiness to support the exchange of antiterrorist information with the secret services and police forces of other European and non-European countries. The British intelligence community enjoyed a strategic position due to the country's special relationship with the United States, close commonwealth ties, traditionally good relationships with many Arab regimes, and the British accession to the European Community in 1973. Thereby, the preconditions for information exchange with a wide array of countries were firmly institutionalized. Already in the early 1970s London explicitly welcomed the exchange of secret information on terrorism, especially with Middle Eastern countries such as Jordan and Israel, but also with Western European countries and the United States.[26]

Traditionally, the British police had a strong standing in the transgovernmental 'old boy networks' of police officers (Dobson and Payne 1982: 27). This must have given the British Government an incentive to support the formalization of European police cooperation, for example by sponsoring the TREVI framework. When the Council of Ministers of the European Community met in Rome in December 1975, the British Foreign Secretary proposed setting up a special working group to combat terrorism in the EC. This working group was established in 1976 and became known, in 1977, under the acronym TREVI (Bunyan 1993: 16).[27] Although the police forces were to develop a preference for the more informal forum of the Police Working Group on Terrorism, which was established with British support in 1979, London continued to champion the intergovernmental TREVI framework (House of Commons 1990a: 5, 43–4).[28]

Much of the initiative for both TREVI and PWGOT had come from the British police. As a police counterpart to the Security Service's Central Liaison Office, in 1976 New Scotland Yard created a European Liaison Section at Metropolitan Police Special Branch. Very soon, the European Liaison Section started systematically collaborating with the police forces of other friendly European countries, regardless of whether they were Members of the European Community or not. For example, collaboration was extended to Sweden, Switzerland, and Spain (Wharton 1981: 13–17). When TREVI became operational in 1977, the European Liaison Section officially became the central contact point for information exchange on terrorist matters between British police forces and their counterparts in the Member States of the European Community (House of Commons 1990a: 42). Since this arrangement might have hampered information exchange with other European states and across the Atlantic, the British Government welcomed the formal extension of the TREVI framework to other Western countries.[29]

It would be unfair to object that TREVI was 'only' an intergovernmental framework. Although this is precisely what TREVI was, it was not until the Thatcher era that international cooperation moved further and the British preference for the intergovernmental method started becoming an impediment to deeper international cooperation (Bigo 1996: 214). Moreover, it is important to note that British collaboration on antiterrorist investigations was not limited to the exchange of information. Already during the 1970s, British police officers were ready to go on joint surveillance operations targeted at international terrorists travelling through Europe (Wharton 1981: 3).

Only with regard to the automatic exchange of computerized information was Britain not as quick as, say, Germany or the United States. While the United Kingdom was happy to receive data from the German facilities in Wiesbaden, in the 1970s the British databases were still under development and not yet sufficiently advanced to allow for reciprocity (Dobson and Payne 1982: 70; Wiesel 1985: 214; Anderson 1989: 88).[30]

France

During most of the 1970s, France was less affected by terrorism than other countries (Cerny 1981). Nevertheless, the French Government was of course persuaded that there was a national interest in improving antiterrorist methods to fight the problem more effectively. Thus, exchanging information with other states was seen as a useful instrument for dealing with terrorism. Insofar as conventional police forces were not suitable to counter the violence of political extremists, Paris also recognized the national interest in following the example of other Western European countries and establishing a special commando unit. As we shall see, however, for a variety of reasons this did not always translate into concrete collaboration. At least until the early 1980s, France was an awkward partner in international cooperation to improve antiterrorist methods.[31]

A few years after the 1972 terrorist assault on the Olympic village in Munich, France established its own special commando unit, the *Groupe d'Intervention de la Gendarmerie Nationale*. As the French Minister of Defence declared at the 30th anniversary of the GIGN, like any other European country France had become aware of the terrorist menace and decided to establish an intervention unit in order to improve its ability to conduct antiterrorist operations.[32] Despite the importance this was given officially, it took a very long time for the French special commando unit to become fully operational (Barril 1984).

By its specific institutional set-up, the GIGN was precluded from operational collaboration and from the exchange of 'best practices' with its foreign counterparts. While foreign units were highly specialized in counterterrorism, the GIGN worked as a sort of fire-fighter coping with a variety of incidents the normal police could not deal with effectively. From the very beginning, the fight against terrorism was only one among many tasks assigned to the unit. Apart from antiterrorist operations, the mandate of the GIGN included raids against ordinary kidnappers, homicidal maniacs, prison mutineers, and even sadomasochists (Barril 1984; Logorjus 1990). As a result the unit was forced to pursue its own, distinct approach towards exercising and drilling, and its ability to learn from the experiences of the special intervention units of other countries, or even to teach them about its own experiences, was seriously impaired. Due to its relative dissimilarity from the institutional format of other units, the GIGN was mostly condemned to learn its tactics by means of trial and error (Barril 1984: 32).

The problem was not so much a lack of will on the part of French professionals. On the contrary, as an emergent organization the GIGN was keen to learn as much as possible from the challenges posed to its foreign counterparts, and from the responses other special commando units were developing to tackle them. For example the GIGN tried to learn from the experience of the German GSG-9 and the British SAS, and its leaders were particularly interested in contacts with the US Delta Force, which despite the 1981 Iranian hostage fiasco was considered to be uniquely advanced and trained (Barril 1984: 31–2; Legorjus 1990: 116, 129; Scholzen and Froese 2001: 25). But although the GIGN was keen to learn from other groups, visited them, followed their training, and went to international conferences to keep up to date on the latest antiterrorist techniques, institutional learning was largely thwarted by its specific mandate as a multi-purpose unit.

As far as can be seen from the literature, throughout the 1970s the GIGN never participated in joint operations with the special commando units of other countries. In 1976, the GIGN and the Foreign Legion freed some hostages at the border between the French colony Djibouti and Somalia, killing more than 40 terrorists (Barril 1984: 28). However, given the considerable losses, which included one agent and two of the hijacked schoolchildren, this was hardly a glorious chapter. Unlike the German GSG-9, with its successful raid on the Lufthansa airplane at Mogadishu, the French GIGN did not handle any truly successful antiterrorist operation during the 1970s.

Another problem was that, as a matter of national interest, France insisted on keeping its discretion to deal with terrorist incidents on a case-by-case basis, especially when hostage-taking situations were at stake. Already in 1970, France had explicitly rejected the idea of an international arbitration organ to decide when a government should or should not be allowed to give in to terrorist demands.[33] Later on, Paris systematically ignored the emergent international norm of non-negotiation and pursued a flexible strategy towards terrorist incidents (John 1991: 96–100).

Still in the 1980s, Paris was notorious as one of the European states most ready to accommodate terrorist demands – especially when there was a chance of achieving the release of French hostages in exchange for 'leniency' towards apprehended extremists or other concessions to Islamic terrorists and their state sponsors (Lodge 1989: 41; Chauvin 1990). The main objective of this policy was, on the one hand, to protect the life of French citizens. On the other hand, Paris avoided anything that could jeopardize its pro-Arab and pro-Palestinian foreign policy. The French Government certainly did not want to alienate the Arab world by a tough line on Middle Eastern terrorism.[34]

Only when no French nationals were endangered and no French foreign policy goals were at stake, did the French Government take the opportunity to offer the world a show of resolve. For example in September 1976, when Croatian terrorists abducted an airplane from Chicago to Paris, the French President, Prime Minister, and Minister of the Interior all excluded negotiations as an undue concession to terrorist blackmail (Bell 1978: 23–7). However this was hardly due to a sea change in French policy, but rather to the fact that in this particular incident there were no national interests involved.

Similarly, the real or perceived national interest was the most important factor in determining the French attitude to the international exchange of information. On the one hand, this kind of collaboration was supported whenever the exchange of secret-service or police information seemed to be expedient. On the other hand, the systematic exchange of information on terrorists was perceived as a potential threat to national autonomy and to the French ability to control sensitive information. Therefore, Paris had a predilection for informal cooperation among top secret-service officials. For the same reason, the French Government made sure that cooperation among police officers was sufficiently formal and bureaucratic to guarantee the closest possible control of the political decision-making apparatus (Police College 1977: 18–20).

Already in the early 1970s Paris emphasized that, while it welcomed the idea of information exchange on a continental or intercontinental scale, this had to take place in a highly informal manner. At critical junctures, a 'hardcore' of selected European agents should gather in order to suggest instant measures, with representatives of third countries admitted only on a case-by-case basis.[35] While a regional system for the exchange of information was thus envisaged, a world-wide system was seen as 'dangerous'.[36] Even the contacts between Western European police services, which were seen as very satisfactory, were not considered to be suitable for institutionalization beyond the informal exchange of antiterrorist information that was already happening at Interpol.[37]

Initially, Paris did not see any need for the establishment of intergovernmental groups to facilitate the exchange of information. The French Government never initiated any forum for the exchange of police information such as TREVI or PWGOT. Nor did Paris support forums for the exchange of secret-service information such as the Vienna Club, which united the secret services of Germany, Italy, Austria, and Switzerland. Only in the autumn of 1982, did Paris finally become more active in the Vienna Club.[38]

According to a top official from the secret-service of the Italian military, French agents were generally more cooperative than their Government (Martini 1999: 177). Apparently, this was also true of French police officers. Already since 1968, chief security officials from France had participated in European meetings.[39] Moreover, the French police disposed an 'international squad' to provide the necessary liaison in cases where Interpol was not entitled to operate.[40] In 1976, another unit known as the *Bureau de Liaison* was set up, with a mandate to facilitate the exchange of 'political intelligence' at the European level (Police College 1977: 20–1).

Once intergovernmental frameworks like TREVI and PWGOT had been established, the French delegates were among the most eager to participate (Bigo 1996: 91). France even headed the TREVI sub-working group on arms and explosives. Over time, this de-facto collaboration at the working level apparently had a conciliatory effect on the French Government. Moreover, since intergovernmental groups such as TREVI and PWGOT were acting outside the formal institutional framework of the European Community, it was easier for Paris to accept and eventually even embrace them.[41]

Since the exchange of information was seen primarily in terms of the national interest, Paris had a general predilection for limiting the exchange of information to those Member States of the European Community that were in urgent need of such collaboration. Especially Germany, Spain, and Italy had serious problems with terrorism, and extremists from those countries often crossed French borders. Due to the Gaullist 'sanctuary doctrine', France had a bad reputation as a rear-guard area for terrorists in exile.[42] To avoid being blamed for terrorist incidents in the neighbouring countries, Paris could hardly afford to withhold available information on terrorists from these states.

Be that as it may, until well into the 1980s France did not significantly invest in modern technologies to expedite exchange of information. The French police were very backward in computer technology and could not actively engage in the exchange of computerized information. In any event, they did not dispose of sufficient computers or the technical infrastructure to build up ample databases and exchange electronic information. While Germany had systematically built up its computer facilities in the course of the 1970s, the first 200 terminals for a comprehensive French computer network were delivered only at the beginning of the 1980s (Dobson and Payne 1982: 138). In 1983, the Ministry of the Interior finally created a special database named VAT: Violence, Assassinations, *Terrorisme* (Guillaume 1993: 133). At least until this database went operational, in the mid-1980s, France was at the receiving end in the exchange of computerized information (Wiesel 1985: 214; Anderson 1989: 88; Bigo 1996: 90).

Apparently, this was related to a typical feature of the French police forces and secret services: the predilection for human intelligence. As a British report put it in 1977, '[t]he French have never been to the forefront in technology and seem to rely less on sophisticated equipment than other countries. The French police put far more faith in personal initiative and experience than they do in gadgetry' (Police College 1977: 24). In line with this philosophy, France mainly relied on the exchange of secret-service information and on the appointment of police liaison officers.

Italy

During the 1970s, Italy was mostly conspicuous by its absence from international efforts to improve antiterrorist methods. Apparently, Rome was not sufficiently convinced that this kind of international cooperation was in the national interest. Neither in the field of special commando units nor in the field of information exchange, was there any significant effort on the part of the Italian Government to foster international cooperation.

In fact, international cooperation on antiterrorist methods hardly seemed to be in the Italian national interest because of both the domestic nature of Italian terrorist groups and a deliberate appeasement policy towards foreign terrorism. On the one hand, Italy was mostly confronted with terrorist gangs that limited their operational area to the national territory.[43] Unlike the

German Red Army Faction, the Italian Red Brigades did not exploit the methods of Palestinian and Latin American terrorists in hijacking and taking hostages on an international scale (Dobson and Payne 1982: 149). On the other hand, Italy had a perceived national interest in the appeasement of Palestinian and Libyan terrorists (R.H. Evans 1994; Martini 1999: 74–89).[44] The objective of this policy was to protect Italy from terrorist attacks and to secure the Italian policy of friendship with the Palestinian people and the regime of Muammar al-Gaddafi (John 1991: 91).

The most important practical impediment was the institutional backwardness of the Italian police and secret services, both of which were in a permanent state of crisis and reorganization.[45] While other European countries established special commando units in the aftermath of the 1972 terrorist assault on the Olympic village in Munich, Italy did little to prepare for scenarios of national or international terrorism. Instead of setting up an outright special commando unit, it relied upon an elite squadron of the paramilitary *Carabinieri* under the leadership of General Carlo Alberto Dalla Chiesa. Between 1974 and 1976, the team was relatively successful in fighting Italian right- and left-wing terrorism. Nevertheless, it is fair to say that Dalla Chiesa's unit was completely home-grown and little endowed with the sophisticated techniques that were developed by other units such as the British SAS or the German GSG-9.

For reasons that were never fully disclosed, Dalla Chiesa's unit was disbanded in 1976. As a replacement, in January 1978 the Italian Minister of the Interior Francesco Cossiga decided to establish an agency for special operations in the Italian police. Apparently, one of his objectives was to establish an outright special commando unit and thereby to improve the standing of the civilian police vis-à-vis the paramilitary *Carabinieri* (Rognoni 1989: 141–2; cf. Della Porta 1993: 159–60).

When the prominent conservative politician Aldo Moro was kidnapped on 16 March of the same year, however, Italy was caught completely unprepared.[46] In the aftermath of the debacle, Dalla Chiesa was reinstated and started suppressing the Red Brigades from the summer of 1978. Once more the General, who had a tough and fairly personal style of leading his elite squadron, was relatively successful in fighting Italian terrorism. And once more, although labelled as 'counter-guerrilla', the policing techniques applied were fairly conventional (Dobson and Payne 1982: 158–9).[47]

While Dalla Chiesa's men were inflicting painful blows on the Red Brigades, the newly founded special commando unit of the civilian police, called NOCS, was slowly becoming operational.[48] NOCS had its baptism of fire in January 1981, when it freed the American general James Lee Dozier from a Red Brigade 'popular prison'.

Even then, however, Italy was still prevented by its perceived national interest from practical cooperation with the antiterrorist experts and special commando units of other countries. Neither in 1981, in the Dozier affair, nor in 1985, at the hostage drama on the ship *Achille Lauro*, did Rome concede any operational role to special forces from the United States. In the Dozier case,

Italy feared a loss of prestige if the hostage was liberated with American help (Genova 1985: 152–5; Rognoni 1989: 139–51;). In the *Achille Lauro* case, the reason for refusing collaboration was a feared loss of credibility. Rome had promised the Palestinian terrorists who had captured the ship a safe conduct, and therefore the Italian Government would not allow the American Delta Force, which had hunted the perpetrators down at a military base in Sicily, to arrest them on Italian soil (Cassese 1989; Silj 1998; Martini 1999: 121–32).

From the beginning, Italy systematically disregarded the no-concessions principle. In February 1973, the Italian navy flew two Arab terrorists, who were alleged to have planned an attack against an Israeli plane, to Libya; another two terrorists from Libya were released in the summer of the same year (John 1991: 93; Lutiis 1991: 321).[49] In 1977, the Italian Minister of Transport allowed a skyjacked Lufthansa airplane to take off from Fiumicino airport (Martini 1999: 82–3).[50] The plane ended up in Mogadishu, where all the hostages were released by the German GSG-9 (see p. 62). And still in 1985, in the aforementioned case of the cruiser *Achille Lauro*, Italy not only negotiated with the Palestinian terrorists but also stuck to its promise that the latter would be provided with safe conduct after the release of the hostages. Consequently, Italy was considered to be the extreme case of a country ready to grant almost any concession to terrorists. Rome was even suspected of having worked out a secret deal with Gaddafi whereby Libya would not conduct terrorist operations against Italians if Italy turned a blind eye on his men and the Palestinian faction under his control (John 1991: 94).

There is a similar picture with regard to the international exchange of antiterrorist information. During the 1970s, the Italian secret services were haunted by a series of scandals due to the unconstitutional behaviour of their administrative and political leaders (Lutiis 1991). Because of the weakness of its secret services, which were constantly under reorganization, Rome was seriously handicapped in its ability to participate in normal cooperation with other Western democracies. For example, when Aldo Moro was kidnapped in 1978, the first reaction of the Italian Prime Minister was not to seek the collaboration of Western European partners, who could have been gathered using the TREVI framework. Instead, Andreotti turned to Arafat's PLO, Tito's Yugoslavia, Gaddafi's Libya, Castro's Cuba, and Boumedienne's Algeria.[51]

In the same year, the Italian Minister of the Interior Francesco Cossiga took the opportunity to propose an informal body, later to be known as the Vienna Club, for the exchange of information among five European countries: Italy, Germany, France, Austria, and Switzerland. Although Italy obviously also used more official channels, in general it seems that informal collaboration was preferred. This can be seen from the fact that the Vienna Club became Italy's favourite framework for the exchange of antiterrorist information – preferred even to the intergovernmental TREVI Group. In continuation of this policy, Cossiga's successor emphasized that Italy was not committed to any particular institutional framework (Rognoni 1989: 87, 133, 138–9).[52]

Nothing can be ascertained for the 1970s or early 1980s about an Italian central bureau for information exchange or about the activities of Italian liaison officers in other European countries. The situation was no better for the exchange of computerized data. Although the Italian Minister of the Interior, during the Moro affair, asked Germany for computerized information and got access to the database in Wiesbaden (Rognoni 1989: 93–4), Italy was still a long way from establishing its own national database. It took until February 1979 before the Italian Government discussed its first plan for a national database system.[53] Two years later, a law was passed setting up a computerized database at the Ministry of the Interior (Della Porta 1993: 160). Nevertheless it seems that, well into the 1980s, Italy lacked the organizational capacity, financial resources, and political will to build up an electronic infrastructure worthy of that name (Clutterbuck 1990: 39; cf. Wiesel 1985: 214).

Even in the case of SISMI, the secret-service of the Italian military, the challenge of electronic intelligence was not seriously tackled before the mid-1980s (Martini 1999: 110–11, 116–17). As a consequence, the kind of information Italy could offer to its partners was mostly limited to so-called human intelligence.

In short, Italy was prevented by the institutional backwardness of its police and secret services from systematic information exchange beyond occasional collaboration in narrowly circumscribed and informal 'clubs', or from setting up an efficient special commando unit that would have been able to collaborate with its counterparts in other countries. Due to the deplorable state of its domestic institutions, it would have been hard for Italian policy makers to make binding commitments to international cooperation. In any case, Rome did not usually perceive a strong national interest in cooperating with other countries, unless the interests of the latter were very similar to Italian ones. Italian decision makers insisted that there had to be a shared risk assessment, as for example in the case of Germany which had similar problems with the Red Army Faction as Italy had with the Red Brigades (Rognoni 1989: 93–4). Needless to say, in most cases Italy did not discern any such harmony of interests.

Exchanging secret-service and police intelligence (2001–06)

With the advent of suicide bombing, special commando units lost much of their usefulness in countering terrorist attacks. This is not to deny that, in the context of military or paramilitary operations in countries such as Afghanistan, specialized units can usefully apply coercive force against terrorists. However, this is happening far away in the military 'war against terrorism'. To the extent that terrorism is fought in Western countries, in contrast, there are few situations left in which special commando units are useful. Terrorists have largely abandoned the tactic of hostage-taking in Western countries, and shootouts for their arrest have become the exception rather than the rule.

While special commando units have lost much of their importance, the elaboration and timely exchange of antiterrorist intelligence has become the single most important method of international police cooperation against terrorism.[54] Antiterrorist intelligence can be defined as information elaborated to help executive agencies, namely the police forces and the secret services, not only to identify and arrest terrorists but also to act tactically or strategically in order to prevent terrorist crime from happening in the first place. To reach this objective, relevant pieces of information are systematically put together in order to gain a picture of the terrorist underworld. This has become particularly important in recent times, since there is a broad consensus that it is not sufficient to capture and convict terrorists after they have committed their crime, but that one must act preventively in order to protect innocent victims from future attacks.

To the extent that terrorists act beyond territorial boundaries, there does not seem to be any alternative to the international exchange of intelligence as a tool in the fight against terrorism. Since terrorism strikes at the heart of state security, however, both states and their national security apparatuses are sometimes reluctant to share sensitive information. One important impediment to international cooperation is constituted by the fact that, even in Europe, a certain degree of distrust is often part of the professional culture of national security apparatuses. Especially among secret services but also among police forces, the exchange of data regarding terrorism presupposes a considerable amount of mutual trust. As the European Commission stated in 2004, 'two different concepts of co-operation can be distinguished in the Union, which determine to a large extent the capacity of the institutional structures to combat terrorism effectively: one between the police services and one between the security/intelligence services'.[55]

In fact, after 9/11 it was a real challenge to make sure that police forces and secret services would share their intelligence. Should the police, and thereby the courts as well, have easy access to secret-service information, or was it more important to protect the confidentiality of sources? Another contested issue was the sharing of information contained in a variety of databases. Should there be a centralized European database, or was it better to connect existing national databases at the European level? And, more specifically, should there be a European database of Islamic fundamentalists, or was it better to connect existing national databases horizontally? Finally, there was an important debate on whether it was necessary to introduce common European standards for the retention of mobile phone and Internet communications data.[56] Mobile phone data in particular can provide crucial information, since it allows for the reconstruction of terrorist networks and for tracking the position of a phone within a few hundred meters.

Over the 1990s, the European Union had probably become the geographical and institutional framework in which the exchange of antiterrorist intelligence had reached the highest level of inter-state and inter-agency cooperation (Walsh 2006). Nevertheless, there were important functional, political, and institutional reasons for preferring other forums such as, for example, transatlantic cooperation (Dalgaard-Nielsen and Hamilton 2006). In fact, many countries had a certain predilection for alternative geographical frameworks.

The same was also true of the institutional commitment of various states towards the exchange of intelligence. The crucial question was whether and to what extent individual states were willing to share sensitive information with Europol. Another good indicator of a country's institutional commitment was its willingness to accept derogations from the intergovernmental framework of the so-called Third Pillar. Was it acceptable to finance certain structures for the exchange of antiterrorist intelligence from the Community budget? Only on one issue did the top five Member States of the European Union all agree: they all opposed the idea, introduced by Austria and Belgium in March 2004, of creating a European equivalent of the CIA (Nomikos 2005: 450).

Germany

After 11 September, German decision makers recognized that the exchange of antiterrorist intelligence was an indispensable means for furthering the international interest in the suppression, and eventually also the prevention, of terrorist crime. However, a significant part of their preference is better explained by the institutional structure of the German security establishment. The international exchange of antiterrorist intelligence resonated well with the institutional specificities of German policing, and this in turn enhanced the support of German decision makers for international cooperation.

In the German policing system, the lead responsibility for the fight against terrorism is not so much with the secret services as with the police in general, and with the Federal Criminal Police Office (*Bundeskriminalamt*, BKA) in particular. While a certain professional 'culture of secrecy' is typical of secret services, police forces tend to be less reluctant to share relevant information. Ever since the times of TREVI and Schengen, the collection and dissemination of data has been a hallmark of the BKA (Aden 1998; Narr 2003).[57] Particularly during the 1990s, Germany was a stout supporter of Europol as a clearing house for information exchange (Bigo 1996; Occhipinti 2003). From the German standpoint, there were attractions in trying to reproduce the German scheme of intelligence-led policing at the European level. It was therefore only consequential for Berlin to declare, immediately after 9/11, that the secret services should collaborate with the police forces at the European level, preferably through Europol.[58]

For similar reasons, it made intuitive sense for Berlin to support, at the level of the European Union, the free and borderless exchange of data contained in a variety of electronic databases. Germany supported the idea of creating a centralized European database system to link up the existing national databases.[59] This would have made it possible to push the high-tech approach of the Federal Criminal Police Office to the European level. Already back in the 1970s, the BKA had conducted so-called dragnet investigations to identify terrorists. The prospect of being able to conduct European-wide dragnet investigations, and thereby project a typical tool of German antiterrorism at the European level, was highly attractive to German experts and decision makers.

A partial exception was the German reaction to the proposal for a centralized European-wide database of Islamic extremists. In this particular case, Germany preferred the horizontal connection of national databases at the European level.[60] Unfortunately, the reason for this surprising departure from the typical German position was not disclosed.

The most hotly debated issue in Germany was the idea of creating common European standards for the retention of mobile phone and Internet communications data. This was placed on the agenda of the European Union after the Madrid bombings of March 2004, on the initiative of Britain, France, Ireland, and Sweden. From the beginning, the idea was very unpopular in Germany, both among civil libertarians and in commercial circles. At the same time, it was also contested in legal circles due to the strict German data protection legislation. In the new telecommunications bill of June 2004, the German Bundestag consequently refused to impose any binding provisions on data retention.[61] Despite all these obstacles on the domestic front, Berlin continued to support the idea. As the Minister of Justice put it, in the face of political consensus in the European Council, Germany could hardly say 'we don't want that'.[62]

While this is hard to understand from a democratic point of view, it reflects a more general pattern. German decision makers are often more loyal towards the European Union than to the preferences of their domestic constituency.[63] Similarly, they sometimes have a normative preference for cooperation in the EU even where cooperation in some other geographical framework would be more useful on functional grounds. After 9/11, it would have been relatively obvious to focus on intelligence cooperation on a more global scale, especially with the United States and with the source countries of Islamic fundamentalism. Nevertheless, German decision makers were more interested in intelligence cooperation within the EU than in any other geographical framework.[64]

This is not to deny that the European Union with its Third Pillar provides a uniquely developed institutional framework for the exchange of antiterrorist intelligence. It certainly appears easier to strengthen this existing framework than to build up institutional alternatives beyond Europe. Taken by itself, however, this does not yet sufficiently explain why Germany was more devoted to the European Union than, for example, Britain and France. The more important explanation seems to be that, even in cases where the national interest and functional considerations would point in a different direction, German decision makers often have a predilection for European solutions due to their normative commitment to the European project (Jachtenfuchs 2002: 162–209).[65]

Of course there were limits even to German support for institution building at the European level. This can be seen from the fact that, like all other large EU Member States, Berlin rejected the idea of a European CIA. However, this was not motivated by considerations of national sovereignty, but rather because the idea was seen as utopian.[66]

Short of a European CIA, Germany was strongly committed to intelligence cooperation. Immediately after 9/11, the German Minister of the Interior requested that 'all relevant data' about terrorism should be shared with Europol.[67] If one considers that both functional considerations and the national interest would have suggested that certain data be kept confidential, such a bold statement is somewhat surprising. Once again, it would seem that German decision makers were driven by their overriding normative commitment to European integration. As we have already seen, they were also emboldened by the fact that the modus operandi of the German security apparatus, which was considered to be at the vanguard of the collection and dissemination of data on terrorist suspects, seemed compatible with the requirements of Europol.

France

Since 9/11, France has been as committed as any other Western country to the fight against terrorism. To prevent and eventually defeat terrorism, France has consistently recognized the international interest in the exchange of antiterrorist intelligence. However, there is one important impediment for Paris in supporting intelligence cooperation: the fragmentation of the French security apparatus in general, and of the French secret services in particular (Anderson 2000: 235–6).

In France, there is a great variety of police forces and secret services concerned with the collection of antiterrorist intelligence.[68] Under the direction of the Ministry of the Interior, there are two competing police agencies operating very much like secret services;[69] moreover, there are three full-blown secret services under the Ministry of Defence;[70] in addition to that, there are several intelligence units in other agencies, as for example in the *Gendarmerie* and in the Customs Service (Brodeur and Dupeyron 2003). Although the competencies of these agencies are delimited in theory, in practice there is often a great overlap between their fields of operation. In general, the system is relatively strong in the infiltration of terrorist cells and the production of court-proof and policy-relevant intelligence (Shapiro and Suzan 2003; Chalk and Rosenau 2004: 17–23). Unsurprisingly, however, in such a fragmented environment turf wars are endemic and inter-agency collaboration is a constant challenge (Cettina 2003: 84). Since collaboration is already difficult at the domestic level, decision makers are careful not to impose too heavy demands on French agencies for cooperation with their foreign counterparts.

In this spirit, the French Minister of the Interior said in 2004: 'Intelligence is the most difficult and most complex thing to be put in common because, to obtain it, one has to protect the sources, which is already difficult within one and the same country'.[71]

In fact, French security professionals adhere to secrecy as a professional principle even more than their counterparts in other European democracies. The secret services in particular, but to a certain extent also the police forces, combine this 'culture of secrecy' with a kind of 'action culture'. The secret services have a predilection for human intelligence, while the police forces tend to favour special operations and covert methods such as infiltration and secret observation (Porch 1995: 469; Joubert and Bevers 1996: 536). In continuation of this tradition, after 11 September French security experts immediately called for more freedom of action to the secret services and accused their counterparts in the United States and in other European countries of being too obsessed with technology instead of promoting human intelligence.[72]

The French President Jacques Chirac and his successor, Nicolas Sarkozy, both stress that one should respect the 'habits' of the secret services.[73] Paris recognizes that the French agencies concerned with antiterrorist intelligence have a distinct tradition and culture. Accordingly, informal cooperation in shifting geographical settings is preferred to automatic data-sharing in fixed geographical and institutional frameworks, whether at the European level or elsewhere. From the standpoint of French decision makers, it would be too harsh to decree a general scheme of cooperation from above.

For quite some time, the French secret services have been successfully working together on a bilateral basis with their British, German, Italian, and Spanish counterparts. As of 2002, there was a new agency called 'Alliance Base' for the exchange of antiterrorist intelligence between the American CIA and the French intelligence services. This agency, which has the full support of the French political elite and also serves as a hub for agents from Britain, Canada, Australia, and Germany, performs an important role as an informal clearing house for the exchange of information among secret services.[74]

In the eyes of Chirac and Sarkozy, the selection of cooperation partners should be guided by the national interest. Some secret services are seen as less important than others, and cooperation with them is seen as less attractive to France.[75] Within the European Union, France has a preference for enhanced cooperation among the secret services of the 'Big Five' (France, Britain, Germany, Italy, and Spain). As the French Minister of the Interior put it in 2004: 'Among the five of us, we have the same intelligence culture, things will move quicker. The ten new countries, let's face it, do not have any intelligence culture, they work differently, not to mention their specific relations with NATO.'[76] Or, as a French antiterrorist expert put it, smart intelligence cooperation 'doesn't have anything to do with the European Union'.[77]

The French predilection for flexible frameworks is not limited to international cooperation between secret services, but extends to the exchange of antiterrorist intelligence among police forces. While Paris supports Europol as a useful framework for setting up task forces and joint investigation teams, French decision makers are wary that institutionalization at the European level might become too heavy or too dense.[78] Instead they extol the virtues of bilateral cooperation, for example with Britain, Germany, and Spain.[79] In May 2005 France gladly signed the intergovernmental Prüm Convention, containing non-enforceable rules on data exchange among seven EU Member States.[80]

In line with the institutional set-up of the French security apparatus, Paris supports a neat separation between international cooperation among secret services on the one hand, and among 'normal' police forces on the other. In a similar vein, French decision makers do not agree that existing national databases should automatically be linked up among all EU Member States.[81] Only when a problem has been solved at the domestic level does France support European initiatives. Paris seems to follow a simple rationale: 'Why not establish on a European level the tools that are used for fighting terrorism at home?' Thus, France has been pushing forward two important issues: the idea of creating a centralized European database of Islamic fundamentalists, and the introduction of European standards for the retention of mobile phone and Internet communications data.

Already in the mid-1990s France had started to establish a database of Islamic fundamentalists.[82] After the Madrid bombings of March 2004, it could therefore take a bold stance on the creation of an analogous database at the European level.[83] Similarly, since the end of 2001 French law has provided that mobile phone and Internet communications data shall be retained for a period of 12 months.[84] It took some time for the law to be implemented in France, with an important decree still pending in March 2004.[85] Given the advanced state of affairs at the domestic level, however, there were no obstacles in the way of France sponsoring a European initiative on the same matter.[86]

At any rate, Paris is hardly willing to accept binding obligations. Instead, France supports the informal exchange of information on a need-to-know basis. French decision makers, as well as their British counterparts, believe that it is in the interest of their countries to preserve the autonomy of the national intelligence system. The French Minister of the Interior therefore opposed the idea, introduced in 2004 by Austria and Belgium, of creating a European equivalent to the American CIA.[87] Moreover, he made it clear that France would not hand over 'anything too sensitive' to Europol and declared that he was opposed to a binding obligation to exchange antiterrorist intelligence because this would jeopardize the protection of sources and endanger the anonymity of informers.[88] Once more, there seems to be a concern that such obligations might be too much for the highly secretive French secret services.

Britain

The intelligence apparatus of the United Kingdom is concentrated in the hands of the secret services, not the police forces. Moreover, it is closely tied to the notion of the national interest. According to a report by the Cabinet Office on the national intelligence machinery,

> In relations to national security, HMG's policies are directed towards the protection of the UK and British territories, British nationals and property, including from terrorist and espionage threats, and towards the protection and promotion of significant defence and foreign policy interests.
>
> (Cabinet Office 2005: 17)

As a Member of the so-called coalition of the willing in the war against terrorism, the British Government has a national interest in the international exchange of intelligence to prevent attacks on British territory and eventually defeat terrorism.

Precisely because of the dominant position of the secret services in the national intelligence machinery, however, British support for the international exchange of antiterrorist intelligence is far from unconditional. In particular the exchange of sensitive data is often hampered by the 'culture of secrecy' of the Security Service, more commonly known as MI5, which in Britain has the lead responsibility for the collection and dissemination of antiterrorist intelligence. Given the pole position of MI5 and other secret services, British security experts and policy makers tend to assume that a generous but voluntary exchange of intelligence among secret services is the best policy option available.[89]

This does not necessarily preclude British support for the international exchange of antiterrorist intelligence among police forces, as long as no secret service information is involved.[90] Whenever police information goes beyond the narrow bounds of criminal intelligence, however, the professional 'culture of secrecy' of MI5 inevitably makes it difficult even for the British police to collaborate with their counterparts in foreign countries. Without explicit authorization by the Security Service, British police forces are understandably hesitant to provide sensitive information to foreign agencies.

This has not always been so. Until the early 1990s, the most important agency responsible for counterterrorism, including intelligence, was the Metropolitan Police Special Branch at New Scotland Yard. As far as the international exchange of antiterrorist intelligence was concerned, the main responsibility was with the European Liaison Section of the Metropolitan Police Special Branch (House of Commons 1990a: 4, 42–6).[91] But then, in May 1992, something changed. Very much to the dismay of New Scotland Yard, the lead responsibility for domestic terrorism was transferred to MI5 (Wilkinson 2000: 106–11; Hollingsworth and Fielding 2003: 131–64).[92]

Although the police continue to play a significant role, and although they work together with the secret services in the Joint Terrorism Analysis Centre, MI5 has become the paramount agency on terrorism in general, and international terrorism in particular. From 1997/98 to 2006/07, the share of MI5's budget allocated to international terrorism has grown from 15.5% to 60.5%.[93] As the British Home Secretary put it in 2002, 'the Security Service has refocused its work with an increased budget, developing its focus on countering al-Qaeda'.[94] Or, as the Cabinet Office stated in the same year, '[t]he Security Service continues to lead on countering the threat from international terrorism to the United Kingdom and UK interests overseas' (Cabinet Office 2002: 16).

To protect British foreign-policy interests, London has a preference for intelligence cooperation in fairly exclusive frameworks, mainly with the United States and a limited number of leading Western countries. While this is certainly not to deny that the British secret services have established links all over the world, since the early days of the Cold War there has always been a very 'special' relationship with the United States and other Anglo-Saxon countries.[95] Since the so-called UKUSA agreement of the late 1940s, Britain is engaged as a junior partner of the United States – along with Canada, Australia, and New Zealand – in a global secret surveillance network that allows the screening of huge amounts of data (Bamford 2002). The most prominent expression of this cooperation is the legendary ECHELON, the world's largest eavesdropping system for the interception of electronic communications data (C. Walker 2003: 34).[96]

In recent times, British-American cooperation has been additionally spurred by the fact that the United Kingdom is part and parcel of the American-led military coalition against international terrorism.[97] To a certain degree, this makes it more difficult for Britain to share secret-service intelligence with countries that do not participate in the 'coalition of the willing'. But even if this were not the case, the 'culture of secrecy' of MI5 would make it difficult for decision makers to impose on British secret services the automatic exchange of sensitive data beyond the intelligence circles of allied countries.

Britain was initially opposed to the exchange of antiterrorist intelligence at a European level. Thus, in the early 1990s Britain opposed the inclusion of terrorism into the remit of Europol (House of Lords 1995: E5). Instead, London would have preferred to see the more informal TREVI cooperation continued, at least as far as terrorism was concerned (House of Commons 1991: 3–4). In the mid-1990s the United Kingdom accepted, although somewhat grudgingly, that Europol should have a competence on terrorism (House of Lords 1995: E49, E90). Whenever there is a choice, however, Britain is still more ready to exchange antiterrorist intelligence on a bilateral basis than at the European level: 'The Agencies co-operate with European partners at both a bilateral and multilateral level. Co-operation on operational matters is primarily bilateral, to ensure that intelligence is shared where necessary and to protect operational sources and information-gathering techniques' (Intelligence and Security Committee 2006: 28).[98]

As long as the secret services have the lead in the collection and dissemination of antiterrorist intelligence, the exchange of sensitive information in a Europe-wide police agency such as Europol is difficult. Britain's preferred framework for intelligence cooperation is therefore still transatlantic and bilateral rather than European and multilateral.

Exchange among secret services on a need-to-know basis is preferred to exchange among police forces in formal institutional frameworks such as Europol. As far as secret-service intelligence is concerned, Britain pushed already in 2004 for a new European intelligence centre to provide high quality strategic intelligence material and to be modelled on Britain's secretive Joint Terrorism Analysis Centre.[99] And indeed, Britain is more than ready to support SitCen, the Joint Situation Centre in the Council Secretariat (Intelligence and Security Committee 2006: 29). As far as police intelligence is concerned, however, the United Kingdom is far from enthusiastic about sharing sensitive intelligence with Europol. The idea is that antiterrorist intelligence is exchanged more easily among secret services and outside the institutional framework of Europol.

Many British decision makers believe that it is in the national interest to preserve the autonomy of the British intelligence system. As Home Secretary David Blunkett said in 2004, 'national security considerations place some necessary limits on what information can be shared'. Countering terrorism is seen as 'a vital issue' and 'an essential state function' to be respected by the EU.[100] At least in part, this explains the negative attitude of the United Kingdom towards binding institutional commitments. For example, London was opposed to the idea of creating a European CIA.[101] Moreover, Britain blocked any opt-outs from the intergovernmental scheme of intelligence cooperation in the so-called Third Pillar. In accordance with the British view that the Third Pillar must remain intergovernmental, London opposed a European Commission proposal to use the Community budget in order to finance certain structures that should facilitate the exchange of intelligence. Britain insisted that European cooperation on the exchange of antiterrorist intelligence should continue to be funded via the normal intergovernmental mechanisms of the Third Pillar (House of Commons 2002: 34–7).[102]

Beyond rhetoric, however, all these reservations on institution building did not prevent London from taking a pragmatic stance on data exchange. In 2004, for example, the Home Secretary demanded that the national databases of Islamic fundamentalists should be integrated at the European level. The idea was to create a European-wide forensic database of terrorist suspects, which should include DNA samples and biometric data such as electronic fingerprints and eye scans.[103] Britain continues to be sceptical about a centralized European database system, but instead supports the idea of connecting the existing national databases containing criminal intelligence.[104] Moreover, the country has been at the forefront on the retention of mobile phone and Internet communications data, being the first to adopt provisions by national legislation in 2001, calling for a European solution in 2002, adopting an apposite national law in 2003, and urging the EU to adopt common rules in 2004.[105] Mainly to increase the chance of preventing terrorist attacks in the United Kingdom, London was ready to support the international exchange of telecommunications data even in the face of determined opposition from industrial stakeholders and civil liberties groups.[106]

Italy

While the Berlusconi Government (2001–06) was fully committed to the global fight against terrorism, the international exchange of antiterrorist intelligence was also seen as a matter of national interest. As the Parliamentary Committee on Intelligence and Security Services established in December 2001, the task of the intelligence apparatus was the 'gathering and analysis of information which could not be obtained otherwise, and which is useful for the protection of national security'.[107]

Especially after 9/11, Rome saw a national interest in the exchange of intelligence on Islamic terrorists planning attacks in Italy or using Italian territory as a rear-guard area to prepare attacks in other countries. Apart from that, the Ministry of the Interior also maintained a certain interest in the international links of violent globalization critics and subversive political anarchists (Camera dei Deputati 2004: 3–4). The Minister of Foreign Affairs left no doubt that certain 'functional missions' could not be realized single-handedly but only by virtue of international cooperation, and that the flow of intelligence among secret services was a common objective of all democratic states.[108]

The problem was certainly not new. Already in the 1970s and 1980s, Italy had experienced serious problems with home-grown terrorist groups and their international links. This experience had convinced Italian decision makers, through a long and painful learning process, that there was a national interest in the exchange of antiterrorist intelligence with other countries. Since the mid-1980s, the country had therefore heavily invested in a network of bilateral treaties on international cooperation against terrorism. At the time, Interior Minister Scalfaro and Prime Minister Craxi visited a considerable number of capital cities such as Paris, Bonn, Belgrade, London, Washington, Cairo, Athens, Ankara, Vienna, and Jerusalem. During these trips, Scalfaro consistently highlighted the importance of antiterrorist intelligence and managed to conclude a series of bilateral agreements. The objective was to build a large intergovernmental network of treaties on the exchange of antiterrorist intelligence (Massai 1990: 95–103).[109]

Over the 1990s, the bilateral network was expanded by a whole series of subsequent Italian Ministers of the Interior. As a result, by 11 September Italy was at the centre of a dense web of bilateral relationships providing for the exchange of intelligence on a regular basis with a large number of countries, including Saudi Arabia, Algeria, and even Libya.[110] Consequently, existing links between domestic agencies and their foreign counterparts could now feed back on the readiness of Italian decision makers to support even more international cooperation on antiterrorist intelligence.

While traditionally Italian agencies have a certain predilection for intelligence cooperation at the bilateral level, in 2004 Minister of the Interior Giuseppe Pisanu said: 'Today our bilateral agreements, though useful, do not allow complete freedom of manoeuvre'.[111] Accordingly, Rome tried to be as active as possible in the framework of Europol and as a Member of the 'Big Five' of the European Union. At the same time, Italy further developed its regional cooperation with the countries on the southern shore of the Mediterranean. Rome also cultivated its ties with moderate Arab regimes. While the exchange of intelligence was particularly intense with large Western countries, Italian decision makers and experts insisted that cooperation had to be extended all over the world (Frattini 2001: 2; Ministero dell'Interno 2003: 76, 114).[112]

However, this does not mean that Italy was unconditional in its support for intelligence cooperation. On the contrary, it was often very difficult for Rome to promote the further expansion of the international exchange of antiterrorist intelligence, or to accept binding institutional obligations. More than in Britain and France, the main impediment was the 'culture of secrecy' of the Italian police forces and secret services.[113] Even at the domestic level, it was far from easy for the Italian Government to ensure cooperation between different police forces on the one hand, and among the military and the civilian branch of the secret services on the other, not to mention inter-agency cooperation between police forces and secret services.[114] The Italian Minister of the Interior talked explicitly about a problematic 'culture of secrecy', and the head of the Italian police mentioned persistent 'difficulties in acquiring a culture of immediately sharing classified investigation activities, for example on terrorism'.[115]

Given this particular state of affairs, it is hardly surprising that Italian decision makers were not among the most vocal supporters of ambitious solutions at the international level. This is particularly evident in the field of technical solutions, the realization of which can never be taken for granted as long as the culture of secrecy and concomitant technological backwardness of Italian agencies remains unaltered.

For example, the Berlusconi Government kept an eloquent silence in discussions about the merger or centralization of national databases at the European level. Nor did Rome articulate any explicit preference on European standards for the retention of mobile phone and Internet communications data. At the national level, Rome initially wanted to make sure that communications data would be stored for 30 to 60 months. Ironically, the provisions were hidden in a legal decree on the administration of water supplies.[116] Despite fierce resistance in the Italian Parliament, consensus was secured for the retention of communications data for 24 to 48 months.[117] Despite this Pyrrhic victory on the domestic front, the Italian Government left it to other Member States to promote common European standards on the retention of telecommunications data. Nevertheless, it did not actively oppose such technical solutions either. For the record, in 2004 the Foreign Minister even declared in an interview that he wanted to foster the exchange of information between the secret services and the police at a European level.[118]

On the one hand, intelligence cooperation was understood to be a delicate plant. Italian decision makers feared that too much binding institutional commitment might actually turn counterproductive and that exaggerated expectations would discourage the police, not to mention the secret services, from sharing sensitive information in the first place. On the other hand, Italian decision makers were aware that the 'culture of secrecy' of Italian police forces and secret services could become detrimental to the national interest. To prevent this from happening, they consciously tried to use Europe as a vehicle to 'open' the Italian agencies and 'socialize' them into Europe. The rationale behind this sort of pedagogical approach was that a modicum of European cooperation might work as a transmission belt to overcome the rigidities of Italian agencies.[119]

On the one hand, it goes without saying that Rome was opposed to the idea of converting Europol into an equivalent of the American CIA.[120] On the contrary, Italy supported a split of the EU committees dealing with Justice and Home Affairs into a normative and an operational branch. This was supposed to allow for higher confidentiality among the security officials who would informally meet in the operational committees. Moreover, Italy was obstinate that the financing of the European infrastructure for information exchange should be tightly controlled. When the technical implementation of the Europol Intelligence System was delayed, the Italian Minister of the Interior was very annoyed and called for a verification of whether the system was actually worth its costs.[121] During the Italian presidency in 2003, this led to a rupture with the consortium that should have delivered the system, and ultimately to an alternative solution (Camera dei Deputati 2004: 6–7; 2006: 15–16).

On the other hand, Rome promoted intelligence cooperation whenever it seemed practicable from an organizational point of view. Apart from the European network of police liaison officers, Italy supported direct contacts among police forces and set great hopes on the European Police Chiefs Task Force.[122] According to the official position of the Italian Government, even sensitive information should be delivered to Europol. Thus, the Italian Ministry of the Interior declared its pride in Italy's 'particularly significant' contribution to Europol's analytical work files on international terrorism, and of having delivered to Europol the data concerning all important antiterrorist operations conducted on national territory (Camera dei Deputati 2003: 12; 2004: 3). In fact, the share of terrorism of all communications reported by the Europol National Unit in Rome increased from 4 per cent in 2001 to 9 per cent in 2002 (Camera dei Deputati 2002: 9; 2003: 22).[123]

5 Extradition of terrorists

Extradition is an age-old institution in international law. Its original purpose was to mitigate an adverse effect of territoriality, namely the opportunity for wrongdoers to find sanctuary in foreign jurisdictions, by authorizing their surrender under the jurisdiction of the prosecuting state (Chauvy 1981; Stanbrook and Stanbrook 2000: 3–18). As long as extradition is a matter of comity among states, there is no inherent tension between extradition and national sovereignty. As soon as there is an obligation to extradite, however, this militates against the absolutist idea that a government should be free to decide whether or not to surrender a person subject to its territorial jurisdiction. For a long time, an automatic obligation to surrender criminal suspects or convicts to the criminal jurisdiction of other states was therefore considered to be irreconcilable with the traditional role of the Leviathan as the final arbiter of jurisdiction on its own territory.

Apart from the conservative notion of national sovereignty, extradition can also enter into sharp conflict with the liberal idea that at least some fugitives deserve political asylum rather than punishment. This is particularly clear in the case of political offences, where asylum is granted to shield dissidents from prosecution by ruthless regimes. Insofar as terrorism is the political offence par excellence, an obligation to extradite terrorists is a tremendous challenge to international cooperation. Well into the twentieth century, the extradition of terrorists was therefore seen as a matter of comity among sovereign states. Depending on the specificities of the case at hand, states were free to decide whether or not to surrender a terrorist suspect or convict. For example, France was notorious for providing safe haven to Spanish and Italian terrorists (Anderson 1989: 133–6). No state was obliged to justify such a decision, as long as the principle of national sovereignty and the logic of *raison d'état* were considered sufficient.

Political offenders, including terrorists, traditionally enjoy particular protection under the political exemption clause. Following the tradition of the liberal constitutional state, ever since the 1830s a clause precluding the extradition of political offenders was written into most bilateral extradition agreements (Stanbrook and Stanbrook 2000: 65–7). Unfortunately, however, this raised the problem that the political exemption clause could be easily abused by undesirable persons. To prevent this from happening, exemptions to the clause were subsequently introduced. Already towards the end of the nineteenth century, attempts on the lives of state leaders and their families were exempted from the political exemption clause in most bilateral extradition agreements. Another famous example is the Genocide Convention, which exempted genocide from the political exemption clause in the wake of World War II.

Already in the 1930s, there was an abortive attempt to exempt terrorism from the political exemption clause. On the initiation of France, the League of Nations had discussed a Convention for the Prevention and Punishment of Terrorism, which would have made it mandatory either to extradite terrorists or to sue them before a domestic court. The Convention was formally adopted in 1937, but never entered into force (Dubin 1991). This was the first in a series of attempts to construct a multilateral regime to expedite the extradition of terrorists.

As we will see in the first part of this chapter, in the 1970s the Council of Europe tried to solve the problem at the regional level, through the European Convention on the Suppression of Terrorism. Once again, the attempt was largely frustrated by a lack of political will among some of the Member States. The second part of the chapter is dedicated to the European Arrest Warrant, which was agreed upon by the Member States of the European Union after the terrorist attacks of 11 September 2001. It is possible, although not yet entirely certain, that this time, at least among the Member States of the European Union, the extradition of terrorists will become a matter of course.

Early moves towards a regime (1972–82)

Until the mid-twentieth century, the extradition regime was exclusively based on bilateral treaties. Then, after World War II, Europe saw some cautious attempts to place extradition on a multilateral basis. The first milestone was the *European Convention on Extradition* (1957), which however left the political exemption clause untouched. To make up for this failure, the European Convention on Extradition was later complemented by the *European Convention on the Suppression of Terrorism* (1977), which contained an obligation to exempt terrorism from the political exemption clause. Both of these conventions were agreed upon under the umbrella of the Council of Europe.[1]

More specifically, the 1957 European Convention on Extradition was designed as a mechanism for bringing offenders to justice across European frontiers. However, there were three remaining loopholes allowing states to derogate from their obligation to extradite:

- First, a state could deny extradition if it deemed that a case involved a political offence (political exemption clause).
- Second, extraditable offences had to be pursuable under the laws of both countries (principle of double criminality).

- Third, a state could deny the extradition of its own nationals and try them under domestic law (*aut dedere aut judicare*).

The 1977 European Convention on the Suppression of Terrorism was mainly an attempt to come to terms with the political exemption clause. The deliberations started in the autumn of 1972, when the Consultative Assembly of the Council of Europe conducted discussions on terrorism parallel to the discussions in the United Nations General Assembly.[2] The result of these talks was a recommendation to the Committee of Ministers that the notion of 'political offence' should be redefined in such a way that it would become possible to refute any political excuse for terrorist acts. On the basis of this recommendation, in 1975 the Committee of Ministers set up a committee of government experts to study the legal aspects of international terrorism. This committee prepared a European Convention on the Suppression of Terrorism, which was opened for signature on 27 January 1977 (Council of Europe 1977; Camera 1981; Gal-Or 1985: 207–73).

Initially, the Council of Europe was only one among several possible frameworks for the negotiation of a multilateral regime on the extradition of terrorists. In theory the most obvious alternative would have been the United Nations, but due to its notorious divisions over the very essence of international terrorism the UN was never seriously considered. Another competitor to the Council of Europe was the European Community, which would have been preferred by most of its Member States. Other European states that were not Members to the European Community, however, preferred the Council of Europe. At the instigation of France, the Council of Europe was finally chosen in May 1975 as the institutional and geographical site for the negotiation of the European Convention on the Suppression of Terrorism.

Nevertheless, rivalry between the Council of Europe and the European Community was a constant obstacle to harmonious cooperation at the Council of Europe. Until the late 1970s the European Parliament and, although to a lesser degree, the European Commission, tried on several accounts to award terrorism a permanent place on the political agenda of the European Community. Despite these efforts, however, the Convention on the Suppression of Terrorism was eventually negotiated at the Council of Europe (Gal-Or 1985: 210–21; cf. Lodge 1981; Freestone 1981; Lodge and Freestone 1982).

In the course of bargaining and ratification, virtually all relevant aspects of the European Convention on the Suppression of Terrorism were subjected to contestation. This started with Article 1, which denies a political character to terrorist acts and to the motivations of their perpetrators. Insofar as there is hardly anything more political than a terrorist act, this denial was somewhat paradoxical. But the political implications were very clear. The plan was simply to make sure that the political character of terrorist acts would be ignored, so that terrorist fugitives would no longer be able to shield behind the political exemption clause. As a consequence, the principles of the 1957 European Convention on Extradition, as well as the 1959 European Convention on

Mutual Assistance in Criminal Matters, would become applicable to terrorist acts as well.

This plan was largely thwarted by two important loopholes in the Convention. First, Article 5 rules that a party may refuse extradition when there is reason to suspect that the requesting state intends to prosecute a person in a discriminatory way. Second, and more importantly, Article 13 provides for the possibility of upholding the political exemption in a national reservation clause at the time of signature or ratification. It is easy to see that the whole purpose of the Convention was thereby almost nullified. Those states that did file such a reservation could continue to reject the extradition of a terrorist on the grounds that the offence in question was considered to be political. What remained was only the obligation to try the person for whom extradition was denied, before a domestic court, according to the principle *aut dedere aut judicare.*

Apart from extradition, Article 8 of the Convention contains an obligation to grant mutual legal assistance in terrorist cases. But even this relatively harmless obligation was too much for some countries. The same was true for the mechanism of dispute settlement under Article 10. Not only was there a spate of reservation clauses filed by a variety of countries, but there was also a considerable delay in ratification. Eventually, the last of the initial signatories who finally ratified the Convention were Italy and Belgium in 1986, France in 1987, Greece in 1988, and Ireland in 1989.

In 1979, there was a half-hearted attempt to apply the principles of the Convention at least among the Member States of the European Community: the *Dublin Agreement concerning the Application of the European Convention on the Suppression of Terrorism among the Member States of the European Communities.*[3] Significantly, the agreement was negotiated under the arrangements for European Political Cooperation and not under the auspices of the Treaty of Rome. For similar reasons as the Strasbourg convention, the Dublin agreement was boycotted by some member states and never entered into force (Lodge 1988: 21–5; Nuttall 1992: 294–6; Vercher 1992: 354–6).

Presumably as a way out of the impasse, already in 1977 the French President had proposed the idea of a full-blown European judicial area, aka *espace judiciaire européen.*[4] Although the proposal was never fleshed out with content, and although it was not at all clear whether and to what extent the European judicial area would cover terrorist offences, the idea was often repeated. In 1982, the French Minister of Justice Robert Badinter submitted an even more ambitious proposal to establish a supranational tribunal for criminal justice in Europe, which was to deal with terrorist offences and other forms of serious crime.[5] Most other Members of the European Community rejected these proposals as unrealistic (Nuttall 1992: 295–7; Vercher 1992: 356–7).

Britain

In comparison to other states, Britain was extremely quick to ratify the new legal instrument. After signing the European Convention on the Suppression of Terrorism in January 1977, it took less than two years for the British Parliament to adopt the 1978 *Suppression of Terrorism Act* and, thereby to fully transpose all the obligations under the Convention into national law (Stanbrook and Stanbrook 2000: 83–7).[6]

In a highly bipartisan ratification debate, it was proudly stressed by the Government that Britain had played a major part in the negotiations. In fact, London saw a national interest in the extradition of Northern Irish activists from the Republic of Ireland. British extradition requests were regularly frustrated by the view of Irish courts that political offenders were not extraditable in principle. A European convention on the extradition of terrorists seemed attractive because it would increase political pressure on Dublin not to grant political asylum to IRA militants (Gal-Or 1985: 253). In addition to that, the British Government declared its conviction that the Council of Europe provided a sufficiently solid institutional environment to allow for 'a response by those European States which share common democratic values and a respect for human rights'. Ostensibly, the British Government was also motivated by moral reasons, such as for example 'punishing offences which everyone feels to be abhorrent'; justice would be served by the extradition of an offender to the place where he had committed the crime, and where the evidence and witnesses were available; and by quickly and unconditionally ratifying the Convention, Britain would give a shining example to the notorious laggards.[7]

London did not file any reservation, neither at the time of signature nor of ratification, despite the fact that all its bilateral extradition agreements with other countries contained the political exemption clause.[8] This is not to deny that, at the time of negotiation, Britain had insisted on the inclusion of Article 5, which rules that a state can refuse extradition when there is reason to suspect that the requesting state intends to prosecute a person in a discriminatory way (Lodge and Freestone 1982: 81).[9] As an additional safeguard, Britain also retained a residual power for the Home Secretary to annul the decision of a tribunal and refute extradition in extreme cases.[10] Apart from these relatively minor loopholes, however, Britain fully embraced the idea that the political exemption clause should be abolished to facilitate the extradition of terrorists among the Member States of the Council of Europe.

Originally, Britain would have preferred to endow the European Community, rather than the Council of Europe, with the task of negotiating a convention on the extradition of terrorists.[11] Although London was ready to give in on this point, Britain had good reasons to be worried about the Council of Europe. The main problem was that, apart from the political exemption clause, British extradition law was based on a series of other legal principles. These principles, which were related to the Common Law tradition and codified in the 1870 Extradition Act, seemed to be incompatible with the harmonizing philosophy of the Council of Europe (Poncet and Gully-Hart 1986).

Due to these incompatibilities, it was only in 1990/91 that Britain finally signed and ratified the 1957 European Convention on Extradition. Even the 1948 UN Genocide Convention, which provides that genocide cannot be considered a political offence, was not ratified until 1969. Still in 1962, the Government had declared in an oral answer to the House of Commons that ratification of the Genocide Convention would involve 'a derogation from this country's traditional right to grant political asylum which the Government do not think it right to accept'.[12] If one takes all this into account, it bears witness to London's strong commitment to the extradition of terrorists that it fully supported the European Convention on the Suppression of Terrorism, raising no serious objections even though the item was referred to Strasbourg and not to Brussels.

During the ratification debate, the British Home Office fully subscribed to the abolition of the political exemption clause, whether for foreigners or for British nationals, and whether for extradition or for mutual assistance in criminal matters. Britain even went beyond its treaty obligations by abolishing the clause not only for the offences enumerated in Article 1, but also for those mentioned in Article 2. The British commitment to the Convention can also be seen from the fact that, during the negotiations, London had successfully demanded the introduction of an obligatory arbitration procedure (Gal-Or 1985: 247). Later the United Kingdom was anxious to be among the first to ratify the Convention, and in the ratification instrument the country undertook 'faithfully to perform and carry out all the stipulations' contained in the Convention.[13] While the British Government declared its regret that so many countries were filing reservations, it was made clear in the ratification debate that Britain would not insist on reciprocity.[14]

There was only one important limitation: Britain was not ready to support legal utopianism. Britain was opposed to the French idea of creating a harmonized 'European judicial area' for the repression of terrorist acts and other forms of serious crime, and also rejected the French suggestion of instituting a supranational European tribunal to deal with terrorist offences (Anderson 1993b: 24, 30).[15] The British Government feared that, apart from being unrealistic, these proposals would imply an unnecessary loss of sovereignty and were therefore incompatible with the national interest.

Italy

On 27 January 1977, when the European Convention on the Suppression of Terrorism was signed in Strasbourg, the Italian Prime Minister welcomed the agreement as an important step in improving international cooperation against terrorism and highlighted the moral significance of this multinational initiative (Andreotti 1981a: 75).

However, the warm words of the Italian Prime Minister by no means meant that the Convention was close to the heart of Italian decision makers. On the contrary, right from the beginning the Italian representative in Strasbourg had declared serious doubts as to whether it was possible to define the concept of 'political offence'.[16] As far as can be seen from the official records, during the negotiations Italy kept a low profile, and did not formulate any strong and explicit preferences on particular points.

Initially, Italy would have preferred a convention among the Member States of the European Community.[17] Later on, however, Rome did not question the choice of the Council of Europe as the appropriate framework for dealing with the extradition of terrorists. In fact, to deal with its domestic terrorism problem Italy had a national interest in receiving more support from other European countries, whether in the European Community or in the Council of Europe.[18] France in particular was granting safe haven to Italian terrorists, and the elimination of the political exemption clause at the European level was seen as a matter of Italian national interest (Rognoni 1989: 89–93).

The main problem, however, was that Italy was torn between constitutional and moral considerations. On the one hand, the Italian Constitution categorically prohibits the extradition of foreigners and Italian citizens for political offences (Articles 10 and 26).[19] Accordingly, there were constitutional reasons for Italy to insist that the political exemption clause had to be included in any international agreement. When signing the European Convention on the Suppression of Terrorism, Rome was forced to reserve the right to refuse extradition for political offences. Apart from extradition, the Italian reservation clause also covered mutual assistance in criminal matters.[20]

On the other hand, moral considerations militated against these constitutional concerns. The Italian Government held the political offence clause to be an unfortunate impediment to the extradition of terrorists, whether foreign or Italian, and to mutual legal assistance among European states. It was seen as desirable to put an end to this loophole. Already in 1978, the Italian Government therefore pledged to ratify the Convention as soon as possible.[21] Presumably for the same reason, the Italian Government did not introduce the reservation clause into the first draft of the ratification laws for the Strasbourg Convention and the Dublin Agreement (Camera 1979, 1980).

In the ratification debate, though, Italy's constitutional problems resurfaced once again. In particular, it turned out that Italy had serious problems in accepting the institutional commitments that were associated with the Convention.[22] On the initiative of some parliamentarians upholding constitutional principles, the reservation clause was reintroduced into the ratification law with only minor modifications. Moreover, due to the fierce opposition of civil libertarian lawyers represented in the Italian Parliament, and due to the weakness of the frequently changing Italian Governments of the time, the ratification of the Convention was protracted until 1986.

Having signed the Convention, however, the Italian Government felt a moral obligation to ratify. Thus, senior politician Andreotti pointed out that Italy had actively participated in drafting the Convention, and that it was therefore wrong to deny ratification.[23] Moreover, in the course of the debate it was increasingly recognized that terrorist offences were 'absolutely not justified by any political motive'.[24] Accordingly, Italy should 'give a signal at the international level of the Italian commitment'.[25]

Towards the end of the ratification debate, the Italian Government became increasingly convinced that a supranational approach was in the common interest of all European nations to defend democracy and liberty, and that European cooperation in criminal matters should be invigorated not only against terrorism but against all forms of serious crime.[26] In the 1980s, senior Italian statesmen were ready to support the French idea of creating a unified 'European judicial area' and a supranational tribunal to deal with terrorist offences. In the words of the Italian President, it was necessary to pool sovereignty for the 'common good of European nations', and 'nobody should think he can go it alone'.[27]

Germany

During the ratification debate, the German Government vowed that it had always supported the European Convention on the Suppression of Terrorism. On the one hand, the Minister of Justice was proud to declare that, at an extraordinary meeting in May 1974, Germany had been the most important initiator of the Convention.[28] On the other hand, a shameful veil of silence was drawn over the original German attitude.

At first, Germany would have preferred to deal with international terrorism among the nine Member States of the European Community rather than among the 17 Member States of the Council of Europe. The idea was that a smaller circle of countries could provide for a more homogenous institutional environment, which would provide the necessary trust and confidentiality for a meeting of minds.[29]

At the beginning of the deliberations, Germany was indeed a relatively awkward supporter of the Convention. Between 1973 and 1974, the German Ministry of Justice raised severe objections against the most important substantive points. In particular, an obligation to extradite terrorists was held to be incompatible with the right of political offenders to obtain asylum under Article 16 of the German Constitution. The same article was also invoked to explain why Bonn could not accept the extradition of German nationals.[30] Furthermore, the Ministry argued that German courts should keep their autonomy to establish when and under what circumstances an offence was political. It was held that an obligation under an international treaty to depoliticize the political exemption clause would interfere unduly with the autonomy of the courts.[31]

Despite these concerns, the idea of a European convention on the suppression of terrorism was welcomed as a further step in the German policy of slowly enhancing the obligation to extradite terrorists. Bonn could point to the fact that Germany had already concluded some bilateral extradition agreements containing derogations from the political exemption clause. Under many agreements, attacks on heads of states were not treated as political crimes; in some cases, this was applied to attacks on the life of any person; in still other cases, there were provisions for the surrender of political criminals in fulfilment of an international obligation, such as the UN convention on genocide or the existing conventions against particular manifestations of terrorism.[32]

In line with this gradualist approach, Germany wanted to reduce the substantive scope of the Convention to a minimum and, at the same time, extend its binding force to a maximum. During the negotiations, Germany successfully called for the introduction of an obligatory arbitration procedure (Gal-Or 1985: 247). Moreover, Bonn was eager to implement the Convention once it had been concluded. After Austria and Sweden, Germany was the third country to ratify the agreement, on 3 May 1978. It was emphasized that, in principle, Germany would have preferred a more binding Convention. The German Minister of Justice deplored the possibility of reservations under Article 13 and emphasized that his country was ready to accept this loophole only because of its strong desire to see the Convention ratified by as many states as possible.[33]

At the end of the day, an obligation for European states to extradite terrorists coincided with the German national interest for a very simple reason: during the 1970s, Germany suffered several serious terrorist incidents. From the 1972 assault on the Olympic village in Munich to the 1977 hijacking of a Lufthansa airplane to Mogadishu, many of these incidents had an international background. Due to the trans-border character of the problem, international cooperation was seen as a necessary complement to national measures.[34] Germany had a clear interest in fighting terrorism effectively and thereby forestalling similar incidents in the future. As Chancellor Schmidt put it,

> At least since the spectacular raid on the Israeli team at the Olympic games in 1972, we are all aware of the dangerousness and international dimension of politically motivated violent crime. (...) Early on, the Federal Government has tackled the problem at two levels: First, the apparatus for the protection of internal security had to be developed further within our state; second, international cooperation in fighting crime had to be improved.[35]

Increasingly, terrorism was not only seen as a challenge to the order of the country under attack, but as an attack on the moral and political values of the international community in general, and of the Western European community of states in particular. Accordingly, a coherent European answer to the problem of violent political crime was deemed necessary. Insofar as terrorist raids were a challenge to the 'common European order', Germany could only welcome an international obligation to extradite terrorists.[36] In the same spirit, in December 1977 Germany supported the French idea of a 'European judicial area' that should unite the Members of the European Community.[37]

France

Together with Ireland and Malta, France was one of the most obstinate opponents of a binding obligation to extradite terrorists. For a long time, Paris persistently refused to ratify the European Convention on the Suppression of Terrorism. Signed in 1977, the Convention was ratified as many as ten years later (Koering-Joulin and Labayle 1988). And even then, despite the considerable delay in ratification, the French Government was eager to declare that the Strasbourg Convention and the Dublin Agreement would not apply retrospectively.[38]

This astounding hesitation was primarily due to the fact that France had, and in part still has, a unique tradition of political asylum. Ever since the liberal revolution of July 1830 France has considered itself as *terre d'asile*, or 'land of asylum'. The first extradition treaty containing the political exemption clause was concluded between France and Belgium, in 1833 (Stanbrook and Stanbrook 2000: 66). Since then, political asylum has been part and parcel of French national identity, and accordingly a treaty to curtail the political exemption clause posed severe normative problems to French decision makers (Harrison 1994). Moreover, French politicians were certainly aware that France was hosting a large community of political refugees. From the standpoint of the national interest, it therefore seemed inconvenient to support a convention that implied a formal obligation to extradite or incriminate members of these refugee communities.[39]

Apart from normative considerations and regardless of the national interest, French decision makers also saw their hands tied on constitutional grounds,

> We couldn't accept a system that would oblige us automatically to extradite the perpetrator of an attempt on the life of a diplomat (or on the life of any other person, when we talk about terrorism in general), without the possibility of taking into consideration the motivation of the offence, which may be political. We are dealing here with a fundamental principle of French law.[40]

According to the predominant understanding of the French Constitution, the extradition of political offenders was strictly prohibited. France could therefore hardly accept the idea of an international obligation to extradite terrorists. Even from the viewpoint of the French Government, the right of political asylum had constitutional rank. This was echoed by the French reservation clause to the European Convention on the Suppression of Terrorism, according to which efficiency in the repression of terrorism had to be

> reconciled with respect for the fundamental principles of our criminal law and of our Constitution, which states in its Preamble that 'Anyone persecuted on account of his action for the cause of liberty has the right to asylum in the territory of the Republic'.[41]

In any case, France was anxious to maintain its discretion to grant or refuse the extradition of terrorists.[42] Take for example two extradition requests submitted in 1977 by Germany, with which France had a bilateral extradition treaty.[43] In the case of Klaus Croissant, a German defence lawyer indicted for terrorist involvement, extradition was granted. On this particular occasion, the French Minister of Justice Peyrefitte even stated that 'it is not possible for France to become a country of asylum for terrorists' (quoted in Mouvement 1977: 70). In the case of the Palestinian terrorist Abu Daoud, by contrast, whose extradition was requested by Germany in connection with the 1972 assault on the Olympic village in Munich, extradition was denied for reasons of political expediency (Carbonneau 1977).[44] While the extradition of foreigners indicted for terrorist offences was already seen as problematic, the extradition of French nationals was considered to be completely impossible (Chauvy 1981: 45–7). Apart from extradition, France also had a restrictive view on mutual legal assistance in criminal matters.[45]

In 1973, the direction of judicial affairs of the French Foreign Ministry had come to the conclusion that France had no interest whatsoever in the Council of Europe undertaking any action in the field of terrorism. It was contemplated, however, that eventually there might be a political opportunity for 'posturing' in response to a recommendation by the Consultative Assembly of the Council of Europe.[46] The time for such posturing came in 1975, when France emphasized the need for concrete talks and initiated a working group to draft the European Convention on the Suppression of Terrorism.[47]

It is possible that, at the end of the day, French decision makers were ready to revise their negative attitude and ratify the Convention. Regardless of whether or not there was any such intention, however, the prospect for the French Government to ratify the Convention was thwarted by domestic public opinion. From September 1976, when the secret deliberations in Strasbourg were made public by a journal of the radical left, Paris witnessed increasing opposition from political and legal pressure groups who protested that human rights in general, and the right of political asylum in particular, were in jeopardy (Gal-Or 1985: 257, 275; Cerny 1981: 114).[48] Some critics even suspected that the venerable French tradition of '*terre d'asil*' and '*patrie des droits de l'homme*' would be sold out to foreign countries such as Germany, which were pursuing the extradition of terrorists in order to solve their own domestic problems (Julien-Laferrière 1979: 45).

After this moral outcry among an important sector of French public opinion, it then became even harder for the French Government to accept a binding obligation to extradite terrorists. While the other delegations in Strasbourg were convinced that a consensus had already been reached, Paris did not hesitate to use its veto in the autumn of 1976 to put the conclusion of the Convention on ice. Most importantly, France insisted that the Convention should be amended to allow for ample reservations. Moreover, France was opposed to a tough mechanism for dispute settlement (Gal-Or 1985: 256–7, 326). Only after the French amendments had been accepted by the other delegations, and presumably to avoid further embarrassment, did France choose to sign the Convention. Needless to say, however, the French Government made wide use of its right to attach reservations and apparently did not have any serious intention of ratifying.[49]

Apparently, France had a particular dislike of the Council of Europe as a geographical and institutional framework for a convention on the extradition of terrorists. According to the French reservation clause, there were doubts over whether there was enough commonality as to ideals of freedom and democracy among the Member States of the Council of Europe to warrant the extradition of political offenders.[50] Quite obviously, Paris was convinced that the French political system was superior and that one could not sufficiently trust the democratic quality of the other Member States of the Council of Europe. In the words of the French President:

> This convention gives a fairly automatic character to extradition. Tomorrow, in Europe there can be dictatorial regimes. Is it possible to easily envisage the extradition of a person who would be reclaimed by these countries? This is where one has to situate the reasons for the French misgivings.[51]

The negative attitude towards the Council of Europe was consistent with the fact that Paris had also failed to ratify the 1957 European Convention on Extradition (which was ratified in 1986, one year before the Convention on the Suppression of Terrorism).

Officially, France had more trust in the European Community. One point in the French reservation clause to the European Convention on the Suppression of Terrorism was that France would not ratify the Convention before the European Community had reached a similar agreement.[52] Arguably, however, this did not reflect a genuine will to come to a binding arrangement in the more exclusive institutional and geographical framework of the European Community. Instead, it would seem that France was rather trying to gain time and show some goodwill to its European partners.

In October 1978, when the European Community had negotiated the Dublin Agreement, France again refused to ratify. This time, the French President declared that an extradition treaty did not solve the problem at its root, and demanded a full-blown *espace judiciaire européen*, or 'European judicial area' (Gal-Or 1985: 327–8). The ostensible rationale for the initiative, which had been launched for the first time in December 1977, was to solve the problems connected with international cooperation in criminal matters on a more general level. While this would not necessarily solve the problems connected with the extradition of terrorists, the harmonization of criminal law amongst the Member States of the European Community would be an important step towards improved cooperation. As the French President pointed out:

> The idea of judicial area is not at all the idea of an area that would deal with the problem of political activities; it is about criminal offences, and about providing a more routine and more systematic character to existing provisions that are posing problems of competencies as far as crimes of a certain seriousness are concerned.[53]

The proposal of creating a 'European judicial area' was a typically French attempt to take the bull by the horns. Apparently, it was connected to the French tradition of promoting ambitious normative ideas to strike intractable political problems at their root, rather than taking concrete action. It was certainly embarrassing for Paris to be seen by other countries as a safe haven for terrorists, and 'thinking big' provided a comfortable alternative to taking more concrete political steps (Lacoste 1982: 197).

In the eyes of the French President, the idea of a 'European judicial area' must have been attractive because, in theory, it would have shaped the legal systems of the other European states in the model of the French tradition, which corresponded to the legal and political ambitions of France in the European Community. At least to some degree, the initiative was apparently sincere although it did not meet serious support from the other Member States. In any case, the French Government was also interested in promoting a new, ambitious idea in order to divert attention from the embarrassing fact that France was unable to ratify the European Convention on the Suppression of Terrorism. Since the idea of a 'European judicial area' was never fleshed out with content, it could be left open whether or not the proposal would cover the extradition of terrorists.

In October 1982, France proposed an even more ambitious idea: the establishment of a supranational tribunal for criminal justice in Europe as an alternative to the European Convention on the Suppression of Terrorism. The tribunal would deal with terrorism and other forms of serious crime. Again, this ambitious project was typical of the French tradition of 'thinking big' on normative issues. Again, the initiative was not welcomed by most other European states. And again, it would seem that the proposal also served to deflect attention from the fact that France was not ready to ratify either the European Convention on the Suppression of Terrorism at the Council of Europe, or even the European Community's Dublin Agreement.[54]

The European Arrest Warrant (2001–06)

As we have seen, when the Council of Europe tried in the 1970s to resolve the problem of the extradition of political offenders by means of the European Convention for the Suppression of Terrorism, the attempt was thwarted by the large number of loopholes in the Convention and by a lack of political will on the part of many Member States. As a result, the 1977 Convention did not fulfil the high expectations that had originally been set in the new legal instrument. Furthermore, attempts by the European Parliament and, to a lesser extent, the Commission of the European Community to put the issue back on the agenda failed due to the concern of some Member States with national sovereignty (Lodge and Freestone 1982).

Only after the end of the Cold War, did the European extradition regime start to gain new momentum. ETA-plagued Spain in particular demanded that, at least among Western European states, extradition should be granted automatically (Anderson 1993b: 32). In the mid-1990s, then, there were two attempts to draw up conventions to foster extradition within the EU.[55] These conventions would have required ratification by all Member States to come into force. However, of the four states examined in this book only Germany was relatively quick to ratify the two conventions, in 1998. Britain took until 2001, and France until 2005; Italy did not ratify at all. In the absence of ratification by all Member States, the conventions could not come into force. As a consequence, in the late 1990s the European extradition regime once more seemed to be stuck.

At that point, Spain started to demand that, at least for cases of particularly serious crime such as terrorism, extradition should be replaced by an entirely new legal principle: the mutual recognition of criminal sentences (J. Vogel 2001: 937). The underlying idea was that, at least among EU Member States, there should be sufficient trust for judicial decisions, such as extradition requests, to be automatically executed.

In 1999, Britain joined Spain in promoting the mutual recognition of criminal sentences at the level of the European Union.[56] In the Presidency Conclusion to the Tampere European Council, of 15 and 16 October 1999, the principle of mutual recognition was endorsed as the 'cornerstone' of judicial cooperation in general, and as the future basis for European extradition law in particular. The European Heads of State declared their intention that 'the formal extradition procedure should be abolished among the Member States as far as persons are concerned who are fleeing from justice after having been finally sentenced, and replaced by a simple transfer of such persons'.[57]

One year later, Italy and Spain signed a bilateral extradition treaty on the basis of mutual recognition for a series of particularly serious offences, most notably terrorism. In 2001, Spain attempted to reach similar agreements with France, Germany, and Britain (in November of the same year, such an agreement was indeed reached with the UK).[58]

As a result, and with the partial exception of France, by 2001 the five largest countries of the European Union were committed to a completely new and simplified scheme of extradition, which would henceforward be based on the principle of mutual recognition. This is not to deny that, while Britain was strongly in favour of mutual recognition, France would have preferred legal harmonization. But although the debate between the supporters of mutual recognition and legal harmonization never reached any conclusion, there was an emerging consensus that mutual recognition was more practicable.

Ultimately, this led to the adoption of a new legal instrument called the 'European Arrest Warrant', which bases extradition among the Member States of the European Union on the principle of mutual recognition (Wagner 2003: 704–8; Kleine 2004: 78–84; Wouters and Naert 2004: 911–25; Blekxtoon and Ballegooij 2005). The framework decision on the European Arrest Warrant was elaborated by the European Commission in the course of 2001, and submitted to the European Council immediately after 9/11. After the shock of this landmark event, the framework decision was negotiated by the Council of Ministers in only three months, and officially released on 13 June 2002.[59]

The European Arrest Warrant abolishes formal extradition between Member States and replaces it by a system of surrender between judicial and executive authorities. The surrender of criminal suspects or convicted criminals is handled directly between the agencies concerned, without any political review. Formally, the principle of mutual recognition means a step away from international to trans-governmental (not supranational) law. The idea is that, among EU Members, the final word on extradition should no longer be given to political decision makers, but that extradition should rather be handled by judicial and executive agencies. Clearly, if the European Arrest Warrant is properly applied, the concomitant loss of sovereignty will be considerable.

Unsurprisingly, though, important differences among national policy preferences surfaced during the process of bargaining and ratification.[60] As in other cases, national positions on the European Arrest Warrant can therefore be examined with regard to the core issues that were debated before and during the bargaining process.

By far the most important innovation of the European Arrest Warrant is the partial abolition of the principle of double criminality or double incrimination. According to this legal principle, extradition can be denied if the offence in question is a criminal offence in the requesting state only, and not in the requested state. Under the European Arrest Warrant, by contrast, a judge in one Member State must automatically validate a warrant issued in another Member State, without any test of double criminality. There are two other indicators which measure the institutional commitment of a country towards the European Arrest Warrant. First, it was an open question whether the other Member States would eventually apply 'enhanced cooperation' and go ahead without Italy, which was opposed to the European Arrest Warrant (Pastore 2003). Second, some countries were more eager to declare their will to ratify the Framework Decision in due time, or even ahead of time, while others openly announced that they were not in a hurry.

Concerning the substantive scope of the new legal instrument, there were four bones of contention. First, the framework decision provides a positive list of 32 offences for which the principle of double criminality shall be abolished. The length of this list, which goes far beyond serious crime such as terrorism and drugs trafficking, was highly contested among EU Member States. Second, it was debated how many years of prison an offence must be punishable with for double criminality to be abolished. Third, there were different viewpoints as to retroactive applicability. Fourth and finally, some countries were so fond of the European Arrest Warrant that they wanted to apply it as a blueprint for other legal instruments, such as the framework decision for the mutual recognition of fines, while other Member States were far less enthusiastic.

Britain

It is interesting to see that the United Kingdom, which is generally considered to be the Euro-sceptic nation par excellence (George 1998), was a uniquely strong supporter of the European Arrest Warrant. This British enthusiasm is all the more surprising if one considers that, in general, British extradition practice vis-à-vis other states is relatively strict. Take as an example the following case from July 2002, when the British Home Secretary ruled that there was insufficient evidence for an alleged Al Qaida supporter to be extradited to the United States:

> Mr. al-Siri's extradition had been sought by the US government. The Secretary of State had to decide by today whether to issue an order to proceed on the information and legal advice available to him. He was not satisfied that the prima facie evidence test was met. He therefore concluded that it would not be right on this occasion to issue an order to proceed.[61]

London nevertheless saw a national interest in a strong European Arrest Warrant for two reasons. On the one hand, British decision makers wanted to make extradition as simple and as practical as possible. On 30 September 2001, Prime Minister Tony Blair said to the BBC: '[W]e cannot have a situation in which it takes years to extradite people'. On the other hand, however, British decision makers also wanted to avoid intrusive schemes of legal harmonization, which might have entered into conflict with their understanding of national sovereignty and legitimate diversity among European states. An extradition scheme based on the principle of mutual recognition was seen as the best way to combine efficient procedure with national sovereignty (Hall and Bhatt 1999: 35–7), thereby providing a middle-of-the-road solution between the status quo, which was considered as inefficient, and full legal harmonization, which was considered too intrusive.[62]

Already before 9/11, key exponents of the Labour Government had embraced the international norm of mutual trust and mutual recognition among the Member States of the European Union. This was already clear in October 1998, when Home Secretary Jack Straw gave a speech on the European Judicial Space at a seminar in Avignon;[63] in March 2001, Prime Minister Tony Blair even demanded explicitly that courts should be able to issue 'Eurowarrants' applicable across all EU Member States.[64]

British support for the European Arrest Warrant was also facilitated by the fact that the Common Law tradition seems to favour mutual recognition. While other countries had to amend their constitutions, in the UK a simple statutory instrument was sufficient. Another supportive factor was that, ever since 1965, Britain had had positive experiences with the *Backing of Warrants (Republic of Ireland) Act*, an agreement which in some respects anticipated the idea of mutual recognition (Home Office 2001: 1). Nevertheless, the British Government was not oblivious to potential clashes with the national interest. Under the British ratification law, the Secretary of State retains a residual right of veto when extradition would be against national security.[65]

Apart from that, the British Government was deeply committed to the project. For example, London demanded the complete abolition of double criminality in order to minimize 'the restrictions on recognition of other people's legal systems'.[66] When Rome threatened to block the framework decision, Britain even considered proceeding without Italy as a sort of *ultima ratio*, although for diplomatic reasons London did not feel very comfortable about this eventuality.[67] Initially, Britain was among those states which committed themselves to applying the European Arrest Warrant at least six months before the deadline. In the end, however, the ratification law entered into force exactly on the deadline foreseen by the framework decision: 1 January 2004.[68]

It is interesting to note that, at least potentially, Britain wanted to expand the geographical range of application of the new legal instrument far beyond the boundaries of the European Union and the Schengen area. The *Extradition Act 2003* draws a distinction between two categories of states. The first category contains states to which the European Arrest Warrant shall be applied, and for the time being it is limited to all those Member States of the EU and the Schengen area that have also ratified the European Arrest Warrant. The second category comprises the rest of the world. In principle, however, nothing would prevent the transfer of a country from the second category into the first, even if the country concerned is not a Member of the European Union.

There was a perceived British national interest in keeping the flexibility to offer to other trusted extradition partners the same conditions as to EU Member States. The United Kingdom has firmly institutionalized ties of judicial cooperation with other Common Law countries, many of which belong to the Commonwealth. To keep the door open to these partners, the Home Office had already declared in March 2001 that it should be possible to extend the European Arrest Warrant not only to all Member States of the European Union and the Schengen area, but eventually to other trustworthy countries as well (Home Office 2001: 5). The warrant might be extended, for example, to 'a trusted Commonwealth or bilateral treaty partner' (House of Commons 2003: 5).[69]

Concerning the content of the new legal instrument, Britain was more ambitious than most other Member States. In particular, the British delegation wanted to see the principle of double criminality abolished for all offences not explicitly mentioned in an apposite 'negative list'. Due to the resistance of some other Member States, however, it was finally decided that there should be instead a 'positive list' of 32 offences for which the principle of double incrimination should be abolished. For all other offences, double criminality would be retained. Despite the considerable length of the 'positive list', the UK was slightly deluded by this solution.[70] Furthermore, early on Britain declared its intention of deliberately going beyond the commitments made, removing double criminality for all offences punishable with a penalty of at least 12 months of imprisonment (instead of 36 months).[71] Moreover, the British Government never raised any problems concerning the retroactive application of the new legal instrument.

London went far beyond its obligations and completely reformed British extradition law. As a spokesman of the British Government put it, the United Kingdom was 'prepared to go further than required and set an example to the EU partners'.[72] Unsurprisingly, the British Government was not amused when criticized by the European Commission for insufficient implementation (House of Lords 2006). In reality, once the European Arrest Warrant had been adopted, Britain was keen to use it as a blueprint for other legal projects in the European Union. For example, in 2003 London supported the idea of the Greek Presidency that the list of 32 offences from the European Arrest Warrant should be used as a template for the mutual recognition of fines.[73]

France

France was also a strong supporter of the European Arrest Warrant, although for different reasons. While France did not feel as immediately threatened by Al Qaida as the United Kingdom, the French Government was convinced that, in the interest of the entire international community, after 11 September it was necessary to forge new legal instruments such as the European Arrest Warrant in order to repress terrorism and other forms of serious crime. Since the time of the Gaullist doctrine of sanctuary for Middle Eastern terrorists and the subsequent *Doctrine Mitterrand*, when France had allowed terrorists from the Italian Red Brigades and from Spanish ETA to find sanctuary in the French *terre d'asile*, the normative consensus of the nation had changed considerably. A tough line on political refugees had become more popular, and the right-wing Government under President Chirac could easily support the European Arrest Warrant.[74]

Indeed, ever since the 1980s a tough line on terrorism in general, and on the extradition of terrorists in particular, was part and parcel of the institutional agenda of the French right. Already in 1986, the first 'serious' antiterrorist legislation was introduced by the right-wing Government of Prime Minister Chirac. Since then, the French right had constantly been trying to harden the French policy on terrorism and other forms of political violence. For example, the European Convention on the Suppression of Terrorism was ratified in 1987; the national security alert system *Vigipirate* was reinforced in 1995; and a considerable number of Italian terrorists were extradited in 2001. From the viewpoint of the right-wing Government under President Chirac, the European Arrest Warrant fitted well into this pattern and was therefore warmly welcomed.

In fact, there was a strong imperative for the modernization of French extradition law. The most important national legislation on extradition was, and still is, from 1927. Since the law is clearly inappropriate for dealing with the requirements of the twenty-first century, a complex system of international treaties and court sentences has been developed to make it work. Over time this has led to a considerable fragmentation of extradition practice, which is often criticized by French lawyers and legal specialists (see Haas 2000). Although the 1927 law does not have constitutional status, it seems to be very difficult to make any legislative changes. As a substitute, the European Arrest Warrant was seen by many as an appropriate move to unravel, at least for the Member States of the European Union, the Gordian knot of French extradition law and practice.

Accordingly, Paris demanded the resolute suppression of double criminality in the name of mutual recognition.[75] Nor did France exclude, in the face of

Italian opposition to the European Arrest Warrant, enhanced cooperation without Rome.[76] Moreover, France committed itself to applying the European Arrest Warrant at least six months before the deadline, that is in the first half of 2003.[77] In the end, it was not because of the French Government but rather due to foot-dragging in the National Assembly that the Framework Decision was ratified only on 9 March 2004, three months after the deadline.[78]

France wanted the European Arrest Warrant to be applied to all EU Member States, past and present. This was explained in normative terms by the French allegiance towards the construction and expansion of a European 'Area of Freedom, Security and Justice'. With its aspiration for becoming such an Area of Freedom, Security and Justice, the EU provided an institutional focal point for deciding which countries should or should not be eligible to become parties to the new legal instrument. The European Arrest Warrant was understood as an exception to the normal extradition procedure that had to be limited to the Member States of the European Union and the Schengen area.[79]

To make the European Arrest Warrant as comprehensive as possible, France proposed a long 'positive list' of offences for which double criminality should be abolished. This was not quite as radical as the idea of a 'negative list' proposed by the United Kingdom, but in principle France supported the idea that double incrimination should become the exception to the rule (Brana 2001: 17, 37–40).[80] Like Britain, France also wanted to apply the European Arrest Warrant to any offence punishable with at least 12 months of imprisonment.[81] In fact, according to the French ratification law the European Arrest Warrant is applicable to all offences liable to at least one year in prison, instead of the minimum penalty of 36 months designated by the Framework Decision.[82] France was even willing to apply the mechanism of enhanced cooperation in order to use the European Arrest Warrant as a template for the mutual recognition of fines.[83]

On one point, however, the French Government was adamant. Paris refused to apply the European Arrest Warrant to crimes committed before 1993, that is before the Maastricht Treaty came into force. This is interesting because Paris was, and still is, an important hub for retired left-wing radicals from Spain and Italy, who had been militant in the 1970s. This is not to deny that the right-wing Governments under President Chirac had taken their distance from the *Doctrine Mitterrand.* On the other hand, however, they were not ready to go beyond the case-by-case examination of requests for the extradition of members of the old generation of leftist radicals. The main reason was that, according to a French tradition, decisions taken by a former president should be respected. The French Minister of Justice Dominique Perben paid tribute to this tradition by refusing the automatic extradition of retired leftist radicals to Spain or Italy.[84]

Germany

While Britain and France were stout supporters of the European Arrest Warrant, Germany did not live up to its reputation of being the epitome of a pro-European Member State (Katzenstein 1997). Although Berlin did support the European Arrest Warrant, the German attitude on many seemingly technical points was somewhat ambiguous (Böse 2004: 109). This was due to the fact that, on the one hand, the European Arrest Warrant was in contradiction to important legal principles that were dear to German law, as the representatives of various ministries rightly pointed out. On the other hand, as Chancellor Gerhard Schröder put it, there was a strong imperative for Germans to behave as good Europeans and not as 'finicky minds'.[85] As a result of these countervailing tendencies, Berlin's attitude on many points was relatively unstable.

At the beginning, the German Ministers of Justice, the Interior, and Foreign Affairs all maintained that the principle of double criminality should be safeguarded as far as possible.[86] It took an energetic intervention by Chancellor Schröder to break, at least in part, the resistance of the Ministries.[87] When Rome threatened to block the European Arrest Warrant, the German Minister of the Interior used very strong language in his condemnation of Italy.[88] At the same time, however, the Minister recognized that Rome did have a right of veto.[89] Together with other Member States, Germany was eager to promise that the European Arrest Warrant would be applied at least six months before the deadline.[90] In the end, however, the entry into force was delayed until 23 August 2004, almost nine months beyond the deadline.[91] The problem was that Bavaria and other German States were using the federal system to obstruct ratification via the *Bundesrat*.[92]

In July 2005, then, the Federal Constitutional Court ruled on the occasion of an extradition request for a terrorist suspect that the ratification law was void because there had been too much unnecessary surrender of constitutional principles (Schorkopf 2006). The revised version of the German ratification law was finally promulgated in July 2006.[93]

The German position was also relatively unstable with regard to the offences for which to abolish the principle of double criminality. After Schröder had put his foot down on the suppression of double criminality, Germany supported its abolition for all offences mentioned in a long 'positive list' of offences. Even then, however, the German delegation called for a more precise definition of the listed offences and wanted to see the application of the European Arrest Warrant limited to offences punishable by a sentence of at least 48 months.[94] Moreover, it seems that Germany initially wanted to apply the European Arrest Warrant only to offences committed after the entry into force of the Maastricht Treaty in 1993.[95] In the first ratification law, however, Berlin showed itself satisfied with a threshold of only 12 months' imprisonment and did not pose any limitation to the retroactive application of the European Arrest Warrant.[96]

Even after the adoption of the European Arrest Warrant, the German Ministry of Justice remained cautious with regard to the abolition of double criminality. At the discussions on the mutual recognition of fines and on the European evidence warrant, for example, the German delegation called for a more restrictive list of offences and wanted to keep as much of double criminality as possible.[97]

Despite all these ambiguities, Germany welcomed the inclusion of the new EU Member States into the regional scheme of the European Arrest Warrant. Quite obviously, this was mainly due to the institutional dynamics of the accession process.[98] However, Berlin never envisaged extending the new legal instrument to third countries outside the European Union and the Schengen area. Apparently, the normative idea of an 'Area of Freedom, Security and Justice', to which Germany is deeply committed, made it obvious for Berlin that the EU was the proper regional framework for the application of a simplified extradition regime based on the principle of mutual recognition.

Italy

The most flagrant case of a country opposing the European Arrest Warrant was Italy. This could not have been predicted at the start, since Rome had not initially been opposed to the idea of applying the principle of mutual recognition to extradition in Europe. As already mentioned, in 2000 the Italian Government had signed a pioneering bilateral agreement with Spain, which foresaw the mutual recognition of court sentences and arrest warrants with regard to a list of six particularly serious infringements: terrorism, organized crime, drug trafficking, sexual exploitation of children, arms trading, and trade in human beings. It could have been expected that Italy would be willing to proceed from this bilateral scheme to a European-wide solution on similar terms (Grevi 2002).[99]

In principle, Italy would have favoured a 'small' solution with less institutional commitment and with a shorter list of serious offences. Although such a solution would have been less ambitious than the European Arrest Warrant, it would still have constituted a European regime for the mutual recognition of arrest warrants. Short of the European Arrest Warrant, a small solution along Italian lines would still have represented considerable progress in comparison to the situation in the 1980s and 1990s. After the terrorist outrage of 9/11, however, such a small solution was out of the question.

From the autumn of 2001, when the European Arrest Warrant was first discussed in the Council of Ministers, the Berlusconi Government acted as a fierce opponent of the project as it was negotiated in the 2002 Framework Decision of the European Council. The first sign of Italian resistance came on 16 November 2001, when Rome expressed scrutiny reservation.[100] After it turned out to be politically impossible for Italy to veto the European Arrest Warrant, Rome protracted the implementation of the Framework Decision and even suspended the ratification of the bilateral agreement with Spain, presumably to avoid the appearance of political inconsistency.[101] In the end, Italy was the last EU Member State to ratify the European Arrest Warrant in April 2005.[102]

How is it possible to explain this fundamental opposition? Arguably, the main problem was neither posed by Prime Minister Berlusconi and his party, *Forza Italia*, nor by Deputy Premier Fini and his post-fascist *Alleanza Nazionale.*

The main problem was the political ideology of a small coalition partner to the Italian Government, the *Lega Nord*, and its leaders Umberto Bossi and Roberto Castelli.

Prominent exponents of the autonomist *Lega Nord* were fearful of a 'Europe of handcuffs' and suspicious of a conspiracy of the so-called Red Robes, that is crypto-communist judges backed by ominous elements from the secret services.[103] In the words of Minister of Justice Castelli: 'If we put together all the pieces of the puzzle, there is a precise objective emerging: power into the hands of the judges (or those behind them).'[104] Or, again in the words of the Minister of Justice, in Europe there was a risk of 'first giving the power to the judges and only then making a common constitution. This is an unacceptable fact'.[105] This was also the mindset of the leader of the *Lega Nord*, Umberto Bossi, according to whom the European Arrest Warrant was 'madness', 'a step towards dictatorship, towards a regime of terror', and 'a crime in itself'.[106]

There was a ferocious national and international campaign to present the entire Italian Government, and not just the *Lega Nord*, as petty-minded opponents to the European Arrest Warrant. However, there is hardly any concrete evidence that Prime Minister Berlusconi and Deputy Premier Fini supported this view. On the contrary, these politicians and their followers tried to moderate the radical stance taken by the *Lega Nord*.[107]

Apart from ideological reasons, however, individual exponents of the Italian ruling elite had a personal interest in avoiding the real or perceived risk of themselves becoming liable to a European Arrest Warrant. Probably for this reason, the Italian delegation insisted that the crimes of corruption, racism, and xenophobia should not be covered by the warrant. Moreover, Bossi feared that he would be the first victim of the European Arrest Warrant.[108] He even warned that one should not surrender a certain 'inhabitant of Arcore' (the hometown of Berlusconi) to 'the land of the gallows' (the EU).[109]

Initially, Italy had not been against the partial abolition of double criminality. On the contrary, its abolition for six very serious crimes had been the basis of the agreement with Spain. In the heat of the controversy over the European Arrest Warrant, however, Italian opposition grew so strong that there was temporarily a risk that the principle would even be tightened. According to one expert from the Italian opposition, the ratification law that was discussed in the Italian Parliament was

> a fraudulent and suicidal law that betrays the European Arrest Warrant, imposing on European partners such as Germany, France and Spain conditions that have never been demanded from them in the last 50 years, and which are much tougher than those required of countries that are not EU Members, such as Turkey or Ukraine.[110]

In fact, the draft ratification law provided that the European Arrest Warrant should be made conditional on the respect of due process in the requesting state, and that every single arrest warrant should be channelled through the

Ministry of Justice together with ample documentation, in the absence of which it had to be rejected. Moreover, an Italian judge would always check whether a warrant had been released on the basis of sufficiently 'serious indices of culpability' – a condition that had previously been abolished among European partners by the 1957 European Convention on Extradition.[111]

The Italian Government was in no hurry to ratify the European Arrest Warrant. Already in December 2001, Berlusconi stated: 'We shall see. As far as we are concerned, we have to modify a fundamental law; we shall see whether we manage to do that by 2004. If not, nothing will happen.'[112] For Rome it would have been an acceptable way out of the quagmire if the European Arrest Warrant had been applied among the other EU Member States, with Italy staying apart. Or, as the Italian Minister of Justice put it: 'England has stayed away from the Euro and hasn't gone into bankruptcy. If Italy stays away from the European Arrest Warrant, one does not have to see this as a drama'.[113] Even when Italy had formally implemented the warrant, 16 months after the deadline of 1 January 2004, the European Commission found serious shortcomings in the ratification law.[114]

From the Italian standpoint, the main problem was the plan to abolish the principle of double criminality for a list of 32 items – far too many in the eyes of Minister of Justice Castelli, who had called for 'a more restricted list of more serious offences'.[115]

In this spirit, Italy had proposed the same list of six particularly serious infringements as in the agreement with Spain: terrorism, organized crime, drug trafficking, sexual exploitation of children, arms trade, and trade in human beings.[116] For the eventuality that the European Arrest Warrant should be extended to other crimes, Italy's fallback position was that its application should be restricted to citizens of the requesting state.[117] And if even that should prove unacceptable to the partners, Italy wanted the warrant not to enter into force before 2008 for 16 crimes (including financial crimes, racism, and xenophobia).[118] In any event, Rome was strictly against retroactive application.[119] Moreover, Italy wanted the European Arrest Warrant to be applied only to crimes punishable with more than four years of imprisonment, as in the agreement with Spain.[120]

Taken all together, it comes as little surprise that Italy was opposed to using the European Arrest Warrant as a blueprint for other legal instruments, such as the decision on freezing assets. At that opportunity, Minister of Justice Castelli even went as far as talking about Italy's 'essential interests', thereby evoking the famous formula used by Charles de Gaulle during the EU crisis of the 1960s. After threatening to block the project, however, Castelli was once again forced to accept a compromise.[121]

Part II

The international fight against drugs

6 International drug prohibition

There is a feeling widely shared across time and space that narcotic drugs are a dangerous borderline phenomenon which can engender considerable harm to the drug user and his or her social environment. But although drug use is mostly associated with a vague feeling of opprobrium, taken by itself this does not lead to coercive action. To legitimize the repression of drug users and traders, it takes a formal prohibition regime specifying which substances, for example cocaine or tobacco, and which kinds of behaviour, as for example trafficking or consumption, shall be proscribed. The twentieth century saw the development of such a 'global prohibition regime', first at the League of Nations and later at the United Nations.[1]

Drug prohibition is about meta-political authority or, in other words, about deciding what is regulated by the free market, and what is manipulated by political fiat (Thomson 1995: 222–3). Since the early twentieth century, the United States has been at the forefront in bolstering the punitive approach towards narcotic drugs. Especially after World War II, when a growing population of addicts in the American homeland was consuming drugs from distant countries, global drug prohibition became a matter of US national interest. Drugs were exempted from the emerging free trade regime and placed instead under a repressive political regime that provided for the mandatory use of coercive power (Thomas 2003). Most of the time, and especially under the Nixon administration (Nixon 1971; Gross 1972), the regime was shaped by the punitive approach of the United States, which tried to commit the world to taking hard measures against drug trafficking (King 1972: 208–28).

Between 1961 and 1972, three landmark agreements were passed at the United Nations: in 1961, the *Single Convention on Narcotic Drugs* simplified the drug prohibition regime and reduced the number of relevant agreements from nine to one; in 1971, the *Convention on Psychotropic Substances* extended international drug prohibition to a new class of substances; and in 1972, the *Protocol amending the Single Convention on Narcotic Drugs* further strengthened the regime (McAllister 2000: 215–39; see also Albrecht 2001 for a short survey). The main focus was, and still is, on supply-side measures, which were further strengthened in 1988 by the *Convention against Illicit Traffic in Narcotic Drugs and Psychotropic Substances*. While states are also formally obliged to take action against the consumption of drugs, there is much more discretion on demand-side measures.

Together, the aforementioned agreements limit the discretion of states to define the drug problem autonomously and thereby to determine under which circumstances the use of force is legitimate. Nevertheless, it is important to emphasize that the regime does not exactly prescribe how a state should deal with drug users. This has led to a never-ending debate over whether it is permissible to pursue non-repressive policies towards drug users. While such policies have been practised for long by small countries such as the Netherlands and Switzerland, since the mid-1990s the punitive approach has also been challenged by large states such as Britain and Germany. It has now become debatable whether and to what extent drug prohibition is still shaped by American hegemony (Gerber and Jensen 2001). Some authors contend that there is instead an alternative European drug regime in the making (Elvins 2003).

According to one author, the tide has been changing since the 1998 UN General Assembly Special Session on drugs. Since then, due to an informal coalition between consumer countries in Europe and producer countries in the South, the so-called balanced approach has 'gained ground in relation to the American law enforcement approach that had been more traditional in UN circles hitherto' (Boekhout van Solinge 2002: 15). Many EU Member States are at least rhetorically promoting this balanced approach. The idea is to combine the international fight against the supply of drugs with appropriate measures to reduce the demand for drugs in the consumer countries.

Of course this does not alter the fact that the right balance between supply-side and demand-side measures remains subject to debate. There is still disagreement on whether and to what extent one must continue to pursue a punitive approach, or whether it would not be better to rely more on prevention and harm reduction.

Expanding the regime (1961–72)

During the crucial period between 1961 and 1972, when the three landmark agreements were adopted at the United Nations, international consensus emerged slowly. In theory all the countries under consideration here were in favour of global drug prohibition, and they all accepted the United Nations as the competent body. But while Britain, France, and Germany insisted that drug prohibition should rest upon the universal consensus of the international community, Italy would have been content with a regime that enlisted 'as many countries as possible' (UN 1973c: 33).

There was profound disagreement over the question of which and how many narcotic drugs and psychotropic substances should be proscribed. Especially with regard to psychotropic substances, considerable commercial interests of the German, British, and Italian pharmaceutical industries were involved. There was also disagreement on whether, and to what extent, the regime should affect the domain of genuine domestic regulation. Should the regime address demand-side measures, and should it provide for the mandatory introduction of counterfoil books for the prescription of drugs?

Moreover, there was also profound disagreement on the institutional strength of the regime. Should there be a strong or rather a weak Commission on Narcotic Drugs (CND) and International Narcotics Control Board (INCB)? Should there be an outright appeals committee, or was it sufficient to create a weaker arbitration committee? Should the US-supported United Nations Fund for Drug Abuse Control (UNFDAC) be empowered to act in the source countries, or was it better to stick to the United Nations Development Program (UNDP)? And was it desirable to introduce the possibility of a mandatory trade embargo against states contravening the regime, or was this an unacceptable interference in the principle of national sovereignty?

There was considerable disagreement on all of these points. In 1961, when the Single Convention on Narcotic Drugs was under negotiation, virtually all continental European states considered drugs to be a specific problem of US society. With the exception of the notorious hardliner France, these states had therefore only a very limited interest in further criminalizing the phenomenon, or in making binding institutional commitments. Only in the 1970s, when European societies were increasingly faced with similar drug problems to the United States, did a more vigorous attitude start to carry the day.

In general, the United Kingdom took a minimalist approach to the further development of the global drug prohibition regime as a whole. Germany and Italy were fairly reluctant to expand the substantive scope of the regime, but favoured a cautious boost to the institutional infrastructure. Only France was supportive of criminalizing as many narcotic and psychotropic substances as possible. On the other hand, however, Paris had misgivings about the introduction of binding institutional commitments.

Britain

Well into the 1970s, the United Kingdom saw drugs as an international problem that hardly affected British society. Britain accepted that global drug prohibition was in the international interest and that the United Nations was the competent body. In the absence of a clear national interest, however, this formal allegiance to global drug prohibition did not translate easily into the approval of specific points. On the contrary, the United Kingdom perceived a national interest in safeguarding British sovereignty against an international regime that was set on restricting the room for manoeuvre for an autonomous drugs policy. At the same time, the British bargaining position was heavily influenced by the professional and commercial interests of the country's powerful medical lobbies, namely doctors and the pharmaceutical industry. Already during the 1950s, Britain had stonewalled a protocol which might have jeopardized the supply of the United Kingdom with opium for medical use (McAllister 2000: 194–5).

At the 1961 Conference for the Adoption of a Single Convention on Narcotic Drugs, the British delegate explicitly emphasized the concern of his country for sovereignty. '[I]t would be difficult, or even impossible, for his government to agree to a convention which included a clause absolutely prohibiting certain drugs on the basis of a decision by an international body' (UN 1964a: 17).[2] At the same time, the delegate highlighted medical considerations: 'It was for governments to decide, after consultation with the medical profession, whether or not the therapeutic properties of a substance justified its prohibition' (UN 1964a: 4; cf. 1964b: 102–3, 106). At the time, the British approach to drugs was shaped by regulation rather than prohibition, and British doctors were allowed to prescribe heroin to addicts (Bruun *et al.* 1975: 131).[3] It certainly would have caused problems to the British Medical Association if the use of counterfoil books had been made mandatory for the prescription of narcotic drugs, and the British delegation therefore could not accept this idea (UN 1964a: 31).[4]

Furthermore, the UK was afraid that certain methods of treatment, as well as legislation against the simple possession of drugs, might one day turn into a mandatory international obligation: 'It was for each country to decide what treatment would be most effective in the circumstances' (UN 1964a: 111).[5] To forestall the risk of jeopardizing sovereignty, the British delegate emphasized that the convention would only be effective if it could rely on the universal consensus of the international community. He went so far as to declare that the United Kingdom preferred a weak but universal drug regime to a more ambitious but less inclusive approach (UN 1964a: 4).[6]

A decade later, at the Conference for the Adoption of a Convention on Psychotropic Substances, Britain's emphasis on the 'professional freedom and judgment' of the medical professions was even stronger. At the Conference, in 1971, the British delegate argued that the British medical profession and other domestic groups did not recognize the danger of certain substances, such as barbiturates (UN 1973b: 112, 121; cf. UN 1968: 27).[7] He therefore insisted that the Protocol should not 'encumber medical practice and scientific research with unnecessary controls' and that 'the truly international problems requiring international solutions should be precisely delimited' (UN 1973b: 8). In any case it would not be right 'to impose an obligation to take action before a country actually had a problem' (UN 1973b: 21). In fact, Britain ratified the Protocol on Psychotropic Substances as late as 1986.

The Single Convention on Narcotic Drugs, by contrast, had already been ratified in 1964. Since then, Britain had formally become a supporter of this particular convention (UN 1973c: 13).[8] The main reason behind the British change of mind was an attempt to assuage the United States. Thus, in September 1972 the UK delegation at the conference to consider amendments to the Single Convention reported back to London that the United Kingdom had 'sought to be active in support of the US position whenever opportunity offered', while ingenuously recognizing that Britain had been a 'reluctant associate', and that the true objective of the exercise was 'widely taken to be a ploy to promote domestic support for the re-election of President Nixon'.[9]

This is not to deny that, in the early 1970s, Britain's attitude on international drug prohibition became more positive for other reasons as well. Due to the emerging drug problem in and around London, the British Government started to convince itself that the international prohibition of narcotic substances could be in the national interest (UK 1971; cf. Bean 1974). Foreign Secretary Douglas-Home cautiously started recognizing that drugs were 'an ever present threat to the UK and Western Europe despite the fact that heroin addiction here is relatively small'.[10] Unsurprisingly, this led to a more positive British attitude towards international drugs prohibition (UN 1973b: 8).

Nevertheless, the United Kingdom was still unwilling to accept stronger institutional commitments towards the regime.[11] In particular, Britain was horrified by the idea that the Commission on Narcotic Drugs and the International Narcotic Control Board could gain 'dictatorial' powers, which might be used against sovereign countries.[12] Britain was opposed to the US proposal that it should be possible for the INCB to decree trade embargoes against notorious source countries of illicit drug trafficking (UN 1974: 43). London had for long been concerned that a strict prohibition regime might endanger the supply of the British market with opium for medical use (UN 1964a: 39),[13] and was fearful of commercial disadvantages, as for example to the British branch of the Coca-Cola Company (UN 1973c: 216–19).[14]

In general, Britain stuck to its preference for limiting international drug prohibition to a small number of general principles and for leaving as much as possible to national legislation.[15] There were only three exceptions to this rule. First, Britain did not want strong powers for the CND and the INCB, but still wanted them to be independent expert bodies (UN 1964a: 90–1; 1973c: 172–5). Second, Britain was initially opposed to the idea of an appeals committee (UN 1964a: 68), but later revised its position. In 1971, the British delegate declared that 'it would not be right in principle to deprive the parties of the right to have recourse to a court after the failure of the procedures' (UN 1973b: 84). Third, Britain also changed its mind with regard to the American suggestion of a United Nations Fund for Drug Abuse Control. Initially, Britain was committed to the United Nations Development Programme (UNDP) as the competent body for activities in developing countries and therefore rejected the American suggestion of creating a United Nations Fund for Drug Abuse Control. After considerable soul-searching and in an attempt to please the United States, however, Britain finally agreed to pay a small contribution.[16]

Germany

Like Britain, for most of the 1960s Germany did not see itself as a country with a serious drug problem. Accordingly, Bonn did not perceive a strong national interest in supporting the global drugs prohibition regime. This does not mean that Germany was not formally committed to global drug prohibition (UN 1964a: 5). However, it was anxious to preserve its national sovereignty in order to be able to take its own policy decisions. In particular, Bonn had serious misgivings that autonomous decisions of the Commission on Narcotic Drugs might harm German interests, and this was the main reason why the ratification of the Single Convention was protracted from 1961 to 1973.[17]

Around 1970, Bonn started to recognize that a growing national drug problem made international drug prohibition more desirable (Briesen 2005: 277–307).[18] In particular, Germany realized that global drug prohibition at the United Nations was essential for the adequate handling of the problem (UN 1973b: 7).[19] The Single Convention on Narcotic Drugs was ratified in 1973, and the Convention on Psychotropic Substances in 1977. At least in part, this change of mind was also due to Germany's desire to avoid international isolation. Bonn recognized a growing international interest in global drug prohibition and did not want to appear as indifferent towards one of the most urgent problems of the time.[20] In addition to that, allegiance to global drug prohibition was also seen as a relatively easy way for Germany to demonstrate political goodwill to the United States.[21]

Nevertheless in the 1970s, as well as in the 1960s, Germany was reluctant to make concessions on many substantive points. One important reason for this was that, as a country with a large pharmaceutical industry and a strong medical lobby, the German Government had an overriding incentive to take the professional and commercial interest of these domestic stakeholder groups into account.[22]

Even before the negotiations for the Single Convention started, Germany was opposed to the idea of the total and mandatory proscription of any drug. Regardless of the substance at hand, medical research and therapeutic use should always remain possible.[23] Germany even defended the therapeutic use of cannabis in homeopathic pharmacopoeia (UN 1964b: 102). Another obvious case in point was the commercial interest of the German pharmaceutical industry in psychotropic substances. At least initially, Bonn was fundamentally opposed to the international control of psychotropic substances (UN 1968: 20, 56). In particular, it was opposed to the international regulation of commercially lucrative psychotropic substances, 'since it was not sufficiently clear that they did give rise to dependence and since no appreciable risk of abuse was involved' (UN 1973b: 7). Germany therefore voted against the inclusion of schedule IV into the Convention on Psychotropic Substances and abstained when the Protocol was voted upon at the end of the Conference (UN 1973b: 54, 121).

Germany was also opposed to the mandatory use of counterfoil books for the medical prescription of drugs. As the German delegate stated, '[h]is government did not think it right that a patient should know that an addiction-producing substance had been prescribed for him' (UN 1964a: 28).[24] It is plausible to assume that this attitude was connected to the professional interests of German doctors. At the same time, Germany was also committed to the popular idea that humanitarian measures to help drug addicts were a necessary complement to a more repressive approach. For example, Bonn was co-sponsor of a proposal to introduce non-repressive measures on the demand side into the Single Convention (UN 1973c: 199; 1974: 95).[25]

Although without great enthusiasm, Germany supported the institutional strengthening of the drug prohibition regime. While this was hardly related to any specific national interest, it was rather typical of Germany to view international institution-building as a value in itself. For example, Bonn supported an institutional reform to strengthen the International Narcotics Control Board and supported an initiative to grant the Board the power to make inspections monitoring compliance.[26] Germany was also committed to the United Nations Fund for Drug Abuse Control as an instrument for fighting the disastrous effects of drug abuse by operating in the source countries, and together with the United States and Canada was one of the first countries to transfer a voluntary financial contribution to the newly founded institution.[27]

But there were certain limits to Germany's institutional commitment. In particular, the country was opposed to the idea that the INCB should have the power to decree trade embargoes against the source countries of illicit drugs. Germany was very concerned that an embargo imposed by a UN organ might be incompatible with the EC treaties (UN 1974: 16).[28] For example, there were preoccupations that the United States might instigate the INCB to impose an embargo on France, where opium was distilled into heroin for the American market. In this hypothetical case, German firms would have been obliged to interrupt their lucrative pharmaceutical trade with an EC partner.[29]

All in all, Germany was a hesitant supporter of global drug prohibition. While opposed to an expansive attitude on proscribing as many narcotic drugs and psychotropic substances as possible, it nevertheless supported a moderate institutional strengthening of the relevant organs for monitoring and implementing the regime.

Italy

While other countries were clearly concerned about international drug prohibition, Rome was initially hardly interested in the issue. At the conference on the Single Convention, in 1961, the Italian delegation failed to display a proper accreditation letter and was therefore excluded from participation (UN 1964a: xix). At the talks on psychotropic substances, ten years later, Italy was allowed to join the conference although the credentials of the Italian delegation again failed to meet the requirements (UN 1973a: 12).

Nevertheless, Italy formally supported global drug prohibition and accepted the United Nations as the competent body. Since Rome had long ignored the rising national drug problem in Italy (King 1972: 226), the Italian Government did not see any problem with talks at the United Nations, which were happening regardless of whether Italy participated or not, as long as these talks did not affect Italian interests. As the regime gained in importance, however, the Italian Government increasingly perceived a national interest in joining the relevant debates and organs.[30]

There was a measure of opportunism in all of this. If Italy formulated a bargaining position at all, most of the time it was distinguished not only by a certain degree of fuzziness but also by a considerable amount of duplicity and inconsistency. This is not to deny that, in the 1970s, the Italian Government sometimes talked about the moral duty of tackling drugs for the sake of mankind (Senato 1973: 5; UN 1973c: 44). Nevertheless, critical experts were right that such lofty talk hardly reflected any real political activity by the Christian-Democrat Governments of the time.[31] This can also be seen from the fact that the 1961 Single Convention was not ratified until 1974, and the 1971 Convention on Psychotropic Substances not until 1981.

While a ban on narcotic drugs did not seem to pose any particular problems, Rome tried to torpedo the international prohibition of synthetic drugs and psychotropic substances. At the conference on psychotropic substances in 1971, Italy declared its misgivings about the international prohibition of these substances because the problem was 'a health one rather than a legal one'; furthermore, 'if a country decided, for example, to prohibit the consumption of alcoholic beverages, it did not necessarily follow that all countries should imitate it' (UN 1973b: 131). While these were the official reasons for Italy's negative attitude, Rome's real concern was quite obviously due to the fact that the Italian pharmaceutical industry earned a lot of money from amphetamines and did not want to lose this source of revenue (Mantelli Caraccia 1973: 48, 79–80; Cancrini *et al.* 1977: 105–7). Similarly, it is likely that commercial interests were behind Italy's diplomatic outrage at the danger that some countries might use drug prohibition as a pretext to reap unfair trade advantages (UN 1973b: 51). Italy kept a fairly low profile during the talks on psychotropic substances, but after the conference Rome led a conspiracy of several EC states not to sign the Convention or at least to agree upon a common form of reservation (UN 1973b: 121).[32]

At the Conference to amend the Single Convention, in 1972, Italy for the first time took a positive interest in international drug prohibition and welcomed the intention of broadening the Convention (Senato 1973: 7; UN 1973c: 44). In an attempt to gratify its American partner, Italy was even co-sponsor of a US resolution calling for wide ratification and announced its own readiness to ratify soon.[33] Nevertheless, the Italian delegate candidly declared that in his country the problem was not 'acute' (UN 1973c: 12). The position of the Italian delegation was also ambiguous on demand-side measures, signalling a clear preference against international regulation and at the same time a considerable level of diplomatic flexibility (UN 1973c: 198).

If one considers that, by the early 1970s, Italy had a growing drug problem, the diplomatic detachment of the Italian delegation appears somewhat bizarre. Nevertheless, it reflected a more general pattern. On the home-front, the national drug endemic was not tackled by the Italian Government until the mid-1970s (Manna and Ricciardelli 1989). Even then, the problem was widely attributed to the pernicious Anglo-Saxon, Dutch, and Danish influence on

Italian teenagers (Senato 1976: 45). Italian decision makers were stubbornly reluctant to recognize that drugs had already hit home.

Although Rome slowly became more interested in global drug prohibition during the 1970s, the position of the Italian Government continued to be ambiguous. Take as an example Italy's stance on the appeals procedure. Rome was not ready to support an independent appeals committee. Instead, Italy filed an amendment to weaken the appeals procedure under discussion (UN 1974: 105–6).[34] The official explanation was that it could not be accepted that an international organ should have the power to pass judgement over sovereign states (UN 1973c: 83–4). This clearly shows that Italy was opposed to a strong institutional mechanism for monitoring the international drug prohibition regime. It is therefore ironic, to say the least, that one year later the ratification law for the Single Convention was recommended to the Italian Parliament precisely on the grounds that the authority and powers provided to the Commission on Narcotic Drugs were an important step forward.[35]

But be that as it may, Italy applied for membership of the INCB in 1970.[36] Four years later, it also applied for membership in the CND.[37] In recognition of the increased importance of the UN organs, apparently Rome was following the maxim 'if you can't beat them, join them'. As a final example of Italian ambiguity, consider its attitude towards the American proposal for a United Nations Fund for Drug Abuse Control. Rome was ready, after some initial hesitation, to support the Fund with a contribution of 100,000 Dollars (UN 1973c: 43). Italian diplomats, however, mainly saw this as a cheap way of gratifying the American partner.[38]

France

In comparison with most other European countries, France presented itself as uniquely concerned with the drugs phenomenon and aware of the potential danger of a spread of the problem. Already in the early 1950s, France had assumed a joint leadership role with the United States in preparing the Opium Protocol (McAllister 2000: 179–82). Certainly, the French Government did not seriously consider that drug addiction might soon become a serious problem for the French homeland (UN 1964a: 110). However, the French Government believed that there was an international interest in the fight against drugs, and that the fight could only be effective if a hard line were pursued at a global level. Paris therefore preferred the widest possible international regime to isolated solutions. Moreover, France was consistently loyal to the United Nations as the competent international body.[39]

France was also motivated by moral reasons. From the perspective of the French Government, a relentless fight against drugs was a matter of moral commonsense. At the Conference to amend the Single Convention, the French delegate did not hesitate to declare in public that, 'unlike other psychiatric cases, drug addicts were normally both liars and active proselytisers'

(UN 1973c: 183). This attitude was connected to a specific feature of the French political culture. In France, drugs are traditionally seen as a dangerous social poison that alienates the individual from the vocation to be an active citizen. From this perspective, the addict's withdrawal into Baudelaire's 'artificial paradises' is not only a risk to personal health but also the expression of a moral ill and a potential threat to the Republic (Ehrenberg 1996: 7–9).

Paris was therefore at the forefront in calling for the prohibition of as many narcotic drugs as possible. At the Conference for the Single Convention, in 1961, France did not object to any of the substances scheduled for prohibition (UN 1964a: 18). In fact, the French delegate went far ahead of the discussion, emphasizing that synthetic drugs – 'a very serious and growing peril' – were the 'real problem for the future' (UN 1964a: 63, 193).[40] France even submitted an unsuccessful draft resolution on the control of barbiturates, and when psychotropic substances had finally been put on the agenda, in 1971, it insisted that no exceptions be made either for barbiturates or for any other psychotropic substance (UN 1973b: 13, 114).

This hard-line was facilitated by the fact that France did not have a large pharmaceutical industry. While other countries had to take commercial interests into account, France could focus on the safety of French citizens. Although the French Government did not yet consider, during the 1960s, that drug addiction might soon become a serious problem for French society, it could only be in the national interest to protect the country from the dangers involved in international drug trafficking. Moreover, at the time France had not yet tackled the 'French Connection', a ring of smugglers based in Marseille and trafficking heroin from Turkey to the United States (Gévaudan 1985; McCoy 2003: 46–76). To divert attention from this shameful state of affairs, it was important for the French Government to demonstrate leadership and send the US an adequate signal that it was not soft on drugs (Cusack 1974: 243–8).[41]

Only as far as demand-side measures were concerned, did France take a more cautious stance. According to the French delegate, '[i]t was difficult to lay down methods of treatment, for drug addiction took many forms' (UN 1964a: 110). Therefore, Paris was opposed to the inclusion of treatment and other harm reduction measures in international agreements. Under any circumstances, the replacement of punishment by treatment or educational measures should be merely optional (UN 1973b: 30). France was more sanguine about the use of counterfoil books in order to control the medical prescription of drugs, but nevertheless insisted that the provision on counterfoil books should not go beyond a mere recommendation (UN 1964a: 30).

While France held relatively stark preferences on the substantive scope of drug prohibition, its stance on binding institutional commitments was more ambivalent. In 1961, it was not satisfied with the creation of a relatively weak arbitration procedure and supported the idea of establishing a stronger appeals mechanism instead (UN 1964a: 65; 1964b: 92). In 1972, however, when the issue was renegotiated, France had reservations on the proposed appeals committee (UN 1974: 43). It officially called for a strong and independent International Narcotics Control Board and was 'in favour of any provision which would ensure the de facto independence of the Board' (UN 1973c: 194; cf. 1974: 5–6, 27–9). Internal sources from the French Foreign Ministry, however, reveal that there were some clear limitations to this preference.[42]

In any event, France was not ready to accept a heavy infringement of drug prohibition upon national sovereignty. For example, Paris was not willing to accept the idea of a trade embargo against states contravening the regime, because the French understanding of national sovereignty did not allow for such far-reaching measures.[43] Moreover, France initially was not ready to support the American proposal for a United Nations Fund for Drug Abuse Control, preferring the United Nations Development Program to remain in charge.[44] Although in the end it did accept the Fund, Paris insisted that France had agreed only 'in a spirit of compromise'.[45] Paris initially refused to pay a contribution, but soon after changed its mind in order to avoid damage to its credibility as a hardliner against drugs.[46]

Regime under fire (1998–2006)

In recent years, global drug prohibition has been coming under increasing stress. Especially since the United Nations General Assembly Special Session on drugs (UNGASS) in 1998, there has been a latent conflict beneath the surface of the regime between countries committed to vigorous drug prohibition and countries hoping for a more pragmatic approach (Jelsma 2003). France and Italy under Chirac and Berlusconi were representatives of the former group, whereas Britain and Germany under Blair and Schröder were committed to the so-called harm reduction approach. While there has always been experimentation with non-repressive approaches, for example in the Netherlands, an alternative EU regime is now appearing on the horizon (Elvins 2003). These approaches affect both the provision and the consumption of drugs, although the UN regime is more clearly under fire on the demand side than on the supply side.

Non-repressive approaches to drug control may become a serious challenge to the global prohibition regime. As far as the supply side is concerned, some contend that violent crop eradication in producer countries is a legitimate means of reducing the availability of drugs. Others object that the destruction of poppy fields and coca farms is counterproductive because of the harmful social consequences. Another contested issue is precursor chemicals. Some contend that these non-intoxicating substances are important for the concoction of narcotics, and that their control is a necessary part of the fight against drugs. Others object that the control of precursor chemicals is an infringement on the principle of free trade that cannot be justified either on normative or practical grounds. It is held that precursor chemicals are mostly used for legitimate purposes, and that any of these substances can be substituted by other chemicals.[47]

On the demand side, some argue that the controlled consumption of narcotics in drug injection rooms is a useful way of minimizing the harm inflicted to drug users, especially when combined with substitution treatment (e.g. methadone). Others object that injection rooms and substitution treatment are in contravention of the drug prohibition regime, and that it is immoral for a state to arrange for the consumption of drugs, whether in injection rooms or in other localities, let alone to provide drugs and utensils such as syringes and needles. There is a similar dispute regarding cannabis. Some argue that it does not make sense to keep prosecuting the users of such a 'soft' drug. Others, however, object that cannabis is an illicit drug according to the Single Convention, and that it is therefore forbidden to decriminalize it, let alone legalize it.

Similarly, different countries have different ideas on how deeply they want to be committed towards the regime.[48] These institutional preferences, regarding both the UN regime and the 'alternative' EU regime, can be seen from the following indicators. At the UN level, one can compare the contribution of a country to the general budget of the United Nations with its voluntary contribution to the United Nations Drug Control Program (UNDCP).[49] In addition to that, one can examine the extent to which a country is otherwise committed to supporting distant countries in their activities against drugs. At the EU level, one can identify the position of a country with regard to minimum standards for drug-related penalties. Moreover, it is interesting to see whether a country calls for coordinated measures at the European level against drug tourism to and from the Netherlands, where soft drugs are freely available in the (in)famous 'coffee shops'. A strongly committed country can be expected to contribute a larger budget share to the UNDCP than to the UN in general, to support distant countries in their fight against drugs, to demand minimum penalties at the EU level, and to call for coordinated measures against drug tourism to the Netherlands.

While all countries are formally committed to drug prohibition, a closer look reveals that there are important differences between 'hardliners' such as France and Italy on the one hand, and 'revisionist' countries such as Britain and Germany on the other.

France and Italy

Under the aegis of Jacques Chirac, France is committed to a global 'crusade' against drugs that involves both producer and consumer countries, and both the supply and demand side of the problem. 'Drugs corrupt. Drugs kill.'[50] At least during the tenure of the second Berlusconi Government (2001–06), Italy took a similar line,

> The objective is that drugs shall not have any market, neither supply nor demand, and that there shall no longer be the need to lament and, where possible, repair the devastation and death that drugs invariably inflict upon whoever approaches them; it's never soft, it's always a drug.[51]

Under Chirac, France fully supports the United Nations regime for global drug prohibition. This approach is still grounded in the national ideology of the 1960s and 1970s. In French political imagery, the drug addict has lost the essential quality of a citizen and is a prisoner of his or her private life. Insofar as drug addiction reduces the person to an 'idiotic' existence, it is not only a 'pact with the devil' and a threat to personal health, but also a public threat to the state (Ehrenberg 1995: 73; 1996). As one critical researcher has characterized this ideology: '[t]he citizen must be liberated from a drug that alienated him/her, just as the social body must be delivered from the evil that besieged it; hence the policy of eradicating drugs' (Bergeron 2003: 44).

Under the impact of psychoanalytical therapy, this national ideology became institutionalized during the 1970s as a therapeutic doctrine. From the perspective of the French 'curative approach', drug addiction is pathological. The only legitimate aim of therapy is therefore to attack the pathology at its roots in order to help the addict become abstinent.[52] There seems to be a large consensus in the French therapeutic community that abstinence is the objective, and that psychoanalysis is the best way of attaining it. This psychoanalytical and curative approach provides an institutional context in which, for normative reasons, there is almost no room for the tolerant handling of the drug problem under the banner of 'harm reduction' (Bergeron 1999; 2003).[53]

For the last four or five decades, France has consistently pursued a hard line, and belongs to the group of countries with the most severe drug policies in Europe. According to the former French President, fighting drugs is 'an absolute priority in France'.[54] French decision makers are convinced that the fight can only be successful if states cooperate on a global scale and if the UN regime is not weakened. Not so much in the French interest as for the sake of the international community as a whole, France is opposed to any opt-outs from the punitive approach. It even supports the idea of repressive supply-side measures such as crop eradication in remote producer countries like Afghanistan, although advocating that such measures should be complemented by alternative development strategies.[55] Moreover, France supports the fight against the abuse of chemical precursor substances (Mission 1999: 110–11; 2004: 50).

At the same time, the French Government also favours a repressive approach on the demand side of the problem. Controlled consumption and drug injection rooms are seen more as a moral outrage than in terms of harm reduction. They are considered to pose severe ethical problems and to be useless against infective diseases such as AIDS.[56] A similar attitude prevails with regard to cannabis. According to the former French President, it is erroneous to talk about 'soft' drugs:[57] 'France will remain firm in its refusal to legalize or de-penalize drug use. Now more than ever the priority must be to fight the use of cannabis and synthetic drugs by young people effectively'.[58] In 2004, the French Minister of the Interior even proposed that Europe should establish compulsory therapy and fines of up to £ 1,000 for cannabis users.[59]

Let us now compare this to the situation in Italy during the Berlusconi Government. While the French hard line on drugs was based upon a nation-wide consensus, the Italian policy rested on the political ideology of two right-wing parties (*Alleanza Nazionale, Lega Nord*) represented in the ruling coalition of Prime Minister Silvio Berlusconi. According to the political ideology of these two parties, there was a moral obligation to criminalize drug users. The Prime Minister himself and his party (*Forza Italia*) coveted more liberal ideas, but mostly left the issue to the other two coalition partners and formally endorsed their hard-line ideology on drugs.

There were two variants of this ideology. On the one hand, there was the 'solidarity' version of Deputy Prime Minister Gianfranco Fini, who considered the full recovery of drug addicts as a moral duty and was

> outraged at the egotism of a society that says to the drug addict: 'I give you the methadone, you stay in a corner like a physical wreck and don't bother society, you don't disturb the calm of the brave citizenry'.[60]

On the other hand, there was a more aggressive breed of un-deconstructed drug warriors in the Ministry of Justice and elsewhere. Regardless of these internal divisions, however, right-wing politicians from both 'schools' were convinced that 'one can never allow the voluntary consumption of drugs to become a right'.[61]

As far as the demand side of drug prohibition was concerned, the preferences of the Italian Government were in fact close to the orthodoxy of the global drug prohibition regime. For example, Italian policy makers were very fond of 'zero tolerance': even the consumption of small quantities had to be sanctioned, since 'there are no soft drugs and hard drugs, there are only drugs and any kind of drug is harmful'.[62] This position was formalized in the new drug law of February 2006, which abolished the distinction between 'soft' and 'hard' drugs for the incrimination of users.[63] The declared aim was not harm reduction but abstinence, that is the 'liberation' and 'recovery' of drug users.[64] Methadone could not be accepted as a solution but only as a last resort when everything else had failed (Ministero del Lavoro 2003: 70). Italian drug officials were outraged at the use of drug injection rooms in Switzerland and Germany.[65]

As far as the supply side was concerned, Italian decision makers were convinced that it was in the national interest to protect Italy as a consumer and transit country from international drug trafficking (Direzione 2004: 49). At the same time, they also saw a collective interest of the international community in the fight against drugs. In the words of Gianfranco Fini, '[e]ither there is a mobilization of the entire international community, or there is a risk of not winning this fight'.[66] From this perspective, the United Nations was clearly the competent international body for drug prohibition.

While Italy was quite resolute in the fight against precursor chemicals, it seems that Rome had more scruples over the violent eradication of crops in the source countries.[67] It was emphasized that 'drug warehouses' had to be destroyed, but there was an eloquent silence on violent measures against drug farmers in Afghanistan and elsewhere.[68]

Overall, French and Italian preferences on drug prohibition were quite similar. Nevertheless, it is fair to emphasize that Italy joined the phalanx of hardliners more recently than France. During the 1990s, Italy had been relatively lenient on the demand side; substitution treatment had become routine in the Italian public health system; there had even been a successful referendum on decriminalizing the personal use of drugs in 1993. This came to an end with the second Berlusconi Government. In October 2001, Deputy Prime Minister Gianfranco Fini announced a radical paradigm shift in drug policy. He explicitly used the word 'repression' in declaring that his Government was going to put an end to the harm reduction approach, and especially to the toleration of cannabis and prescription of methadone.[69] From then onwards, Fini personally made sure that Italy would become more resolute on drug prohibition. The Italian Government was for 'zero tolerance not only of the trafficking but also of the personal consumption of drugs'.[70]

Clearly, then, both France and Italy had strong preferences on the substantive scope of global drug prohibition. But were these preferences matched by institutional commitments? As a first cut, a good measure of institutional commitment is the share of a country's contribution to the United Nations Drug Control Program (UNDCP) in comparison to its share as a contributor to the general UN budget.

In 2004, Italy was second only to the United States in donating to the UNDCP. In the same year, it was the sixth largest contributor to the UN as a whole. France, by contrast, was the fourth largest contributor to the UN, but only the seventh largest contributor to the UNDCP (spending roughly the same amount as tiny Luxembourg).

Ever since 1982, when the flamboyant Giuseppe di Gennaro took office, there has been a veritable dynasty of Italian directors succeeding to each other at the head of first the UNFDAC, and later the UNDCP. Since then, Italy has always been a leading contributor to UN activities against drugs in the source countries (G. di Gennaro 1991; Fazey 2003: 163). Especially under the Berlusconi Government, Italy was very proud of this leading position and called upon other states to fund the Program more generously.[71] From the standpoint of Italian policy makers, after so many years at the forefront of the UN bodies it was simply 'normal' for Italy to continue supporting the United Nations as the competent body for global drug prohibition.[72]

As we have seen, Italian generosity towards the UNDCP went beyond the French readiness to fund this body. The picture does not change very much when taking activities outside the institutional framework of the United Nations into account. Italy was not very busy in this field, although it did organize some seminars and courses for participants from all over the world (Ministero del Lavoro 2003: 85–96). This relative inactivity is understandable, because Italy was already a champion at the UNDCP. In the French case, by contrast, one would expect a leadership role in program activities outside the United Nations, given the fact that Paris keeps a low profile at the UN.

Interestingly, however, France lends only limited support to distant countries in their fight against drugs. Nominally, Paris contributed to dozens of bilateral projects in countries like Russia, Turkey, Uzbekistan, Niger, and Burkina Faso between 2002 and 2005. However, the total amount of money spent on these projects is even lower than the amount contributed to the UNDCP (Mission 2003: 11–12). In theory, France is convinced that drugs are a global phenomenon that requires a global response, and that 'international legitimacy has its home in the United Nations'.[73] It would seem, however, that there are budgetary reasons why France's rhetorical support for vigorous international supply reduction is not matched by adequate financial commitments.

Traditionally, France has always considered demand-side policies as a matter of political choice for sovereign nation-states or as a field where states could exchange best practices. More recently, however, Paris perceives a national interest in making sure that drug prohibition is not diluted in the European Union (Mission 2004: 8, 58).[74] To further this end, French decision makers would very much like to raise the repressive French demand-side policy to the EU level and thereby coerce countries with soft drug policies, such as the Netherlands, to take a harder line. When the Council of Ministers finally adopted a framework decision on minimum standards for drug penalties in 2003, the French Minister of Justice warmly welcomed the agreement. The Minister was happy to announce that it finally allowed for effective judicial cooperation against trafficking in small quantities. He was also delighted that the agreement would help to fight drug tourism to Dutch coffee shops, which had been a bone of contention between France and the Netherlands for many years.[75]

On minimum standards for drug penalties, the Italian Minister of Justice could only agree. He even declared that this had been the primary objective of his EU presidency. As far as drug tourism to Dutch coffee shops was concerned, however, the Minister pointed out that the principle of subsidiarity had to be respected.[76] This was certainly not connected with any sympathies for drug users in Dutch coffee shops, but rather with the apprehensions of his party (*Lega Nord*) that too much legal harmonization might imply a transfer of power to Brussels.[77] On the other hand, however, the Italian Minister of Justice called for more uniformity among European countries in the fight against drugs and condemned the 'hypocrisy' of those European countries who were fighting drug trafficking and, at the same time, tolerating personal consumption.[78] Against this hypocrisy, Italy wanted to use its influence in the EU in order to get European drug policies in line with its own views and with the spirit of the UN regime. It fully supported global drug prohibition and expected its EU partners to adjust their policies to its own restrictive interpretation of the regime (Ministero del Lavoro 2003: 69).

To summarize, France and Italy both took a hard line on international drug prohibition. The French hard line, which goes back to the 1950s and 1960s, was hardly backed by an adequate institutional commitment. In the Italian case, the hard line was the result of a policy change in 2001. Both Italy and France had serious misgivings that certain European states might be undermining the global drug prohibition regime. Accordingly, France (and, to a lesser extent, Italy) supported the nascent EU drug regime while insisting that this should not touch the principles of drug prohibition.

Britain and Germany

Britain and Germany are exactly the type of countries Italy and France would criticize for their lax drug policies. However, a closer look reveals both similarities and differences between the German and British attitude on international drug prohibition.

Although Germany is not opposed to the idea that there should be a global drug regime, it is hard to find a statement to the effect that global drug prohibition is in the German national interest. Of course Berlin agrees that, in the international interest, it is necessary to cooperate with other countries to forestall the dangers posed by drug trafficking and related organized crime (Drogenbeauftragte 2003: 51–2). However, Germany has serious normative misgivings about the repressive 'philosophy' underlying the global drug prohibition regime. Since the late 1980s, it has become more and more uneasy with many of the beliefs that are used to justify the crackdown on consumers and producers (Friman 1996: 106–12). Since then, the German soft-line policy seems to rest upon a bipartisan consensus that has survived the Government changes in 1998 and 2005.

Britain, by contrast, is 'soft' on the demand side but 'tough' on the supply side. On the demand side, Britain wants to retain the autonomy to pursue an independent national approach geared towards harm reduction. London adopts a relatively tolerant policy towards drug users at home, and has thereby come into conflict with the international obligation to criminalize the consumption of drugs. On the supply side, however, the current British Government has inherited the international role of a hardliner and American 'deputy' in the global 'war on drugs'. In fulfilment of this traditional role, London is deeply committed to the suppression of drug trafficking.[79]

Already during the 1990s, Britain provided logistic support to the United States in the drug war in Colombia (Klein 2000). In late 2001, after the military invasion in Afghanistan, the UK took the lead responsibility for counter-narcotic efforts in that country (Home Office 2002b: 26–9). Although Britain in the end largely refrained from violent crop eradication, it is fair to say that this was mostly for pragmatic reasons and because the United States were fearful of alienating Afghan farmers.[80] In principle, Britain kept as committed as ever to the idea of crop eradication and was even more ready to destroy crops than the United States.[81] In a similar spirit, from the early 1990s Britain persisted in supporting the prohibition of chemical precursor substances in order to curtail the supply of drugs (Dorn *et al.* 1992: 164–8).[82]

On the demand side London is so 'soft' that it touches the limits of what is permissible under international law. By 2002, most British policemen 'did not think that criminalizing young people was a good use of their time' (May *et al.* 2002).[83] In order 'to free the considerable amount of police time currently spent in dealing with minor cannabis possession offences', London reclassified cannabis from Class B to Class C (Home Office 2002b: 36–7; 2002c: 3). In practice, the decision to declassify cannabis was tantamount to decriminalizing the personal use of this drug. The British Government expected that this would serve the professional interests of the British police by allowing 'enforcement agencies to focus resources in disrupting the supply of the drugs that cause the most harm' (Home Office 2002c: 5–6).

London claimed that the reclassification of cannabis was in conformity with international law insofar as cannabis was not formally legalized (Home Office 2002c: 27). The International Narcotics Control Board did not agree and sharply criticized the measure. In response, a top British official rejected the Board's 'selective and inaccurate use of statistics' and the 'failure to refer to the scientific basis on which the UK Government's decision was based'. It would do 'great damage to the credibility of the messages we give to young people about the dangers of drug misuse if we try to pretend that cannabis is as harmful as drugs such as heroin and crack cocaine'.[84] Apart from the decriminalization of cannabis, the guardians of global drug prohibition were irritated by another British affront to the international drug prohibition regime. Not only do British state officials supervise the consumption of drugs but, in pursuit of harm reduction, the UK has even turned back to a practice that had been effectively abandoned since the 1970s: prescribing heroin to drug addicts (Home Office 2002c: 20).[85]

While Britain is 'tough' on the supply side and 'soft' on the demand side, Germany seems to have an aversion against the punitive approach to drug prohibition in general. For altruistic or even idealistic reasons, Berlin favours non-repressive solutions and would like to see a substantive reduction of the current UN regime. Ever since the early 1990s, and to some extent even before, German drug policy has been guided by the notion that drug addiction is an illness rather than a crime, and that addicts deserve treatment. Since 1998 there has been an even stronger emphasis on harm reduction, with the Ministry of Health playing a more important role in German drug policy (Friman 1996: 112; Friesendorf 2001: 84–5; Drogenbeauftragte 2003: 27–43).

In 2000, Berlin amended the German Narcotics Bill to legalize drug injection rooms, that is facilities where narcotics can be used under the supervision of state employees.[86] The German Drug Commissioner defended this measure as 'survival assistance' to drug users.[87] Drug injection rooms are in clear contradiction to the punitive 'spirit' of the UN regime, although it is possible to argue that they are in technical compliance with the relevant international agreements.[88] Germany even experimented with the distribution of heroin to incurable users.[89] The German policy towards cannabis is also contentious. After the 2002 Federal Elections, the coalition agreement of the centre-left Government explicitly re-endorsed a 1994 sentence of the Federal Constitutional Court that had effectively decriminalized the possession of small amounts of cannabis.[90] Germany is aware that the full legalization of cannabis would violate international law and has therefore not considered such a radical step.[91]

On the supply side, Germany has no problem with market-centred measures such as the control of precursor chemicals. It even calls for new 'global strategies to control chemicals which can be misused for the production of narcotic drugs'.[92] More directly repressive measures, however, are rejected. In particular, Berlin has serious misgivings about violent crop eradication in producer countries and openly denounces the US emphasis on destruction.[93] Instead, Germany is strongly in favour of 'alternative development' and vigorously promotes the scheme of 'development-oriented drug control' as a normatively superior way of curtailing the supply of drugs (Bundesministerium 2004).[94] This is in full continuity with the policy of the conservative Governments of the early 1990s (Friman 1996: 106–7).[95]

In short: Britain is 'soft' on demand and 'tough' on supply, while Germany is 'soft' on both demand and supply. This is also reflected in each country's commitment towards the institutional dimension of global drug prohibition.

Since the global drug prohibition regime is so focused on the supply side, it is easy for Britain to sustain multilateral cooperation at the global level. At the same time, commitment to the UN regime is also seen as a means to pursue the national interest. London hopes to keep drug supplies away from British streets, influence international drug policy, and further the interests of the British pharmaceutical industry (Foreign and Commonwealth Office 2003a: 35). In 2004, Britain was the fifth largest contributor *both* to the UNDCP *and* to the regular UN budget. London supports counter-narcotics activities all over the world with a priority on tackling the key heroin and cocaine routes to the UK (Foreign and Commonwealth Office 2003b). In 2000, Prime Minister Blair called for minimum penalties for dealers and smugglers to be introduced all across Europe, and in 2002 Britain was 'pushing hard' for a framework decision on minimum penalties for trafficking drugs and precursor chemicals in the EU.[96] The United Kingdom has also made considerable efforts to bring the Central and Eastern European countries into line with the state of the art in the fight against drug trafficking (Home Office 2002b: 30).

Germany, by contrast, is unhappy with the punitive approach taken by the UN organs. On the one hand, it is convinced that the drug problem can only be solved multilaterally. On the other hand, it does not seek conformity with the current global drug regime at any cost. In 2004, Berlin was the third largest contributor to the general UN budget but provided only the sixth largest budget share to the UNDCP. To build up a non-repressive alternative, the Federal Republic is pursuing bilateral projects of 'alternative development'. The Ministry of Development plays a very important role in German drug policy, and between 1990 and 2003 Germany spent 140 Million Euros on projects of 'development-oriented drug control', for example offering treatment to local addicts in Afghanistan – ten times as much as the amount contributed to the UNDCP in the same period (Drogenbeauftragte 2003: 52; Bundesministerium 2004: 17, 30; cf. Friesendorf 2001: 97–100, 144).

In short, Germany is silently opting out of the UN regime and prefers bilateral projects as an outlet for international solidarity in response to the drug problem. One will not of course find any explicit statement rejecting the UN as the competent international body to tackle drugs. However, in the words of the Ministry of Health, cooperation between Germany and the UN institutions is far from optimal.[97]

To avoid the appearance of a German *Sonderweg*, which would be harmful to the German interest in being seen as a good international partner, Berlin supports the European Union as an alternative platform for international drug policy. Former Minister of the Interior Otto Schily never hesitated to remind his European colleagues that EU action against drugs needed to be tough. For example, Berlin took part in peer-pressuring the Netherlands to take steps against drug tourism and supported European-wide standards for minimum penalties on trafficking in small amounts of drugs.[98] In a position paper outlining Germany's view during the negotiations for the new European Drug Strategy, Berlin underscored the German preference for a harmonized European drug policy and recommended its own approach concerning drug injection rooms and other elements of the harm reduction scheme.[99] It has often been noted that Europe is becoming more important in the drugs field and that the German approach is embedded in the EU strategy (Drogenbeauftragte 2003: 51–8).[100]

In fact, Germany can expect to exert more influence in the European Union than at the United Nations. Its attempt to expand the EU regime along the lines of harm reduction is based on the assumption that this approach, which is relatively unpopular at the UN, has a better chance of success at the European level (cf. Boekhout van Solinge 2002: 113). Moreover, a liberal European demand-side policy would add an important share of legitimacy to Germany's silent opt-out from the UN regime (Friesendorf 2001: 144). Berlin therefore has an interest in a strong EU regime, which will provide the necessary institutional coverage for an alternative drug policy.

Britain, by contrast, makes no effort at camouflaging its determination to follow its own approach towards demand reduction. The Blair Government inherited this will to maintain national autonomy from its predecessor Governments (Fazey 2003: 156–7). As we have seen, already in the 1970s British Governments rejected binding international rules on demand reduction. London traditionally sees demand reduction as a matter of autonomous national policy that should not be regulated in any way by international agreement. Correspondingly, British policy makers do not usually address the issue of drug tourism to Dutch coffee shops. Moreover, after the reclassification of cannabis they would rather avoid peer-pressure among European countries; each country should keep the flexibility to set penalties of its own choice. London is also sceptical about expanding the competencies of the European Union, especially in the field of demand reduction. In British eyes, Europe should primarily 'add value to national efforts' (House of Commons 2004: 18–19).

In summary: Britain is 'tough' on supply but 'soft' on demand. In particular the British policy of harm reduction touches the limits of acceptability under the international drug prohibition regime. The Federal Republic is as 'soft' on demand as the United Kingdom, and pursues a similar policy of harm reduction. At the same time, however, Germany is also 'soft' on supply and has some reservations about the punitive aspects of the UN regime. As an alternative to the punitive approach of the UN, Germany supports bilateral projects of 'development-oriented drug control' and the emergent drug policy of the European Union. Britain, by contrast, is sceptical about any attempt to regulate demand reduction policies at the international level.

7 Drug enforcement methods

The fight against drug trafficking is the epitome of international policing (Sheptycki 2000b). Ever since the early twentieth century, the United States has not only been the most conspicuous market for the consumption of drugs, but its police have also led in the development and promotion of new drug enforcement techniques. In 1930, the Federal Bureau of Narcotics (FBN) was created with the mandate to fight drug traffickers in the US and abroad in order to curb the supply of drugs on American streets. In 1968, the Bureau was reorganized and renamed Bureau of Narcotics and Dangerous Drugs (BNDD). Since 1973, after another reorganization, it has been called the Drug Enforcement Administration (DEA). Despite these institutional metamorphoses, American agencies have always been able to shape the investigative methods with which drug traffickers are fought at the international level.[1]

This was particularly true in the early 1970s, when President Nixon declared a global war on drugs (Nixon 1971; cf. Epstein 1977). Roughly at the same time, European societies were for the first time confronted with a serious drug problem. To deal with the problem, European police forces slowly came to converge on a homogenous spectrum of law enforcement techniques similar to the methods adopted in the United States. Although these techniques posed serious problems to the legal and constitutional traditions of continental European states, over the 1970s and 1980s even the most obstinate civil law countries like France and Italy accommodated to controversial investigative techniques such as undercover policing (Fijnaut and Marx 1995).

Nevertheless, drug trafficking was not seriously defeated by these methods. Incrementally over the 1980s, the cutting edge of US drug enforcement therefore shifted from man-hunting to the fight against the financial base of criminal organizations (Nadelmann 1986; Dorn *et al.* 1992: 68–70; Sheptycki 2000a). Once again, European states accommodated to a technique that had serious implications for venerable principles such as banking secrecy or the professional confidentiality of lawyers. Especially during the 1990s, there was a growing consensus that the fight against criminal finance was the best strategy to fight drug trafficking.[2] This is remarkable if one considers the fact that the very idea of fighting criminal finance had been largely unknown in the 1970s.

Leading scholars assume that, in the case of investigative techniques, legislative politics tends to be determined by executive practice. According to this view, law enforcement officers form transnational networks whereby investigative techniques travel from one country to another. As new investigative practices become established, officers succeed in convincing their governments that they should be accommodated by national legislation. At the most general level, Mathieu Deflem (2002) argues that this amounts to a global pattern of bureaucratic diffusion. Other authors propose similar arguments about the institutional effects of inter-police networking at the European level (Bigo 1996; Elvins 2003).

With particular regard to the diffusion of drug investigation techniques, Ethan Nadelmann (1993) talks about the 'Americanization of European drug enforcement'. He assumes that American law enforcement agencies have performed as mentor agencies to promote the diffusion of their techniques all over the world. In the European case, the adoption of the new techniques was thereafter sanctioned by national legislation in the target countries. By and large, nation-states in Europe are seen as reactive to the investigative techniques adopted by their own police forces, which in turn are shaped by the modus operandi of the American law enforcement agencies.

While these are highly suggestive hypotheses, whether and to what extent they are accurate is an empirical question. It is certainly true that American law enforcement agencies play an important role in the diffusion of investigative techniques, and it is clear that national policies are sometimes influenced by domestic and transgovernmental networks of police practitioners. In this chapter, however, the internationalization of drug enforcement methods is analysed from the vantage point of state preferences. On closer analysis, it turns out that states are more often motivated by reasons other than the professional interests of their law enforcement agencies.

Novel ways of tackling drugs (1969–76)

In the late 1960s and early 1970s, when the United States intensified its global fight against drug trafficking, the Bureau of Narcotics and Dangerous Drugs was assigned the task of institution building, which included training drug enforcers in foreign countries to increase the efficiency of their investigative techniques. These techniques included extensive undercover operations, intrusive forms of surveillance, and offers of reduced charges or immunity from prosecution to known drug dealers in order to 'flip' them into becoming police informers. At least initially, however, the problem in continental Europe was that these investigative techniques posed serious legal problems to many countries (Nadelmann 1993: 139–50, 189–249).

The largest problem was undercover investigation and infiltration tactics. These methods were very popular in American law enforcement circles (Marx 1974, 1988; Wilson 1978). However, the use of undercover techniques conflicted with the 'rule of compulsory prosecution' that held sway in the civil law countries of continental Europe. Whenever the police infiltrated a criminal structure without arresting the culprits, even if it were for investigative purposes, then it actually let a crime happen. This was seen as legally problematic, because state authorities were formally obliged to act when a crime was occurring. Moreover, the traumatic memory of 'agents provocateurs' from Europe's illiberal past made undercover investigation and infiltration tactics suspect of being illegitimate attempts at 'entrapment', with the police instigating a crime that otherwise would not have happened. Although by 1968 all Interpol member agencies considered undercover investigation and infiltration tactics useful in the fight against drug trafficking (Schenk 1968: 301), in many European countries it took well into the 1990s for these techniques to become lawful (Joubert 1995).[3]

Another challenge was the American law enforcement doctrine of going for 'Mr. Big'. The idea underlying this doctrine was to abandon the street-level policy of arresting addicts and seizing small amounts of drugs, and instead to concentrate efforts on the major traffickers smuggling the bulk of the drug supply. By the end of the 1960s this had become accepted wisdom in American law enforcement circles (Epstein 1977: 107), but in most European countries the modus operandi of the law enforcement agencies was still to make as many seizures as possible.[4]

Although to different degrees, the diffusion of American investigation techniques was supported by the political elites in continental countries such as France, Germany, and Italy. Paris, Bonn, and Rome also supported institutional learning, from European drug enforcers visiting the United States up to more intense forms such as courses and internships. Only in the British case, active state support for American investigation techniques was not necessary due to the constitutional autonomy of the police.

In any case, the Americanization of drug enforcement techniques is only part of the story. At the same time, there was also a conscious attempt on the part of European decision makers to 'Europeanize' the methods of dealing with the problem. Most notably, in August 1971 the French President launched his famous 'Pompidou initiative'. This was a clear attempt at embedding drug enforcement into a multidisciplinary approach that would include education and health care. Another objective was the legal harmonization of drug policies among European countries. Moreover, the Pompidou group intended to be a regional forum for facilitating the exchange of information, thereby creating an institutional alternative to Interpol. Although the group was not very successful in terms of policy output, most European decision makers welcomed the French President's ambitious initiative.

France

In theory, France had always recognized the interest of the international community in more efficient drug enforcement methods. As we have seen in the last chapter, France is a longstanding supporter of global drug prohibition.

This alone, however, was not yet sufficient to motivate Paris to actively support the modernization of drug enforcement techniques. In fact, during the 1950s and most of the 1960s France paid little interest to drug enforcement. This was a source of annoyance to the United States, considering the infamous 'French Connection'. In fact, after the end of the Second World War France had become the most important hub of the opium route from Turkey to the US. The raw opium arriving from Turkish poppy crops was processed into heroin in the area of Marseille. The refined product was then forwarded via different channels to New York (Cusack 1974; Gévaudan 1985; McCoy 2003: 46–76). In the late 1960s and early 1970s, the Nixon administration was desperate to finally tackle the French Connection (Epstein 1977: 93–5; Friesendorf 2007: 37–78).

Franco-American cooperation was unavoidable for the achievement of this aim. Already in the 1950s, investigators from the Federal Bureau of Narcotics had regularly visited France from their regional headquarters in Rome, with French investigators making counter-visits to the US. Around 1960, the FBN had reinforced the Franco-American link of police cooperation by establishing branch offices in Paris and Marseille (Nadelmann 1993: 130–1). Unfortunately, however, none of these efforts were even remotely sufficient to curb the heroin supply that ran from France to the United States. Despite the American pressure on Paris to allocate more resources to drug enforcement, the amount of drugs trafficked from Marseille to New York was constantly increasing.

In August 1969, President Nixon and President Pompidou took the decision to intensify contacts between American and French drug enforcement agencies.[5] In the same month, the US Bureau of Narcotics and Dangerous Drugs (BNDD) transferred its regional headquarters from Rome to Paris. Also in August 1969, a young man died from a heroin overdose on the French Riviera. These two events were widely publicized by the French press, and Paris had to wake up to the fact that the French Connection was more than a myth (Cusack 1974: 252; Gévaudan 1985: 45).

At this point, the ice had been finally broken. It was clear that there was a serious national drug problem looming on the horizon. From then on, Paris acted on the premise that it was not only in the American interest and that of the international community, but also in the French national interest to increase the efficiency of drug enforcement. The French Government defined the fight against drugs as one of its priorities and devoted substantial resources to supporting the US authorities in the investigation of drug trafficking. French police officers were eager to cooperate with their American colleagues and to learn the latest investigation techniques from the BNDD. According to the French Minister of the Interior, the suppression of drug trafficking was a global fight in which France was ready to participate 'with an iron will to succeed'.[6]

As the documentary evidence[7] shows, Franco-American police cooperation was greatly facilitated by the fact that the French police had a professional interest in international cooperation. While French police officers were relatively inexperienced, their American colleagues were at the cutting edge of drug enforcement methods. Franco-American police cooperation was therefore seen not only as an operational instrument for tackling the French Connection, but also as an opportunity for institutional learning. It was expected that cooperation would help the French police to become more familiar with the state of the art in drug enforcement methods. This was acknowledged by the Minister of the Interior, who declared that the Nixon administration and his Government fully agreed about the methods to be used in the fight against international drug trafficking.[8] Or, as the president of the French criminal police said to the director of the BNDD: 'We need your experience to try to avoid and strangle this problem and not to be over-awed by it. That is why we welcome any contact that we may have with any members of the Bureau.'[9]

The most important innovation for the French police was undercover investigation and infiltration tactics. The problem was that these techniques, which were the bread and butter of BNDD investigations, where highly problematic in France due to their uncertain legal status. Up until 1991, they were employed in a legal grey zone (Lévy 2002). Police investigators were forced to conceal their use in order to circumvent the legal problems involved (Monjardet and Levy 1995: 41; Nadelmann 1993: 231–2). Nevertheless, the French police gratefully accepted American support to make undercover investigation and infiltration tactics possible. It was secretly agreed that the French police would supply informers to the BNDD, and that these informers would be directly paid by the BNDD with the French police kept informed.[10] This even led to an agreement on the exact amount of money the BNDD would pay to French informers: 500 dollars per kilo of heroin with a ceiling of 25,000 dollars.[11] In 1970, the regional director of the BNDD in Paris wrote to the director of the French *Police Nationale*: 'My administration will continue to collect information and recruit informers for your specialized services in Paris and Marseille'.[12]

Apparently, all this was to circumvent the problem that infiltration techniques could not appear in the French budget due to their problematic legal status. Nevertheless, it is quite obvious that the services paid by the BNDD were often instrumental to French investigations. Due to the intricate legal situation, French politicians could not, of course, publicly welcome the use of such questionable techniques. However, they certainly approved of the fact that undercover investigation and infiltration tactics were widely used by the French police. After all, the French ministerial bureaucracy was kept fully informed about the talks between the French police and the BNDD.

Another innovation proved even more problematic: the American doctrine of hunting down 'Mr. Big' instead of arresting small dealers. In 1971, amidst the heat of a scandal involving the French secret service SDECE, the American chief investigator Cusack accused the French of not having enough bite in fighting the drug criminals based in Marseille (Gévaudan 1985: 121–34).[13] This caused considerable diplomatic annoyance, and it took a month for the affair to be amicably resolved.[14] Nevertheless, France learned its lesson and from then on fully supported the BNDD in dismantling the French Connection and arresting the *gros bonnets* (McCoy 2003: 70).

Franco-American police cooperation was quickly institutionalized. In October 1969, the French Ministry of the Interior supported the idea of creating a Franco-American committee that would coordinate efforts and avoid 'certain misunderstandings'.[15] In December, it was convened that the committee should meet alternately in the US and France on a quarterly basis. On the political level, the committee would meet as the 'intergovernmental committee'. On the technical level, French police officers would submit their problems and desires to a 'scientific sub-commission' composed of French and American experts. On the investigative level, the committee would meet as a 'working group'.[16] It met for the first time in February 1970.[17]

Right from the start, the American side proposed a protocol that would place Franco-American police cooperation on a formal basis (Gévaudan 1985: 51). The French Minister of the Interior fully supported this idea, since a protocol would sanction the cooperation that was already going on.[18] Indeed, the French police were suffering from the fact that cooperation with the BNDD, including the investigation techniques employed, lacked a legal basis. The French criminal police were therefore interested in an agreement 'to legalize the methods, procedures and techniques which have been tried and tested, and which must not keep their semi-clandestine character'.[19]

Apart from the Ministry of the Interior, the Ministry of Justice also supported the draft for this agreement, which was elaborated by the BNDD and the *Police Nationale*. From the standpoint of the French Government, a formal agreement would further the French national interest. While informal collaboration between the BNDD and the French criminal police had become unavoidable, a formal agreement sanctioning this collaboration would preserve the appearance of French sovereignty. At least nominally, the direction of investigations on French territory would rest with the French authorities. As a matter of prestige, Paris was also proud to be the official host of the regional BNDD headquarters for Europe, the Middle East, and Africa.[20]

On 26 February 1971, the Franco-American agreement was signed in Paris by the French Minister of the Interior Raymond Marcellin and the US Attorney-General John Mitchell.[21] Apart from frequent visits of French officials to the United States, the agreement also established more demanding forms of institutional learning. In particular, Articles 23 and 24 of the agreement provided that the BNDD and the French police would provide each other with technical help, exchange training materials, and offer training to qualified candidates. While the French Minister of the Interior highlighted the reciprocal nature of these provisions, in practice it was obvious that the BNDD would be at the providing, and the French police at the receiving end.[22] The truth was that, as the French Foreign Minister had mentioned in a high-level meeting with the US Secretary of State the year before, Paris hoped that Franco-American police cooperation would improve the skills of French personnel.[23]

With the signature of the Franco-American agreement, France placed itself at the forefront of international drug enforcement cooperation. Thereafter, it saw it as a kind of mission to adopt Franco-American police cooperation as a blueprint for similar arrangements in Europe. Apparently, Paris was hoping to become the centre of a system of bilateral protocols modelled on the Franco-American agreement.

With similar speed, France also advanced from apprentice to master in a more technical sense. In the spring of 1971 the BNDD was involved in two seminars which were intended to initiate French policemen into the state of the art in drug enforcement. The seminars – one in Paris, one in Marseille – were graciously called the 'Circus' by one high-ranking police official. In the summer of the same year, France had the honour of co-organizing an 'international seminar on illicit drug traffic and abuse' in Washington (Gévaudan 1985: 130). Paris also planned seminars in Bonn, London, Rome, and elsewhere to increase the efficacy of drug enforcement. In the words of the French Interior Minister: 'If we really want to succeed, all police forces must cooperate like France and the United States are presently cooperating'.[24]

Moreover, in August 1971, the French commitment towards international drug enforcement took a multilateral and multidisciplinary turn: President Pompidou launched the famous 'Pompidou initiative' with a letter to the five other EC Members and Britain.[25] At the core of the initiative, there was the idea that repressive methods were certainly an important aspect of a successful drug policy, but that legislative, educational, and health issues were also paramount. Pompidou proposed that the participating Ministers should meet at least twice a year in order to 'assess the situation, exchange information, and eventually place the resources of each at the disposal of concerted action'. At the working level, there should be permanent bodies of experts on the legal, police, health, and educational aspects to support the Ministers.

One of these bodies, the expert committee on law enforcement, should have a mandate to exchange experience on drug enforcement methods and eventually coordinate law enforcement efforts. In other words, the Pompidou Group was at least in part meant to become a regional forum for shortcutting cooperation via Interpol. This was despite the fact that the French Foreign Minister paid lip-service to Interpol as the international organization responsible for mutual legal assistance.[26] Another goal of the Pompidou initiative was to achieve a harmonization of national legislation among European states.[27] The idea was to foster information exchange on legislative matters. 'Every state must benefit from the experience acquired by its neighbours'.[28] Ultimately, however, the Pompidou initiative is best understood as a French attempt at setting standards for a European approach to the drug problem.

According to the French Foreign Minister, the European Community was 'the adequate framework for strengthening the drug enforcement activities of international and multinational organizations'. It was envisaged that the Pompidou initiative should include not only the Member States of the EC and the United Kingdom, but also the other accession countries. But no matter what the French Foreign Secretary declared in public, at the negotiation table Paris was reluctant to extend membership in the Pompidou Group to Norway, Ireland, and Denmark, or the European Commission.[29]

Germany

During the 1950s and 1960s, the only significant group of drug users in Germany were American soldiers deployed across the country. To deal with the problem, the German police relied on the aid and guidance of the US army and maintained close relationships with its military police. Ever since the American occupation of Germany, the Criminal Investigation Department of the US army has been allowed to conduct investigations on the territory of the Federal Republic, even outside the American military bases (Nadelmann 1993: 125–6; Friman 1996: 101; Briesen 2005: 145–51).

Around 1968, the student movement brought the drug problem to the attention of German policy makers. While this may still not have caused great worries to leading experts, in the 1970s the country also had a growing problem with heroin abuse (Briesen 2005: 295–305). Bonn perceived a national interest in protecting German youth from the detrimental effects of illicit drug consumption, and so was motivated to increase the efficiency of drug enforcement methods. At the same time, the German Government believed that the issue had to be addressed internationally. In part this was also the result of US drug diplomacy, which tried to persuade other countries that drugs were a common threat to international society (Gross 1972).

On 17 June 1971, US President Nixon declared war on drugs and identified international cooperation as one of the keys to successful drug enforcement (Nixon 1971). The manuscript of Nixon's special message to Congress was sent to foreign leaders, including the German Minister of the Interior and the German Chancellery Minister. In their response to the US ambassador, the two politicians stressed the importance of enhanced cooperation between the American and German authorities and expressed their satisfaction that cooperation with the Bureau of Narcotic and Dangerous Drugs (BNDD) had already been intensified the year before.[30]

Indeed, American law enforcement agencies had a decisive impact on the German response to the problem. The German police absorbed the American theoretical discourse and came to believe that drug criminality was dominated by 'Organized Crime', that is international syndicates of professional gangsters. Whether or not this was accurate, the operational code of the US authorities could thereby spread into the discourse and practice of German drug enforcement circles (Pütter 1998; Busch 1999: 24).

This is not to deny that professionals from the German police also participated in framing the problem and devising counterstrategies. Drug enforcement offered a welcome opportunity for the police, and especially for the Federal Criminal Police Office (BKA), to gain importance and expand their role. The sympathy of the German police for American ideas may have been influenced by the gains in power and resources which were to accrue from a crackdown on international drug trafficking. Indeed, one could argue that drugs posed a new challenge to society and therefore required a new kind of response and a significant transfer of resources (Herold 1972: 133–7). If drug criminality was in the hands of crime syndicates, it could only be countered by exceptional policing powers such as 'conspiratorial' policing. Moreover, if drugs were connected to international crime syndicates, the BKA was needed for international liaison with the police forces of other countries.

Consequently, the role of the BKA was greatly enhanced. Initially, the federal structure of the German police envisaged a limited role for the Federal Criminal Police Office. In the 1970s, terrorism offered the BKA an opportunity to gain new powers. Drugs were another opportunity (Anderson 1989: 88; Nadelmann 1993: 204–5; Busch 1999: 14–33). As the director of the BNDD, Ingersoll recalled from a meeting in November 1969,

> I had a very lengthy conversation with [the director of the BKA] Dr. Dickopf who is somewhat aware of the information concerning the traffic in Germany but his jurisdiction is restricted and so he has to rely on the states to enforce these laws. He is aware of the growing problem and intends to do all he can to become involved.[31]

In 1970, then, the BKA was transformed into the national centre for international drug investigations. In 1971, the German Government envisaged a further centralization of drug enforcement in the hands of the BKA, which took place in 1973.[32]

In the course of the 1970s, the German police were eager to adopt American investigation methods (Nadelmann 1993: 229). Although politicians did not often address specific points in the public, the German Government clearly embraced this American influence. According to the US Coordinator for International Narcotics Matters,

> [o]ur exchanges on narcotics matters continue to be excellent at all levels of government. Our program embraces increased cooperation with the Germans on training and education programs, the sharing of narcotics control techniques, and increased exchange of intelligence data (...), and further coordination of US-German diplomatic efforts in producer countries.
>
> (Gross 1972: 511)

At the European level as well, the German Government promoted international cooperation to improve drug enforcement methods. This general preference for transatlantic and European cooperation was fleshed out with specific content by the law enforcement agencies themselves.

In the late 1960s, the German police developed an interest in undercover investigation (Busch and Funk 1995: 58–9). At an expert conference in 1972, leading German policemen argued that conspiratorial policing was necessary to deal with the challenges posed by organized crime (Ellinger 1972: 265). Over the first half of the 1970s, American-style infiltration techniques were therefore increasingly practised by the German police (Pütter and Diederichs 1994: 25–7; Dietl 2004: 160–74).

The advent of undercover investigation was connected to a more general change in the way the German police understood the fight against drug trafficking. Similar to the US strategy of going after 'Mr. Big', German policemen increasingly aimed at putting the heads of well-organized drug syndicates behind bars. Other American-style techniques, such as the extensive use of secret observation, were also considered necessary to achieve this end (Busch 1999: 19–21).

The willingness to use international cooperation as a vehicle for increasing the efficiency of German law enforcement practice found its expression in concrete institutional collaboration. For example, in 1974 and 1978 Germany sent officers to seminars organized by the American Drug Enforcement Administration (Stoessel 1979: 11).[33]

In August 1971, Georges Pompidou launched his famous initiative. In his response to the French President, Chancellor Brandt proudly pointed to the fact that Germany had already opted for a multidisciplinary approach to the drug problem, and that the Federal Government had already stressed the importance of international cooperation the previous year in an action plan.[34] Although the German Ministry of the Interior had serious doubts about whether and to what extent the Pompidou initiative was sincere, the philosophy of the French proposal was fully in line with German policy.[35] For example, Bonn could easily endorse the idea that the drug problem should be tackled through a multidisciplinary approach including components of education, prevention, and health care, in addition to law enforcement.

Moreover, Germany supported the goal that legislation should be harmonized across Europe. During the Pompidou talks, the German delegation suggested that, as a first step towards legal harmonization, agreement should be reached on general principles for European legislation.[36]

Germany wanted the Pompidou talks to be as inclusive as possible. It not only welcomed the fact that Britain had been invited to join the Members of the European Community in the Pompidou Group, but also proposed the involvement of the other candidate countries, namely Denmark, Ireland, and Norway. Even the European Community itself (namely the European Commission) should be invited to participate. To make this claim more plausible, Chancellor Brandt took refuge in the rather tenuous argument that drug trafficking fell under the jurisdiction of the treaty of Rome because it was related to the free movement of goods.[37]

Finally, Germany accepted that drug enforcement could only be effective if the exchange of intelligence among European police agencies was improved. Formally, Interpol held a monopoly on the exchange of information on drug criminality. But since communication via Interpol was cumbersome in practice, it was necessary to create a regional alternative. To shortcut communication via Interpol, the German police therefore called for the deployment of liaison officers abroad. Once the home secretaries of the German regions had reached a consensus to this effect, the German delegation at the Pompidou talks was authorized to support the idea that liaison officers be exchanged among European states (Busch 1999: 26–7).[38]

Germany chose transatlantic and European cooperation because its decision makers and security experts were convinced that drug criminality was a problem of advanced industrial societies, and that for the benefit of the entire Western community this problem required a common solution (Maihofer 1975). Moreover, it fell within the logic of the German 'strategy of multilateralism' to make credible commitments to international cooperation and to gain a say in international affairs in return (Haftendorn 2001: 15). Germany also had a foreign policy interest in not opposing its partners, particularly the United States. For similar reasons, European cooperation in the Pompidou Group was very attractive.

Italy

Since the end of the Second World War, Italy has been notorious for its mafia problems. Accordingly, one would expect Italy to have been keen to improve its drug enforcement methods. From 1951 to 1969 Italian law enforcement agencies could easily have benefited from the experience of the US Federal Bureau of Narcotics, which had its European headquarters at the American embassy in Rome (Cusack 1974: 244, 252). But while cooperation between US law enforcement representatives and Italian authorities was excellent at all levels, Rome did not publicly recognize that there was a drug problem in Italy. To avoid public embarrassment, the Italian Government even pretended that the Sicilian mafia had been defeated in the mid-1960s (McCoy 2003: 72).

By the mid-1970s, however, this attitude had gone bankrupt. Italian society itself had an increasing drug problem (Gardner 1979; Pantaleone 1979). Maybe for the first time, Rome perceived a strong national interest in cracking down on the drug mafia and was open to international cooperation to improve enforcement methods. Now, at last, Italian law enforcement agencies were seriously committed to international cooperation and the modernization of investigative techniques. In particular, the fact that the US had longstanding experience with the drug problem and was actively promoting innovative investigation methods gave a strong incentive for the adoption of these methods. The Italian police were now eager to collaborate with the US authorities in order to bring Italian law enforcement practice up to date.

Nevertheless, Rome's readiness to adopt the investigation techniques promoted by the BNDD was limited by what could be accepted on constitutional grounds. Despite all the noble intentions to make the country more efficient in the fight against drug trafficking, there were serious constitutional problems with American-style undercover tactics and infiltration techniques. The main problem was the constitutional principle of compulsory jurisdiction, also known as the legality principle. According to this rather theoretical principle, a police officer must immediately arrest, and a public prosecutor must immediately prosecute, anyone known to have committed a crime, whether or not it is expedient for investigative purposes (McDonald 1990).

Since the principle of compulsory jurisdiction had constitutional standing, it was difficult for Italian politicians to support, and for Italian police officers and public prosecutors to adopt these techniques. The problem was that the police could not be actively or passively involved in the commitment of crimes. 'An undercover agent who purchased drugs was, according to the dominant legalist interpretation, as guilty of violating the law as the illicit drug dealer from whom they were purchased' (Nadelmann 1993: 227). Accordingly, it must have been difficult for Italian state officials to sustain or even support these techniques (Nadelmann 1993: 216–17).

Clearly, public prosecutors sometimes conspired with the police to leave conspiratorial investigation techniques unchallenged (Iezzi 1990: 140; Nadelmann 1993: 228). Already in 1952, the Italian Ministry of Justice had tolerated joint sting operations with the US Federal Bureau of Narcotic Drugs (Oliva 1967: 453–4). Nevertheless, the use of American-style techniques remained problematic (Manna and Ricciardelli 1989: 205–6). European-style wiretapping, for example, created much less problem than the use of the so-called agent provocateur (Nadelmann 1993: 244).[39]

In the 1970s, the Italian legislator and the Italian legal doctrine were not yet ready to officially accept the new techniques. The situation only started to change in the 1980s. In 1982, Italy concluded an innovative mutual legal assistance treaty with the United States, and thereafter American law enforcement officials found in Italy 'accommodating allies eager to break new ground in forging ever-closer law enforcement relations' (Nadelmann 1993: 394, cf. 352–5). In 1986, the US-French police agreement from 1971 was extended to include Italy (Anderson 1989: 89, 152). Nevertheless, most of the intrusive techniques utilized were only fully legalized in 1990, when the 1988 *United Nations Convention against Illicit Traffic in Narcotic Drugs* was implemented (Iezzi 1990; Pepino 1991: 157–9; Ministero dell'Interno 1992: 20–2).

Despite all the problems with the rule of compulsory jurisdiction, it was recognized that American-style infiltration techniques were necessary to penetrate and eventually destroy mafia structures (Senato 1976: 6). But since infiltration techniques were legally so problematic, the Italian Ministry of the Interior avoided any more concrete commitment to these methods. Instead, the Ministry pragmatically put the focus on an item that was in itself difficult, but at least not completely impossible to tackle in the Italian context. It was suggested that Italy should follow the American drug enforcement doctrine of targeting big traffickers instead of small dealers (Senato 1976: 14). Other American-style techniques, such as 'flipping informants', were not addressed.

In any event, it was recognized that US officials were better trained and more experienced than their Italian colleagues. Rome therefore supported transatlantic cooperation between the Italian law enforcement agencies and their American counterparts. For example, an Italian expert visited the US in order to learn more about the American approach (Senato 1976: 41). Moreover, officers from the Italian military police attended specialization courses at the FBI and DEA (Senato 1976: 20–1). The first in-country course ever conducted by a US drug enforcement agency was held in Rome in 1971, and by 1979 the US Drug Enforcement Administration had provided training to more than 200 Italian police officers (Gardner 1979: 14).

At the European level, Italy followed the European trend of pursuing a multidisciplinary approach, involving the Ministries of Health and Education (UN 1973c: 12; Senato 1976: 25–60). The Italian Government hoped that legal harmonization among the countries represented in the Pompidou Group would help Italy bring its legislation and practice closer to the standards of other European countries.[40] Clearly, the national interest in modernizing Italian drug legislation motivated the study of the legislative experience of other European states.[41]

Italy agreed with France that the EC was the appropriate framework for fighting drug trafficking in Europe.[42] Nevertheless, Rome wanted neither the participation of Denmark, Ireland, and Norway, nor any involvement of the European Commission in the discussions.[43] Moreover, the Italian commitment to the Pompidou Group was hampered by the fact that decision makers from the Ministry of the Interior were extremely eager to ensure that Interpol was maintained as the privileged channel for the exchange of investigative information (Senato 1976: 8, 11).

There were, in fact, serious domestic reasons for Italy's allegiance to Interpol against any attempt at creating an alternative forum for the exchange of investigative information. To understand these rather bizarre reasons, it is necessary to appreciate Interpol's vital importance to Italian law enforcement agencies. It was an indispensable clearing house for the exchange of investigative information, not only at the international level but also among different Italian police forces. In the absence of Interpol, the Ministry of the Interior would have had serious difficulties imposing a central bureau upon Italy's reluctant law enforcement agencies (Senato 1976: 7, 18). Even so, the various agencies had difficulties collaborating. Under certain circumstances, the *Carabinieri* and the *Guardia di Finanza* preferred to communicate via Interpol rather than sharing their information directly with one another or with the *Pubblica Sicurezza* (Senato 1976: 21–3). As late as the 1980s, Italy caused irritation at Interpol because messages from Rome were sometimes unnecessarily marked urgent and information was sent which seemed to be of Italian interest only (Anderson 1989: 89).

In short, Interpol was necessary to guarantee a minimal information flow amongst Italian law enforcement agencies. To compensate for a fatal lack of internal coordination among its law enforcement agencies, Italy was forced to stick to Interpol as the privileged channel for the international exchange of information. Presumably to prevent the Pompidou Group from becoming a regional alternative to Interpol, Italy even suggested that Interpol should be involved in the Pompidou talks.[44] It must have been very difficult for the Italian Government to envisage institutional alternatives to police cooperation via Interpol, despite the limited efficiency of the international police office.

Britain

The British case is actually a non-case because, in the 1970s, British decision makers abstained from formulating explicit national preferences with regard to the investigation techniques that should (or should not) be adopted by the police in the prosecution of drug trafficking. In other words, London chose not to interfere with the institutional autonomy of the British police. This hands-off attitude was possible because, in the British common law system, the police can operate in the absence of any formal authorization by statute law. As long as there are no explicit impediments, British police are free to shape their own investigative practice (Mark 1977: 79).

London consistently abstained from intruding on British police autonomy. Already in 1961, Britain had expressed doubts about courses on investigation techniques to be offered by the United Nations Commission on Narcotic Drugs and recommended the more informal forum of Interpol instead (UN 1964a: 196). In 1971, British decision makers once again defended the status quo against French attempts at creating a more formal framework for the exchange of investigative information. On the one hand, it was conceded that 'the opportunity to establish direct links between national administrations, particularly at this time, should not be lost'. On the other hand, it was made clear that direct contacts were only intended to be used 'in cases of extreme urgency. In all other cases the usual Interpol channels should be used'.[45]

When Georges Pompidou proposed the harmonization of drug legislation in Europe, Britain took a very cautious stance.[46] It was not until the Thatcher reforms of the 1980s that Britain made serious and systematic efforts to set up a multidisciplinary and inter-ministerial machinery to streamline its drug policy (MacGregor 1998). In the 1960s and 1970s, however, the autonomy of British policing was still by and large uncontested.

Only once, in 1972, did the Home Office interfere in drug enforcement practice when it established, together with New Scotland Yard, a Central Drug Intelligence Unit (Bunyan 1976: 83–5; Offenbach and Dolan 1978: 152; Hain 1980: 96–7). Even in this exceptional case, however, the Home Office tried to avoid the appearance of encroaching on police autonomy. When the issue was raised in the House of Commons, it was assured that '[t]he operational activities of the police are a matter for the Chief Constables concerned; they are not normally subject to Parliamentary control'. In a similar mood, the British Home Secretary emphasized that the police themselves were responsible for their authority and strategy in any situation.[47]

The most important reason for this remarkable abstention was that, until relatively recent times, policing in the UK was based on the *doctrine of constabulary independence*, which in its turn was based on the legal notions of *original powers* and *local governance*. Whereas in other countries the police are directed by the Ministry of the Interior and closely supervised by public prosecutors, in the UK they were considered to be directly accountable to the law. In England and Wales, there were as many as forty-three police forces which all enjoyed a considerable degree of constitutional autonomy from the state, and even from the Home Office (Bunyan 1976: 74).[48]

Whereas the more legalistic culture on the continent was posing obstacles to undercover policing, in Britain many new drug enforcement methods could creep in inadvertently, without any explicit authorization from political decision makers. This is not to deny that, even before the 1970s, there was a certain centralization, bureaucratization, and judicialization of British policing. In comparison to other European countries, however, and particularly in England and Wales, police constabularies held the authority to investigate and prosecute crime with minimal central command or external review (Brogden 1982; Busch 1995: 200–19; Sheptycki 2002b: 526–7).

Due to the autonomous status of the British police, the adoption of new law enforcement techniques was relatively unproblematic. Under these particular circumstances, British decision makers could simply rely on the self-interest of the police forces to renew the armoury of their investigation techniques. And indeed, despite the silence of political decision makers on the issue, in the 1970s and 1980s the British law enforcement agencies were at the forefront of innovations in crime control and drug enforcement methods (Bigo 1996: 80–95).

Controversial practices such as 'entrapment' through undercover agents could be challenged before British courts. Thus the boundaries of lawful enforcement developed spontaneously from the interaction between police practice and court jurisdiction, and there was no need for the British Government to take sides and expose itself to potential criticisms.[49] It was safe for the Home Office to lend the police forces moral and financial support in their fight against crime without giving them clear prescriptions on the dos and don'ts of proper policing (Levi 1995: 195–201). As one scholar has put it somewhat maliciously, 'poor communications between the police and the Home Office left the police to forge ahead, and in the absence of government control the police made their own arrangements' (Sheptycki 2002b: 536–40).

This made it possible for the British police to follow their own convictions about which investigation techniques were most efficient in the fight against crime in general, and drug trafficking in particular. Due to legal similarities and a common pragmatic philosophy, the British police intuitively followed the US rather than continental Europe with regard to undercover policing and other drug enforcement techniques. Many authors have stressed the British emulation of US practices. According to one, 'the general influence of the United States on thinking about multilateral law enforcement cooperation is considerable', whereas history and geography have 'allowed Britain to maintain a certain distance from European arrangements' (Anderson 1993a: 303–5; cf. Dorn *et al.* 1992: 63–77, 148–75; Bean 2001: 93).

Apart from the constitutional autonomy of British policing, which made it possible for politicians to keep a neutral stance on the issue of drug enforcement techniques, the British police actively defended their autonomy on normative grounds. As a former Commissioner of New Scotland Yard put it in 1977, central control was unacceptable because autonomy from political interference represented 'one of the most sophisticated and valuable social institutions to emerge from the British way of life'.[50] In a similar way, the Chief Constable of Devon and Cornwall, John Alderson, was outraged at 'the French tradition, which itself had come down in spirit from the central bureaucracy of ancient Rome, and had been adjusted to suit Napoleonic bureaucracy'. Against this, Alderson defended the discretion rooted in Common Law and insisted that 'the police in England and Wales [were] not political animals and should never be so'.[51] This served as another reason for the British Government to not impose any guidelines on international cooperation to improve drug enforcement methods.

Fighting criminal finance (1988–2002)

The fight against criminal finance as a drug enforcement method has three aspects. First, the suppression of money laundering is expected to make drug trafficking a more risky, and therefore less rewarding, business. Second, 'following the money trail' is expected to lead to the identification of drug criminals and those who support them. Third, some countries consider drug trafficking a major threat to the national and international economy; from their standpoint, the fight against criminal finance may help to protect the financial infrastructure. Taken together, these considerations have provided the rationale for the crackdown on criminal finance since the late 1980s.

Consequently, there is now an international regime against criminal finance that cuts deep into the penal code, financial sector regulation, and privacy laws of individual states. This does not necessarily mean that the regime is efficacious, but the concomitant legal changes have certainly had a serious impact on national interests and on the interests of domestic groups such as bankers and lawyers. Sometimes these lobby groups, often making reference to constitutional principles, have been able to hinder the swift adoption of measures. Nevertheless, the regime has grown increasingly more intrusive (Savona 1997; Gilmore 1999; Sheptycki 2000a; Corradino 2002; Mitsilegas 2003; Masciandaro 2004).

Formally, this regime started in 1988 with the *United Nations Convention against Illicit Traffic in Narcotic Drugs and Psychotropic Substances*. A further milestone in its development was a convention by the Council of Europe in 1990.[52] Since then, the regime has gained momentum as a result of a long series of recommendations by the Financial Action Task Force (FATF), which operates as a technical body of the OECD under the mandate of the leading industrial states (G7).

Gradually, all these norms have been, or are still being, transposed into the national legislation and judicial practice of individual states. This is remarkable if one considers that 20 years ago, before the 1988 UN convention, there was no international regime against money laundering. In the Member States of the European Union, the norms of the emerging regime have been transposed into national law by virtue of a directive, which was adopted in 1991 and amended in 2001 and 2005.[53]

Most states have an interest in taking vigorous action against criminal finance. For some of them, the anti-money laundering regime also provides an excuse to re-regulate the financial sector and, as a desirable side effect, to crack down on tax evasion (Rixen 2005). Eventually, the regime may even provide an antidote against some of the more problematic aspects of globalization (Thomas 2003). As a matter of fact, the fight against criminal finance has considerably expanded over the last fifteen years to include unlawful transactions other than drug trafficking.

In any case, different states have different attitudes on how exactly the fight against criminal finance should be conducted. More often than not, these differences are hardly visible. According to a survey on global financial relations in the post-war era, there are few examples of outright conflict among state actors on global financial matters (Dombrowski 1998: 15). In particular, states are very careful not to appear as 'soft' on drug trafficking and transnational organized crime. The norm that a 'decent' state has to crack down on criminal finance is so compelling that states do not often explicitly declare their reservations on specific measures against money laundering. Nevertheless, there are considerable political differences. Not only the 'usual suspects' such as Switzerland, Luxembourg, Bermuda, and Barbados oppose measures that would harm their interests. Apart from such notorious fiscal paradises, this section will show that political differences have also existed among other states.

The core question was which professions, which types of crime, and which kinds of transactions should be controlled under the anti-money laundering regime. Inevitably, this meant that some longstanding traditions from Europe's liberal past had to be sacrificed. The first and most important victim was the banking community. It is obvious that, as long as banks were allowed to withhold information on suspicious transactions, the international regime against money laundering could not be effective. Therefore, banking secrecy started crumbling in the late 1980s and at the beginning of the 1990s. After the abolition of banking secrecy, criminal finance moved into less obvious channels such as bureaux de change and casinos. To stop this trend, these alternative channels were also absorbed into the regime. The professions connected to these channels were obliged by law to collaborate with state authorities against clients suspected of money laundering.

In particular, lawyers and other members of the legal professions may gain important knowledge about the criminal transactions of their clients. Accordingly, the most crucial step after the abolition of banking secrecy was the lifting of the professional confidentiality of lawyers. However, this proved particularly difficult because professional confidentiality is another crown-jewel of liberalism, enshrined in procedural law and sometimes even in constitutional principles. Nevertheless, in 2000 a majority of the Member States of the European Union was determined to oblige lawyers to report information about suspicious transactions by their clients.[54] One year later the professional confidentiality of lawyers was seriously curtailed, although not entirely abolished, by the second EU directive against money laundering.[55]

Which types of crime should be covered was also contested. Initially, the anti-money laundering regime had been designed only for the fight against drug trafficking. Over the 1990s, then, there was an increasing consensus that the regime should include all sorts of serious crime. But the most important point was never settled: should tax evasion be incorporated into the anti-money laundering regime, or does it constitute a distinct kind of offence? Around 2000, it seemed for a while that the regime against money laundering would be extended to tax evasion. On an initiative by the Clinton administration, there were discussions at the OECD to fight 'harmful tax competition' among states. An extension of the regime to tax evasion would have been in the interest of high-tax jurisdictions such as France and Germany. However, the initiative was watered down by the new Bush administration, which considered tax competition as a positive feature of international life in the era of globalization (Stessens 2001; Gilligan 2004; Rixen 2005).

Another challenge was the control of large transactions in cash. This was important because, at least at the street level, drug trafficking is a cash economy. Money laundering typically commences with the 'placement' of cash; then the money is laundered, through various layers, in the financial system or elsewhere; finally, its criminal origin is so well concealed that the money can be integrated into licit business. The control of large transactions in cash was obviously desirable from the law enforcement standpoint, in order to detect money laundering activities at the placement stage. Nevertheless, some countries were reluctant to place individuals under a sort of general suspicion simply because they prefer to pay large sums in cash.

In general, it is difficult to convict money launderers because it is often hard to demonstrate the illegal origin of financial assets. One obvious solution to this problem is to shift the burden of proof to those who are suspected of money laundering, and to force them to demonstrate their innocence instead of leaving it to the prosecution to show their culpability. Since this constitutes an obvious challenge to the legal system of any liberal constitutional state, a reversal of the burden of proof is a good indicator of the institutional commitment of a state to the international fight against criminal finance. Another indicator is the willingness of a state to control suspicious offshore activities of domestic investors. The more willing a state is to control these activities, the larger its commitment to the anti-money laundering regime. It is particularly interesting to see whether countries such as Britain and France, which have their own bank havens in offshore territories, are willing to suppress money laundering in these areas.

A country's level of commitment to the fight against criminal finance can also be seen from whether it has a policy towards vulnerable countries, particularly in the Third World, either to support their efforts to adopt anti-money laundering standards or to coerce them into compliance. Does a country provide assistance to vulnerable countries to develop anti-money laundering capacities? Is developmental aid made conditional on cooperation against criminal finance? Less important perhaps, but still a good indicator of institutional commitment, is the willingness of a state to underwrite binding international agreements on the sharing of confiscated assets. After an international coup against money laundering, who shall get the proceeds from confiscation? Shall they accrue to the confiscating country, or shall they be divided among the states that have taken part in the coup (Zagaris and Kingma 1991: 506–7)?

France

France was a pioneer in the international fight against criminal finance. French legislation against money laundering started in 1987, one year before the adoption of the UN convention against drug trafficking.[56] Since then, France has demonstrated a considerable and continuing willingness to fight criminal finance in all its forms. In general, there are two reasons for this. First, France recognized that there was an international interest in tackling transnational crime. The fight against criminal finance was seen as a useful instrument in the service of the international community. Second, Paris saw the fight against money laundering as an opportunity to serve the national interest, namely to keep criminal finance away from France and to promote the French vision of crime fighting.

French politicians agree that the systematic abolishment of banking secrecy is 'one of the means necessary to improve the transparency of financial transactions'.[57] For similar reasons Paris planned to abolish the professional confidentiality of lawyers, that is their privilege to withhold information on the money-laundering activities of their clients. In the legislative process, however, the French Government was forced to compromise with the corporate interests of the legal professions. As in other countries, they held on stubbornly to their professional privileges and managed to constrain the policy of the Government on this particular issue. The result was a typical compromise. In 2001, the Minister of the Interior declared his satisfaction that, under the new EU directive, the legal professions would be obliged to denounce money launderers. To his own regret, however, he was forced to concede that the new French law on money laundering did not cover defence attorneys.[58]

As a high-tax jurisdiction, France has a national interest in the suppression of tax evasion to fiscal paradises. To suppress 'harmful tax competition', in 2000 Paris championed an attempt to bring the weak international regime against tax evasion up to the standards of the regime against money laundering.[59] Quite obviously, France was as concerned with tax evasion as it was with money laundering. Presumably to suppress both of these harmful activities, France amended its customs law in order to impose harsh sanctions on travellers who fail to declare cross-border cash transfers of more than 7,622.45 Euro. The French arrangement was so tight that the European Commission considered it to be dangerous to the principle of the free movement of capital and sued France before the European Court of Justice.[60]

In some aspects, France appears to be deeply committed to the fight against criminal finance. The French Prime Minister even declared that his Government was willing to make development aid to Third World countries conditional on a credible effort against criminal finance.[61] Moreover, in an effort to raise the credibility of the French policy, Paris took a surprisingly strong stance against suspicious activities in its own offshore territories. Acknowledging that these fiscal paradises offer many possibilities for money laundering, the French Minister of the Interior pointed out his 'total' determination to force French offshore territories like Saint-Martin or Saint-Barthélémy to apply tight anti-money laundering measures.[62] Apparently, French politicians were following the normative idea that France had, or should have, a sort of civilizing mission in the fight against criminal finance. Moreover, the French Minister of Economic Affairs declared that the fight against criminal finance was also helpful in pushing forward a specifically French normative agenda, namely the idea that globalization should be regulated by means of international cooperation.[63]

In other aspects, the institutional commitment of the French Government was hampered by concerns about the compatibility of certain measures with the national legal order. For example, Paris would have liked to shift the burden of proof from the prosecution to the defence, but faced severe legal problems. Following the failure of a legal project in 1996, there was an eloquent silence on the part of the Minister of Justice regarding plans in 2001 to reverse the burden of proof.[64] Nevertheless, the French Government did not give up on this issue. In 2002, the Minister of Justice could celebrate the fact that a new article in the French criminal code had shifted the burden of proof considerably towards the defence.[65] International agreements on asset sharing were also seen as problematic. To avoid all sorts of legal problems, Paris proposed a compromise: forfeited assets should accrue to the state that had issued the confiscation order, but the executing state should be able to withhold its expenses.[66]

Britain

The United Kingdom, like France, recognized the national and international interest in fighting criminal finance as a means of tackling transnational organized crime. With the *Drug Trafficking Offence Act*, of 1986, Britain was among the first countries to follow the lead of the United States in the construction of a vigorous regime for the forfeiture of criminal assets derived from drug trafficking (Rutherford and Green 1989: 394–403). The most important goal of the early British anti-money laundering legislation was to lift banking secrecy; in fact, British banking secrecy was virtually dead by the early 1990s (Levi 1991; Dorn *et al.* 1992: 220–1). Since then, Britain has sought and continues to seek ways to undercut the profits gained from organized crime. Under the *Proceeds of Crime Act*, of 2002, any kind of criminal conduct, from serious crime to petty credit-card fraud, can be prosecuted under the British anti-money laundering legislation (Whitehouse 2003: 143).[67]

However, Britain was rather hesitant to tighten the cord on some important points. For example, the professional confidentiality of lawyers was explicitly maintained in the 2002 *Proceeds of Crime Act*, at least as far as information obtained under 'privileged circumstances' is concerned. Apparently, Britain was prevented by the adversarial system of British procedural law from removing professional confidentiality. In the adversarial system, a lawyer is not just allowed but even expected to be biased in favour of a client when defending his legal interests. This must have made it more difficult for the United Kingdom than for other European countries to embrace the idea of lifting professional secrecy (Mitsilegas 2003: 148).

From the beginning, Britain had been opposed to a fusion of the two regimes against money laundering and tax evasion. Nevertheless, in 2000 London suddenly started to recognize that an international response to the problem of tax evasion was desirable. However, it is not quite clear whether this preference change was genuine or motivated by strategic considerations.[68] Similarly, the British Government for a long time failed to make sure that suspicious cash transactions would be confiscated at the British borders. Only after the adoption of the 2001 EU regulation on money laundering, did it order that suspicious cash transactions beyond £10,000 be confiscated.[69]

Despite these reservations on important substantive points, the British Government was almost as ready as France to commit the country towards the international regime against money laundering. Already in 1986, Britain accepted the reversal of the burden of proof. Since then, British law has required suspected drug criminals and their banks, when accused of money laundering, to show their innocence (Rutherford and Green 1989: 394–403).[70] This is remarkable because in most other European countries there were serious difficulties in accepting a reversal of the burden of proof. Moreover, Britain has actively supported other countries such as Colombia and Turkey in building up their anti-money laundering capacities, for example by offering training seminars.[71] Britain is also very much in favour of international agreements on sharing the assets seized in joint anti-money laundering operations.[72] Agreements have been concluded, amongst others, with the United States, Colombia, Trinidad and Tobago, and Canada.[73]

Appealing to the moral consensus of the nation, London wanted to make sure that crime does not pay. In the words of the British Home Office, it would be wrong to allow drug criminals a 'champagne lifestyle'. Apparently, this was linked to a typically British trust in the power of rational utility-maximization. Given the fact that most criminals are motivated by money, 'taking the profit out of crime' was supposed to dissuade them from their harmful behaviour.[74] In the same spirit, the British Government trusts in the power of positive incentives to shape the behaviour of police officers. As the Home Office depicts this 'incentive scheme', the police will work more successfully if they are given a stake in the assets confiscated from criminals. The British Home Office finds it unobjectionable for the police to be granted a material reward for successful strikes against the financial basis of unlawful abundance.[75]

Nevertheless, the United Kingdom is sometimes accused of duplicity. Britain takes a strong stance on money laundering, while at the same time protecting the financial interests of the bank havens in its own offshore territories. In fact, Britain's dependent territories in Europe and overseas such as the Channel Islands, the Isle of Man, Bermuda, the Cayman Islands, and so on provide an important basis for money laundering and tax evasion (Nakajima 2004). But be that as it may, London was hesitant to pursue the matter. The reason most frequently given for this inaction, the constitutional autonomy of the British offshore territories, feels like a poor excuse. The most likely reason seems to be successful lobbying by British financial circles, whose interests are closely intertwined with those of the offshore centres. In 2001, a well-documented report by the French Parliament revealed serious doubts as to Britain's willingness to suppress money laundering in its own dependent territories (Montebourg 2001).

Italy

As we have seen earlier, in the 1970s Italy was notoriously backwards in the fight against drugs. After a mutual legal assistance treaty with the US, which was signed in 1982 and came into effect in 1985, however, Rome developed from a laggard into one of America's best drug enforcement partners. There was an Italian-American working group on organized crime and, most prominently, intense cooperation in the international coup against the 'Pizza Connection' (Nadelmann 1993: 352–5).

Due to its experience with organized crime, Italy was a pioneer in the fight against criminal finance. Already in 1971, Rome was proud of its legislation on the confiscation of criminal assets (UN 1973b: 34). In 1978, Italy enacted its first explicit anti-money laundering law against the attempts of kidnappers to launder ransom money (Santino 1997: 153). In 1990, this legislation was extended to drug traffickers, and in 1993 to all other forms of serious crime. As a result, anti-money laundering legislation in Italy was more advanced than in other European states (Cornetta 1996: 19–43). As was often the case in Italy, however, implementation kept lagging behind.

After the demise of the 'old' Christian Democratic regime, the technocratic and centre-left Governments of the 1990s saw the fight against organized crime and criminal finance as a matter of the national interest, if not survival. Given the reality of the *Mafia* and other criminal organizations in the country, there appeared to be hardly any reasonable alternative to the fight against criminal finance. Insofar as organized crime operates internationally, the international interest was seen as another important reason for establishing a strong regime against money laundering.[76] Over the 1990s, Italian Governments showed considerable willingness to expand the regime. The Berlusconi Governments of 1994 and 2001–06 were less enthusiastic about certain measures, but mostly honoured the commitments undertaken by their predecessors.[77]

To begin with, Italy took an incredibly bold step in limiting the use of cash. In a law of 1991, Rome introduced a limit of 12,500 Euro[78] beyond which it would be forbidden to transfer cash outside authorized circuits. At the same time, special controls were required for transactions beyond 12,500 Euro. Banks would even be obliged to actively denounce suspicious transactions (Cornetta 1996: 28; Dini 1997: 4). Since these provisions were hardly compatible with the mobility of capital in the EU, they were openly criticized by the European Commission (Fauceglia 1996: 252–3; Ciampicali 1998: 117). Despite these criticisms, however, in the late 1990s the Italian Government was resolutely set to convince the rest of Europe to take similar steps.[79]

By a ratification law introduced in 1992, Italy undertook to expand the remit of its anti-money laundering legislation to cover all sorts of serious crime. From the beginning, the plan was to automatically recognize foreign sentences on money laundering.[80] Six years later, the Government was still proud that Italy had been among the first to expand anti-money laundering beyond the fight against drug trafficking.[81] By then, the new frontier of anti-money laundering was the fight against tax evasion. Prime Minister Romano Prodi declared that Italy was 'very interested in international cooperation to fight tax evasion', and the Minister of Justice went as far as to equate 'fiscal paradises' with 'money-laundering paradises'.[82] In 1999, under the next Prime Minister Massimo d'Alema, the Minister of Justice demanded that the remnants of banking secrecy should be vigorously tackled at the European level.[83]

The best explanation for this proactive stance at the international level is that, by the early 1990s, Italy had already built up a strong national anti-money laundering regime. Being a pioneer by virtue of its domestic legislation against money laundering, it was easy for Italy to posture as an international leader. The only exception was the professional confidentiality of lawyers, on which the technocratic and centre-left Governments of the 1990s kept an eloquent silence. Since liberal lawyers were key exponents of these Governments (Pizzorno 1998), it would have been hard for any of them to abolish this professional privilege. The Berlusconi Governments, by contrast, had a difficult relationship with lawyers and consequently had less scruples in lifting their professional secrecy. In fact, it was only after the third EU directive of 2005 that Italian lawyers were for the first time running a real risk of losing part of their professional secrecy, namely the right to maintain the confidentiality of information about money laundering.[84]

While Italy supported most of the substantive points of the emerging international regime, there were certain ambiguities with institutional matters. On the one hand, the country had a national interest in the fight against criminal finance and was thereby motivated to make institutional commitments against money laundering. For example, when there were discussions at the European Union on controlling the offshore activities of domestic companies, the Prodi Government was ready to take a leadership role.[85] Moreover, in 1992 the Italian legislator had tried to shift the burden of proof against suspected money launderers.

On the other hand, however, the issue was silently buried two years later, after a ruling by the Constitutional Court that it was unconstitutional to prosecute a person simply because he or she could not justify the possession of valuables.[86] When dealing with vulnerable countries, Italy was also very cautious. In particular, Rome tried as much as possible to honour the international institution of sovereign equality. In 1998, the Italian Prime Minister stressed how important it was to make sure that the fight against criminal finance was compatible with the sovereignty of foreign countries.[87] Finally, Italy has not been very active in support of Third World countries needing help to build up and consolidate their national anti-money laundering regimes.

Germany

In 2005, when the German red-green Government was replaced by a grand coalition of Christian and Social Democrats, German law met all international standards of anti-money laundering, and German banking secrecy had been relegated to history.[88] Three years before, Germany had passed a tough anti-money laundering bill, fully implementing the EU directive of 2001.[89] Despite some legal rearguard battles, Germany was in full compliance with its international obligations.

That had not always been so. Up until 1998, when the Social Democrats defeated the conservative Government of Helmut Kohl, there were narrow limits to German support for the anti-money laundering regime. Since the conclusion of the 1988 *United Nations Convention against Illicit Traffic in Narcotic Drugs*, the opposition could accuse the German Government of dragging its feet. While the Social Democrat opposition pushed for strong regulations, the Christian Democratic Government acted as a brake rather than a motor in the fight against criminal finance.

Of course it is true that Germany was among the founding Members of the FATF and had subscribed to the 1988 Vienna Convention, the 1990 Council of Europe Convention, and the 1991 EU directive. Nevertheless, the country was rather slow to implement these obligations. It took until 1992 for money laundering to become a criminal offence under German law, and until 1993 for the first specific anti-money laundering bill to be passed.[90] This first law was weak, and the second one of 1998 did not lead to major changes. The 1990

Council of Europe *Convention on Laundering, Search, Seizure and Confiscation of the Proceeds from Crime* was ratified by Germany only in 1998 – two years after France, four years after Italy, and six years after Britain.

It seems that even these cautious steps were mostly the result of entrapment in an institutional logic of appropriateness (Müller 2004). Caught up in the momentum of an increasingly dense anti-money laundering regime, Germany simply could not avoid joining in for long. Berlin embraced the global fight against criminal finance reluctantly at first, and more eagerly after the Government change in 1998.[91] Especially after press reports that Germany had become a Mecca for money laundering, German decision makers started to perceive a national interest in tackling criminal finance.[92] Nevertheless, the Government tried to deny that Germany had a serious problem with money laundering until well into the mid-1990s (Pütter 1998: 121).

How can it be explained that, for such a long time in the 1990s, Germany lagged behind its European partners? Most importantly, domestic interest groups successfully prevented the German Government from taking steps that were to diminish their professional autonomy. Presumably for this reason, Germany had a particularly hard time in abolishing banking secrecy. In 1990, when the EU Council negotiated its first directive against money laundering, Germany found itself allied with Luxembourg in trying to maintain its strong safeguards for banking secrecy.[93] Similarly, due to considerable misgivings in the banking community, Germany was relatively slow to impose an obligation to report large cash transactions (Friman 1996: 110).

In 2000, when a majority of the EU Council of Ministers was determined to abolish professional confidentiality for lawyers, Germany was once again among the few countries opposed. The German Minister of Finance said he had wanted to vote against the measure, but had failed to rally a sufficient number of countries to block the agreement.[94] While this obstructionism was officially due to constitutional concerns, other sources seem to suggest that in reality the German Government was constrained by the professional interests of the legal professions.[95] Neither Helmut Kohl's centre-right Government, nor the Social Democrats, who determined German policy after 1998, could ignore these corporate interests.[96]

Only with regard to the inclusion of tax evasion in the anti-money laundering regime, was Germany quick to declare its full support. Although this did not work out at the international level, in 2001 the German Government decided to add tax evasion to its new anti-money laundering legislation.[97] Since Germany is a notorious high-tax jurisdiction, the side effects of anti-money laundering policy on the suppression of tax havens must have been one of the most appealing elements of the emerging regime. Germany, as a high-tax jurisdiction, had a perceived national interest in using the OECD as a transmission belt for making tax evasion riskier and more difficult.

Nevertheless, Germany was fairly reluctant to commit itself towards the anti-money laundering regime. In comparison to other countries, the German Government did not show a particularly strong will to combat suspicious offshore activities of German investors. Similarly, its efforts to support foreign countries in their fight against money laundering have been relatively weak. In late 2004, Germany was still opposed to the very idea of international asset sharing.[98]

Most importantly, the German Government was not ready to shift the burden of proof. According to the predominant interpretation, Article 14 of the German constitution rules that property cannot be confiscated if its illegal origin is not certain. Conversely, suspicious transactions must be considered to involve legal money as long as enforcement authorities have not proved otherwise. A proposal by the Social Democrat opposition to reverse the burden of proof for suspected cases of organized crime failed in the mid-1990s.[99] On the one hand, subsequently, the criteria for the prosecution to prove the illegal origin of proceeds were carefully relaxed. On the other hand, even the Social Democrats started recognizing that a reversal of the burden of proof was problematic for constitutional reasons (Meyer 2001: 57).

Final note

As we have seen, from the late 1980s to the early 2000s there were considerable differences between the attitudes of different states on how to conduct the fight against criminal finance. Take as a final example the different attitudes regarding the preferred geographical framework for international cooperation. Officially Britain and France, Germany and Italy are all active in many different forums. Their representatives meet at the United Nations, the Financial Action Task Force (FATF), the EU, and elsewhere. Nevertheless, different countries have a predilection for different geographical frameworks. Britain is a global player in the world financial system, France and Germany are medium-sized financial powers with stakes beyond Europe but not all over the globe, and Italy is a regional financial centre in Europe. Apparently, the preferences of each of these countries for a specific institutional forum are constituted and constrained by its position in the world financial system.

Since the City of London is a financial centre of global dimensions, Britain had a national interest in avoiding a bad reputation for the City and wanted to create a level playing field for financial transactions all over the globe.[100] Accordingly, Britain preferred a global approach towards anti-money laundering. In this spirit, a representative of the British Home Office stated as early as 1989 that the ultimate goal was the realization of a universal regime.[101] France and Germany had an interest in influencing the anti-money laundering regime at the level of the leading industrial states. Accordingly, they preferred the FATF as a forum for the coordination of anti-money laundering activities.[102] In fact, it was more realistic for these countries to influence the fight against criminal finance via the FATF rather than through the UN. For analogous reasons, Italy had a predilection for anti-money laundering activities in the European Union. As a regional financial power it preferred the EU, rather than the FATF or the UN, for the international coordination of anti-money laundering activities.[103]

8 Investigation across borders

Cross-border police cooperation to fight drugs or other forms of serious international crime has a long tradition that goes back, at least, to the period after the First World War. Already in the 1930s, for example, the US Federal Bureau of Narcotics had deployed a number of drug liaison officers to Europe (Nadelmann 1993: 99), and Franco-American investigations into the heroin trade from France to the United States were also conducted (Cusack 1974: 235). In those early days, however, cross-border drug enforcement was hardly an issue of high politics. This changed dramatically in the early 1970s, when the Nixon administration increased bilateral and multilateral efforts to intensify drug abuse control (Nixon 1971; Gross 1972).

As we shall see in the first part of this chapter, in the early 1970s the French and German Governments raised international drug enforcement to the level of an official policy goal, while Britain and Italy were still somewhat lagging behind for different reasons. During the 1970s, arrangements for cross-border police cooperation were mostly bilateral and/or informal. However, Germany and France were already trying out different forms of multilateral and more formal cooperation. While this was expanded during the 1980s (Anderson 1989: 161–2), what was still missing in the 1990s and early 2000s was a legal framework which could solve two fundamental problems.

First, cross-border police cooperation is often in conflict with the classical instrument for international cooperation in criminal matters: mutual legal assistance. Traditionally, this consists of formal letters of request (*commissions rogatoires*) being exchanged between judicial authorities in order to obtain information. Unfortunately, it is a notoriously bureaucratic and time-consuming endeavour. This is precisely the reason why police officers are tempted to cooperate informally, that is without a formal request for legal assistance. However, due to demanding standards of procedural law it is almost never certain whether information obtained outside the formal channels of mutual legal assistance can subsequently be used for criminal prosecution. Police officers are therefore often forced to resort to awkward charades, such as convincing the legal authorities to file letters of request for information that is already in their possession, simply to make sure that it is legally admissible. From the standpoint of efficient law enforcement, this is an extremely unsatisfactory state of affairs.

Second, police officers on mission abroad run considerable personal risk when joining their foreign colleagues in bi- or multinational teams for the investigation of crime. Since the civil and criminal liability of police officers is usually unregulated, in the worst case an officer may himself end up under prosecution if for some reason a cross-border operation gets out of hand.

To solve these problems, between 1997 and 2003 there was an attempt in Europe to create a legal template for 'Joint Investigation Teams' and other forms of cross-border investigation. Despite the high hopes set on Joint Investigation Teams (Schalken and Pronk 2002; Plachta 2005), however, the ratification and implementation of the new legal instrument turned out to be more cumbersome than expected (Commission 2005a, 2005b). It remains to be seen to what extent Joint Investigation Teams will stand the test of time as a means of encouraging European law enforcement agencies to intensify cross-border collaboration.

In any case, cross-border investigation has always been and continues to be possible without a formal legal framework. Policing across borders is much older than its institutionalization by the European Union. The EU regime has only complemented – not superseded – an existing system of bilateral agreements and customary arrangements. Accordingly, the regulation of Joint Investigation Teams and their twins, Multinational Ad Hoc Teams, must be seen as an institutional rather than a substantive innovation.

Joint efforts in the Nixon years (1969–74)

When President Nixon launched his war on drugs, one obvious challenge was to facilitate on the one hand the exchange of information, and on the other of personnel in joint investigations against drug traffickers. Another challenge was to encourage Western countries to support American efforts at 'drug diplomacy', so that they would exert diplomatic pressure on drug producing and transit countries such as Turkey, Iran, or Burma. Finally, there was a clear need to integrate the separate efforts of police authorities and customs services, and to encourage both of these organizational branches to engage jointly in international cooperation.

The governments of some countries, such as Germany and France, were active in all of these regards. Bonn and Paris encouraged their police forces to exchange information and take part in joint investigations, supported the US in its diplomatic efforts to influence drug producing and transit countries, and tried to combine international police cooperation with international customs cooperation. We shall see that other governments, for example in Britain and Italy, took a more parochial approach and left it to the law enforcement agencies themselves to take the necessary steps.

This was also reflected in different attitudes about the proper institutional depth of international cooperation. France and Germany were relatively readier than Britain and Italy to conclude bilateral agreements, deploy and receive liaison officers and/or special envoys, and provide technical help for drug producing countries to build up their enforcement capacities. Only on one point were even Paris and Bonn adamant. At least in theory, executive powers for foreign officers on national territory were considered to be an unacceptable encroachment on national sovereignty. To prevent this from happening, the power to use coercion was upheld as the exclusive prerogative of the law enforcement agencies of the countries concerned.

Germany

During the 1970s, Germany was the uncontested champion in international cooperation against drug trafficking. This becomes clear when one compares the situation in the late 1960s with the situation in the early 1980s. Up until the late 1960s, Germany collaborated purely because the US authorities requested it. Collaboration was mostly elicited by US initiatives and consisted of joint operations with the military police of the American army. From the German perspective, it was important to accommodate the interest of the United States in curtailing the supply of drugs to American soldiers stationed in Germany (Busch 1999: 23). As a 'semi-sovereign state' (Katzenstein 1987), Germany did not object to this American interest and was ready to formulate its policy according to the preferences of its most important ally.

Little more than a decade later, in the early 1980s, Germany was at the centre of a dense web of cooperation. The network comprised a variety of bilateral and multilateral arrangements for international police cooperation with a wide range of countries. The German police forces cooperated with their counterparts in the United States and Canada, in most of Western Europe and even in some Eastern European countries, and in drug producing countries such as Turkey and Afghanistan. Most importantly, in 1978 Germany and the United States had concluded a formal agreement on mutual cooperation between their drug enforcement agencies (Stoessel 1979). Another protocol on police cooperation was signed with Turkey, in 1981 (Rebscher 1981: 168–9). Apart from close collaboration with foreign police forces, there were also agreements for customs cooperation with a considerable number of countries.

The turning point from accommodation to activism was around 1970, when the German Government realized that there was a growing drug problem in Germany (Briesen 2005: 295–305). To address the problem, Bonn started perceiving a genuine national interest in cooperating with foreign authorities (Bundesminister 1972). With the full support of the German Government, a dense network of working groups and liaison officers began to coordinate international police cooperation. Out of this grew a policing network with the United States, Canada, and many of Germany's neighbours. The Federal Criminal Police Office (BKA) was at the centre of this network, which was extended to the most important drug producing and transit countries.

American agencies were particularly important partners because of their expertise and because American soldiers in Germany played an important part in the drug distribution chain. Moreover, the BNDD believed in the theory that Munich was an important transit point for the so-called French connection, with Turkish opium base transported via the Balkans to Munich and from there to Marseille, and ultimately to the United States (Friman 1996: 102–3). If this was correct, German–American police cooperation was not only in the American but also in the German interest. Germany had an interest in cooperating with US law enforcement agencies in order to prevent drugs from 'spilling' into the German market. Moreover, the German Ministry of the Interior hoped that drug enforcement cooperation with US authorities would help the German police obtain potentially valuable criminal intelligence.

A look into the documentary evidence[1] shows that there was only one important limitation to German cooperativeness. Bonn was determined not to allow foreign law enforcement agencies to exercise executive powers on German territory. This is not to say that, in practice, Germany was particularly jealous of its territorial sovereignty. In theory, however, executive powers for foreign officers could not be accepted. This became clear in September 1972, when the BNDD proposed a US-German taskforce to tackle the presumed Bavarian transit point of the French connection. While the German Ministry of the Interior was clearly interested, there were serious concerns that such a US-led taskforce would overstep its mandate and engage in executive operations. To prevent this from happening, Germany devised a clever strategy of institutional embracement. German–American police collaboration was encouraged while, at the same time, US agents were tightly knit into a dense cooperation network so that it would be difficult for them to overstep their mandate.

Under the auspices of an inter-ministerial working group, instituted in late 1971, the BKA hosted a commission on the exchange of information between the German police and the law enforcement agencies of the US military presence in Germany (Gross 1972: 511; Briesen 2005: 343). In September 1972, when the BNDD proposed the aforementioned taskforce, the German Ministry of the Interior did not follow the suggestion. Instead, the Ministry instituted another multi-agency working group under the auspices of the BKA and under the direction of the Bavarian criminal police office. Its original mandate was to deal with the presumed role of Munich as a transit point in the French connection. But although the transit point theory was never confirmed by criminal evidence, the working group continued to meet. The group was quickly extended to Austria and Bulgaria. Later, Hungary, Romania, Yugoslavia, and Canada were also included (Bigo 1996: 94).

The next step was the institutionalization of a platform for German–American police cooperation at the federal level. In December 1972, the Ministry of the Interior created a permanent working group on narcotics (*Ständige Arbeitsgruppe Rauschgift*, STAR), which would serve as a meeting ground for officials from German and foreign law enforcement agencies. On the German side, the BKA, customs, the border guard, and the regional criminal police offices were the main participants. On the American side, the group was joined by the BNDD, US Customs, and the Army's CID and OSI.

When appropriate, the group was also opened to interested parties from other countries.

Over the years STAR founded a series of regional working groups, which were modelled on the Bavarian-American working group. The first of these new working groups was established in May 1973 and included Germany, the Netherlands, and the United States. The group was quickly extended to Belgium and Luxembourg.[2] At the end of the 1970s, regional working groups for the South-East, South-West, and North included most German regions and their neighbouring countries (Bigo 1996: 94).

The main task of all these groups and committees was to facilitate the exchange of information among agencies. At the same time, however, they also had a capacity for joint investigations. In fact, joint investigations were sometimes conducted by the regional working groups, under the auspices of the Federal Criminal Police Office. They not only involved police officers, but also customs officials. As provided for by the Ministry of the Interior, both the police and the customs service participated in the STAR working groups. Moreover, in the course of the 1970s Germany negotiated several bilateral agreements for customs cooperation in order to provide for closer cooperation against drug trafficking. In 1972, such agreements were already in force with the Member States of the EEC, plus Spain and Austria. Similar agreements were to be concluded with Sweden and Yugoslavia (Bundesminister 1972). Most importantly, a cooperation agreement with US Customs was signed in 1973.

Ever since the formulation of the first German drug strategy (Bundesregierung 1970: 1666), cooperation with drug producing and transit countries was deemed to be essential. Initially, the action was focused on Turkey as the most important source country. Apparently for diplomatic reasons, Germany took a rather cautious view on a ban on opium production in Turkey. The German Government acknowledged that the political situation in many drug producing and transit countries did not allow for much German influence. Nevertheless, it explored all possible avenues of exerting influence on Turkey.[3] Next to Turkey Germany was also active in Afghanistan, where local police were trained to develop their drug enforcement capacity (UNDND 1973). There were discussions on whether to send German officers as capacity builders to Afghanistan, either through the UN or directly as liaison officers.

Germany was also willing to control migration flows in order to keep drugs away from German borders (Bundesregierung 1970: 1664). In 1971, the Minister of the Interior released a circular advising that all foreigners convicted for drug trafficking should be deported after serving their sentence. A year later, this was transformed into a mandatory requirement. Accordingly immigration, or the renewal of residence permits, could be denied, while access to new residence permits could be restricted. These measures applied even in the absence of a verdict when there was a suspicion based on sufficient evidence.[4]

It is not clear to what extent the BKA, customs, and the criminal police offices of the German regions had been emboldened by the German Government to intensify their international cooperation efforts, and to what extent they acted on their own initiative. Already in November 1969, the director of the BKA had informally invited the BNDD to station a man in Frankfort. As the director of the BNDD recalled, Mr. Dickopf was aware of the drug problem and intended to do all he could to become involved (see p. 142). This was several months before the first official contact of the German Ministry of the Interior with the BNDD, which occurred at some point in 1970.[5]

Although the next director of the BKA, Horst Herold, was more concerned with terrorism than drugs (Dietl 2004: 156–7), the German police developed a professional interest in international drug enforcement cooperation. In particular, they were deeply impressed by the frontline approach taken by the BNDD. After a study visit to the United States and Canada in 1973, they lobbied their Government to emulate the American model, namely by creating a web of bilateral relationships around the BKA. Thus, the internationalism of the German police led to a political and institutional situation that emboldened Bonn to encourage even more cooperation.

The thorniest problem remained the flow of intelligence from American to German law enforcement agencies. Between 1973 and 1975, STAR came up with several proposals to improve the exchange of intelligence. Apparently, the US authorities had serious problems in funnelling their information to the proper authorities in the complex German policing system. To resolve this and similar problems, plans had already been made in the autumn of 1972 to formulate a comprehensive German–American program for drug enforcement cooperation. When the draft cooperation protocol was submitted by the Americans in 1974, the German Ministry of the Interior once more insisted that executive powers for foreign officials were out of the question. After several years of lengthy negotiations, the agreement was finally ready for signature in June 1978 (Rebscher 1981: 168). It set up four new working groups and thereby led to a further institutionalization of German–American drug enforcement cooperation.

In the course of the 1970s, Germany also provided technical aid to drug producing countries (Friman 1996: 106). For example, in 1971 it considered sending tanker lorries to Turkey which would fuel helicopters surveying areas of illegal opium production.[6] While the budget numbers for the 1970s are unclear, it is known that in 1981 Germany forged a deal with Turkey on technical aid worth 15 million DM (Rebscher 1981: 169). Since 1982, the BKA had a special fund of initially 2 million DM per year for technical aid to drug producing countries. The money was used for training and for the provision of technical equipment (Busch 1995: 168).

While Germany was ready to send police officers on missions to drug producing and transit countries, Bonn was reluctant to send out permanent liaison officers. Although the BNDD already had officers positioned in Germany since 1969 (Friman 1996: 102), Bonn was hesitant to reciprocate the measure. The issue was discussed and formally approved by the police in July 1971, but the Ministry of the Interior voiced legal concerns. In early 1974, STAR decided unanimously that a German liaison officer should be sent to the DEA headquarters in Washington.[7] After the aforementioned study visit to the

United States and Canada in 1973, STAR also discussed about the deployment of liaison officers to the drug producing countries. However, this was not put into practice until 1983 (Fröhlich 1985: 12; Busch 1995: 169; Dietl 2004: 212). The only exception was a BKA official at the German consulate in Istanbul, who had been stationed in 1972 to facilitate information exchange and mutual legal assistance.

To summarize, apart from executive powers for foreign law enforcement agencies and despite Bonn's unwillingness to deploy drug liaison officers, the burgeoning horizontal relationships between German and foreign law enforcement agencies were fully supported by the German Government. The most extreme case was at a meeting of the intergovernmental Pompidou Group, where the German delegation urged France to accept that the police agencies of different European states should be able to directly exchange investigators, without waiting for the formal consent of their ministries.[8] While cooperation was particularly close with the United States, Germany embraced any form of international drug enforcement cooperation, from formal intergovernmental coordination in the Pompidou group to horizontal arrangements with the police forces and customs services of other countries, be they in Western or in Eastern Europe, or in drug producing or transit countries.

France

Alongside Germany, France was the other champion in international cooperation against drug trafficking.[9] Most prominently, the final crackdown on the so-called French Connection from 1971 to 1973 was a joint operation of the French law enforcement agencies and their American counterparts (Gévaudan 1985; Friesendorf 2007: 37–78).

This was in sharp contrast to the previous French attitude in the 1950s and 1960s, when American drug enforcers had hardly been able to count on French support. As we have seen in the last chapter, until the summer of 1969 the French Government understood the fight against drug trafficking as a global fight to which France, in the interest of the international community, would lend moral support with little practical involvement. Very much to the chagrin of the United States, taken by itself the French normative commitment to fighting drugs was not yet a sufficient motivation for Paris to cooperate in the crucial case of the French Connection.

Then, in the summer of 1969, there was a sharp change in policy when Paris realized the growing national drug problem in France.[10] After that date, Paris started acting on the premise that the fight against drug trafficking was not only in the international but also in the French national interest. Incidentally, France also had a national interest in a healthy political climate between Paris and Washington. Although France had resisted for a long time American pressure to tackle the French Connection, Paris could no longer afford to ignore the issue when US President Nixon raised drug trafficking to the level of high politics and declared war on drugs. At that point, the French Minister of the

Interior Raymond Marcellin declared in public that the fight against drugs was one of his main concerns.[11] Moreover, the Minister pointed out that the French police had the greatest interest in benefiting from the criminal intelligence American officers could collect at the very source of drug trafficking.[12]

In less than two years, France developed from a notorious laggard into an eager participant in the American fight against drug trafficking. In November 1969, The French Minister of the Interior was delighted when the US Bureau of Narcotics and Dangerous Drugs proposed that the French criminal police should send a liaison officer to New York, just as the BNDD had deployed a number of special agents to France. The French police was clearly interested in the bonanza of information it could potentially obtain at the BNDD headquarters. Moreover, given the fact that the United States maintained several special agents in France, the French Minister of the Interior was very much pleased by this American gesture of diplomatic reciprocity.[13]

The French enthusiasm to join the American fight against drug trafficking was reflected by a unique and unprecedented institutional commitment. In late 1969, an intergovernmental commission was instituted to deal with the coordination of joint investigations. In November 1970, membership of the intergovernmental commission was extended to Canada (Gévaudan 1985: 113–20). The primary task of this cooperation was concrete law enforcement operations against the French Connection in Marseille. However, officers from the French criminal police were worried that the burgeoning Franco-American law enforcement collaboration was without a formal basis. Accordingly, the French criminal police supported the American idea of concluding a formal agreement that would relieve them from this 'semi-clandestine' situation.[14]

To be sure, there was one important limit to French cooperativeness. Paris was not ready to endow foreign officers with executive powers on French soil, because this was seen as incompatible with the national interest in upholding territorial sovereignty. As the French Minister of the Interior pointed out in 1970: 'These American agents do not have any operational powers or prerogatives'.[15] Be that as it may, in February 1971 the BNDD and the French criminal police concluded a formal agreement to institutionalize their ongoing cooperation and facilitate further joint investigations.[16]

First and foremost, the Franco-American police agreement rubber-stamped the participation of officers from both countries in joint investigations. The agreement provided for the exchange of information and personnel and sanctioned the cross-posting of special agents. The BNDD kept three officers deployed in Paris and another three in Marseille; to reciprocate, the French criminal police maintained two officers in New York. For concrete operations, these special agents could be supported by additional envoys. In case of an accident, they would benefit from the statutory guaranties of their country of deployment. France and the United States would even coordinate press releases in order to avoid the leakage of relevant information.

Officially, France was also ready to support American pressure on drug producing countries. Turkey was the most important target, since the French

Connection was trafficking in Turkish morphine base. On several occasions, the French declared their willingness to take diplomatic and police initiatives in order to influence the behaviour of Turkey or other drug producing countries. In practice, however, France did not take any concrete steps to help these countries suppress the production of drugs. It was hot air when the French Minister of the Interior emphasized that one had to fight 'not only against drug traffickers but also to control the entire production of opium, whether in Afghanistan, Turkey, or in the Golden Triangle, that is Burma, Laos, and Thailand'.[17] In reality, France was not at all motivated to take a 'total' approach towards the fight against drug trafficking, but merely seconded the United States in their attempt to eliminate the supply of morphine base and other commodities.

In addition, French policy makers were motivated by a perceived national interest to protect citizens from 'depraved people', namely the 'students, beatniks, tramps' who were bringing small amounts of drugs from their trips to Central Asia. 'We have Scandinavians, English, Americans, Germans and they are starting to convert the French youth who were at one time completely outside of the problem of drug abuse. And this is the French problem'. Apart from cooperation with the United States, Paris was very much motivated to support measures that would fend off drug trafficking from French soil. In pursuit of the national interest, France expanded its efforts to countries from which drug traffickers could reach French territory. Turkey, as the most important of these countries, was asked to watch its borders more carefully and 'really search and go in depth on all those individuals that return to France'.[18]

Police agreements alone were not considered sufficient to protect French soil from the dangers of drug trafficking. Customs agreements with neighbouring countries, especially with Spain, were also seen as helpful to ensure border control. Moreover, France seriously intended to deport foreigners suspected of trafficking or using drugs. The main suspects were migrant workers from North Africa, Western European students, and US soldiers stationed in Germany. Furthermore, Paris wanted to make sure that suspicious individuals would be prevented from entering France in the first place. For example, in 1970 the French Minister of the Interior agreed with his German colleague that the fight against drug trafficking would be intensified at the Franco-German border.[19] In the same spirit, France held a systematic discussion with the United Kingdom on the prospects for enhanced drug enforcement cooperation.[20] In the case of North-African migrant workers, the plan was to cooperate with the local police authorities in the countries where these workers were recruited.[21]

Britain and Italy

While both Bonn and Paris were very much engaged in international action to suppress drug trafficking, the same could not be said about London and Rome. Neither the British nor the Italian Government was sufficiently motivated to formulate a coherent set of national preferences for this policy field. This is not to deny that, horizontally and on a case-by-case basis, British and Italian law enforcement agencies were cooperating with their foreign counterparts. While this certainly did not happen against the will of their Governments, however, international drug enforcement cooperation was not awarded the status of an issue of high politics until well into the mid-1970s.

The relevant ministries in both London and Rome kept a relatively low profile, and did not develop any coherent set of preferences on international drug enforcement cooperation. The main reason for this remarkable inactivity was that, in the early 1970s, the political elites in the United Kingdom and Italy had not yet fully understood that drugs were becoming a problem that affected not only the United States and remote countries in the Third World, but also British and Italian society in general, and metropolitan life in London and Rome in particular.

Since Britain was not much used as a transit country for international drug trafficking towards the United States, the UK Government did not initially perceive a strong interest in taking vigorous action against the phenomenon. British decision makers were convinced that international drug trafficking was not a serious threat to British interests, and accordingly they showed little interest in expanding international cooperation to suppress the phenomenon. This was amplified by the fact that there was a widespread conviction in the United Kingdom that, as long as drugs were prescribed by doctors to notorious addicts, there would not be any illicit market beyond the control of the political authorities (see pp. 115–17).

Moreover, as we have already seen (pp. 147–9) there was a consensus that politics should interfere as little as possible with police activity. Policing in England and Wales enjoyed a considerable degree of constitutional autonomy from the state, and the Government could therefore trust that the police would deal with cases of international drug trafficking as they emerged. This is also an important reason why Britain abstained from bilateral agreements on police and customs cooperation. Another important fact of life was the absence of a central police agency which could have concluded agreements with its foreign counterparts. Under any circumstance, the fragmentation of the British police forces would have made it difficult for London to impose more international police cooperation from above.

In Italy, the heroin problem was officially 'discovered' only in the middle of 1973 (Senato 1976: 12). Although it was no secret that Italian society had a problem with heroin and other drugs (Mantelli Caraccia 1973; Vannucci 1973), the political elite was little accountable to the public and stubbornly continued to pretend that Italy was primarily a transit country for opium products destined for the US market. Even in the mid-1970s, when the clandestine heroin market in Italy was finally recognized, Rome continued to emphasize that the market was based on small quantities imported by tourists, rather than organized or mafia crime (Senato 1976: 14; cf. Mancusi 1976: 7, 24). Accordingly, Italian decision makers kept behaving as if there was only a limited national interest in taking action against the phenomenon.

This is surprising, since the cases of Tommaso Buscetta and Zizzo Benedetto should have warned Rome that there was indeed a national interest in tackling transnational mafia structures. Since the end of the Second World War, the Italian mafia had had a stake in the drugs trade (McCoy 2003: 24–45). Nevertheless, in the 1970s it was still fairly common for Italian decision makers to maintain that the mafia had been miraculously defeated 'the other year', and that there was no urgent need for action.

Furthermore, in the 1970s coordination among Italy's diverse law enforcement agencies was notoriously poor. The agencies were so fragmented that it was almost impossible to control, from above, their cooperation with the agencies of other countries. Only the police forces (*Pubblica Sicurezza*) were, at least in theory, under the control of the Ministry of the Interior. The military police (*Carabinieri*) was headed by the Ministry of Defence, while the financial police (*Guardia di Finanza*) was under the Ministry of Finance. Given the unavoidable problems of inter-agency coordination, Rome had to move with caution at the international level in order to avoid the embarrassment of making unrealistic commitments. Had the Italian Government ordered an increase in the scope of international police cooperation, it would not have been clear to which extent the Italian law enforcement agencies would have been able to deliver.

Of course this is not to say that Rome was actively opposed to the idea of international drug enforcement cooperation. Already in the 1950s, it had succumbed to American pressure in proscribing heroin production and hardening its legislation against drug trafficking (Siragusa 1966: 100–1). Unencumbered by the Italian Government, over the 1950s and 1960s the regional headquarters of the Federal Bureau of Narcotics was working from its base at the US embassy in Rome (Cusack 1974: 244–5; Gardner 1979). In the 1970s Italian police forces were free to cooperate with their foreign counterparts in Tunisia and Algeria, and Italian officials could even interrogate suspects in Algiers and Oran. The Italian police sent an investigative mission to Lebanon, and cooperated with Brazil and Canada to arrest notorious drug traffickers (Senato 1976: 8–16). Despite such horizontal collaboration between Italian law enforcement agencies and their foreign counterparts, however, Rome was careful not to attach programmatic status to international drug enforcement cooperation.

The first bilateral agreement with another country on police or customs cooperation against drug trafficking was an executive deal concluded in the late 1970s with the United States. The agreement was exempt from ratification by the Italian Parliament and could therefore be kept secret until its first revision in the mid-1980s.[22] Otherwise, it was difficult for Rome to accept the idea of bilateral police agreements sidestepping the established communication channel via Interpol. As we have seen in the last chapter (pp. 146–7), the main reason for Italy's remarkable loyalty to Interpol was the importance of the international police office as an external platform for facilitating information exchange among the Italian law enforcement agencies.

In the British case, too, cooperation was mostly limited to horizontal collaboration between British law enforcement agencies and their counterparts in other countries. In the first half of the 1970s, it seems that Britain did not conclude any bilateral agreements with other countries on police or customs cooperation against drug trafficking. Although there are some interesting exceptions from the rule that London did not articulate explicit preferences on drug enforcement cooperation, on balance these exceptions do not warrant the conclusion that London had a coherent policy on the issue.

In September 1971, there was an Anglo-French discussion at the British embassy in Paris, at which the British stated a slight preference for customs rather than police cooperation. However, this was simply due to the fact that British customs, unlike the police, was under the control of the central Government. On a French initiative, in the same year the Home Office drafted a *Circular for urgent drug cases involving France* for the British police. However, it is unclear whether the circular was ever launched.[23] In 1974, Britain took a spontaneous initiative to amend its extradition treaties with France and Belgium to make drug trafficking an extraditable offence.[24]

Furthermore, in 1973 the British ambassador in Tehran acted on a US request for British support in convincing the Iranian authorities to become more active against drug smuggling.[25] However, this support did not flow from any consistent British policy. Already in 1971, the US Coordinator for International Narcotics Matters Nelson Gross had put pressure on the UK to intervene with the authorities in Hong Kong and Burma to act more vigorously against drug trafficking.[26] When considering the two cases of Hong Kong and Burma, it becomes clear that London did not pursue any consistent policy on how to deal with drug producing and transit countries.

In the case of Hong Kong, the response sounded very much like an excuse: as a British crown colony, Hong Kong would be glad to co-operate, but it would not be easy to control all the commerce taking place there. In the case of Burma, Britain was even more reluctant to be used as a proxy for US action. In this particular case, Nelson Gross wanted Britain to buy off the opium manufactured in the Golden Triangle and to supervise its destruction. As the British embassy in Washington reported:

> Asked how one could tell confiscated Opium from that grown to order, Gross allowed that it would be desirable to have some form of outside check. (…) However to some extent the volume of Opium surrendered would speak for itself. There was a limit on how much could be grown to order.[27]

Taking into account the astounding naiveté of the US approach, it is hardly surprising that the British Foreign Office was dragging its feet and declared that the American proposals were either not practicable or even counterproductive.

Cross-border investigation in Europe (1999–2006)

In the second half of the 1990s, there were talks at the United Nations on the creation of a legal template for Joint Investigation Teams. Since many Member

States were deeply concerned with territorial sovereignty, however, it was impossible to reach a consensus. As a result of these disagreements, the 2000 UN Convention against Transnational Organized Crime only contains a soft provision on Joint Investigation Teams (Plachta 2005: 285–7). Given the difficulties in reaching a consensus at the United Nations, Europe turned out to be the only region in the world where the idea of a legal framework for Joint Investigation Teams could be further pursued.

With its 'Third Pillar' of Justice and Home Affairs and its ambition to become an 'Area of Freedom, Security and Justice', the EU provided, maybe for the first time in history, a sufficiently 'thick' legal regime to regulate cross-border investigation. In 1997 (Amsterdam) and 1999 (Tampere), the EU Member States agreed that a legal framework for Joint Investigation Teams should be set up in order to combat trafficking in drugs and human beings, as well as terrorism. In 2000, Joint Investigation Teams were foreseen in the EU Convention on Mutual Assistance in Criminal Matters. Unfortunately, however, the ratification of this treaty was delayed – although for reasons that had nothing to do with Joint Investigation Teams (Plachta 2005: 292).[28]

To overcome this deadlock, a week after the terrorist attacks of 11 September 2001 the Justice and Home Affairs Council decided that Joint Investigation Teams should be brought into *advance effect* by means of an apposite framework decision, which was released nine months later (Council 2001, 2002). As one expert points out, never before had a treaty offered police officers the possibility of carrying out joint cross-border investigations on so many issues and for such an extended period of time (Fijnaut 2004: 252). When properly implemented, Joint Investigation Teams offer the police ample leeway for shortcutting the tedious procedure of mutual legal assistance. Moreover, they clarify the problem of civil and criminal liability.

Apart from Joint Investigation Teams, there was another initiative on 'Multinational Ad Hoc Teams for Exchanging Information on Terrorists'. This went back to an idea of the Spanish presidency of the European Council in 2002, which was further pursued by the Italian presidency in 2003. The idea was to go beyond the investigation of terrorist crimes that have already happened. Whereas Joint Investigation Teams work under the control of judicial authorities and have the objective of bringing culprits to justice, Multinational Ad Hoc Teams aim at the prevention of terrorism. Police forces and secret services collaborate without judicial involvement in order to monitor alleged terrorists and thwart their plans. The Italian proposal was passed in March 2004, putting this highly secretive instrument in place.[29]

Initially, there was some debate on whether Joint Investigation Teams should be restricted to particularly serious offences such as trafficking in drugs and human beings, and terrorism, or whether they should be open to any kind of criminal investigation. The plans to establish Multinational Ad Hoc Teams were kept relatively confidential. Nevertheless, some states stood up for these plans in public while others didn't.

While cross-border investigation conventionally takes place under informal and bilateral arrangements, the legal framework for Joint Investigation Teams provides a European umbrella for these practices. At the time of their institution, there was no reasonable alternative to the EU as a geographical and institutional framework for the regulation of Joint Investigation Teams. As already mentioned, the EU was the only international legal regime sufficiently developed for this sort of cooperation. After Joint Investigation Teams had been instituted at the level of the European Union, Germany, and Austria sponsored a convention to expand cross-border investigation, including Joint Investigation Teams, to the Western Balkans.[30]

When Joint Investigation Teams were negotiated, a number of institutional points were contested. Should it be possible for Europol to participate in Joint Investigation Teams? Should Europol have a right to initiate investigative activities? Should foreign officers have coercive powers when on missions abroad in the context of Joint Investigation Teams? At the end of the day, many European states had difficulties in ratifying and implementing the new legal instrument (Commission 2005a, 2005b).

Joint Investigation Teams are especially interesting because, while all the states under examination supported them, there was a lot of variation. On the one hand, it was fairly easy to reach a consensus on their desirability and to release a framework decision. On the other hand, Member States were motivated for different reasons and to a different degree to support the new legal instrument. On one extreme are Germany and France, which in 2005 moved even further ahead and stipulated in Article 24 of the Prüm Convention that '[e]ach contracting party may (...) confer sovereign powers on other contracting parties' officers involved in joint operations'.[31] On the other extreme is the United Kingdom, which would hardly embrace a similar provision.

France

France is as a long-standing pioneer in multinational cross-border investigation. As we have already seen, in the 1970s Franco-American teams were constituted to tackle the 'French Connection'. In the 1990s, Franco-Spanish teams started prosecuting Basque terrorists across the Pyrenees.[32] At the Tampere Summit, in 1999, and during its Presidency of the European Union, in 2001, France called for a European-wide framework for Joint Investigation Teams to fight drug trafficking and other forms of serious crime.[33] A week after 9/11, France was among the initiators of the EU Framework Decision on Joint Investigation Teams (Council 2001a).[34] While the initial proposal was geared towards the fight against trafficking in drugs and human beings, as well as terrorism, the initiators made clear in an explanatory note that Joint Investigation Teams should be applicable to any sort of crime (Council 2001b).

Since then, France has been an enthusiastic supporter of the idea. This included support for a right for Europol to initiate such teams and to participate in their activities. In 2003 and 2004, Paris was actively engaged in the establishment of a considerable number of Joint Investigation Teams and celebrated every single move towards the creation of a new team as an important step towards improved police cooperation.[35] In addition to Joint Investigation Teams, the French Government also supported the idea of Multinational Ad Hoc Teams for Exchanging Information on Terrorists.[36]

French politicians believed that Joint Investigation Teams were in the interest of their country, since they could serve as a 'European device for fighting in common against serious crime, money laundering, and drug trafficking'.[37] At the same time, French support for multilateral investigation in Europe was part of a wider strategy to shape police cooperation in the EU according to the operational habits of the French executive. Insofar as Paris had reason to believe that French law enforcement agencies were particularly strong at multinational investigations, the institutional development of Joint Investigation Teams at the European level was in the French national interest. French support for Joint Investigation Teams could be expected to increase the French influence in the field of European police cooperation and to provide additional leverage to influence the future development of this important policy field.

All this was fully in line with the French vision of an 'Area of Freedom, Security and Justice' in which Europol would become a European coercive authority with a capacity to investigate across borders, and in which under certain circumstances the authorities of one Member State would be able to take coercive measures on the territory of another Member State (Fischer and Villepin 2002). Considering French negotiating behaviour in the past, however, is seems unlikely that France was really going to accept coercive powers for foreign officers operating on French territory. Take as an example the negotiations for the Schengen Implementing Convention, in 1989. In these negotiations, Paris had also started as a visionary but then became concerned with national sovereignty and pulled the communication cord as plans for cross-border hot pursuit got too concrete (Friedrichs 2006b: 244).[38]

Britain

Joint Investigation Teams were a 'key priority' of the British Government (Home Office 2004: 18). In the eyes of the Home Office, the greatest benefit of Joint Investigation Teams was that they would make it possible to avoid lengthy negotiations and, under certain circumstances, to dispense with letters of request for mutual legal assistance.[39] The British Government believed that Joint Investigation Teams were in the British interest because they would help fight crime more efficaciously, and saw them primarily as a practical device for defeating transnational criminal structures. As a Home Office spokesman said to the House of Commons, the purpose of these teams was to 'investigate organized crime groups across the full range of their activities'.[40] Together with

France, Britain was therefore among the initiators of the Framework Decision on Joint Investigation Teams (Council 2001a, 2001b).

Clearly, Joint Investigation Teams offered a vehicle for 'speedy and efficient team working' that coincided with the professional interests of the British police.[41] From their standpoint, the regulation of the civil and criminal liabilities of police officers working abroad was an important advantage. The UK Government acknowledged this point and supported Joint Investigation Teams as a formal legal umbrella for multinational investigation in Europe.[42] It even declared its readiness to apply the provisions before the EU Framework Decision was formally adopted.[43] In early 2002, that is four months before the formal adoption of the Framework Decision, the British Home Office was proud to inform the public about plans to install two Joint Investigation Teams to tackle trafficking in cocaine and precursor chemicals.[44]

Soon after the release of the framework decision, the British Home Office recommended the early involvement of Europol in a technical and advisory capacity. In a circular, it emphasized that Britain had supported successive EU presidencies in their endeavours to amend the Europol Convention for that purpose.[45] Nevertheless, for the sake of national autonomy and territorial sovereignty, there were clear limitations to Britain's institutional commitment to the new legal instrument. In particular, the British Government was not ready to consider coercive powers for foreign police officers on British soil.[46] Moreover, London did not wish to see Europol developing independent investigative powers (House of Lords 2003: 23).

The British Government believed that informal cooperation among law enforcement agencies was often more efficient than cooperation under a legal framework. Therefore it did not cast Joint Investigation Teams into binding statutory law. While Joint Investigation Teams were recommended to the British police, they were not turned into a mandatory tool for international police cooperation in Europe. In a Home Office Circular of September 2002, the decision on whether to use the EU framework or some more informal procedure was pragmatically left to the discretion of the law enforcement agencies concerned,

> There is no obligation to set up a joint investigation team under the Framework Decision. If less formal ways of working together with other EU countries are appropriate, then teams may continue to be set up as is already the case, outside the arrangements in the framework decision.[47]

It is interesting to note that, while London was relatively supportive of Joint Investigation Teams, the British Government kept silent on the idea of Multinational Ad Hoc Teams for Exchanging Information on Terrorists. As in the case of antiterrorist intelligence, one may reasonably suspect that this was due to the fact that in Britain the Security Service (MI5) is the lead agency for international investigations on terrorism. As a secret service, MI5 had a vested interest in keeping international cooperation as informal as possible. While

Multinational Ad Hoc Teams were designed as an informal tool from the standpoint of the police, from the standpoint of a secret service they must have looked like a superfluous framework for the formal institutionalization of a confidential kind of cooperation that in practice was going on anyway.[48]

Germany

Berlin had more ambitious plans than only to facilitate horizontal collaboration among police officers (Funk 2000). Germany would have wanted to place multinational investigation in Europe on a supranational basis. Joint Investigation Teams certainly did not satisfy such high-flown aspirations. Given the strong German commitment to Europol and other supranational schemes for European police cooperation, there must have been some disappointment limiting the German enthusiasm for the new legal instrument. Being in favour of supranational policing in Europe, however, Berlin could hardly afford to oppose such a pragmatic instrument of multinational investigation. For reasons of normative and political consistency, Germany had no other choice than to support Joint Investigation Teams.

Already in 1984, the German Ministry of the Interior had endorsed the vision of a European police with executive competences (Fröhlich 1985: 15). Helmut Kohl had launched initiatives for the creation of a 'European FBI' with independent investigative powers twice, once in 1991 and again in 1996 (Busch 1999: 143–7; Occhipinti 2003: 34–5, 53–4). At the Amsterdam Intergovernmental Conference, Germany was among the strongest supporters of supranational police cooperation.[49]

Under Chancellor Gerhard Schröder and Foreign Minister Josef Fischer, Germany continued to demand that Europol be granted investigative and coercive powers. In its effort to place police cooperation in Europe on a supranational basis, Germany called, among other things, for the following measures: the introduction of majority voting for matters related to police cooperation; a right of initiative for the European Commission; the involvement of the European Parliament to increase democratic accountability and control; and a supervisory role for the European Court of Justice (Fischer and Villepin 2002; Occhipinti 2003: 58–63, 93–112).

For all of these reasons, it was a must for Berlin to support Joint Investigation Teams. Already in 1999, the German Foreign Minister had expressed his support for the establishment of such teams.[50] Berlin also supported the participation of Europol, and the German Interior Minister called for it to be granted the power of initiating cross-border investigations.[51] However, Germany was not among the initiators of the Framework Decision on Joint Investigation Teams, nor was it particularly committed to its implementation. It even declared that there was no need for a ratification law (Commission 2005b: 8). As we have seen, Berlin would have preferred to go much further and to grant real investigative and coercive powers to Europol. Insofar as Joint Investigation Teams can be seen as a transgovernmental surrogate for European institutions being endowed with true supranational competences, Germany was far from enthusiastic about such a pragmatic instrument.

In 2003, the German Government also supported the establishment of Multinational Ad Hoc Teams for Exchanging Information on Terrorists.[52] To some degree, the German Minister of the Interior may have seen Multinational Ad Hoc Teams as an instrument to overcome resistance from domestic institutions. In Germany, the police and secret services work within strong legal and institutional constraints against the intrusion into the privacy of citizens. Due to this legalistic tradition, German authorities are often hesitant to embark on multinational investigations when legally problematic practices are involved. The Interior Minister could expect that an agreement at the European level would give him a certain purchase to overcome such domestic constraints.

Italy

Italy also supported Joint Investigation Teams, although rather half-heartedly. The main reason for this may appear somewhat bizarre.[53] Italian policy makers and police leaders perceived a strong national interest in Italy's law enforcement agencies being more outward-looking. They hoped that Joint Investigation Teams would have an important socializing effect on the Italian police. Eventually, working in such Teams might help the Italian police forces overcome their difficulties in collaborating with their foreign counterparts and with Europol.[54] Already in 2000, Italy was one of the few countries to support the suggestion of the Portuguese presidency that there should be a framework decision on Joint Investigation Teams.[55] Presumably for similar reasons, in 2003 Italy was one of the key sponsors of Multinational Ad Hoc Teams for Exchanging Information on Terrorists.[56]

However, Italian lawyers had problems with the prospect that Joint Investigation Teams could lead to a situation where evidence that had not been gained according to Italian procedural standards could be used before Italian courts.[57] Apparently, this is also the reason why the ratification of the Framework Decision proved so difficult for the Italian Parliament. After the Government introduced an apposite draft in 2002, the legal project got stuck. Two years after the deadline, the European Commission noted that Italy had still not ratified the framework decision (Commission 2005b: 26). In fact, one may reasonably wonder whether, and to what extent, certain components of the Berlusconi Government were really committed, beyond lip-service, to the new legal instrument of Joint Investigation Teams.[58]

But be that as it may, at the negotiation stage Rome welcomed the right of Europol not only to take part in Joint Investigation Teams but also to initiate investigations.[59] In the case of Multinational Ad Hoc Teams, the Italian Minister of the Interior even declared that their final objective was 'to entrust Europol with the coordination of European investigations on terrorism'.[60] Given that there remain some doubts as to whether Rome would really have been ready to accept coercive powers for foreign police officers operating on Italian territory, it is remarkable that Italy remained silent on this delicate point.

On the one hand, the Italian Government perceived a national interest in using Joint Investigation Teams and Multinational Ad Hoc Teams as an instrument for striking at serious organized crime and terrorism more effectively. On the other hand, however, there was a widely shared belief among Italian security experts and politicians that international cooperation against serious crime should take precedence over the fight against lesser forms of crime. As in the case of the European Arrest Warrant Italy therefore would have preferred to see the competences of Joint Investigation Teams restricted to particularly serious forms of crime such as drugs, terrorism, and trafficking in human beings (G. de Gennaro 2003: 5).

9 Results

This book is somewhat like a sandwich with a rich dense filling. The main nutritional value lies in the six chapters of the main part, which offer plenty of contextual information about European state preferences on international police cooperation. You cannot handle a sandwich by the filling, though. To remain in our culinary metaphor, the bread and butter of the book is therefore provided not so much in the central chapters, but rather in the encompassing parts. The first two chapters provided the necessary background and the essentials for (con)textual understanding. The present chapter, then, is going to provide the results.

A lot of ground has been covered in the core chapters (3 to 8). State preferences on fighting terrorism and drugs were dealt with in two separate parts. A distinction was made between three levels on which international police cooperation can take place: legitimization, methods, and authorization. Preferences were examined in two different time periods: the 1960s/1970s on the one hand, and the 1990s/2000s on the other. This was done for each of the four largest and most important Western European states: Britain, France, Germany, and Italy. These countries were examined as member of the international system and not only as EU Members.

Roughly, the book consists to about 75 per cent of qualitative case studies following the methods of structured-focussed comparison and process tracing. Due to the considerable number of overlapping distinctions in the description and explanation of state preferences, the empirical evidence reaches a complexity that cannot be mastered by a purely qualitative and hermeneutic approach. Therefore, all the case studies were formally coded into a database.

The database consists of three datasets, containing information on all 48 of the case studies. This makes it possible to embark on the path of formal statistical analysis, and thereby to detect the patterns of similarity and difference inherent in this enormous amount of information.

- The first dataset contains positive, negative, or neutral values (1; -1; 0) for the preferences of each of the four countries, on all of the 88 specific issues discussed with regard to broadening and deepening international police cooperation.[1]

- The second dataset contains, for each case study, ordinal data measuring the willingness of a country to cooperate with other countries on three dimensions: scope, range, and depth (see the indices introduced on pp. 25–8).[2]
- While the first two datasets are descriptive, the third one is explanatory. It contains eight causal pathways per case study, differentiating between the general attitude of a country and its preferences on scope, range, and depth.[3]

The datasets are reprinted in the three appendices to this book, and published on a supporting website: <http://www.joerg-friedrichs.de/policingdata>.[4] On the website, you can view the data in a synoptic format, including comments on all values and scores, and thereby connect the quantitative evidence back to the qualitative cases (see p. 37 for further information).

On the basis of the descriptive and explanatory datasets, it is possible to detect patterns of similarity and difference by means of simple but rigorous tools of statistical analysis. The statistical methods applied include rank order correlation, cross tabulation, frequency counts, and mean standard deviation. Despite the use of such technical tools the reader should be careful never to lose sight of the main analytical objective of this book, which is to better understand how European states formulate their preferences on international policing. For example, it is important to note that the statistical findings have all been checked against the qualitative record as documented in the core chapters. Whenever a statistical finding could not be reasonably interpreted in qualitative terms, it was dropped as spurious.

While most of the results presented in this chapter pass statistical significance tests, the more exacting and meaningful criterion for confidence is intelligibility in terms of the qualitative evidence. Remember the original meaning of statistical significance: controlling the risk that a generalization is due to chance rather than systematic reasons. When you work with a prefabricated dataset without really knowing your data apart from their nominal or numerical values, statistical significance tests are the only option. Where possible, however, the better alternative is to check quantitative findings against qualitative case knowledge. If the two fit together and make good sense, the risk of a generalization being due to chance is negligible. Nevertheless, it is better to err on the side of caution. No bold claims for universal validity are therefore raised in this study. This is not however to exclude the empirical possibility that the patterns detected may provide a useful guide for better understanding international policing, or even international cooperation in general.

Descriptive patterns

Using the first dataset, it is possible to examine the degree to which the four countries in the sample differ in their preferences on specific issues.[5]

When examining the dataset as a whole, it emerges clearly that international police cooperation is a contested policy field. The average degree of contestation for all 88 issues is indeed relatively high, scoring 0.75 on a scale between 0 and 1.15. When examining the dataset by sub-samples, it turns out that a similar degree of contestation is ubiquitous throughout the field under investigation.[6]

True, the fight against terrorism is somewhat more contested than the fight against drugs.[7] Although international cooperation against drugs has become more contested from the 1960s to the 2000s, it has still not reached the level of contestation of terrorism.[8] This is in line with the qualitative record. The fight against terrorism is clearly more politicized than the fight against drugs. Nevertheless, the difference is statistically hardly significant.

It is fair to conclude that, despite subtle differences, international policing is consistently contested between states. This should warn us against an overly harmonious view of international cooperation. The only partial exception to this rule can be found at the authorization level, where cross-border investigation in Europe is fairly unproblematic.[9] However the same does not apply to the extradition of terrorists, which is the most contested sub-sample of the dataset.[10]

Leaders and laggards

The analysis of the second dataset shows that some countries are more willing to engage in international police cooperation than others.[11] By means of descriptive statistics, it is possible to identify the 'leaders' and 'laggards'. Table 9.1 shows that France and Germany tend to be more ready for international police cooperation than either Britain or Italy (values are on a scale between 0 and 4; higher values denote a more internationalist stance).

A further dissection into sub-samples shows interesting patterns by countries. Thus, France has always been a leader in the fight against drugs, and since the 1970s has become slightly more proactive in the fight against terrorism.[12] Be it in terms of scope, range, or depth, and at the legitimization, methods, or authorization level, Paris is truly committed to international policing and often tries to be at the forefront of international cooperation.[13]

Germany is second only to France.[14] Berlin is even more committed than Paris to international cooperation against terrorism, but has become one of the 'laggards' on drugs.[15] Interestingly, Germany is more 'internationalist' than any other country on the institutional depth (but less so on the substantive scope) of cooperation.[16] This indicates that Berlin views the improvement of international police cooperation very much as an institutional project.

Britain, by contrast, seems to honour its reputation as a pragmatic country. Unlike Germany, London has problems with institutionally binding commitments

Table 9.1 Mean ranks of state preferences (n = 12)

	Britain	*France*	*Germany*	*Italy*
Mean rank	2.0	3.0	2.8	2.1

and international cooperation at the legitimization level, while being much more proactive at the authorization level.[17] A quick glance into the qualitative chapters is sufficient to confirm that, while London is most sceptical about drug prohibition and the definition of terrorism, cross-border investigation and the extradition of terrorists do not seem to pose any major problems. Interestingly, Britain has consistently been more ready to cooperate against terrorism than against drugs.[18]

Italy offers the picture of a 'laggard' anticipating its own implementation problems. The country is relatively cautious in supporting cooperation at the authorization level, where compliance is particularly difficult and non-compliance particularly visible.[19] In the 1970s, Rome gave little support to cross-border drug enforcement or information exchange on terrorism. In the 2000s, the European Arrest Warrant is another case in point. Recently, Rome has brought up the rear in the fight against terrorism while taking a far more proactive stance on drugs.[20]

Synergies and tradeoffs

Throughout this book, preferences have been determined separately for substantive scope, membership range, and institutional depth. This distinction (see pp. 25–8) is connected to the familiar debate about possible synergies and/or tradeoffs between broadening, widening, and deepening international cooperation in general, and European integration in particular.

In principle, there are two equally plausible hypotheses as to the relationship between preferences on scope, range, and depth. The first hypothesis follows functionalist theory in assuming that the relationship is characterized by a virtuous cycle, whereas the second hypothesis is of a more realist nature and assumes that there are tradeoffs rather than synergies.

Hypothesis 1: There are synergies. Preferences on scope co-vary with preferences on range and depth. In statistical terms: there are positive correlations between the variables.

Hypothesis 2: There are tradeoffs. In statistical terms: there are two negative correlations between the three variables (whereas the third correlation is by necessity positive).[21]

Take as an example the debate about broadening, widening, and deepening the European Union. From an optimistic viewpoint there is, or should be, a virtuous cycle among the three dimensions of integration. Enlargement enhances the readiness of new Member States to share the goals and values of the EU, this in turn reinforces the process of institutional reform and makes it possible to bring new policy fields under the competence of the EU, which further increases the incentives for even more Member States to join, and so on and so forth.

Against this, Euro-sceptics emphasize the risk of a vicious cycle. In their view, an increase in substantive scope makes it more difficult to reach a common denominator on institutional reform; expanded membership impedes an

Table 9.2 Correlations between scope, range, and depth

Relationship	*Strength*	*Significance*	*N*
Scope ∘ Range	0.542	0.000**	48
Range ∘ Depth	0.572	0.000**	40
Scope ° Depth	0.715	0.000**	40

Note: Double asterisks indicate statistical significance at the highest level (<1%).

increase in the scope of activities; the prospects for institutional reform are hampered by enlargement; and if the EU is institutionally strengthened, then Member States will be less ready to enhance substantive scope.[22]

Thus, both a negative and a positive relationship between state preferences on scope, range, and depth would be theoretically plausible. Fortunately, the two rival hypotheses are subject to empirical scrutiny. The second dataset allows for settling the dispute at least with regard to European state preferences on international police cooperation. Table 9.2 shows that *Hypothesis 1* is vindicated by the empirical evidence, while *Hypothesis 2* must be rejected. There are highly significant and strong positive correlations between state preferences on substantive scope, membership range, and institutional depth.[23]

A further examination of the data by sub-sets clearly confirms the pattern. The only significant exception is the sub-set for German preferences in the 1970s, for which there is a strong negative correlation between preferences on scope and depth.[24] For all other sub-sets, broadening, widening, and deepening international police cooperation go together.

Interestingly, there is a certain trend towards stronger consistency between state preferences on scope, range and depth. While a synergetic pattern is already visible for the data on the 1960s/1970s, the correlations are stronger and more significant for the 1990s/2000s.[25]

Explanatory patterns

To the social scientist, the more interesting part is not so much the description but rather the explanation of state preferences. To that end, 18 causal pathways were formulated in Chapter 2 (pp. 29–31) in order to make the explanatory data amenable to statistical analysis. Each pathway indicates whether a given state preference was determined by interests, institutions, or ideas; whether these interests, institutions, or ideas came from a domestic, national, or international source; and whether this resulted in a positive or a negative effect.

Eight causal pathways have been coded for each of the 48 case studies: two for the general readiness of a state to support international police cooperation; two for its readiness to support an increase in the substantive scope; two on its

Table 9.3 Frequency of causal pathways

	Interests		*Institutions*		*Ideas*	
Domestic	5.4	Pos: 2.3	11.2	Pos: 4.4	3.1	Pos: 0.5
		Neg: 3.1		Neg: 6.8		Neg: 2.6
National	37.5	Pos: 23.2	5.9	Pos: 1.0	10.4	Pos: 7.3
		Neg: 14.3		Neg: 4.9		Neg: 3.1
International	10.2	Pos: 10.2	12.5	Pos: 7.3	3.6	Pos: 3.6
		Neg: –		Neg: 5.2		Neg: –

readiness to enhance the membership range; and two for its readiness to increase the institutional depth of cooperation.[26]

As a result of this coding exercise, there is an ample dataset containing as many as 384 explanations. This large number of data-points makes the dataset amenable to a simple but rigorous form of descriptive statistical analysis. Table 9.3 quantifies the frequency of each of the 18 possible causal pathways, that is, how often it occurs within the dataset (values are percentages).

Even without further analysis, there are some interesting patterns emerging. The general picture is that national sources account for half of the empirical evidence, while domestic and international sources account for roughly a quarter each. Similarly, interests account for about half of the picture, while institutions make up for a third and ideas for only a sixth. Interestingly, international interests and international ideas never have a negative impact.

To make these findings theoretically more meaningful, in Chapter 2 I have introduced a variety of baseline hypotheses against which to assess the empirical evidence. These hypotheses were derived from existing theoretical perspectives: the liberal theory of international politics, liberal intergovernmentalism, orthodox realism, normative approaches, institutional approaches, social institutionalism, and neoclassical functionalism (see pp. 31–5)

Different theoretical perspectives would suggest different combinations of causal pathways to explain the lion's share of state preferences. This can be easily deduced from the overview in Table 9.4, which simply repeats Table 2.3 for the reader's convenience.

One popular strand of explanation is absent from the list. There is an important part of the policing literature which relies on what one may term 'grassroot transgovernmentalism' (Anderson 1989; Nadelmann 1993; Busch 1995, 1999; Bigo 1996; Deflem 2002; Sheptycki 2002a; Elvins 2003; Lavenex and Wagner 2006). This literature suggests that states mostly enact the preferences or professional inclinations of police practitioners, as well as the preferences of executive stakeholders in ministerial bureaucracies.[27] These people and their organizations, it is argued, have a vested interest in the promotion or prevention of specific policy choices. They will lobby states for more international policing whenever they anticipate that this is going to enhance their autonomy and make

Table 9.4 Causal expectations of existing explanatory approaches

Explanatory approach	*Causal expectations*
Liberal theory of international politics	Domestic interests/institutions/ideas (with positive/negative impact)
Liberal intergovernmentalism	Domestic interests (with positive/negative impact)
Orthodox realism	National interests (with negative impact)
Normative approaches	Domestic/national/international ideas (with positive/negative impact)
Institutional approaches	Domestic/national/international institutions (with positive/negative impact)
Social institutionalism	International institutions (with positive impact); national/domestic institutions (with negative impact)
Neoclassical functionalism	National/international interests (with positive impact); international institutions (with positive impact)

their organizations grow. Conversely, when they fear a loss of autonomy or pressure to adapt their organizations to exacting international standards, they will urge 'their' governments against increased cooperation.

Prima facie, this sounds like a plausible explanation. At least for our purposes, however, the theory must be discarded despite its apparent plausibility and despite its popularity in the literature. Among the 384 explanations in the dataset, there are few examples where states are directly influenced by the interests of executive stakeholders and their networks. This is not to deny that security professionals may try to influence their governments. Nor is it to exclude the possibility that shadowy networks of police practitioners and executive stakeholders are the *prime movers* (see p. 30) behind international police cooperation. In this study, however, we are concerned with empirical evidence. Moreover, we concentrate on the *efficient causes* of state preferences.[28] If grassroot transgovernmentalism was applicable to our research question, we would expect decision makers to frequently say: 'Our experts all agree, so this is what we have to do'. In reality, however, we rarely find this kind of statement.

Leaving aside 'grassroot transgovernmentalism', let us now confront the empirical findings with the expectations derived from the other existing explanatory approaches. Table 9.5 shows the relative aggregate strength of the different possible sources of explanation. The second column of the table uses a simple system of abbreviations to name the causal pathways mobilized.[29] The third column quantifies, by way of mathematical addition, the amount of the empirical evidence each of the different explanatory approaches can account for. Based on these values, it is possible to specify exactly which of the explanatory approaches can account for how much of the empirical evidence. How preference

Table 9.5 Relative strength of explanatory approaches

Explanatory approach	*Causal expectations*	*Cumulative percentage*
Liberal theory of international politics	DomIntPos, DomIntNeg, DomInstPos, DomInstNeg, DomIdPos, DomIdNeg	20%
Liberal intergovernmentalism	DomIntPos, DomIntNeg	5%
Orthodox realism	NatIntNeg	14%
Normative approaches	DomIdPos, NatIdPos, IntIdPos DomIdNeg, NatIdNeg, IntIdNeg	17%
Institutional approaches	DomInstPos, NatInstPos, IntInstPos, DomInstNeg, NatInstNeg, IntInstNeg	30%
Social institutionalism	DomInstNeg, NatInstNeg, IntInstPos	19%
Neoclassical functionalism	NatIntPos, IntIntPos, IntInstPos	41%

formation actually works in the policy field of international policing thereby becomes more transparent.

It turns out that neither version of liberal theory can suitably account for European state preferences on international policing. Of course this is not to deny that liberal theories are useful to explain the formation of state preferences in other policy fields such as market integration. In the particular field of international police cooperation, however, domestic factors simply do not play a sufficient role for any version of Moravcsik's theories to be vindicated. Liberal theory of international politics uses a third of the causal pathways to explain a fifth of the evidence, while liberal intergovernmentalism can only account for a tiny 5 per cent.

Relying on only one causal pathway, orthodox realism can account for an impressive 14 per cent of the empirical record. In absolute terms, 'national interests with a negative impact' is indeed the second most frequent causal pathway. Contrary to realist predictions, however, national interests are more often an incentive (23 per cent) than an impediment (14 per cent) to international police cooperation. This is the exact opposite of what orthodox realism, with its notorious obsession with national sovereignty, would predict.[30] Accordingly, it is fair to say that orthodox realism does not offer a convincing key to the empirical evidence.[31]

Nor is the role of ideas sufficiently significant to commend the explanatory power of normative approaches. National ideas in particular sometimes do constitute an incentive for preferences on international police cooperation, but the result is relatively meagre if one considers the causal impact of normative ideas in comparison to interests or institutions. While normative ideas cover a third of the possible causal pathways, they can account for less than a fifth of all empirical explanations contained in the dataset.[32]

Institutional approaches, by contrast, do account for a significant share of the empirical evidence. Covering a third of the causal pathways, they cover an almost equivalent proportion of the explanations contained in the dataset. The result is even better for social institutionalism. As we have seen in Chapter 2, social institutionalism predicts that international institutions should have a positive net effect on the readiness of states to cooperate with one another, while national and domestic institutions should have a negative effect. Indeed, these three causal pathways account for 19 per cent of the empirical evidence.

The palm, however, goes to neoclassical functionalism, where only three causal pathways can account for as much as 41 per cent of the empirical evidence. A look into the qualitative record confirms that expectations derived from neoclassical functionalism are largely met. States tend to support international police cooperation when they believe that this will help them tackle problems connected with terrorism and drug trafficking. Since they are aware that the challenge is international by nature, their preferences are not only determined by the national interest but also by the interests of the international community as a whole. In line with functionalist expectations about institutional feedback, existing international institutions further increase the willingness of states to cooperate with other states.

Neoclassical functioalism

As should have become clear by now, what I am suggesting is a reformulation of classical functionalism. This 'neoclassical functionalism' is fairly remote from EU studies, viz. 'neo-functionalism'. It is closer to classical functionalism as formulated by David Mitrany in his seminal text *A Working Peace System* (1943; see also Groom and Taylor 1975).

In a nutshell, the functionalist theory of preference formation runs like this: States are ready for international cooperation when they believe that this will contribute to meeting important challenges. They do this because they want to pursue not only their national, but also the international interest in problem solving. Over time, this leads to a situation in which upcoming international institutions call for even more cooperation.

As expected by functionalism, there is a gradual shift of loyalty to the international sphere.[33] When we split the dataset into two sub-samples, one for the 1960s/1970s and one for the 1990s/2000s, it is confirmed that, over time, the motivating force of international interests and institutions has become relatively more (and the constraining force of national interests and institutions relatively less) important for the determination of state preferences.[34]

Furthermore, a functionalist would expect that 'form follows function', that is, preferences on institutional depth and membership range should follow preferences on substantive scope. As we have seen in the last section, there is indeed a strong and significant correlation between state preferences on the substantive scope, membership range, and institutional depth of international police cooperation (see also Friedrichs *et al.* 2005).

Finally, and again as predicted by neoclassical functionalism, there is a spill-over from international cooperation against one form of crime to international cooperation against another. For example, anti-money laundering started as a drug enforcement method and was subsequently applied to other forms of serious crime and, since 9/11, to the financing of terrorism. Conversely, the systematic international exchange of intelligence started as an element in the European counter-terrorist strategy of the 1970s, and was subsequently expanded world-wide to include other offences such as drug trafficking and even football hooliganism.

Political functionalism

As we have seen, neoclassical functionalism can account for 41 per cent of the empirical evidence by virtue of three causal pathways only. While no other explanatory approach reaches a similar score, one may argue that a good social scientific theory should cover at least half of the phenomenal class for which it is designed. To reach this threshold, let us blend neoclassical functionalism with another theory that scores high, namely institutional approaches.

Functionalism and institutionalism are indeed compatible theories, and there is no conceptual reason why one should not merge the causal pathways mobilized by both of them. If we combine neoclassical functionalism with institutional approaches, we can account for as much as 63 per cent of the empirical evidence by virtue of eight causal pathways.[35]

It is more parsimonious, however, to merge neoclassical functionalism with social institutionalism. In this case, a combination of five pathways (national and international interests with positive impact, international institutions with positive impact, domestic and national institutions with negative impact)[36] accounts for 52 per cent of the empirical evidence, while the remaining 48 per cent of the evidence is explained by the other 13 pathways.

Orthodox realism consists of only one causal pathway: 'national interests with negative impact'. If we add this to the picture, clearly not as a complement but as a weaker but significant countervailing theory, then one third (6) of the causal pathways explain two-thirds (66 per cent) of the empirical record, while the other two-thirds (12) of the pathways explain the remaining third (34 per cent) of the evidence. Such a fit between theory and evidence is quite remarkable for an empirically grounded social scientific theory.

This theoretical fusion may be labelled 'political functionalism', to distinguish it from the apolitical functionalism à la David Mitrany. Its quintessence is that (1) the driving force behind international police cooperation is the collective and individual interest of states in solving practical problems, and that (2) this impetus is often fostered by the socialization effects of international institutions, and hampered by the constraints imposed by existing national and domestic institutions, while (3) the national interest in the preservation of territorial sovereignty frequently poses a significant obstacle to international cooperation.

Variation by countries

A closer look at the data reveals some interesting variation. Different countries at different times tend to be driven to pursue or eschew international police cooperation for a variety of different reasons. Cooperation against terrorism is not necessarily and not always supported or avoided for the same reasons as cooperation against drugs. It also makes a difference whether cooperation is to be envisaged at the level of legitimization, methods, or authorization. Accordingly, let us dissect the dataset by countries, threats, time periods, and levels.

Country-wise, the analysis broadly confirms conventional wisdom on the foreign policy orientations of Germany and France on the one hand, and Britain and Italy on the other. It is hardly surprising to find that French and German preferences seem to reflect a stronger functionalist inclination towards problem solving;[37] that both countries are more often motivated by international reasons;[38] that they more often follow normative 'visions';[39] and that Germany in particular is most often concerned with normative ideas and hardly ever constrained by domestic reasons or national interests.[40] In a nutshell, there seems to be a kernel of truth in the folk wisdom about Germany being the epitome of an internationalist and Europeanist country, and about France pursuing a sort of 'civilizing mission' at the international level.

Since the early 1970s, Germany has perceived a clear national interest in fighting terrorism and drugs. At the same time the country has also pursued a 'strategy of multilateralism', viewing international cooperation as an end in itself. This multilateralism is typically mirrored by the 'internationalism' of domestic law enforcement agencies, which actively lobby their Government for enhanced cooperation. Domestic factors hardly ever have a negative influence on German preferences. And even in the few instances where they do, at the end of the day Berlin is usually entrapped in an international logic of appropriateness. Similarly, constitutional concerns are sometimes raised, but in the long run they tend to be overruled by Germany's typical commitment to international cooperation. A good case in point is the European Arrest Warrant, where Berlin accepted the extradition of German nationals regardless of a constitutional principle to the contrary. There are few cases where Germany has opposed international cooperation due to concerns with national sovereignty. Sometimes, there is a conflict between two alternatives: cooperation in the EU or in some wider framework. In such cases, Germany tends to favour the EU. Normative considerations often play an important role, as in the case of drug prohibition where Germany prefers a non-repressive approach.

France tends to view terrorism and drugs not only as threats to national and international security, but also in moral terms. On the one hand, the international community as embodied by the United Nations should vigorously fight terrorism. On the other hand, France sees a moral obligation to understand the root causes of the problem. For quite a long time, France even held more sympathies for political fugitives than for foreign prosecutors seeking the extradition of terrorists. Like terrorism, drugs are also viewed both as a security threat and as a moral problem. Paris has always condemned narcotics, and ever since the late 1960s and early 1970s has supported concrete international cooperation to tackle the perceived emergency. In the 1990s, international cooperation was seen as the key to tackling criminal finance. In particular,

Paris had an interest in fending off the infiltration of criminal finance into the French banking system, and eventually also in stopping the clandestine exodus of taxable money to fiscal paradises. Despite its internationalist inclinations, however, France is quite often concerned with national sovereignty and the preservation of its territorial monopoly of force. Sometimes, Paris also pursues foreign policy objectives such as manipulating transatlantic relations or influencing other countries through international institutions like the European Union or the Pompidou Group. Occasionally, the idiosyncrasies of domestic institutions or legal arrangements are another reason for France to pursue or eschew international cooperation.

Britain and Italy, on the other hand, are far less often motivated by international factors than Germany and France.[41] Britain is the country most driven by national interests and least by normative ideas.[42] Furthermore, it is the only country where national interests are more often an impediment than an incentive to the pursuit of international policing.[43] In the Italian case, there are significant domestic constraints hampering Government preferences.[44]

In fact, Britain is most often concerned with sovereignty. Moreover, the country often perceives a strong national interest in the maintenance of political autonomy. In the case of terrorism, for instance, Britain is unwilling to see a definition of the international public enemy codified at the United Nations. Similarly, London consistently tries to maintain the necessary room for manoeuvre for an autonomous national drug policy. On the other hand, the British Government tends to support international cooperation whenever this seems to be warranted by the national interest. The common law tradition sometimes makes cooperation more difficult, but in the long run this usually does not prevent London from cooperating. Due to the high professionalism of British agencies, Government support for international policing is relatively unproblematic. However, there is a flipside to this. British agencies tend to be characterized by a rather informal culture, and this sometimes hampers the ability to ordain international cooperation from above. In general, British preferences are very much driven by institutional considerations. On some occasions this gives an incentive for international policing, for example when the UK performs as America's 'deputy' in the global 'war on drugs'. On other occasions it places a constraint on Government support for international policing, as in the 1970s when London avoided encroaching on the autonomy of the British police.

Italy frequently strives to solve national problems through international cooperation, but often faces severe domestic constraints militating against this wish.[45] Examples range from the institutional backwardness of the Italian police and secret services in the 1970s to the 'culture of secrecy' of the same agencies in the 2000s, and from the commercial interests of the pharmaceutical industry opposing the prohibition of psychotropic substances in the 1970s to the populist *Lega Nord* stonewalling the European Arrest Warrant in the 2000s. Usually, such domestic constraints lead the Italian Government to be relatively cautious on international police cooperation. In some cases, however, they have the opposite effect, and international cooperation is seen as a vehicle for modernizing Italian structures. In the 1970s, for example, this motivated Rome to cautiously support the Americanization and Europeanization of Italian drug enforcement techniques. Again, in the 2000s, Italy supported Joint Investigation Teams in the hope that they would have a kind of socialization effect on the Italian police.[46] Under the Christian Democratic Governments in the 1960s and 1970s, Rome was often motivated by a desire to be a good 'international citizen'. During the second Berlusconi Government (2001–06), however, this tradition was at least in part neutralized by the Euro-scepticism of the *Lega Nord.*

All this seems to be consistent with – but also to add to – conventional views: Germany and France are uniquely internationalist countries; Britain tends to behave like a maverick in pursuit of the national interest; and fragmented Italy is notoriously driven by internal rifts.

Variation by policy fields

Conventional expectations are also broadly confirmed when comparing the fight against terrorism with the fight against drugs. On the one hand, the national interest in international cooperation is more obvious in the latter case: drugs are a transnational problem in search of an international solution, while terrorism tends to hit states more unevenly. In line with such functional expectations, one would therefore expect the national interest in solving the problem through international cooperation to be more important in the case of drugs. On the other hand, terrorists pose a frontal challenge to the state monopoly of the legitimate use of force, while drug traffickers are primarily profit-oriented criminals trying to evade the state. One would therefore expect that concerns with territorial sovereignty should place a more important constraint on state preferences with regard to fighting terrorism.

These expectations are met.[47] What is more, in the fight against terrorism national interests are as often an impediment as an incentive to international cooperation.[48] In the fight against drugs, by contrast, they are more than twice as often an incentive as an impediment.[49] The qualitative record confirms that European states agree that there is a clear interest in tackling drugs internationally. Disagreement is mostly limited to the question of whether it is better to focus on the supply or demand side of the problem, and whether a curative approach is better than a repressive approach. In the case of terrorism, by contrast, states sometimes perceive a national interest in defining the public enemy on their own, controlling the exchange of sensitive information, and granting or denying extradition on a political basis.

Interestingly, institutions are more important in the fight against terrorism than in the fight against drugs.[50] The main reason is that the presence or absence of appropriate domestic and international institutions is even more decisive in the politically sensitive field of terrorism. For example, the 'culture of secrecy' of the British, French, and Italian police and secret services poses a serious obstacle to the automatic exchange of antiterrorist intelligence. Or take as another example the extradition of terrorist offenders, which was a serious problem in the 1970s when Western European states did not yet sufficiently trust each other's legal and political systems. In the 2000s, however, the 'Area of Freedom, Security and Justice' of the EU finally provides the necessary institutional underpinning for the European Arrest Warrant.

Variation by time periods

A comparison between the 1960s/1970s and the 1990s/2000s reveals that the predictions of neoclassical functionalism are confirmed. As previously mentioned, neoclassical functionalism predicts that over time international cooperation should create an institutional environment at the international level that feeds back positively on the readiness of states to engage in further cooperation. In fact, from the 1960s/1970s to the 1990s/2000s there has been a decrease in the importance of interests, and an increase in the importance of institutions and normative ideas.[51] Moreover, the national level has become significantly less, and the international level significantly more important in accounting for European state preferences on international police cooperation.[52] Apparently, this is mainly due to the increasing transferral of authority to international institutions, such as the United Nations with its drug prohibition machinery, the European Union with its Third Pillar, and the Financial Action Task Force (FATF).

Variation by levels

If one looks at different levels on the chain of coercion, there are some interesting surprises. At the authorization level, one would expect a high salience of interests because here the physical use of the monopoly of force is most directly at stake. However, this expectation is not confirmed. Normative ideas are most, and interests are least important when compared to the other two levels.[53] The pattern is most articulate in the case of the European Arrest Warrant, which was supported by Britain, France, and Germany (and opposed by Italy) for strong normative reasons. This puzzle offers an interesting starting point for future research.

At the methods level, we find that states are very much driven by institutions, mostly at the domestic level.[54] This is exactly what one would expect, since crime fighting methods are of particular concern to domestic institutional stakeholders. Especially in the 1960s/1970s such domestic stakeholders exerted an important influence on drug enforcement methods, the international exchange of antiterrorist information, and cooperation between special commando units. In the 1990s/2000s their influence on anti-money laundering is somewhat lower, but it is still considerable with regard to the exchange of antiterrorist information.

Since the legitimization level is most remote from physical law enforcement, we would expect domestic reasons to be largely irrelevant for national preference formation. This is indeed the case.[55] The domestic level hardly interferes with the definition of terrorism or with international drug prohibition. Nor do national institutions play any role at this level.[56] Surprisingly, however, interests are particularly important at the legitimization level.[57] Moreover, the national interest has a mainly negative impact.[58] Apparently, states watch even more jealously over the legitimization of the monopoly of force than over the control of its physical use. The struggle over the definition of international terrorism is a striking case in point.

Variation by dimensions

The dataset can be decomposed in yet another way. Preferences may differ according to whether they are related to the general willingness of a country to cooperate with other countries in a particular case, or to the substantive scope, membership range, and institutional depth of cooperation. Let us therefore analyse variation by the following dimensions: general mindset, substantive scope, membership range, and institutional depth.

To begin with 'general mindset', governments are most likely to have assertive national interests on whether or not to embrace international police cooperation in a given case. Hence, one would expect that, for good or ill, the general readiness of a state to support international police cooperation should be crucially determined by its perceived national interests. This is indeed the case. Very often, we find state preferences of the type: 'Our country has a national interest in tackling this challenge, and the way to an appropriate solution goes by necessity through international cooperation'.[59] Less often we find state preferences of the type: 'Our country simply cannot cooperate in this case, because it would lose too much of its sovereignty'.[60]

For preferences on substantive issues, domestic factors should play a decisive role. Particularly the police and other executive stakeholders should actively lobby their governments with regard to the nuts and bolts of international cooperation. Once again, this expectation is met. While domestic factors generally explain only a small share of the empirical evidence, their contribution to explaining preferences on substantive scope is considerable.[61] Preferences on substantive issues are often affected by the availability or lack of executive units willing, or able, to engage in international cooperation. Other domestic groups influencing state preferences are the pharmaceutical industry and doctors in the case of drug prohibition, bankers and lawyers in anti-money laundering, and judges and politicians in extradition.

For almost tautological reasons, institutional factors should explain an important share of state preferences on institutional issues. To a slightly lesser degree, the same should hold true for the range of institutional membership. And indeed, states are typically concerned with the 'goodness of fit' between existing institutions and the arrangements to be created.[62]

However, this comes in many different and often contradicting forms. If an international organization, such as the United Nations or the European Union, is already competent for an issue, then it is likely to become a focal point for new institutional arrangements. International cooperation can be 'locked' into an existing international organization, and this makes it more difficult for states to consider wider or deeper alternatives. In still other cases, states see their national legal or constitutional orders as incompatible with certain options. Moreover, perceived institutional strengths of domestic agencies are often projected to the international level. Or, conversely, countries sometimes see their domestic agencies as too backward-looking or closed-minded for increased cooperation. On the other hand, international cooperation is sometimes seen as a vehicle for improving the performance of domestic agencies.

Conclusion

This book is an attempt at combining the best from three different academic worlds: theoretical focus, methodological rigor, and empirical accuracy. Moreover, it is based on a combination of qualitative and quantitative analysis. Despite the linear progression of the argument, the reader shall not be betrayed. The book is an exercise in a pragmatic research strategy, namely abduction, and not in deductive theory testing, the inductive accumulation of theoretical facts, or any other familiar social scientific template.

At the beginning of my research, I was not in a position to derive testable hypotheses from ready-made theories. The only truly elaborate theories of state preference formation were Moravcsik's liberal theory of international politics and liberal intergovernmentalism. Neither of the two seemed easily applicable to international police cooperation. In the absence of plausible theories to be tested, a more modest procedure seemed to be warranted. Abduction provided a reasonable alternative to 'cavalier' deduction and 'myopic' induction.

In any case, abduction is not simply a weaker alternative to theory testing when the latter option is unavailable. On the contrary, abduction can lead to analytic and synthetic results, even of a theoretical nature, that are unattainable by any other method. In fact, other scholars have attempted deductive theory testing, for example with regard to European state preferences on Common Foreign and Security Policy (Koenig-Archibugi 2004) and European integration more in general (Aspinwall 2002, 2007). While I certainly admire these attempts and their results, it is hard to imagine that a similar approach would ever have allowed for a comprehensive mapping of international police cooperation, as offered in the present study.

The procedure employed rests on a combination of induction, deduction, and – most importantly – conceptual analysis. A variety of distinctions was tried and tested for their importance in structuring the field under investigation. While it would be presumptuous to pass the results as a general theory of national preference formation, it has been possible to construct a domain-specific theory of state preferences on international police cooperation from the careful study of a relatively large set of empirical cases.

On the descriptive side, the study has produced plenty of contextual knowledge on systematic patterns of European state preferences with regard to international policing, both in the field of terrorism and in the field of drugs, and both for the 1960s/1970s and for the 1990s/2000s. The most useful conceptual distinction was between different levels on the 'chain of coercion', as well as between the 'scope', 'range', and 'depth' of international cooperation.

On the explanatory side, I started from concepts loosely associated with social scientific theories: material interests, institutional frameworks, and normative ideas. This was combined with a distinction between the three familiar levels of analysis: domestic, national, and international. Although these concepts are loosely connected with broader strands of international relations theory such as realism, institutionalism, or normative theory, rather than 'testing' such 'isms' I moved back and forth between the conceptual and the phenomenal world in order to find patterns of similarity and difference within a class of phenomena. The formulation of a 'new' theory was only the final step, and not the first one, in this hermeneutic process.

In a nutshell, the main results can be summarized in two propositions:

1 There is a positive relationship between state preferences on the substantive scope, membership range, and institutional depth of international police cooperation. Preferences on broadening, widening, and deepening cooperation tend to be mutually supportive.
2 State preferences on international policing are mainly determined by functional incentives, while the constraining effect of the national interest in sovereignty, as well as the positive and negative socialization effects of institutions should also be taken into account.

As an adherent of pragmatism, I should certainly handle theoretical labels with care. However since social scientific theories always sail under some terminological flag, let me call the first proposition the *synergetic theory of preference constellations*. For the second proposition, which reconciles neoclassical functionalism with the political insights of orthodox realism and social institutionalism, my favourite label is *political functionalism*.

While the synergetic theory of preference constellations and political functionalism are clearly appropriate to capture European state preferences on international police cooperation, it is legitimate to speculate about their wider applicability. A conclusive answer to this question would require furthur empirical research.

10 Postscript

The best thing about abduction is that the researcher, instead of only confirming, modifying or disconfirming hypotheses derived from prefabricated theories, actually learns something new about his field of inquiry. For example, I personally sympathize with the conservative view that the monopoly of force is the core of sovereign statehood, which states should be careful not to surrender beyond their territorial reach of control. So my own cognitive and emotional bias was that, in this particular policy field, national sovereignty should play a more important role than functional incentives. To my own surprise, however, I have found that states are more concerned with problem solving than with territorial sovereignty even in this most unlikely field of international cooperation (Mitrany 1943: 25–7, 34; Morgenthau 1963).

While I appreciate well-intentioned attempts at using international cooperation to solve intractable problems such as terrorism and drugs, my feelings as a citizen of a European nation-state are rather mixed. The fact that states believe that international cooperation will be helpful in solving some problem does not really reassure me that this belief is actually warranted. After all, states have cooperated against terrorism, drugs, and other forms of serious international crime for more than a century, and still it does not seem that a definitive solution to any of these problems is in sight (Andreas and Nadelmann 2006).

Should I now invert the expectations suggested by my initial cognitive and emotional biases, and conclude from my findings that a European Leviathan, or even a world state, is simply inevitable (Wendt 2003)? Not necessarily! While a problem solving attitude explains an important part of the empirical evidence, it does not explain everything. States quite frequently oppose international cooperation for sovereignty reasons, and for many other motives. Abduction has made it possible to ponder the relative importance of these reasons.

In any case, in the political world one cannot simply deduce outcomes from preferences. Regardless of well-known systemic effects such as the so-called security dilemma, this becomes immediately clear if one thinks about international cooperation in terms of a policy cycle.[1]

A policy cycle starts with a real-world problem. If dealing with the problem unilaterally is perceived as too costly, states are induced to formulate preferences on the desired terms of international cooperation. Provided that there is sufficient consensus for an agreement to seem at all possible, states can be expected to negotiate with each other. In some cases, although certainly not always, the bargaining process will engender a substantive and institutional outcome, which will be implemented more or less faithfully. Due to problems of incomplete contracting, deliberate and involuntary defection, and unintended consequences, more often than not the result turns out to be unsatisfactory. Compliance is not automatic, nor are the 'real' problems always dealt with effectively. Due to these and similar difficulties, states will formulate new preferences on future international cooperation, and the cycle will start anew.

For a full understanding of the political process, one would have to start from the beginning of the policy cycle, with state preferences, and then work through the bargaining stage to the agreements finally reached. Furthermore, one would have to consider how problems with implementation and compliance can feed back into new preferences in a new policy cycle. While it was clearly beyond the scope of this book to discuss the entire policy cycle, it would be interesting to know more about the other stages.[2] There is reason to hope that a careful analysis of state preferences is a good starting point for future research on political process.

There are other interesting avenues for future research. Now that systematic patterns of similarity and difference have been detected for European state preferences on international police cooperation, other researchers are free to 'test' my findings in a more positivist mood. Furthermore, theories of preference formation can be developed for other actor constellations, policy fields, or regions. It will be interesting to examine the preferences not only of states but also of non-state actors; not only in Europe but also in other areas of the world; and not only on police cooperation but also with regard to other fields of international relations, as for example military cooperation, environmental policy, or regional integration.

By following the procedure outlined in this book, or a modified version thereof, it should be possible to construct theories of preference formation for virtually any kind of actor, policy field, time period, and world region. Beyond that, nothing should prevent other researchers from using the pragmatic research strategy of abduction, as practised in this book, as a useful template for any kind of empirical research they may wish to conduct.[3]

In our scholarly quest to understand the international political process, we can be greatly helped by domain-specific theories of national preference formation. Although it is important to understand 'who gets what, when, how' in international politics, this is not sufficient. The question of 'who wants what, when, why' is equally relevant. Similarly, it is possible that decision makers and diplomats seeking to make good bargains in the international arena will greatly benefit from better understanding the preferences of their fellow actors.

There is reason to be confident that further exercises in abduction may foster results that are interesting not only to academics concerned with international relations theory, but also to practitioners in need of useful roadmaps in order to be better prepared for the contingencies of concrete situations. Ultimately, abduction furthers one of the noblest tasks of social science: getting an analytical grasp on important segments of what we experience as reality.

Appendix 1

First dataset

This dataset contains positive, negative, or neutral values for the preferences of each country on individual issues regarding the substantive scope and institutional depth of international police cooperation (the first eight values on institutional depth are missing). For every single issue, the standard deviation (SD) measures the degree to which it was or is contested. Please see pp. 25–8 for furthur details on coding.

An electronic version of the dataset, including comments on all scores, is available at <http://www.joerg-friedrichs.de/policingdata>.

				Issue	Britain	France	Germany	Italy	SD
01–04	Terrorism	Legitimization	1970s	Scope 1	–1	1	–1	–1	1.00
				Scope 2	–1	1	–1	1	1.15
				Scope 3	1	0	1	–1	0.96
				Scope 4	–1	0	1	–1	0.96
				Depth 1	—	—	—	—	—
				Depth 2	—	—	—	—	—
				Depth 3	—	—	—	—	—
				Depth 4	—	—	—	—	—
05–08	Terrorism	Legitimization	2000s	Scope 1	–1	0	1	0	0.82
				Scope 2	–1	1	1	0	0.96
				Scope 3	1	0	1	1	0.50
				Scope 4	–1	–1	–1	–1	0.00
				Depth 1	—	—	—	—	—
				Depth 2	—	—	—	—	—
				Depth 3	—	—	—	—	—
				Depth 4	—	—	—	—	—
09–12	Terrorism	Methods	1970s	Scope 1	1	1	1	0	0.50
				Scope 2	0	–1	0	–1	0.58
				Scope 3	1	–1	1	1	1.00
				Scope 4	–1	–1	0	0	0.58
				Depth 1	1	1	1	1	0.00
				Depth 2	1	0	–1	–1	0.96
				Depth 3	1	1	1	1	0.00
				Depth 4	0	0	–1	1	0.82
13–16	Terrorism	Methods	2000s	Scope 1	–1	–1	1	1	1.15
				Scope 2	0	–1	1	0	0.82
				Scope 3	1	1	0	0	0.58
				Scope 4	1	1	1	0	0.50
				Depth 1	–1	–1	–1	–1	0.00
				Depth 2	–1	–1	1	1	1.15
				Depth 3	–1	–1	1	1	1.15
				Depth 4	–1	0	0	–1	0.58
17–20	Terrorism	Authorization	1970s	Scope 1	1	–1	–1	0	0.96
				Scope 2	1	–1	–1	0	0.96
				Scope 3	1	–1	0	0	0.82
				Scope 4	–1	1	1	1	1.00
				Depth 1	1	–1	1	1	1.00
				Depth 2	1	–1	1	–1	1.15
				Depth 3	1	–1	1	0	0.96
				Depth 4	–1	1	0	1	0.96
21–24	Terrorism	Authorization	2000s	Scope 1	1	0	0	–1	0.82
				Scope 2	1	1	–1	–1	1.15
				Scope 3	1	0	–1	–1	0.96
				Scope 4	1	1	–1	–1	1.15
				Depth 1	1	1	0	–1	0.96
				Depth 2	1	1	0	–1	0.96
				Depth 3	0	1	0	–1	0.82
				Depth 4	1	1	1	–1	1.00

Table Continued

				Issue	*Britain*	*France*	*Germany*	*Italy*	*SD*
25–28	Drugs	Legitimization	1970s	Scope 1	–1	1	–1	0	0.96
				Scope 2	–1	1	–1	–1	1.00
				Scope 3	–1	–1	1	0	0.96
				Scope 4	–1	0	–1	0	0.58
				Depth 1	–1	1	1	0	0.96
				Depth 2	–1	–1	1	0	0.96
				Depth 3	–1	1	0	0	0.82
				Depth 4	–1	–1	–1	0	0.50
29–32	Drugs	Legitimization	2000s	Scope 1	1	1	1	1	0.00
				Scope 2	1	1	–1	0	0.96
				Scope 3	–1	1	–1	1	1.15
				Scope 4	–1	1	–1	1	1.15
				Depth 1	0	–1	–1	1	0.96
				Depth 2	1	0	1	0	0.58
				Depth 3	1	1	1	1	0.00
				Depth 4	0	1	1	–1	0.96
33–36	Drugs	Methods	1970s	Scope 1	0	1	1	0	0.58
				Scope 2	0	1	1	1	0.50
				Scope 3	0	1	1	0	0.58
				Scope 4	0	1	1	1	0.50
				Depth 1	0	1	1	1	0.50
				Depth 2	0	1	1	1	0.50
				Depth 3	0	1	1	1	0.50
				Depth 4	–1	1	1	0	0.96
37–40	Drugs	Methods	2000s	Scope 1	1	1	–1	1	1.00
				Scope 2	0	1	–1	0	0.82
				Scope 3	–1	1	1	1	1.00
				Scope 4	1	1	–1	1	1.15
				Depth 1	1	1	–1	1	1.00
				Depth 2	–1	1	0	1	0.96
				Depth 3	1	1	0	–1	0.96
				Depth 4	1	0	–1	0	0.82
41–44	Drugs	Authorization	1970s	Scope 1	0	1	1	0	0.58
				Scope 2	0	1	1	0	0.58
				Scope 3	0	1	1	0	0.58
				Scope 4	0	1	1	0	0.58
				Depth 1	0	1	1	0	0.58
				Depth 2	0	1	0	0	0.50
				Depth 3	0	0	1	0	0.50
				Depth 4	0	–1	–1	0	0.58
45–48	Drugs	Authorization	2000s	Scope 1	1	1	1	1	0.00
				Scope 2	1	1	1	1	0.00
				Scope 3	1	1	1	–1	1.00
				Scope 4	0	1	1	1	0.50
				Depth 1	1	1	1	1	0.00
				Depth 2	–1	1	1	1	1.00
				Depth 3	–1	1	1	0	0.96
				Depth 4	0	1	0	–1	0.82

Appendix 2

Second dataset

This dataset contains, for all 48 case studies, ordinal data measuring the willingness of a country on three dimensions of international police cooperation: substantive scope, membership range, and institutional depth (the first eight values on institutional depth are missing). A general index (Ξ) is computed from these three sub-indices on scope, range, and depth. Please see pp. 25–8 for further details on the seven parameters (P1–P7) from which all indices are computed.

An electronic version of the dataset, including a codebook and comments on all scores, is available at <http://www.joerg-friedrichs.de/policingdata>.

					P1	P2	P3	P4	P5	P6	P7	Scope	Range	Depth	Ξ
01	Terrorism	Legitimization	1970s	Britain	1	–2	0	0	0	—	—	–0.25	0.00	—	–0.13
02	Terrorism	Legitimization	1970s	France	1	2	4	4	4	—	—	0.75	1.00	—	0.88
03	Terrorism	Legitimization	1970s	Germany	1	0	2	4	4	—	—	0.25	1.00	—	0.63
04	Terrorism	Legitimization	1970s	Italy	1	–2	2	4	4	—	—	0.00	1.00	—	0.50
05	Terrorism	Legitimization	2000s	Britain	–1	–2	0	0	0	—	—	–1.00	–1.00	—	–1.00
06	Terrorism	Legitimization	2000s	France	1	0	2	4	4	—	—	0.25	1.00	—	0.63
07	Terrorism	Legitimization	2000s	Germany	1	2	4	4	4	—	—	0.75	1.00	—	0.88
08	Terrorism	Legitimization	2000s	Italy	1	0	0	4	4	—	—	0.00	1.00	—	0.50
09	Terrorism	Methods	1970s	Britain	1	3	4	3.5	3.5	4	4	0.88	0.88	1.00	0.92
10	Terrorism	Methods	1970s	France	1	–2	0	2	2	–1	0	–0.25	0.50	–0.13	0.04
11	Terrorism	Methods	1970s	Germany	1	2	4	3.5	3.5	4	4	0.75	0.88	1.00	0.88
12	Terrorism	Methods	1970s	Italy	0	–2	0	0.5	0.5	0	0	–0.25	0.00	0.00	–0.08
13	Terrorism	Methods	2000s	Britain	1	1	2	1	0	–4	0	0.38	0.13	–0.50	0.00
14	Terrorism	Methods	2000s	France	1	0	2	1	0	–3	0	0.25	0.13	–0.38	0.00
15	Terrorism	Methods	2000s	Germany	1	3	2	2	0	1	2	0.63	0.25	0.38	0.42
16	Terrorism	Methods	2000s	Italy	1	1	2	3	0	0	2	0.38	0.38	0.25	0.33
17	Terrorism	Authorization	1970s	Britain	1	2	2	2	2	2	2	0.50	0.50	0.50	0.50
18	Terrorism	Authorization	1970s	France	–1	–2	0	0	0	–2	0	–1.00	–1.00	–1.00	–1.00
19	Terrorism	Authorization	1970s	Germany	1	–1	0	2	2	3	2	–0.13	0.50	0.63	0.33
20	Terrorism	Authorization	1970s	Italy	1	1	0	2	2	1	0	0.13	0.50	0.13	0.25
21	Terrorism	Authorization	2000s	Britain	1	4	4	3	2	3	4	1.00	0.63	0.88	0.83
22	Terrorism	Authorization	2000s	France	1	2	4	2	2	4	4	0.75	0.50	1.00	0.75
23	Terrorism	Authorization	2000s	Germany	1	–3	2	2	2	1	2	–0.13	0.50	0.38	0.25
24	Terrorism	Authorization	2000s	Italy	–1	–4	0	0	0	–4	0	–1.00	–1.00	–1.00	–1.00

(continued)

Table Continued

					P1	*P2*	*P3*	*P4*	*P5*	*P6*	*P7*	*Scope*	*Range*	*Depth*	Ξ
25	Drugs	Legitimization	1970s	Britain	1	–4	0	4	1	–4	0	–0.50	0.63	–0.50	–0.13
26	Drugs	Legitimization	1970s	France	1	1	2	4	0	0	2	0.38	0.50	0.25	0.38
27	Drugs	Legitimization	1970s	Germany	1	–2	0	4	0	1	2	–0.25	0.50	0.38	0.21
28	Drugs	Legitimization	1970s	Italy	1	–1	0	3	0	0	0	–0.13	0.38	0.00	0.08
29	Drugs	Legitimization	2000s	Britain	1	0	0	2	0	2	0	0.00	0.25	0.25	0.17
30	Drugs	Legitimization	2000s	France	1	4	0	3	1	1	2	0.50	0.50	0.38	0.46
31	Drugs	Legitimization	2000s	Germany	1	–2	–2	1.5	–0.5	2	0	–0.50	0.13	0.25	–0.04
32	Drugs	Legitimization	2000s	Italy	1	3	2	4	2	1	2	0.63	0.75	0.38	0.58
33	Drugs	Methods	1970s	Britain	0	0	0	0	0	–1	0	0.00	0.00	0.00	0.00
34	Drugs	Methods	1970s	France	1	4	4	3	3	4	4	1.00	0.75	1.00	0.92
35	Drugs	Methods	1970s	Germany	1	4	4	3	2	4	4	1.00	0.63	1.00	0.88
36	Drugs	Methods	1970s	Italy	1	2	2	3	3	3	2	0.50	0.75	0.63	0.63
37	Drugs	Methods	2000s	Britain	1	–1	2	4	4	2	2	0.13	1.00	0.50	0.54
38	Drugs	Methods	2000s	France	1	4	4	3	3	3	2	1.00	0.75	0.63	0.79
39	Drugs	Methods	2000s	Germany	1	–2	0	3	3	–2	0	–0.25	0.75	–0.25	0.08
40	Drugs	Methods	2000s	Italy	1	3	4	2	2	1	2	0.88	0.50	0.38	0.58
41	Drugs	Authorization	1970s	Britain	0	0	0	0	0	0	0	0.00	0.00	0.00	0.00
42	Drugs	Authorization	1970s	France	1	4	4	3	3	1	4	1.00	0.75	0.63	0.79
43	Drugs	Authorization	1970s	Germany	1	4	4	3	2	1	2	1.00	0.63	0.38	0.67
44	Drugs	Authorization	1970s	Italy	0	0	0	0	0	0	0	0.00	0.00	0.00	0.00
45	Drugs	Authorization	2000s	Britain	1	3	0	2	1	–1	0	0.38	0.38	–0.13	0.21
46	Drugs	Authorization	2000s	France	1	4	0	2	1	4	2	0.50	0.38	0.75	0.54
47	Drugs	Authorization	2000s	Germany	1	4	0	3	2	3	4	0.50	0.63	0.88	0.67
48	Drugs	Authorization	2000s	Italy	1	2	0	2	1	1	2	0.25	0.38	0.38	0.33

Appendix 3

Third dataset

This dataset contains eight causal pathways for each of the 48 case studies, differentiating between the general attitude of a country ('Mindset') and its preferences on substantive scope ('Scope'), membership range ('Range'), and institutional depth ('Depth'). For further details on coding please see pp. 29–31 and the list of abbreviations at the bottom of this dataset.

An electronic version of the dataset, including comments on all values, is available at <http://www.joerg-friedrichs.de/policingdata>.

					Mindset	*Scope*	*Range*	*Depth*
01	Terrorism	Legitimization	1970s	Britain	NatIntPos	NatIntNeg	NatIntNeg	IntInstNeg
					NatIntNeg	NatIdPos	NatIntNeg	NatIntNeg
02	Terrorism	Legitimization	1970s	France	NatIdPos	NatIdPos	IntIntPos	IntInstNeg
					NatIntNeg	NatIntPos	IntInstPos	NatIntNeg
03	Terrorism	Legitimization	1970s	Germany	NatIntPos	NatIntNeg	NatIntPos	IntInstNeg
					IntIdPos	IntIdPos	IntInstPos	NatIntPos
04	Terrorism	Legitimization	1970s	Italy	NatIdPos	NatIntNeg	NatIdPos	IntInstNeg
					NatIntPos	NatIdNeg	IntIntPos	NatIdPos
05	Terrorism	Legitimization	2000s	Britain	NatIntNeg	NatIntNeg	NatIntNeg	NatIntNeg
					IntInstNeg	IntInstNeg	IntInstNeg	IntInstNeg
06	Terrorism	Legitimization	2000s	France	IntIntPos	NatIntPos	IntIntPos	IntInstPos
					NatIntPos	NatIdPos	IntIdPos	IntInstPos
07	Terrorism	Legitimization	2000s	Germany	IntIdPos	IntIntPos	IntIdPos	IntIntPos
					IntIntPos	NatIdPos	IntIntPos	IntInstNeg
08	Terrorism	Legitimization	2000s	Italy	NatIntNeg	NatIntPos	IntInstPos	NatIntNeg
					IntInstPos	IntInstNeg	NatIntNeg	IntInstPos
09	Terrorism	Methods	1970s	Britain	NatIntPos	NatIntPos	DomInstPos	DomInstPos
					DomInstPos	DomInstPos	NatInstPos	DomInstPos
10	Terrorism	Methods	1970s	France	NatIntPos	NatIntNeg	DomInstPos	DomInstNeg
					NatIntPos	DomInstNeg	NatIntPos	NatIntNeg
11	Terrorism	Methods	1970s	Germany	NatIntPos	DomInstPos	DomInstPos	NatIntPos
					DomInstPos	NatIdNeg	NatIntPos	NatIntPos
12	Terrorism	Methods	1970s	Italy	NatIntNeg	DomInstNeg	NatIntNeg	DomInstNeg
					NatIntNeg	NatIntNeg	DomInstNeg	NatIntNeg

13	Terrorism	Methods	2000s	Britain	NatIntPos DomInstNeg	DomInstNeg NatIntPos	NatIntNeg DomInstNeg	NatIntNeg DomInstNeg
14	Terrorism	Methods	2000s	France	IntIntPos DomInstNeg	DomInstNeg DomInstPos	NatIntNeg DomInstNeg	NatIntNeg DomInstNeg
15	Terrorism	Methods	2000s	Germany	IntIntPos DomInstPos	DomInstPos NatIdPos	NatIdNeg IntInstNeg	NatIdPos DomInstPos
16	Terrorism	Methods	2000s	Italy	IntIntPos NatIntPos	DomInstNeg NatIntPos	IntInstPos DomInstPos	DomInstNeg NatIntPos
17	Terrorism	Authorization	1970s	Britain	NatIntPos IntInstPos	NatIntPos NatIntNeg	NatInstNeg IntInstPos	NatIntPos NatIntNeg
18	Terrorism	Authorization	1970s	France	NatIdNeg NatIntNeg	NatInstNeg NatIdPos	NatIdNeg IntInstPos	DomIdNeg NatIdPos
19	Terrorism	Authorization	1970s	Germany	NatIntPos IntIdPos	NatInstNeg DomInstNeg	IntInstNeg NatIntPos	NatIntPos IntIdPos
20	Terrorism	Authorization	1970s	Italy	IntIntPos IntIdPos	NatInstNeg NatIdPos	NatIntPos IntIntPos	NatInstNeg NatIdPos
21	Terrorism	Authorization	2000s	Britain	NatIntPos IntIdPos	NatIntPos IntIdPos	NatIntPos IntInstPos	NatInstPos NatIntNeg
22	Terrorism	Authorization	2000s	France	IntIntPos NatIdPos	IntIntPos NatIdNeg	IntIdPos IntInstPos	NatInstPos DomInstPos
23	Terrorism	Authorization	2000s	Germany	IntIdPos NatInstNeg	IntIdPos NatInstNeg	IntIdPos IntInstPos	IntIdPos NatInstNeg
24	Terrorism	Authorization	2000s	Italy	DomIdNeg DomIntNeg	DomIdNeg DomIntNeg	DomIdNeg DomIntNeg	DomIdNeg DomIntNeg

(continued)

Table Continued

					Mindset	*Scope*	*Range*	*Depth*
25	Drugs	Legitimization	1970s	Britain	NatIntNeg NatIntPos	DomIntNeg NatIntNeg	NatIntPos IntIntPos	NatIntNeg IntInstNeg
26	Drugs	Legitimization	1970s	France	IntIntPos NatIdPos	IntIntPos NatIntPos	IntIntPos IntIntPos	IntIntPos NatIntNeg
27	Drugs	Legitimization	1970s	Germany	NatIntNeg NatIntPos	DomIntNeg NatIdPos	NatIntPos IntIntPos	NatIdPos IntInstNeg
28	Drugs	Legitimization	1970s	Italy	IntInstPos NatIntPos	DomIntNeg NatIntPos	IntInstPos NatIntPos	NatIntNeg NatIntPos
29	Drugs	Legitimization	2000s	Britain	IntInstPos NatIntNeg	IntInstPos DomIntNeg	IntInstPos NatIntNeg	NatIntPos NatIntNeg
30	Drugs	Legitimization	2000s	France	NatIdPos IntIntPos	DomInstPos IntIntPos	IntIntPos IntIntPos	NatIntPos NatIntNeg
31	Drugs	Legitimization	2000s	Germany	IntIntPos NatIdNeg	NatIdNeg NatIdNeg	IntInstNeg NatIntPos	IntIntPos NatIntPos
32	Drugs	Legitimization	2000s	Italy	DomIdPos NatIntPos	DomIdPos NatIntPos	IntIntPos IntInstPos	IntInstPos DomIdNeg
33	Drugs	Methods	1970s	Britain	NatInstNeg DomIdNeg	NatInstNeg DomIdNeg	NatInstNeg DomIdNeg	NatInstNeg DomIdNeg
34	Drugs	Methods	1970s	France	IntIntPos NatIntPos	DomIntPos NatIntPos	NatIdPos NatIntPos	DomIntPos NatIdPos
35	Drugs	Methods	1970s	Germany	NatIntPos IntIntPos	IntInstPos DomIntPos	IntIntPos NatIntPos	DomIntPos NatIntPos
36	Drugs	Methods	1970s	Italy	NatIntPos NatInstNeg	NatIntPos NatInstNeg	NatIntPos NatIntPos	NatIntPos DomInstNeg

37	Drugs	Methods	2000s	Britain	NatIntPos IntIntPos	NatIdPos NatInstNeg	NatIntPos NatIntPos	NatIdPos DomIntNeg
38	Drugs	Methods	2000s	France	IntIntPos NatIntPos	NatIntPos NatIntPos	NatIntPos NatIntNeg	NatIdPos NatInstNeg
39	Drugs	Methods	2000s	Germany	IntInstPos NatIntPos	DomIntNeg NatIntPos	NatIntPos NatIntNeg	IntInstPos NatInstNeg
40	Drugs	Methods	2000s	Italy	NatIntPos IntIntPos	DomInstPos DomIntNeg	NatIntPos NatIntNeg	NatIntPos IntInstNeg
41	Drugs	Authorization	1970s	Britain	NatIntNeg NatInstNeg	NatIntNeg DomInstNeg	NatInstNeg DomInstNeg	NatIntNeg DomInstNeg
42	Drugs	Authorization	1970s	France	IntIntPos NatIntPos	IntIntPos NatIntPos	IntIntPos NatIntPos	DomIntPos NatIntNeg
43	Drugs	Authorization	1970s	Germany	IntIntPos NatIntPos	NatIntPos DomIntPos	NatIntPos DomIntPos	NatIntPos NatIntNeg
44	Drugs	Authorization	1970s	Italy	NatIntNeg DomInstNeg	NatIntNeg DomInstNeg	NatIntNeg DomInstNeg	NatIntNeg DomInstNeg
45	Drugs	Authorization	2000s	Britain	NatIntPos DomIntPos	NatIntPos DomIntNeg	IntInstPos IntInstNeg	NatIntNeg DomIntPos
46	Drugs	Authorization	2000s	France	NatIntPos NatIntPos	NatIntPos NatIntPos	IntInstPos IntInstNeg	NatIntPos NatIntNeg
47	Drugs	Authorization	2000s	Germany	NatIdPos NatIdNeg	NatIdPos NatInstPos	IntInstPos IntInstNeg	NatIdPos NatIdNeg
48	Drugs	Authorization	2000s	Italy	NatIntPos DomInstNeg	NatIntPos NatIdNeg	IntInstPos IntInstNeg	NatIntPos DomInstNeg

Abbreviations
First syllable: Dom = Domestic; Nat = National; Int = International.
Second syllable: Int = Interests; Inst = Institutions; Id = Ideas.
Third syllable: Pos = Positive impact; Neg = Negative impact.

Notes

1 Introduction

1 For a recent introduction to international police cooperation see Andreas and Nadelmann 2006; concerning transatlantic counter-terrorism cooperation see also Rees 2006; for monographs on various aspects of international policing see especially Anderson 1989; Nadelmann 1993; Fijnaut and Marx 1995; Busch 1995; Bigo 1996; Busch 1999; Reinares 2000; Wilkinson 2000; Koenig and Das 2001; Alexander 2002; Deflem 2002; Shepticky 2002a; Buckley and Fawn 2003; Leeuwen 2003; Alexander 2006. On Justice and Home Affairs (JHA) in the EU and other aspects of European police cooperation see Anderson and Boer 1993; Fijnaut 1993; Anderson *et al.* 1995; Hebenton and Thomas 1995; Tupman and Tupman 1999; Boer 2003; Elvins 2003; Mitsilegas *et al.* 2003; Occhipinti 2003; Apap 2004; Kleine 2004; N. Walker 2004; Glaeßner and Lorenz 2005; Balzacq and Carrera 2006; and the annual updates on Justice and Home Affairs in the supplement to the *Journal of Common Market Studies* (e.g. Monar 2006).

2 On the 'logic of appropriateness' vs. the 'logic of consequences' see March and Olsen 1989; 1998: 949–54.

3 While some constructivists stick to the concept of preferences (e.g. Risse 2000; Adler 2002), it becomes questionable why one should talk about preferences in the first place. It is only consequential that many constructivist authors avoid this technical term.

4 I am concerned with 'preferences over outcomes' and not with 'preferences over actions or policies' (see Powell 1994: 318).

5 While still using the term 'endogenous preferences', a similar understanding of preferences is employed in Hug and König 2002; Hug 2003.

6 To the extent that this is true, there is no need to follow social constructivists in abandoning the analytical distinction between national preference formation and inter-state bargaining.

7 In domestic politics, the picture is complicated by the role of parliaments, referenda, etc.

8 Weber himself uses the terms 'monopoly of legitimate physical coercion' and 'monopolization of legitimate violence'. Since the English noun 'force' already implies the real or perceived legitimacy of coercion or violence, I use the term 'monopoly of force' as a shortcut. For a good discussion in German language see Busch *et al.* 1985: 37–49.

9 For the partisan account of a right-wing professional advocate of private gun ownership see LaPierre 2006.

10 Totalitarian states are a partial exception to this rule (cf. Garland 2001: 109–10).

11 Readers not interested in reflections on 'Big Structures, Large Processes' (Tilly 1984) are kindly invited to skip this section and move immediately to p. 12.

12 Along with the elimination contest among territorial units, some authors state that there was also an elimination contest among types of political order. At the end of this process, large and centralized territorial units with a monopoly of force won out against competing types such as city-states (Tilly 1990; Spruyt 1994).

13 This went hand in hand with the formation of national collective identity (Hall 1999).

14 Under exceptional circumstances, well into the twentieth century continental European states sometimes called the military to interfere in domestic affairs (Johansen 2005).

15 For a sociological discussion of military power see Poggi 2000: 180–202. For a sociological discussion of the police, from a French standpoint, see Monjardet 1996.

16 For a more cynical account see Tilly 1985.

17 An interesting exception is, perhaps, the intensification of surveillance that has a tendency to shift policing techniques from last-resort control to the prevention of crime (Ball and Webster 2003).

18 However, globalization may lead to a situation where certain constituencies (e.g. resident aliens of Muslim religion) are not loyal enough to their state of residence (e.g. Britain or France) to accept violent measures inflicted upon members of their own community (e.g. suspected Islamic extremists).

19 In 2002, the Dutch Government fell because it had *not* committed its troops to using violence during the humanitarian intervention in Bosnia (Sion 2006: 456–7).

20 For a critique see Loader and Walker 2006, 2007.

21 Southern Africa constitutes a partial exception (Elrena Van der Spuy, personal communication; cf. id. 1997).

22 To my knowledge, the only serious attempt to study national preferences on international police cooperation in a systematic and theoretically meaningful way is Kleine 2004.

23 I owe this example to Kerstin Friedrichs.

24 See also Kolb 1984 on experiential learning.

25 For the vast literature on case-study research see only George and Bennett 2005; Gerring 2007.

26 In cases of doubt, it will be useful to turn to practitioners or scan the relevant literature in order to find the most important or the most typical cases.

27 When the research programme is more advanced, one can move towards the frontiers to sound out how far the concepts applied can be stretched without losing their analytical value.

28 For further references see George and Bennett 2005: 67–72.

29 A pragmatic approach is more radical than simply moving from 'variable-oriented research' to 'case-oriented research', where the final objective is still to detect necessary or sufficient causation (Ragin 2004). Instead, it moves further towards 'problem-oriented' and 'concept-oriented' research. Recent attempts at typological theory, as valuable as they are in expanding the boundaries of what is accepted as legitimate by the mainstream, fall short of this requirement since they still reduce causality to the search for law-like regularities in terms of dependent and independent variables (George and Bennett 2005: 233–62; Elman 2005).

2 Essentials

1 As the Italian Red Brigades put it, the aim of their fight was to create 'a new legality, a new power' (leaflet distributed in Milan in the spring of 1970).
2 The only topic that can, since the 1980s, compete in importance is the fight against illegal immigration (Mitsilegas *et al.* 2003; Pastore 2004).
3 The most abstract level – discursive conceptualization of deviant behaviour – is excluded here because it is better examined through discourse analysis (Leander 2005). The most concrete level – operational law enforcement – is excluded because, empirically, hardly any international cooperation can be observed at this level. At first glance, there seem to be some developments in the EU pointing in this direction, such as joint management of external borders and cross-border hot pursuit. On a closer look, however, it turns out that at least for the time being the formal power of arrest remains almost exclusively subject to territorial sovereignty (Friedrichs 2006b).
4 As in the field of terrorism, the case sample was submitted for approval to scholars and decision makers in different European countries.
5 The Single Convention on Narcotic Drugs was amended in 1972.
6 At the same time, the Pompidou group was set up on a French initiative in order to provide a European framework for the discussion of adequate methods of tackling drugs.
7 See also Marx 1988.
8 Since 11 September, the regime against money laundering has been muddled with the fight against terrorist finance. In this particular case, the analytical focus is therefore on the 1990s.
9 On the implementation of Joint Investigation Teams see Commission of the European Communities 2005a; 2005b.
10 For further details see Friedrichs *et al.* 2005.
11 The assumption underlying P1 is that, if a country is either opposed to an agreement or indifferent, then its preferences on details are hypocritical, and therefore irrelevant.
12 For empirical and categorical reasons, there are some minor but unavoidable problems. The parameters, none of which is interval-scaled, combine nominal (P1) and ordinal (P2–P7) scales. Not all of them are in the same interval, nor do they all have their arithmetical mean at {0}. The latter problem also applies to the indices, which are computed from the parameters. However, there is a justification for all of this. This book engages in a combination of 'cross-case analysis' with 'within-case analysis'. It is typical for this kind of analysis to combine different levels of measurement (Mahoney 2003: 360–1). Since the level of measurement and format of my data is somewhat debatable, for safety reasons I consistently assume that the three indices are ordinal and not interval-scaled, and use them for rank-order correlations only. This should be sufficient to remedy the problems mentioned.
13 On interests, institutions, and ideas see Goldstein and Keohane 1993; Garrett and Weingast 1993.
14 On levels of analysis see Waltz 1959; J.D. Singer 1961.
15 See also Moravcsik 1993a; Zürn 1997; Freund and Rittberger 2001.
16 For a critique of this article see Lieshout *et al.* 2004.
17 Apart from orthodox realism, there are 'softer' versions that expand realism to become a theory of (almost) everything. Since it is hardly possible to derive coherent expectations from such theories, they are not considered here (see Legro and Moravcsik 1999).

18 On institutionalism in general, see Hall and Taylor 1996; Simmons and Martin 2004.

19 According to Hall and Taylor (1996) there is a third variant: rational-choice institutionalism. This theory is not considered here because it does not understand institutions as a source of state preferences. Instead, it assumes that states have an instrumental interest in international institutions in order to overcome collective-action problems (Keohane 1982, 1989; Keohane and Martin 1995). Preferences are not explained by institutions but by interests. Accordingly, rational-choice institutionalism mostly seems to come down to the causal pathway 'national interests with a positive effect', which is covered by neoclassical functionalism.

20 See also the other contributions in Checkel 2005.

21 Cf. the notion of 'issue-specific interdependence' in Moravcsik and Nicolaïdis 1999: 60–9.

3 The comprehensive approach

1 Council Framework Decision of 13 June 2002 on Combating Terrorism (2002/475/JHA), published in *Official Journal of the European Communities* L 164, 22 June 2002, pp. 3–7; see also the proposal by the Commission contained in *Official Journal of the European Communities* C 233 E, 27 November 2001, pp. 300–304.

2 On defining terrorism more in general see Walter 2004.

3 For further details see Friedrichs 2006a: 72–4. As evidenced by recommendations 684 (1972) and 703 (1973) of the Parliamentary Assembly, there were also attempts at the Council of Europe to find a common understanding of international terrorism. However, there was no consensus among the Member States of the Council of Europe to establish a legal definition, and instead, the bargaining process ended with the adoption of the European Convention on the Suppression of Terrorism (see Chapter 5).

4 UN Doc. A/C.6/L.850: Draft convention, 25 September 1972.

5 UN Doc. A/RES/3034: GA resolution, 18 December 1972.

6 UN Doc. A/9028: Report of the Ad Hoc Committee, 1973, p. 20.

7 See the reports and summary records of the Ad Hoc Committee in UN Docs A/32/37, 28 April 1977; A/34/37, 17 April 1979; A/AC.160/SR.11–19, 1979. For secondary literature see Franck and Lockwood 1974; Dugard 1974, 1982; Murphy 1975, 1989; Hoveyda 1977; Levitt 1986; Toman 1991. Specifically on the position of the non-aligned countries and the communist world see Abellán Honrubia 1975; Rosen and Frank 1975; Blishchenko and Zhdanov 1984: 208–31.

8 UN Doc. A/9028: Report of the Ad Hoc Committee, 1973, annex 7b.

9 UN Doc. A/C.6/SR.1355–1374: Verbatim records of the Sixth Committee, November 1972.

10 UN Doc. A/32/37: Report of the Ad Hoc Committee, 28 April 1977, p. 14.

11 See the observations of states and the analytical study by the Secretary General in UN Docs A/AC.160/1, 16 May 1973; A/AC.160/1/Add.1, 12 June 1973; A/AC.160/2, 22 June 1973.

12 UN Doc. A/32/37: Report of the Ad Hoc Committee, 28 April 1977, p. 14.

13 See the following files from the British National Archives: CO 323/1466/11, 1937; HO 189/7, 1937; HO 189/8, 1937.

14 See the following files from the British National Archives: FCO 41/938, 1972; FCO 58/667, 1972; FCO 14/1078, 1972.

15 British National Archives FCO 41/938: Speaking note for meeting with MPs delegates to the Council of Europe, Autumn 1972 (undated).
16 British National Archives FCO 14/1078: Briefing for UN General Assembly, 19 October 1972.
17 Ibid.
18 British National Archives FCO 41/938: Letter by Mr. Gore Booth from the Near East and North Africa Department, 10 October 1972.
19 British National Archives FCO 14/1078: Briefing for UN General Assembly, 19 October 1972; see also Freeland in UN Doc. A/C.6/SR.1359, 15 November 1972.
20 British National Archives FCO 76/633: Confidential letter from New York, 23 November 1973.
21 Freeland in UN Doc. A/C.6/SR.1310, 25 September 1972.
22 For the most important British contributions to the debate consult the following UN documents: Douglas–Home in A/PV.2042, 27 September 1972; Freeland in A/C.6/SR.1390, 11 December 1972; Crowe in A/PV.2114, 18 December 1972; A/AC.160/1, 16 May 1973; A/9028, 1973, p. 28; Fifoot in A/C.6/SR.1581, 4 December 1975; A/32/37, 28 April 1977, pp. 33–4; A/C.6/32/SR.58, 29 November 1977; A/AC.160/SR.15, 28 March 1979; A/34/37, 17 April 1979, pp. 26–7.
23 For the debate at the Council of Europe see British National Archives FCO 41/938, 1972; FCO 41/1085, 1973.
24 French Diplomatic Archives NUOI 1409, Cote S. 50: Note on international terrorism from the Foreign Ministry in Paris to the French delegation at the United Nations in New York, 19 June 1973.
25 UN Doc. A/9028, 1973, p. 21.
26. Guiringaud in UN Doc. A/BUR/SR.201, 21 September 1972.
27. French Diplomatic Archives NUOI 1409, Cote S. 50: Note on international terrorism from the Foreign Ministry in Paris to the French delegation at the United Nations in New York, 19 June 1973. France did not address the problem of state terrorism.
28 French Diplomatic Archives NUOI 1409, Cote S. 50: Telegrams by the French representative at the United Nations M. de Guiringaud, 19 September 1972, 24 September 1972, and 3 October 1972.
29 Bessou in UN Doc. A/C.6/SR.1360, 15 November 1972; French Diplomatic Archives NUOI 1409, Cote S. 50: Note on the 51st meeting of the Committee of Ministers of the Council of Europe, 12 December 1972; Deniau in Council of Europe, CM (74) PV.2, 1974 (exact date unknown), p. 19; d'Haussy in UN Doc. A/32/37, 28 April 1977, p. 20.
30 France kept a critical distance from the Ad Hoc Committee and usually abstained from voting.
31 Lennuyeux-Comnenk in UN Doc. A/AC.160/SR.12, 28 March 1979.
32 See the case studies in the next two chapters.
33 Foreign Minister Giuseppe Medici in a plenary meeting of the Italian Senate, 6 October 1972.
34 Migliuolo in UN Doc. A/C.6/SR.1389, 11 December 1972.
35 Italian Diplomatic Archive: Telegram from New York, 20 January 1974.
36 Bensi in Council of Europe Doc. CM (74) PV.2, 1974 (exact date unknown), pp. 17–18.
37 Italian Diplomatic Archive: Telegrams of the Foreign Ministry to and from New York, November 1972.

38 UN Docs A/C.6/L.879, 27 November 1972; A/C.6/L.879/Rev.1, 8 December 1972; Vinci in UN Doc. A/C.6/SR.1386, 8 December 1972; Migliuolo in UN Docs A/C.6/SR.1389, 11 December 1972; A/AC.160/1, 16 May 1973, pp. 14–16.
39 A/AC160/1, 16 May 1973: Observations of states, pp. 14–16.
40 Ibid.
41 Italian Diplomatic Archive: Telegram from New York, 9 May 1973.
42 Danovi in UN Doc. A/32/37, 28 April 1977, pp. 22–3.
43 Bosco in UN Doc. A/C.6/32/SR.58, 29 November 1977, pp. 16–18.
44 Serafini in UN Doc. A/AC.160/SR.16, 28 March 1979, pp. 5–6.
45 Ibid.
46 'Una alleanza antiterrorismo fra Ovest, Est e non allineati' (interview with Giovanni Spadolini), *Corriere della Sera*, 28 September 1986.
47 Council of Europe Doc. CM (72) 187 revised, 7 December 1972.
48 German Federal Archive B 141/57344: Exchange of telegrams, September 1972–February 1973.
49 UN Doc. A/AC.160/1, 16 May 1973: Observations of states, pp. 10–11.
50 German Federal Archive B 141/57349: Position paper for UN deliberations (undated).
51 UN Doc. A/C.6/SR.1521, 9 December 1974; UN Doc. A/C.6/SR.1581, 4 December 1975.
52 Bracklo in UN Doc. A/C.6/SR.1521, 9 December 1974.
53 German Federal Archive B 141/57349: Briefing of the Foreign Ministry for the 29th General Assembly, 6 August 1974.
54 UN Doc. A/31/242, 28 September 1976: Letter from Foreign Minister Hans-Dietrich Genscher.
55 For further details see Friedrichs 2006a: 74–7.
56 UN Doc. A/RES/51/210: GA resolution, 16 January 1997; UN Doc. A/C.6/51/6: Draft convention submitted by India, 11 November 1996.
57 UN Doc. A/RES/54/110: GA resolution, 2 February 2000.
58 UN Doc. A/C.6/55/1: Revised draft convention submitted by India, 28 August 2000.
59 Reports of the Ad Hoc Committee: UN Docs A/56/37, 27 April 2001; A/57/37, 21 February 2002; A/58/37, 25 April 2003; A/59/37, 22 July 2004; A/60/37, 18 May 2005. Reports of the Working Group: UN Docs A/C.6/55/L.2, 19 October 2000; A/C.6/56/L.9, 29 October 2001; A/C.6/57/L.9, 16 October 2002; A/C.6/58/L.10, 10 October 2003; A/C.6/59/L.10, 8 October 2004; A/C.6/60/L.6, 14 October 2005.
60 UN Doc. A/59/894: Letter containing draft Comprehensive Convention, 12 August 2005, p. 9.
61 UN Doc. GA/L/3008: Press release, 4 October 1996.
62 Malaysia on behalf of the OIC Group, in UN. Doc. A/C.6/55/L.2: Report of the Working Group, 19 October 2000, p. 38.
63 See for example UN Doc. A/57/730–S/2003/178: Verbal note by Syria, 13 February 2003.
64 UN Doc. L/2993: Press release, 1 February 2002.
65 UN Doc. A/57/37: Report of the Ad Hoc Committee, 11 February 2002, p. 17.
66 UN Doc. A/59/894: Letter containing draft Comprehensive Convention, 12 August 2005.

67 UN Docs A/C.6/60/3: Letter from the Chairman of the OIC, 5 October 2005; Alsaidi on behalf of the OIC in A/C.6/60/SR.3, 24 October 2005, p. 6.
68 OIC Resolution No. 64/27-P, June 2000; a more recent formulation of the OIC position can be found in UN Doc. A/60/440–S/2005/658, 19 October 2005, p. 15.
69 Nesi in UN Doc. A/C.6/58/SR.6, 10 November 2003.
70 Terrorism Act, 2000; cf. the Prevention of Terrorism Act, 1989.
71 Greenstock in UN Doc. A/56/PV.12, 1 October 2001, p. 18.
72 See UN Doc. A/AC/252/2003/INF/1, 18 June 2003.
73 Merill House conversation, 27 February 2002, Carnegie Council on Ethics and International Affairs, <http://www.cceia.org> (accessed 2 August 2004).
74 Only once, in 2001, did the British Foreign Secretary Jack Straw declare to the Security Council that the UK would 'continue to work to complete the comprehensive convention on terrorism', while at the same time stressing the paramount importance of taking concrete measures (UN Doc. S/PV.4413, 12 November 2001, p. 15).
75 'World leaders seek terror definition', *New York Sun*, 8 July 2005; State Department, 'United States urges completion of terrorism convention', press release, 20 July 2005.
76 On the British position see 'London attacks should spur new efforts toward terrorism convention, diplomats say', *Associated Press*, 8 July 2005; 'British diplomats push Annan for a "no excuses" definition of terrorism', *Sunday Telegraph*, 24 July 2004.
77 The US and British initiative was in part prepared by Security Council resolution UN Doc. S/2000/792, 8 October 2004 and, in particular, by the elements for a definition suggested in the report of the High-Level Panel on Threats, Challenges and Change: UN Doc. A/59/565, 2 December 2004, p. 49.
78 'UN struggles to agree on definition of terrorism', *Agence France Presse*, 12 September 2005; 'The obstacles that block the way to a watertight definition of terrorism', *The Herald*, 17 September 2005; 'A reckless salesman: Blair's approach to terrorism will not suit all members', *Financial Times*, 19 September 2005.
79 'Blair frustrated as UN fails to agree on anti-terror action', *The Independent*, 15 September 2005.
80 Levitte in UN Doc. S/PV.4242, 6 December 2000, p. 19.
81 Chirac in UN Doc. SG/SM/7964: Press release, 19 September 2001.
82 Levitte in UN Doc. A/56/PV.13, 1 October 2001, p. 22; Védrine in UN Doc. S/PV.4413, 12 November 2001, p. 7.
83 Villepin in UN Doc. S/PV.4688, 20 January 2003, p. 26.
84 In French domestic law, terrorism was legally defined in 1986 (see UN Doc. S/2001/1274, 27 December 2001, p. 3; W. Vogel 2003: 39).
85 Barnier in UN Doc. A/59/PV.7, 23 September 2004, p. 28.
86 Levitte in UN Doc. S/PV.4242, 6 December 2000, p. 19; UN Doc. S/2001/1274, 27 December 2001, p. 3; Védrine at a meeting of the North Atlantic Council, 6 December 2001, <http://www.doc.diplomatie.fr> (accessed 26 June 2006); Villepin in UN Doc. S/PV.4688, 20 January 2003, p. 26.
87 'Germany not to allow any terrorist activity against India', *Press Trust of India*, 26 June 2001.
88 Fischer in UN Doc. A/56/PV.48, 12 November 2001, p. 12.
89 Fischer ibid. p. 11.
90 Kastrup in UN Doc. A/56/PV.15, 2 October 2001, p. 10.
91 Fischer in UN Doc. S/PV.4688, 20 January 2003, p. 5.

92 Fischer in UN Doc. A/56/PV.48, 12 November 2001, p. 11.
93 Kastrup in UN Doc. A/56/PV.10, 25 September 2001, p. 2.
94 Fischer in UN Doc. S/PV.4688, 20 January 2003, p. 6.
95 Personal communication with a diplomat of the German Foreign Ministry, April 2004; 'Germany says UN reform agenda falls short on disarmament and terrorism', *Agence France Presse*, 15 September 2005.
96 This is the line of argument taken in Friedrichs 2006a.
97 'Terrorismusbekämpfungin den Vereinten Nationen', <http://www.auswaertiges-amt.de> (accessed 26 June 2006).
98 Ruggiero in UN Doc. A/56/PV.46, 11 November 2001, p. 25.
99 Vento in UN Doc. A/56/PV.17, 3 October 2001, p. 23.
100 Italian House of Representatives, proceedings of 9 October 2001, p. 94; cf. also 'Putin und Berlusconi für Verabschiedung umfassender Konvention gegen internationalen Terrorismus', *RIA Novosty*, 3 November 2004.
101 Personal communication with a diplomat of the Italian Foreign Office, April 2004.
102 Italian House of Representatives, proceedings of 9 October 2001, p. 96.

4 Antiterrorist methods

1 Intelligence is understood here as elaborated information to help the forces of order act tactically or strategically in order to forestall terrorist incidents and/or prosecute terrorist fugitives.
2 Most of the literature on special commando units is unscientific (see for example Ryan *et al.* 2003).
3 Delta Force was established a bit later than most Western European special commando units.
4 TREVI = *Terrorisme, Radicalisme, Extremisme, Violence Internationale.*
5 British National Archives CAB 130/616: Meeting of the Cabinet Working Group on Terrorist Activities, 20 October 1972, p. 20.
6 GSG-9 = Grenzschutzgruppe 9; BKA = Bundeskriminalamt; BfV = Bundesamt für Verfassungsschutz.
7 For the GSG-9, see Wegener as quoted in Tophoven 1985: 82; for the BKA see Herold 1980; Becker 1980; Horchem 1980: 52.
8 Wegener in Shaw 1979: 134.
9 Genscher as quoted in Scholzen and Froese 2001: 10.
10 Wegener in Shaw 1979: 134.
11 The first Anti-Terror Workshop was organized in 1979; the Combat Team Competition took place from 1983 on a biennial basis (Tophoven 1985: 95; Scholzen and Froese 2001: 146–7).
12 Others contend that Wegener attended only on an observer mission (see for example Taillon 2001: 50).
13 Statements by Ulrich Wegener and Charles Beckwith, as quoted in Beckwith and Knox 1983: 223.
14 Von Putkamer, as quoted in John 1991: 79.
15 For journalistic accounts of foreign missions see Dietl 2004: 175–9; Schröm 2005.
16 PIOS = Personen, Institutionen, Objekte, Sachen.
17 British National Archives CAB 130/616: Protocol on a meeting of the Cabinet Working Group on Terrorist Activities, 20 October 1972, p. 20.

18 British National Archives CAB 130/616: *Working Group on Terrorist Activities*, 1972.
19 See Bonner 1993 for a clear and concise overview of the UK approach to antiterrorism in the 1970s and 1980s; for the 1990s see Bonner 2000.
20 British National Archives FCO 76/633: Letter from the Security Department of the Foreign and Commonwealth Office to the British embassies in the countries of the European Community, 28 March 1973.
21 British National Archives FCO 14/1078: *Measures to Combat Terrorism Including Hijacking*, 1972.
22 British National Archives FO 973/466: *Background Brief: International Terrorism and the European Response*, June 1986, p. 5.
23 But see note 11.
24 On the organizational setup of the British antiterrorist machinery see Smith 1987.
25 Margaret Thatcher, as quoted in British National Archives FO 973/440: *Background Brief: International Reaction to Terrorism*, January 1986, p. 7.
26 British National Archives CAB 130/616: Meetings of the Cabinet Working Group on Terrorist Activities, 9 October 1972 and 20 October 1972.
27 See Home Office Circular 153/77, quoted in Bunyan 1997: 33–4; Council of the European Communities 1978.
28 See also Bresler 1992: 160–2.
29 In House of Commons 1990b: 163, 166, a Government representative mentioned the following countries as the seven 'Friends of Trevi': Sweden, Austria, Morocco, Norway, Switzerland, USA, and Canada.
30 On the beginnings of British databases see Hain 1980: 96–109; Busch 1995: 211–15.
31 For a general overview see Centre des Archives Contemporaines 19910302: Inventory of files from the General Direction of the National Police, 1929–1982.
32 French Minister of Defence Michèle Alliot-Marie, 'GIGN: trente ans d'interventions', speech held on 15 June 2004 in Satory, France <http://gign.org/evenements/30ans-1.php> (accessed 20 July 2006).
33 French Diplomatic Archives NUOI 1409, Cote S. 50: Letter from the French Foreign Ministry to the French permanent representative at the United Nations, 8 August 1970.
34 For a good example of the French negotiating behaviour see British National Archives CAB 130/636: Report on the attack on the Saudi embassy in Paris, 12 September 1973.
35 French Diplomatic Archives NUOI 1409, Cote S. 50: Letter from the French Foreign Ministry to the French permanent representative at the United Nations, 8 August 1970.
36 French Diplomatic Archives NUOI 1409, Cote S. 50: Instructions concerning a report of the International Law Commission, 2 September 1972.
37 French Diplomatic Archives NUOI 1409, Cote S. 50: Note for the Political Affairs Direction of the Foreign Ministry on Recommendation 703 of the Consultative Assembly of the Council of Europe, 18 June 1973.
38 'Le club des Cinq redoute une réaction des "durs" de l'O.L.P.', *Le Monde*, 4 September 1982.
39 Centre des Archives Contemporaines 19910302: Inventory of files from the General Direction of the National Police, 1929–1982, p. 78.
40 Up until the mid-1980s, there was a consensus that Interpol was precluded by Article 3 of its statute from the exchange of information on terrorists.

41 During the 1970s, France was opposed to the further institutionalization of the European Community.
42 On the French sanctuary doctrine see Plenel 1986; Wieviorka 1990; Shapiro and Suzan 2003; see also pp. 95–9 and 104–5 in this volume.
43 For two staggering analyses of left-wing terrorism in Italy see Drake 1982; Jamieson 1989.
44 But see also the denial in Andreotti 1981b: 551.
45 For the general response of the Italian state to terrorism see Weinberg and Eubank 1987: 119–33; Della Porta 1993; R.H. Evans 1993; for the police response see Dobson and Payne 1982: 149–62; Rodotà 1984; Stortoni-Wortmann 2000; Andreassi 2000: 13–14; for the response of the secret services see Lutiis 1991.
46 In the heat of the Moro affair, Minister of the Interior Francesco Cossiga asked the British SAS, the German GSG-9 and the American CIA for help (Dobson and Payne 1982: 155).
47 For a very positive appraisal of Dalla Chiesa's work see Clutterbuck 1990: 31, 39–41. The main reason, however, why Italian terrorism was defeated in the end was the de-facto impunity, in the 1980s, for 'repentant' terrorists providing king's evidence.
48 NOCS = Nucleo Operativo Centrale di Sicurezza.
49 See also Jarach 1979: 215–17; Jamieson 1989: 163.
50 Subsequently the Italian Minister of the Interior Francesco Cossiga tried to make up for the failure of the Minister of Transport in preventing the terrorists from taking off (Martini 1999: 82–3; for a more negative version see Sievert 2004: 131–2).
51 Andreotti 1981a: 26 April 1978, 30 April 1978, 6 May 1978. The Prime Minister was also opposed to involving the International Committee of the Red Cross or the UN Secretary General (Andreotti 1981a: 14 April 1978, 16 April 1978, 25 April 1978, 26 April 1978).
52 For example, in 1978 Rome agreed to the establishment of a direct hotline between senior police officials from Italy, Germany, Austria, and Switzerland (Wilkinson 1979: 22).
53 Andreotti 1981a: 27 February 1979; see also Della Porta 1993: 159.
54 For early reflections on the importance of antiterrorist intelligence see Barr *et al.* 1979: 11–20; Kerstetter 1979.
55 Commission of the European Communities (2004) *Enhancing Police and Customs Cooperation in the European Union: Communication from the Commission to the European Parliament and the Council*, COM (2004) 376 final, 18 May 2004, pp. 26–9.
56 The importance of telecommunications data became most salient after the Madrid bombings of 9 March 2004, when mobile phones had served as detonators; see Council of the European Union, Doc. 8958/04, 28 April 2004: Draft framework decision on the retention of mobile phone and Internet communication data, submitted by Britain, France, Ireland and Sweden; see also Directive 2006/24/EC of the European Parliament and of the European Council of 15 March 2006 on the retention of data, contained in *Official Journal of the European Union* L 105, 13 April 2006, pp. 54–63.
57 International cooperation gradually enabled the BKA to reap more competences than were foreseen by Germany's federalist post-war constitution (Anderson 1989: 88; Busch 1999: 26–7).
58 'Europa rüstet sich: mehr Sicherheit statt Freiheit', *Spiegel Online*, 25 September 2001; see also 'Der Anschlag von Madrid und die Folgen: Europas Geheimdienste sollen künftig enger zusammenarbeiten', *Süddeutsche Zeitung*, 22 March 2004.

59 Federal Ministry of the Interior, 'Schily will EU-Informationsaustausch verbessern', press release, 19 March 2004.
60 'Schily lehnt Zentraldatei für Islamisten ab', *Frankfurter Allgemeine Zeitung*, 12 July 2004.
61 *Telekommunikationsgesetz*, published in *Bundesgesetzblatt I*, No. 29, 2004, pp. 1190–1243; 'Zankapfel Datenschutz: EU prüft Langfristspeicherung', *Frankfurter Rundschau*, 18 May 2004.
62 'Datenschutzbeauftragter gegen Datenspeicherung zur Terrorabwehr', *Agence France Presse*, 14 March 2005.
63 See for example 'Einigung auf EU-Datengesetz', *Süddeutsche Zeitung*, 3 December 2005.
64 See for example 'EU will Nachrichtendienste enger zusammenbinden', *Frankfurter Rundschau*, 9 June 2004.
65 On 27 May 2005, Germany signed the intergovernmental Prüm Convention for enhanced cooperation among seven EU Member States. It was hoped that this so-called 'Schengen III' agreement would play a pioneering role and would later be incorporated under the legal umbrella of the European Union (Balzacq *et al.* 2006; Kietz and Maurer 2007; for the text of the Convention see Council of the European Union 2005).
66 Federal Ministry of the Interior, 'Schily will EU-Informationsaustausch verbessern', press release, 19 March 2004.
67 'Europa rüstet sich: mehr Sicherheit statt Freiheit', *Spiegel Online*, 25 September 2001.
68 For a general overview see Cettina 2003.
69 Direction de la Surveillance du Territoire, Renseignement Généraux.
70 Direction Générale de la Sécurité Extérieure, Direction du Renseignement Militaire, Direction de la Protection et de la Sécurité de la Défense.
71 'Sécurité: les vues communes des Vingt-Cinq', *Libération*, 20 March 2004.
72 See for example 'La guerre contre le nouveau terrorisme pousse les services à se remettre en cause', *La Tribune*, 13 September 2001.
73 'Le Conseil JAI s'engage à respecter des délais précis pour rattraper les retards et adopter de nouvelles mesures pour la lutte antiterroriste', *Agence Europe*, 20 March 2004; Jacques Chirac, press conference at the European Council in Brussels, 25 March 2004, <http://www.elysee.fr> (accessed 15 July 2004).
74 'Help from France key in covert operations: Paris's "Alliance Base" targets terrorists', *Washington Post*, 3 July 2005; 'Die Agenten-Allianz', *Die Tageszeitung*, 5 July 2005.
75 'Le Conseil JAI s'engage à respecter des délais précis pour rattraper les retards et adopter de nouvelles mesures pour la lutte antiterroriste', *Agence Europe*, 20 March 2004; Jacques Chirac, press conference at the European Council in Brussels, 25 March 2004, <http://www.elysee.fr> (accessed 15 July 2004).
76 'Paris et Berlin lancent un "G 5" de l'antiterrorisme', *Le Figaro*, 20 March 2004.
77 'L'Europe chasse les terroristes en ordre dispersé', *Le Figaro*, 23 March 2004. This is not to deny that there are also some French experts promoting intelligence cooperation at the European level (*e.g.* Mermet 2001).
78 See for example 'Sarkozy: rendre pleinement efficaces les outils antiterroristes de l'UE', *Agence France Presse*, 18 March 2004.
79 Dominique de Villepin, 'La lutte contre le terrorisme et l'enjeu démocratique', speech held at the Universidad Complutense de Madrid, 12 July 2004, <http://www.interieur.gouv.fr> (accessed 16 July 2004).

80 See Note 65. Since the Prüm Convention was concluded outside the institutional framework of the EU, it was unofficially called by some the 'Schengen III' agreement.
81 'Le Conseil JAI s'engage à respecter des délais précis pour rattraper les retards et adopter de nouvelles mesures pour la lutte antiterroriste', *Agence Europe*, 20 March 2004.
82 'La France, Vigipirate et les Islamistes', *Le Figaro*, 13 September 2001.
83 'L'esprit d'après-Madrid souffle sur le G5', *Agence France Presse*, 6 July 2004.
84 Council of the European Union, Doc. 14107/02, 20 November 2002: Answers to a questionnaire on traffic data retention.
85 'Surveillance électronique: les Quinze se mobilisent après les attentats de Madrid', *ZDNet.FR*, 26 March 2004.
86 Council of the European Union, Doc. 8958/04, 28 April 2004: Draft framework decision on the retention of mobile phone and Internet communication data.
87 'Le ministre de l'Intérieur français rejette l'idée de CIA européenne', *Le Figaro*, 19 March 2004; 'Sécurité: les vues communes des Vingt-Cinq', *Libération*, 20 March 2004.
88 'Le Conseil JAI s'engage à respecter des délais précis pour rattraper les retards et adopter de nouvelles mesures pour la lutte antiterroriste', *Agence Europe*, 20 March 2004; 'Member states' failure to share intelligence saps Europol work', *European Voice*, 25 March 2004.
89 Apart from the Security Service (MI5), there is the Secret Intelligence Service (MI6), and Government Communications Headquarters (GCHQ). For a concise overview see Chalk and Rosenau 2004: 7–15.
90 Minister of State in the Home Office Hazel Blears in House of Lords 2005: E134.
91 There are Special Branches in other British police constabularies as well, but Metropolitan Police Special Branch is by far the most important one (for an overview see Her Majesty's Inspectorate of Constabulary 2003).
92 Secretary of State Kenneth Clarke on behalf of the Home Department in House of Commons Debates, vol. 207, col. 297, 8 May 1992.
93 Source: <http://www.mi5.gov.uk/print/Page19.html> (accessed 18 October 2006); see also Intelligence and Security Committee 2006: 13. The figures do not include domestic (Northern Irish) terrorism.
94 '9/11 one year on', *The Observer*, 8 September 2002.
95 'A special relationship? The US and UK spying alliance', *Financial Times*, 6 July 2004.
96 'London fails to head off MEP's inquiry into economic spying', *The Guardian*, 6 July 2000; 'Britain is untrustworthy, say MEPs in spy inquiry', *The Guardian*, 25 April 2001; 'Big Brother: the eavesdroppers', *The Guardian*, 14 September 2002.
97 Home Office, 'Unprecedented co-operation between UK/US Governments fighting terrorism: David Blunkett', Press Release 100/2003, 1 April 2003.
98 On a strategic level, Britain prefers cooperation among the leading industrial states (G7/G8) and the five leading EU Member States (G5). See 'A step change in the response to international terrorism', open speech by Foreign Minister Jack Straw in the House of Commons, 4 October 2001; Home Office, 'European co-operation to secure borders, ensure effective policing and implement tough counter-terrorism measures', Press Release 221/2004, 6 July 2004.
99 Home Office, 'Government steps up its fight against terrorism with £15M cash boost for Special Branch policing', Press Release 127/2004, 19 March 2004.

100 Home Secretary David Blunkett in House of Lords 2005: E128–9.
101 'Time to cut waffle and tackle terror, Blunkett tells EU', *The Daily Telegraph*, 20 March 2004.
102 Somewhat surprisingly, in 2004 the Minister of Interior said: 'We would also be content for Europol to be financed from the Community budget'. This was immediately qualified: 'We attach importance to Europol continuing to function in support of Member States' own investigations' (House of Commons 2004: 17–18).
103 'Blunkett calls for terror database', *The Guardian*, 6 July 2004.
104 Minister of State in the Home Office Hazel Blears in House of Lords 2005: E135.
105 *Anti-terrorism, Crime and Security Act 2001*; Answer to question 6 in Council of the European Union, Doc. 14107/02, 20 November 2002: Answers to a questionnaire on traffic data retention; *Retention of Communications Data Order 2003*; 'Britain urges EU to tighten security intelligence: Blunkett calls for common rules on data retention', *The Guardian*, 19 March 2004.
106 'Blunkett reviews plan to trawl phone and net users' records', *The Guardian*, 13 September 2003; speech by Home Secretary Charles Clarke to the European Parliament, 7 September 2005.
107 Quoted in Lutiis 2003: 107.
108 Minister of Foreign Affairs Franco Frattini in the Italian Senate, plenary assembly of 6 May 2003.
109 See also 'Un piano europeo contro il terrorismo', *Domenica del Corriere*, 23 March 1985; 'Scalfaro: "Ecco il mio progetto per un'Europa più sicura"', *Corriere della Sera*, 20 June 1985; 'A noi l'Oscar dell'antiterrorismo', *Europeo*, 9 August 1986.
110 France, Greece, USA, Austria, Israel: 1986; Spain, Morocco: 1987; Egypt: 1988; UK: 1989; Cyprus: 1991; Chile, Argentina: 1992; Israel: 1994; Saudi Arabia: 1995; Morocco: 1996; Hungary: 1997; Turkey, India: 1998; Czech Republic, Algeria, Argentina: 1999; Uzbekistan, Libya: 2000; Slovakia: 2002. Source: List provided as a courtesy by the Italian Ministry of the Interior (27 April 2004).
111 Minister of the Interior Giuseppe Pisanu in 'Intelligence e prevenzione per battere il terrorismo', *La Repubblica*, 17 March 2004.
112 For Mediterranean cooperation, a source from the Ministry of the Interior (personal interview at the DG for Preventive Policing, April 2004) mentioned the following groups: EUROMED and FOROMED.
113 For the necessary background see Lutiis 1991, 2003.
114 Police: Polizia di Stato, Carabinieri, Guardia di Finanza. Secret Services: Servizio per le Informazioni e la Sicurezza Democratica (SISDE), Servizio per le Informazioni e la Sicurezza Militare (SISMI).
115 Police Chief Giovanni de Gennaro in Resoconti del Comitato parlamentare Schengen, Europol e immigrazione, 5 December 2002, p. 8; Minister of the Interior Giuseppe Pisanu in 'Intelligence e prevenzione per battere il terrorismo', *La Repubblica*, 17 March 2004.
116 Legal decree No. 354, 24 December 2003.
117 Law No. 45, 26 February 2004. For the debate see the proceedings of the Italian House of Representatives, 26 January 2004, 28 January 2004; and of the Italian Senate, 12 February 2004, 17 February 2004, 18 February 2004.
118 Foreign Minister Franco Frattini in 'Il terrorismo colpisce la libertà: fronte commune anche in Italia', *La Repubblica*, 3 September 2004.
119 The following interpretation is mostly based on a personal interview at the Italian Foreign Ministry (DG European Integration), April 2004.

120 Minister of the Interior Giuseppe Pisanu in 'Intelligence e prevenzione per battere il terrorismo', *La Repubblica*, 17 March 2004; Foreign Minister Franco Frattini in 'Il terrorismo colpisce la libertà: fronte commune anche in Italia', *La Repubblica*, 3 September 2004. Paradoxically, Prime Minister Berlusconi declared immediately after 9/11: 'It is essential to renew as soon as possible the backbones of western secret services, creating a "supranational intelligence" capable of working in close coordination' ('Berlusconi: "Guerra è la parola giusta"', *ANSA*, 17 September 2001). Unsurprisingly, no similar statement was ever repeated.

121 Minister of the Interior Giuseppe Pisanu in a hearing of the bicameral Schengen-Europol Committee (Comitato parlamentare Schengen, Europol e immigrazione), 24 July 2002.

122 Joint Investigation Teams were meant to be another instrument for engendering trust and international exchange among European police forces (see pp. 171–8).

123 In 2000, communications on terrorism and counterfeit scored only 3% (Ministero dell'Interno 2001).

5 Extradition of terrorists

1 Council of Europe Treaty Series No. 024 and 090; see also *Protocol amending the European Convention on the Suppression of Terrorism*, European Treaty Series 190, opened for signature in 2003; for further information consult <http://conventions.coe.int>.

2 For the UN discussion see pp. 40–8.

3 Concluded 4 December 1979.

4 Valéry Giscard d'Estaing in 'L'espace judiciaire', *Le Monde*, 16 December 1977.

5 'Extraditions: la volte-face', *Libération*, 11 November 1982.

6 Unfortunately there is little information on the British bargaining position during the negotiations. We are thereby forced to reconstruct many preferences from the time preceding the negotiations (British National Archives FCO 41/938: *Motion for Recommendation on International Terrorism*, 1972; FCO 41/1085, *Council of Europe: Consultative Assembly Recommendation 684 on International Terrorism*, 1973) and from the ratification debate (see next note).

7 Shirley Summerskill, Under-Secretary of State for the Home Office, before the Second Reading Committee of the House of Commons, 26 April 1978; Brynmor John, Minister of State, before the House of Commons, 9 June 1978.

8 Council of Europe Doc. JUR/Tr. No 90 Decl./Res. United Kingdom, 24 July 1978.

9 'Good intentions on combating terrorism', *The London Times*, 25 August 1978.

10 Shirley Summerskill, Under-Secretary of State for the Home Office, before the Second Reading Committee of the House of Commons, 26 April 1978.

11 British National Archives FCO 87/200: Draft reply for parliamentary question, to be answered on 23 May 1971 (undated).

12 Statement by Her Majesty's Government, given on occasion of oral answers to questions in the House of Commons, 18 July 1962.

13 Council of Europe Doc. JUR/Tr. No 90 Decl./Res. United Kingdom, 24 July 1978.

14 Shirley Summerskill, Under-Secretary of State for the Home Office, before the Second Reading Committee of the House of Commons, 26 April 1978.

15 'Terrorist tribunal proposal rebuffed', *The Guardian*, 26 October 1982.

16 Council of Europe Doc. CM/Del/Concl. (73) 224 Item V, 1973, p. 13.

17 British National Archives FCO 41/1085: Note on Belgian proposal of the nine EC countries on the extradition of terrorists, 1973 (undated).

18 Under-Secretary of State Speranza in a commission of the Italian House of Representatives (Commissioni riunite III Affari esteri e IV Giustizia), 4 December 1980.
19 See Council of Europe Doc. DPC/CEPC (73) 26: Reply from the Government of Italy to the questionnaire concerning legal aspects of the problems raised by international terrorism, 20 July 1973.
20 Council of Europe Doc. JUR/Tr. No 90 Decl./Res. Italy, 27 January 1977.
21 Italian Foreign Ministry, reply to enquiry No. 4-00964 of 26 May 1978 by Senator Minnocci, reproduced in Camera 1981: 223.
22 On the ratification debate see Chiavario 1986: 437–40; Massai 1990: 93–5.
23 Giulio Andreotti before a commission of the Italian House of Representatives (Commissioni riunite III Affari esteri e IV Giustizia), 4 December 1980, p. 12.
24 Minister of Justice Mino Martinazzoli in a plenary debate of the Italian Senate, 14 November 1985, p. 15.
25 Minister of Justice Mino Martinazzoli before a commission of the Italian House of Representatives (Commissioni riunite III Affari esteri e IV Giustizia), 14 March 1985, p. 7.
26 Under-Secretary of State at the Ministry of Justice Antonio Carpino in a plenary debate of the Italian House of Representatives, 24 May 1985, pp. 28165–6.
27 'Consultazione Cossiga-Craxi sulla risposta antiterrorismo: Intervista con Francesco Cossiga, Presidente della Repubblica', *La Repubblica*, 20 September 1986; Virginio Rognoni, Minister of Justice, in 'Una Corte europea per i reati di terrorismo radicale alternativa all'estradizione', *Corriere della Sera*, 14 January 1987; see also Raimondi 1990: 132–4.
28 Minister of Justice Hans-Jochen Vogel in a plenary debate of the Bundestag, 10 February 1977, p. 653.
29 German Federal Archive B 141/44303: Briefing for a meeting of the Permanent Representatives at the Council of Europe in Strasbourg, 15 November 1972.
30 German Federal Archive B 141/44306: Position of the Ministry of Justice on Recommendation 703 (1973) of the Council of Europe on international terrorism, 19 June 1973.
31 German Federal Archive B 141/44307: Report for the Ministry of Justice on a meeting (14–16 May 1974) of the European Committee on Crime Problems of the Council of Europe, 29 July 1974.
32 Council of Europe Doc. DPC/CEPC (73) 24: Reply from the Government of the Federal Republic of Germany to the questionnaire concerning legal aspects of the problems raised by international terrorism, 1973.
33 Minister of Justice Hans-Jochen Vogel in a plenary debate of the Bundestag, 25 November 1977, p. 4531.
34 Minister of Justice Hans-Jochen Vogel, ibid. p. 4530.
35 Chancellor Helmut Schmidt in a plenary debate of the Bundestag, 20 April 1977, p. 1445.
36 Minister of Justice Hans-Jochen Vogel in Bundestag, plenary debate, 25 November 1977, p. 4531.
37 'Rasche Einigung im Europäischen Rat', *Süddeutsche Zeitung*, 7 December 1977.
38 Plenary debate of the National Assembly, 29 June 1987, p. 3317.
39 French Diplomatic Archives NUOI 1409, Cote S. 50: Telegram from the Foreign Ministry to the French permanent representative at the United Nations, 6 October 1972.
40 French Diplomatic Archives NUOI 1409, Cote S. 50: Instructions concerning a report of the International Law Commission, 2 September 1972.

41 Council of Europe Doc. JUR/Tr. No 90 Decl./Res. France, 27 January 1977.
42 French Diplomatic Archives NUOI 1409, Cote S. 50: Instructions for the French delegates at the International Law Commission of the United Nations, 1972, p. 5.
43 Signed 1951, ratified 1959 (Greenfield 1977: 563–5; Haas 2000: 66).
44 See the documentation provided in Greenfield 1977: 561–82.
45 French Diplomatic Archives NUOI 1409, Cote S. 50: Instructions for the French delegates at the International Law Commission of the United Nations, 1972, p. 6.
46 French Diplomatic Archives NUOI 1409, Cote S. 50: Position paper for the 217th meeting of the permanent representatives at the Council of Europe, 3 January 1973, p. 2.
47 Pleanary debate of the National Assembly, 20 October 1976, p. 6780; Gal-Or 1985: 215–16.
48 'Le projet scélérat du Conseil de l'Europe sur la répression du "terrorisme:" répression sans frontières', *Rouge*, 20 September 1976.
49 Council of Europe Doc. JUR/Tr. No 90 Decl./Res. France, 27 January 1977.
50 Ibid.
51 Giscard d'Estaing, as quoted in 'L'Assemblée de Strasbourg souhaite une entrée en vigueur rapide de la convention contre le terrorisme', *Le Monde*, 28 January 1977.
52 Council of Europe Doc. JUR/Tr. No 90 Decl./Res. France, 27 January 1977.
53 Valéry Giscard d'Estaing in 'L'espace judiciaire', *Le Monde*, 16 December 1977; cf. 'Dans six mois, l'"espace judiciaire européen"?', *Le Monde*, 13 October 1978.
54 'Extraditions: la volte-face', *Libération*, 11 November 1982.
55 Convention of 10 March 1995 on Simplified extradition procedure between the Member States of the European Union (*Official Journal of the European Communities* C78, 30 March 1995, pp. 2–10); Convention of 27 September 1996 relating to Extradition between the Member States of the European Union (*Official Journal of the European Communities* C 313, 23 October 1996, pp. 12–23).
56 'Britain calls for "eurowarrant"', *The Observer*, 10 October 1999; 'Allarme inglese sul crimine: serve un coordinamento UE', *Il Sole 24 Ore*, 13 October 1999; 'A Tampere difficile vertice UE su criminalità e immigrati', *Il Sole 24 Ore*, 15 October 1999.
57 Articles 33 and 35. For the wider agenda on mutual recognition see Communication from the Commission COM(2005)195 final, 19 May 2005.
58 Trattato bilaterale tra la Repubblica Italiana e il Regno di Spagna per il perseguimento di gravi reati attraverso il superamento dell'estradizione in uno spazio giudiziario comune, signed 28 November 2000; Tratado entre el Reino de España y el Reino Unido de Gran Bretaña e Irlanda del Norte relativo a la entrega judicial acelerada para delitos graves en un espacio común de Justicia, signed 23 November 2001; <http://www.mju.es/prensa/espacio_europeo.htm> (accessed 20 October 2004); 'Commission announces definition of terrorist crime', Agence Europe, 9 February 2001.
59 Council Framework Decision of 13 June 2002 on the European Arrest Warrant and the surrender procedures between Member States, *Official Journal of the European Communities* L 190, pp. 1–18.
60 For a summary appraisal of the ratification process see Commission 2006a; 2006b.
61 Quoted in 'Extradition to US of Al Qaida suspect fails', *The Guardian*, 30 July 2002.
62 Parliamentary Under-Secretary of State for the Home Office, Mr. Bob Ainsworth, in House of Lords 2001: 4.
63 Quoted in Home Office 2001: 1.

64 'Straw wants faster extradition', *BBC News*, 12 March 2001; 'Straw plan to give up extradition role', *The Guardian*, 13 March 2001; for the time after 9/11, see Parliamentary Under-Secretary of State for the Home Office, Mr. Bob Ainsworth, to the European Standing Committee B, 3 December 2001, and in House of Commons 2003: 6.
65 Extradition Act 2003, Section 208.
66 'United Kingdom: What the Permanent Representative Nigel Sheinwald is expecting from the Laeken Summit', *Agence Europe*, 7 November 2001; Parliamentary Under-Secretary of State for the Home Office, Mr. Bob Ainsworth, to the European Standing Committee B, 3 December 2001, and in House of Lords 2001: 10.
67 Parliamentary Under-Secretary of State for the Home Office, Mr. Bob Ainsworth, to the European Standing Committee B, 10 December 2001.
68 'Six countries decide to jump the gun on entry into force of European Arrest Warrant', *Agence Europe*, 15 February 2002; Extradition Act 2003. The 1995 and 1996 Conventions on simplified extradition in Europe were put into force on 20 March 2002 as a sort of interim measure pending ratification of the European Arrest Warrant.
69 See also Home Office 2002a: 3. Apparently, the sentence echoes a clause in the British ratification law to the 1977 European Convention on the Suppression of Terrorism (see Warner 1994: 31–2).
70 'Tricky negotiations over the European arrest warrant', *Agence Europe*, 17 November 2001.
71 Extradition Act 2003; House of Commons 2003: 5–6.
72 Parliamentary Under-Secretary of State for the Home Office, Mr. Bob Ainsworth, in House of Commons 2003: 6.
73 'Greek Presidency and Commission programmes', *Agence Europe*, 24 January 2003.
74 On the French sanctuary doctrine and its gradual abatement see Shapiro and Suzan 2003; see also Plenel 1986; Wieviorka 1990, 1991; Hermant and Bigo 2000; S. Gregory 2003.
75 'France proposes compromise on European arrest warrant', *Agence Europe*, 17 October 2001; 'Le paquet "Anti-terrorisme" progresse timidement', *Europolitique*, 20 October 2001.
76 'Spotlight on Italy for blocking European arrest warrant', *Agence Europe*, 8 December 2001; 'Mandat d'arrêt européen: Paris "n'exclut pas" un accord sans l'Italie', *Les Echos*, 10 December 2001.
77 'Six countries decide to jump the gun on entry into force of European Arrest Warrant', *Agence Europe*, 15 February 2002.
78 Law N. 2004–204, 9 March 2004 (the so-called '*Loi Perben II*').
79 Jacques Chirac and Lionel Jospin, joint press conference at the informal European Council in Ghent, 19 October 2001, <http://www.elysee.fr> (accessed 8 September 2004).
80 'Le paquet "Anti-terrorisme" progresse timedement', *Europolitique*, 20 October 2001.
81 'Tricky negotiations over the European arrest warrant: agreement on idea of listing crimes', *Agence Europe*, 17 November 2001.
82 Law N. 2004-204, 9 March 2004 (the so-called '*Loi Perben II*').
83 Audition de la Ministre délégué aux Affaires européennes Mme Noëlle Lenoir devant la délégation pour l'Union européenne de l'Assemblée Nationale, 16 December 2003, <http://www.doc.diplomatie.fr> (accessed 7 September 2004).

84 'Dominique Perben prêt à de nouvelles extraditions', *Les Echos*, 12 September 2002.
85 'Summit adopts a 79-point action plan', *Agence Europe*, 21 October 2001.
86 'EU favours Commission proposals but agreement on European arrest warrant will be close-run', *Agence Europe*, 21 September 2001; 'Detailed discussion but little result: criticism from several Foreign Ministers', *Agence Europe*, 18 October 2001.
87 'Summit adopts a 79-point action plan', *Agence Europe*, 21 October 2001.
88 'EU kritisiert Blockadehaltung Italiens scharf', *Süddeutsche Zeitung*, 8 December 2001.
89 'Schily: una scelta inacettabile, Roma mette in pericolo il suo ruolo nella UE', *Corriere della Sera*, 8 December 2001.
90 'Controversy over arrest warrant', *Agence Europe*, 16 February 2002.
91 Europäisches Haftbefehlsgesetz, published in *Bundesgesetzblatt I*, No. 38, 26 July 2004, pp. 1748–52.
92 Ostensibly Bavaria blocked the ratification of the arrest warrant because of a small detail in the ratification law, namely the extension to resident aliens of the right to serve their sentence in Germany (see 'EU will Nachrichtendienste enger zusammenbinden', *Frankfurter Rundschau*, 9 June 2004). The true motivation was probably an attempt by the conservative opposition to obstruct the Federal Government.
93 Europäisches Haftbefehlsgesetz, published in *Bundesgesetzblatt I*, No. 38, 25 July 2006, pp. 1721–26.
94 'Tricky negotiations over the European arrest warrant', *Agence Europe*, 17 November 2001; 'Il Belgio accusa l'Italia di puntare a una lista ristretta di crimini', *Il Sole 24 Ore*, 17 November 2001.
95 'Deadlock in talks over European arrest warrant due to block by Italy', *Agence Europe*, 7 December 2001.
96 Europäisches Haftbefehlsgesetz, published in *Bundesgesetzblatt I*, No. 38, 26 July 2004, pp. 1748–52.
97 'Greek Presidency and Commission programmes', *Agence Europe*, 24 January 2003; 'Greek minister Philippos Petsalnikos has confirmed that there is still disagreement', *Agence Europe*, 4 March 2003; 'Ausnahme für Deutschland: nur begrenzte Kooperation bei Verbrecherjagd in der EU', *Süddeutsche Zeitung*, 2 June 2006.
98 Federal Ministry of the Interior, 'Ute Vogt: Europea muss seine Chancen nutzen', press release, 19 March 2004.
99 'Patto giudiziario tra Italia e Spagna', *Il Sole 24 Ore*, 29 November 2000; 'Nei reati gravi riconoscimento immediato dei mandati con l'Italia', *Il Sole 24 Ore*, 9 November 2001.
100 'Presidency compromise on arrest warrant and terrorism', *Agence Europe*, 16 November 2001.
101 'Quei ritardi italiani in Europa', *Il Sole 24 Ore*, 4 February 2004.
102 Commission 2006a: 2; see also 2006b.
103 'A Milano la Lega va in piazza contro le "toghe rosse" di tutta Europa', *CNN Italia*, 9 December 2001; 'Camera: via libera all'euromandato', *Il Sole 24 Ore*, 13 May 2004.
104 'Castelli: c'è un progetto per la dittatura delle toghe', *La Padania*, 19 March 2003.
105 'Mandato d'arresto europeo: L'UE "avanti anche senza l'Italia" ', *CNN Italia*, 8 December 2001.

106 'The day in politics', *Agence Europe*, 23 October 2003.
107 'The day in politics', *Agence Europe*, 15 December 2001; 'Il Presidente del Consiglio: voteremo il mandato di cattura europeo', *La Stampa*, 23 October 2003.
108 'The day in politics', *Agence Europe*, 23 October 2003.
109 'A Milano la Lega va in piazza contro le "toghe rosse" di tutta Europa', *CNN Italia*, 9 December 2001.
110 'Camera: via libera all'euromandato', *Il Sole 24 Ore*, 13 May 2004.
111 Ibid.
112 'Mandato di cattura Ue: sì italiano ma solo dopo la riforma della costiuzione', *CNN Italia*, 11 December 2001.
113 'Castelli si difende: "Nessun dramma, l'Italia resterà fuori" ', *La Stampa*, 7 December 2001.
114 Commission 2006a: 2; see also 2006b.
115 'Tricky negotiations over the European arrest warrant', *Agence Europe*, 17 November 2001.
116 'Contacts between ministers on difficult question of European arrest warrant', *Agence Europe*, 29 November 2001.
117 'Castelli si difende: "Nessun dramma, l'Italia resterà fuori"', *La Stampa*, 7 December 2001.
118 'Spotlight on Italy for blocking European arrest warrant', *Agence Europe*, 8 December 2001.
119 'Final details before Justice and Home Affairs Council', *Agence Europe*, 6 December 2001; cf. the statement made by Italy in *Official Journal of the European Communities*, L 190, 18 July 2002, p. 19.
120 'Mandato di cattura europeo: sui reati si inceppa l'accordo', *Il Sole 24 Ore*, 17 November 2001.
121 'Adoption of decision on freezing assets on Thursday depends on Italy', *Agence Europe*, 28 February 2002; 'Provisional agreement on freeze of assets and proof', *Agence Europe*, 1 March 2002.

6 International drug prohibition

1 On global prohibition regimes see Andreas and Nadelmann 2006: 17–58 (a more up-to-date version of Nadelmann 1990).
2 See also British National Archives FO 371/161047: Statement made by the British representative Green, 25 January 1961.
3 On the 'British system' of drug prescription and medical treatment see Schur 1962; cf. Trebach 1982.
4 In the 1950s, the British Medical Association had won a showdown with the Home Office when the latter wanted to prohibit the manufacture of heroin (King 1972: 112–14; Mott and Bean 1998: 39–40).
5 The standpoint was reiterated in 1971 and 1972 (UN 1973b: 164, 166; 1973c: 158).
6 See also British National Archives FCO 61/947: Briefing for the British delegation, 2 March 1972.
7 See also British National Archives FCO 61/947: Letter from Mr. Beedle, 7 July 1972.
8 See also British National Archives FO 371/172755: Letter from Mr. Green, 8 February 1963.
9 British National Archives FCO 61/947: Report by the British delegation, September 1972; cf. OD 33/138, 1972.

10 British National Archives FCO 61/947: Letter from Foreign Secretary Douglas-Home, 6 March 1972.
11 Needless to say, Britain was fiercely opposed to the idea that the European Commission might get a role to play in the drugs field (British National Archives FCO 33/2297, 1974).
12 British National Archives FCO 61/800: Letter from Mr. MacInnes, 30 September 1971; see also UN 1964a: 81; 1973b: 184; 1974: 42.
13 See also British National Archives FO 371/172755: Letter from Mr. Green, 8 February 1963.
14 See also British National Archives FCO 61/947: Briefing for the British delegation, 2 March 1972.
15 British National Archives FO 371/161047: Statement made by the British representative Green, 25 January 1961; cf. UN 1973b: 8.
16 British National Archives FCO 61/800, 1971; FCO 61/801, 1971; OD 33/138, 1972.
17 German Federal Archive B 106/39470 and B 106/39471: Exchange of letters between ministries, 1961–1973.
18 German Federal Archive B 189/3727: Assessment by the Ministry of the Interior on problems of drug addiction, 17 October 1969; B 106/39470: Statement by the Minister of Health, 28 September 1970.
19 German Federal Archive B 106/91290: Memorandum by the Minister of the Interior Hans-Dietrich Genscher, Autumn 1972.
20 German Federal Archive B 106/39470: Statement by the Minister of Health, 4 November 1970; B 106/91331: Report from a meeting of the CND, 22 February 1973.
21 German Federal Archive B 106/91331: Report from a meeting of the CND, 20 December 1973.
22 German Federal Archive B 141/58372: German position on draft Single Convention, 6 September 1959; B 106/39470: Statement by the Minister of Health, 7 January 1966; B 106/91326: Statement by the Foreign Office, 26 January 1972.
23 German Federal Archive B 141/58372: German position on draft Single Convention, 6 September 1959.
24 See ibid.
25 German Federal Archive B 106/91326: Policy draft for the Conference to consider amendments to the Single Convention, undated.
26 German Federal Archive B 106/91326: Policy draft for the Conference to consider amendments to the Single Convention, undated, and Report from the German delegation, 28 March 1972.
27 German Federal Archive B 141/58376: Speech by the Minister of Justice, 22 February 1972.
28 German Federal Archive B 106/39470: Instructions for the COREPER in Brussels, 4 January 1972.
29 German Federal Archive B 106/91326: Statement by the Foreign Office, 21 October 1971.
30 Italian Diplomatic Archive: Telegrams of the Foreign Ministry to and from Geneva, March 1970.
31 Pasquale Curci in Istituto per la Documentazione e gli Studi Legislativi 1976: 8–16.
32 Italian Diplomatic Archive: Telegram from the Foreign Ministry to New York, 28 November 1972; British National Archives FCO 61/947: Report by the British delegation, September 1972.

33 Italian Diplomatic Archive: Telegram from the Foreign Ministry to New York, 2 December 1972.
34 Italy proposed a quasi-judicial arbitration committee to be appointed by the president of the International Court of Justice.
35 Under-Secretary of State Granelli in the Italian House of Representatives, 21 May 1974.
36 Italian Diplomatic Archive: Telegrams of the Foreign Ministry to and from Geneva, March 1970. From 1971, Italy was represented in the INCB (Mantelli Caraccia 1973: 44).
37 Italian Diplomatic Archive E/CN/7/3a-4a-5a, February–May 1974.
38 See Italian Diplomatic Archive: Telegrams of the Foreign Ministry to and from Geneva, September and October 1970.
39 France ratified the Single Convention in 1969, and the Convention on Psychotropic Substances in 1975.
40 A similar attitude was still applied in 1972, when the amended version of the Single Convention on Narcotic Drugs was under discussion (UN 1973c: 23).
41 French Diplomatic Archives NUOI 1307, Cote S. 50.3.8.7: Instructions for the 24th meeting of the CND (27 September–21 October 1971).
42 French Diplomatic Archives NUOI 1307, Cote S. 50.3.8.7: Instructions for an extraordinary session of the CND (28 September–2 October 1970).
43 French Diplomatic Archives NUOI 1307, Cote S. 50.3.8.7: Telegram from the Foreign Ministry to the permanent representation at the UN, 9 October 1971.
44 French Diplomatic Archives NUOI 1307, Cote S. 50.3.8.7: Telegram from the Foreign Ministry to the permanent representation at the UN, 23 September 1970.
45 French Diplomatic Archives NUOI 1307, Cote S. 50.3.8.7: Telegram from the Foreign Ministry to the permanent representation at the UN, 9 October 1971.
46 UN Doc. SG/C/218/Rev.1, 'France to contribute $100,000 to United Nations Fund against Drug Abuse', press release, 3 November 1971.
47 Around 1970 France and Germany had been in favour of, and Britain and Italy opposed to the international control of precursor substances (UN 1968: 16–18; 1973a: 61; 1973b: 180–1).
48 The preferences concerning institutional depth are typically limited to the supply side of the regime, because binding commitments on demand are not (yet) in sight.
49 The budget numbers are a courtesy of the United Nations Office on Drugs and Crime (UNODC).
50 Jacques Chirac in UN Doc. A/S-20/PV.1, 8 June 1998, pp. 15–16.
51 Alfredo Mantovano, speech at the 47th meeting of the CND, 15 March 2004, <http://www.interno.it> (accessed 1 March 2006).
52 For the canonic formulation of this doctrine see Pelletier 1978.
53 It seems that Bergeron's (2002) farewell to the curative approach was premature; see also the account provided by Boekhout van Solinge (2004: 79–103).
54 'Chirac propose la solidarité dans la lutte anti-drogue', *Reuters*, 15 March 1997.
55 Jacques Chirac, speech at the opening ceremony of the international conference on drug routes in Paris, 22 May 2003, <http://www.elysee.fr> (accessed 1 March 2006).
56 'Les salles de shoot divisent l'Europe', *Agence France Presse*, 25 November 2004.
57 Jacques Chirac in UN Doc. A/S-20/PV.1, 8 June 1998, p. 16.
58 Jacques Chirac, speech at the opening ceremony of the international conference on drug routes in Paris, 22 May 2003, <http://www.elysee.fr> (accessed 1 March 2006).

59 'Europe's new hard line on drugs', *Druglink*, January/February 2004, p. 3.
60 'Droga, per Fini tolleranza zero', *La Repubblica*, 23 September 2003.
61 Gianfranco Fini, speech at the 46th meeting of the CND, April 2003, <http://www.governo.it> (accessed 21 January 2004).
62 'Fini: tolleranza zero', *La Stampa*, 26 September 2002.
63 'Passa la legge sulla droga', *Corriere della Sera*, 9 February 2006.
64 Alfredo Mantovano, speech at the 48th meeting of the CND, 7 March 2005, <http://www.mantovano.org> (accessed 1 March 2006).
65 Personal interview at the Presidency of the Council in Rome, May 2004.
66 'Droga, per Fini tolleranza zero', *La Repubblica*, 23 September 2003.
67 Personal interview at the Presidency of the Council in Rome, May 2004.
68 'Il Vicepremier a Vienna', *La Stampa*, 16 March 2002.
69 'Droga, la svolta di Fini: repressione, la strada giusta', *La Repubblica*, 27 October 2001.
70 'Droga, per Fini tolleranza zero', *La Repubblica*, 23 September 2003.
71 Gianfranco Fini, speech at the 46th meeting of the CND, April 2003, <http://www.governo.it> (accessed 21 January 2004).
72 Personal interview at the Ministry of Foreign Affairs in Rome, May 2004.
73 Jacques Chirac in UN Doc. A/S-20/PV.1, 8 June 1998, p. 15.
74 'Paris accueille avec une satisfaction prudente le plan antidrogue de l'Union européenne', *Le Monde*, 27 June 2000.
75 Minister of Justice Dominique Perben, quoted in 'Lutte contre la drogue: plus de sanctuaire dans l'Europe des 15', *Agence France Presse*, 3 December 2003; see also 'France asks Netherlands for anti-drug mechanism in port of Rotterdam and other measures', *Agence Europe*, 16 February 1996.
76 'Accordo tra i quindici sulle pene minime per chi coltiva, produce e spaccia', *La Stampa*, 28 November 2003; 'Accordo politico sulla sanzione del traffico di droga', *Agence Europe*, 28 November 2003.
77 Cf. Italy's position on the European Arrest Warrant (see pp. 107–9).
78 'Droga, per Fini tolleranza zero', *La Repubblica*, 23 September 2003.
79 For a general introduction see Leishman and Wood 2000.
80 'Afghanistan opium crop threatens Europe', *Financial Times*, 18 February 2002; 'Lethal crop that leads to deaths like Rachel's', *Daily Mirror*, 6 March 2002.
81 'Blair sets up team to stem tide of Afghan heroin into UK', *The Observer*, 24 March 2002; 'Poverty and terrorism fuel booming drug trade in Afghanistan', *The Daily Telegraph*, 24 August 2004; Foreign and Commonwealth Office, 'Speech by the Foreign Secretary at the International Institute for Strategic Studies', press release, 28 October 2004; 'Britain losing war on Afghan heroin', *Scotland on Sunday*, 7 November 2004.
82 Bob Ainsworth in House of Commons, written answers for 9 December 2002, Hansard c115W; cf. Home Office, 'International cooperation is vital in tackling drugs menace', press release, 8 September 1994.
83 'Blunkett's cannabis strategy flawed', *The Guardian*, 2 September 2002.
84 Bob Ainsworth, 'Publication of the International Narcotic Control Board annual report', open letter, 3 March 2003.
85 Home Office, 'New guidance to treat heroin addiction', Press Release 136/2003, 16 May 2003.
86 3. BtmG-Änderungsgesetz, published in *Bundesgesetzblatt* I, 2000, p. 302.
87 Marion Caspers-Merk, 'Modellprojekt heroingestützte Behandlung', speech of 27 August 2002, <http://www.bmg.bund.de> (accessed 23 February 2006).

88 'Den Krieg gegen das Rauschgift haben die UN noch lange nicht gewonnen', *Frankfurter Allgemeine Zeitung*, 19 April 2003.

89 'Letzter Schuss vor dem Jahreswechsel', *Süddeutsche Zeitung*, 22 April 2006.

90 Coalition Treaty 2002, <http://www.bundesregierung.de> (accessed 1 December 2004).

91 German Ministry of the Interior, factsheet 'Rauschgiftkriminalität', <http://www.bmi.bund.de> (accessed 27 February 2006).

92 Marion Caspers-Merk, opening speech at an international conference in Feldafing, 8 January 2002, <http://www.bmg.bund.de> (accessed 23 February 2006).

93 'Kampf gegen Terror zum Kampf gegen Rauschgift nutzen', *Frankfurter Allgemeine Zeitung*, 1 October 2001.

94 Marion Kaspers-Merk, statement at 45th session of the CND in Vienna, 12 March 2002, <http://www.bmg.bund.de> (accessed 23 February 2006).

95 'Kinkel will nicht kapitulieren', *Frankfurter Allgemeine Sonntagszeitung*, 14 June 1998.

96 'Blair praises work of Scots parliament', *Financial Times*, 10 March 2000; Bob Ainsworth in House of Commons, written answers for 9 December 2002, Hansard c115W.

97 German Ministry of Health, 'Internationale Zusammenarbeit bei der Lösung von Drogenproblemen soll gestärkt werden', press release, 15 July 2002, <http://www.bmg.bund.de> (accessed 27 February 2006).

98 'EU in der Drogenpolitik zerstritten', *Frankfurter Rundschau*, 20 December 2002.

99 'EU Drugs Strategy 2005-2012: contribution of the Federal Republic of Germany', <http://www.dpna.org> (accessed 27 February 2006).

100 Erich Stather, speech at the opening of the international conference 'Eindämmung der grenzüberschreitenden Kriminalität', Bonn, 16 December 2002, <http://www.bmz.de> (accessed 27 February 2006); Marion Caspers-Merk, 'Das Programm entwicklungsorientierte Drogenkontrolle', speech of 28 January 2004, <http://www.bmg.bund.de> (accessed 27 February 2006).

7 Drug enforcement methods

1 Interesting insights into the development of American drug enforcement techniques can be gained by a comparison of Lyman 1989 with Lyman 2002.

2 For a simple practical reason, I focus on the time between 1988 and 2002. After 9/11, the fight against terrorist finance was incorporated into the anti-money laundering regime (Shelley and Picarelli 2002) despite the fact that, in the case of terrorism, what is 'dirty' is usually not the source but the destination of the money. After 2002, the fight against criminal finance has become so much entangled with the fight against terrorism that a clear analytical distinction has become almost impossible.

3 Even in the American legal system, undercover investigation and infiltration tactics are somewhat problematic (Chambliss 2001).

4 The doctrine of going for 'Mr. Big' was eventually accepted in most countries (Dorn *et al.* 1992: 63–8), along with 'buy and bust' operations, intelligence gathering, and controlled deliveries.

5 Minister of the Interior Raymond Marcellin in a plenary debate of the National Assembly on 23 October 1970, *Journal Officiel* 1970–71, p. 4629.

6 Ibid., at p. 4630.

7 Mostsources used for this section are taken from a file of the French Ministry of the Interior available at the *Centre des Archives Contemporaines* (file n. 19920026/1–6).
8 Centre des Archives Contemporaines 19920026/1–6: Declaration of Minister of the Interior Raymond Marcellin to Agence France Presse, 29 July 1970.
9 Centre des Archives Contemporaines 19920026/1–6: Minutes of the first meeting of the Franco-American intergovernmental committee on drug control, 4 February 1970, p. 13.
10 Centre des Archives Contemporaines 19920026/1–6: Memorandum on the talks between the director of the BNDD John E. Ingersoll and the Director of the French Criminal Police (*Police Judiciaire*) Pierre Epaud, 21–24 October 1969.
11 Centre des Archives Contemporaines 19920026/1–6: Note on the execution of agreements resulting from the talks of 21 October 1969, undated (1970).
12 Centre des Archives Contemporaines 19920026/1–6: Letter by John T. Cusack to Max Ferret, 26 March 1970.
13 'M. Heath accepte une coopération des pays européens contre la drogue', *Le Monde*, August 1971 (exact date unknown).
14 Centre des Archives Contemporaines 19920026/1–6: Protocol on a meeting of the French Foreign Minister and the US Ambassador, 13 September 1971.
15 Minister of the Interior Raymond Marcellin in a plenary debate of the National Assembly on 23 October 1970, *Journal Officiel* 1970–71, p. 4629; Centre des Archives Contemporaines 19920026/1–6: Letter from the Minister of the Interior to the Foreign Minister, 18 November 1969.
16 Centre des Archives Contemporaines 19920026/1–6: Report from a Franco-American meeting at the French Ministry of the Interior, 13 December 1969.
17 Centre des Archives Contemporaines 19920026/1–6: Minutes of the first meeting of the Franco-American intergovernmental committee on drug control, 4 February 1970.
18 Minister of the Interior Raymond Marcellin in a plenary debate of the National Assembly on 23 October 1970, *Journal Officiel* 1970–71, p. 4629.
19 Centre des Archives Contemporaines 19920026/1–6: Letter from the Central Director of the Criminal Police (*Police Judiciaire*) to the General Director of the National Police (*Police Nationale*), 13 February 1970.
20 Centre des Archives Contemporaines 19920026/1–6: Note from the Ministry of the Interior to the General Director of the National Police, 1 December 1969; Letter from the Minister of Justice to the Minister of the Interior, 30 December 1969.
21 Centre des Archives Contemporaines 19920026/1–6: Accord entre la Direction Générale de la Police Nationale Française (Direction Centrale de la Police Judiciaire) et The United States Bureau of Narcotics and Dangerous Drugs, signed by the French Minister of the Interior Raymond Marcellin and the US Attorney General John Michell, 26 February 1971.
22 Centre des Archives Contemporaines 19920026/1–6: Speech by the Minister of the Interior before signing the agreement, 26 February 1971.
23 Centre des Archives Contemporaines 19920026/1–6: Verbal note on President Pompidou's visit to the USA, 8 May 1970.
24 Centre des Archives Contemporaines 19920026/1–6: Press conferences by the Minister of the Interior, 26 February 1971 and 31 March 1971.
25 German Federal Archive B 106/91288, Letter from President Pompidou to Chancellor Brandt, 6 August 1971; British National Archives PREM 15/911, Letter from President Pompidou to Prime Minister Edward Heath, 6 August 1971.

26 German Federal Archive B 106/91288: Memorandum by the French Foreign Minister, 20 September 1971.
27 Centre des Archives Contemporaines 19920026/1–6: Introductory statement on behalf of the French Minister of Interior at the first expert meeting of the Pompidou Group, Paris, 4 November 1971.
28 Centre des Archives Contemporaines 19920026/1–6: Report by Pierre Arpaillage of the Ministry of Justice on European cooperation in legislative and judicial matters, 18 October 1971.
29 'Drogue: le plan européen de M. Schumann', *Combat*, August 1971; German Federal Archive B 106/91288: Protocol on the first expert meeting of the Pompidou Group, Paris, 4 November 1971.
30 German Federal Archive B 106/91288: Letter by Chancellery Minister Ehmke to US Ambassador Cash, 5 July 1971; Letter by Minister of the Interior Genscher to US Ambassador Cash, 13 July 1971.
31 Centre des Archives Contemporaines 19920026/1–6: Minutes of the first meeting of the Franco-American intergovernmental committee on drug control, 4 February 1970, p. 10.
32 German Federal Archive B 106/91288: Protocol on a conservation between the German Chancellery Minister and the US Ambassador, 9 November 1971.
33 German Federal Archive B 106/85199: Memo of the BKA on the 15th meeting of the *Ständige Arbeitsgruppe Rauschgift der Arbeitsgemeinschaft Kripo* (Hamburg, 18–20 June 1974), 21 June 1974.
34 German Federal Archive B 106/91288: Letter from Chancellor Brandt to President Pompidou, August 1971.
35 German Federal Archive B 106/91288: Memo of the Ministry of the Interior on the Pompidou initiative, 28 October 1971.
36 German Federal Archive B 141/58375: Note on the German position regarding legislative harmonization, 1971 undated.
37 German Federal Archive B 106/91288: Letter from Chancellor Brandt to President Pompidou, August 1971; Protocol on the first expert meeting of the Pompidou Group, Paris, 4 November 1971.
38 German Federal Archive B 106/91289: Memo of the Ministry of the Interior on an expert meeting on improved international drug enforcement (Paris, 16–17 December 1971), 14 January 1972.
39 Personal interview at the Ministry of the Interior in Rome, April 2004.
40 French Diplomatic Archives NUOI 1307, Cote S. 50.3.8.7: Telegram from Rome about the Italian stance on the Pompidou Group, 22 September 1972.
41 British National Archives FCO 33/1404: Note on the first expert meeting of the Pompidou Group, Paris, 4 November 1971.
42 'Drogue: le plan européen de M. Schumann', *Combat*, August 1971.
43 German Federal Archive B 106/91288: Protocol on the first expert meeting of the Pompidou Group, Paris, 4 November 1971.
44 British National Archives FCO 33/1404: Note on the first expert meeting of the Pompidou Group, Paris, 4 November 1971. On the other hand, and ironically, the Italian Ministry of Health supported the 'famous European cooperation for the fight against drugs' in the Pompidou Group precisely because this would be a decisive step towards better coordination at the national level (Senato 1976: 46).
45 British National Archives FCO 33/1404: Draft for a Home Office Circular 'Procedure for dealing with urgent drug cases involving France', 1971.
46 British National Archives FCO 33/1404: Note on the first expert meeting of the Pompidou Group, Paris, 4 November 1971.

47 Minister of State Carlisle, as quoted in Bunyan 1976: 85; Home Secretary Merlyn Rees, according to Offenbach and Dolan 1978: 151.
48 For a more recent restatement of this doctrine see Tupman and Tupman 1999.
49 After some embarrassing entrapment cases in the early 1970s, though, a Home Office Circular imposed some limits (Bunyan 1976: 221; parts of the original circular are reprinted in Commissioner 1974: 48).
50 'Sir Robert Mark opposes national police force', *London Times*, 23 June 1977.
51 'National police force would put power in wrong hands chief constable says', *London Times*, 4 May 1977.
52 Council of Europe Convention on Laundering, Search, Seizure and Confiscation of the Proceeds from Crime (1990).
53 European Community Directive on Prevention of the Use of the Financial System for the Purpose of Money Laundering (1991).
54 'New rule will force lawyers to inform on clients' cash', *Financial Times*, 30 September 2000.
55 The result was a compromise that allows states to exempt information obtained by lawyers while giving legal advice or defending a client in criminal proceedings.
56 Loi relative à la lutte contre le trafic des stupéfiants, N. 87–1157, 31 December 1987.
57 Special European Council of Tampere, joint press conference of President Jacques Chirac and Prime Minister Lionel Jospin, 16 October 1999, <http://www.doc.diplomatie.fr> (accessed 14 March 2007).
58 Daniel Vaillant, 30 January 2002, in Montebourg 2002, vol. 2, pp. 625–35.
59 'France co-hosts 60-states meeting on tax havens', *Agence France Presse*, 28 June 2000.
60 'Commission takes France before the Court for what it considers disproportionate use of sanctions for failure to declare money transfers', *Agence Europe*, 25 January 2002.
61 Lionel Jospin, 8 February 2002, quoted in Montebourg 2002, vol. 1, pp. 101–2.
62 Daniel Vaillant, 30 January 2002, in Montebourg 2002, vol. 2, pp. 625–35.
63 Laurent Fabius, 13 February 2002, in Montebourg 2002, vol. 2, pp. 647–58.
64 'La chancellerie renforce les moyens des pôles financiers', *La Tribune*, 27 June 2001.
65 Marylise Lebranchu, 9 January 2002, quoted in Montebourg 2002, vol. 1, p. 159.
66 'Hésitation du Conseil sur le partage des avoirs criminels confisqués', *Europe Information Service*, 14 March 2003.
67 Home Office, 'Proceeds of Crime Bill receives royal assent', Press Release 213/2002, 25 July 2002.
68 'Offshore financial havens caught up in tax debate', *Financial Times*, 20 March 2000.
69 UK Statutory Instrument 2002, No. 3016.
70 In 2004, Tony Blair declared his intention to push this even further: 'English FBI-style law-enforcement agency "will help tackle Scotland's crime"', *The Scotsman*, 30 March 2004.
71 On Colombia see House of Lords, debate on 15 October 1997, *Hansard* column 540; on Turkey see 'FCO drugs and crime fund', <www.fco.gov.uk> (accessed 18 October 2004).
72 'Money laundering cash for UK', *Financial Times*, 9 November 1990; in the late 1980s, Britain had still been sceptical (see Anderson 1989: 120, note 15).
73 See for example Home Office, 'New extradition treaty and asset sharing agreement signed in USA by David Blunkett', Press Release 097/2003, 31 March 2003.

74 Home Office, 'Cracking down on crooked money transfers', Press Release 188/2003, 1 July 2003; 'New police scheme to keep criminal proceeds taking the profit out of crime: one year on', Press Release 071/2004, 24 February 2004; see also Wagstaff and Maynard 1988; Home Office 2002b: 34.
75 Home Office, 'Using criminals' cash to invest in our communities and frontline agencies', Press Release 267/2003, 2 October 2003.
76 Prime Minister Carlo Azeglio Ciampi, 14–15 May 1993, in Camera 1993: 51–6.
77 Personal interview at the Presidency of the Council in Rome, December 2004 (under a Berlusconi Government).
78 At the time: 20 Million Lire.
79 Minister of Finance Vincenzo Visco, 9–10 July 1998, in Senato 1999: 214.
80 Italian Senate, 11th legislature, Disegno di legge n. 688: Ratifica ed esecuzione della Convenzione sul riciclaggio, la ricerca, il sequestro e la confisca dei proventi di reato, fatta a Strasburgo l'8 novembre 1990, comunicated to the Presidency of the Council on 12 October 1992.
81 Minister of Justice Giovanni Maria Flick, 9–10 July 1998, in Senato 1999: 219.
82 Prime Minister Romano Prodi, 9–10 July 1998, in Senato 1999: 103; Minister of Justice Giovanni Maria Flick, 9–10 July 1998, in Senato 1999: 222.
83 'Ministers determined to step up fight against financial crime and money laundering', *Agence Europe*, 17 September 1999.
84 'Il segreto sul filo del rasoio', *Il Sole 24 Ore*, 22 April 2006.
85 'Open debate', *Agence Europe*, 29 May 1998.
86 'Corte costituzionale: illegittimo il delitto di possesso ingiustificato di valori introdotto dal decreto antimafia', *Il Sole 24 Ore*, 18 February 1994. Presumably due to a fear of legal problems, Italy did not formulate any explicit preferences on the international sharing of confiscated assets.
87 Prime Minister Romano Prodi, 9–10 July 1998, in Senato 1999: 104.
88 'Deutsches Bankgeheimnis am Ende', *Süddeutsche Zeitung*, 3 January 2005.
89 Gesetz zur Verbesserung der Bekämpfung der Geldwäsche und der Bekämpfung der Finanzierung des Terrorismus, published in *Bundesgesetzblatt* I, 2002, p. 3105.
90 Gesetz zur Bekämpfung des illegalen Rauschgifthandels und anderer Erscheinungsformen der Organisierten Kriminalität (OrgKG), published in *Bundesgesetzblatt* I, 1992, p. 1302, outlawing money laundering through a new §261 of the criminal code; Gesetz über das Aufspüren von Gewinnen aus schweren Straftaten (GwG), published in *Bundesgesetzblatt* I, 1993, p. 1770.
91 On the situation towards the end of the Kohl Government see Hoyer and Klos 1998.
92 'Germany proposes law to halt money laundering in its banks', *The Independent*, 9 April 1992.
93 'Brussels airs its dirty washing', *The Independent*, 4 December 1990.
94 'New rule will force lawyers to inform on clients' cash', *Financial Times*, 30 September 2000.
95 'EU will Geldwäsche-Meldepflicht ausdehnen', *Frankfurter Allgemeine Zeitung*, 27 September 2000.
96 However Germany did use constitutional arguments to defend professional secrecy for lawyers.
97 'Germany pressing EU to shut UK tax havens', *Dow Jones International News*, 8 December 1996; 'Oasen bekommen den Segen', *Süddeutsche Zeitung*, 19 November 2001; 'Steuerhinterziehung auch Geldwäsche', *Frankfurter Allgemeine Zeitung*, 23 November 2001.

98 Personal communication with the Federal Criminal Police Office, November 2004.
99 'SPD will Einzug von Gangster-Besitz erleichtern', *Reuters*, 27 January 1994.
100 'City is laundering drug cash says Parliament', *The Times*, 28 February 1990.
101 Mr. Angel, Home Office, in House of Commons 1989: 14.
102 France: Minister of Economic Affairs Laurent Fabius, 13 February 2002, in Montebourg 2002, vol. 2, pp. 647–58; Germany: Federal Ministry of the Interior, 'Geldwäsche mit modernen Instrumentarien effektiv bekämpfen', press release, 20 February 2002.
103 Personal interview at the Ministry of Foreign Affairs in Rome, May 2004.

8 Investigation across borders

1 Unless otherwise stated, the sources are from the following files of the German Federal Archive: B 106/107358: German–American drug enforcement cooperation, 1972–1974; B 106/85197–B 106/85199: High-level meetings of drug-enforcement officials and meetings of the *Ständige Arbeitsgruppe Rauschgift* (STAR), 1969–1974.
2 Formal cooperation with France started in 1975; there were plans to include Scandinavian countries since 1976.
3 See Bundesminister für Jugend, Familie und Gesundheit 1971, 1972.
4 German Federal Archive B 141/58379: Letter from the Ministry of the Interior to the Health Ministry on an expert meeting of the Pompidou Group concerning legal harmonisation, 1 June 1973.
5 German Federal Archive B 106/91326: Letter from the Ministry of the Interior to the Chancellery Office on cooperation with the BNDD, 2 August 1971.
6 Ibid.
7 It is not clear when and if the officer was sent.
8 German Federal Archive B 106/91290: Protocol on an expert meeting of the Pompidou group, 23 May 1972.
9 Most of the sources used for this case study are taken from a file of the French Ministry of the Interior available at the *Centre des Archives Contemporaines* (file n. 19920026/1–6).
10 For a different explanation that links the French policy shift to the change in government from De Gaulle to Pompidou see Krüger 1980: 91–2, 114.
11 Interview with the French Minister of the Interior Raymond Marcellin, *France Soir*, 9 January 1970.
12 Raymond Marcellin, Minister of the Interior, before the National Assembly, 23 October 1970, *Journal Officiel* 1970–71, p. 4629.
13 Ibid.
14 Centre des Archives Contemporaines 19920026/1–6: Letter from the Central Director of the Criminal Police (*Police Judiciaire*) to the General Director of the National Police (*Police Nationale*), 13 February 1970.
15 Raymond Marcellin, Minister of the Interior, before the National Assembly, 23 October 1970, *Journal Officiel* 1970–71, p. 4629.
16 Centre des Archives Contemporaines 19920026/1–6: Accord entre la Direction Générale de la Police Nationale Française (Direction Centrale de la Police Judiciaire) et The United States Bureau of Narcotics and Dangerous Drugs, signed by the French Minister of the Interior Raymond Marcellin and the US Attorney General John Michell, 26 February 1971.
17 'Il faut qu'on sache toute la vérité, déclare M. Raymond Marcellin lors d'un interview télévisé', *Le Monde*, 28 November 1971.

18 Centre des Archives Contemporaines 19920026/1–6: Minutes of the first meeting of the Franco-American intergovernmental committee on drug control, 4 February 1970, p. 6.
19 Centre des Archives Contemporaines 19920026/1–6: Notice on Franco-German drug enforcement cooperation, 28 November 1970.
20 British National Archives FCO 33/1404: *Co-operation between UK and France on problems of drug addiction and drug trafficking*, 1971.
21 Centre des Archives Contemporaines 19920026/1–6: Protocol on a meeting at the Ministry of the Interior on the interception of cannabis, 27 January 1970.
22 Italian Presidency of the Council, personal interview, May 2004; Italian Ministry of the Interior, personal interview, April 2004.
23 British National Archives FCO 33/1404: *Co-operation between UK and France on problems of drug addiction and drug trafficking*, 1971.
24 British National Archives FCO 33/2297: *European Drug Co-operation*, 1974.
25 National Archives FCO 61/1083: *Initiatives of the USA on Narcotics*, 1973.
26 British National Archives FCO 61/800: *Visits by US Narcotic Officials to UK*, 1971. On Nelson Gross see Epstein 1977: 158–62.
27 British National Archives FCO 61/800: Letter from the British Embassy in Washington to the Foreign Office, 29 October 1971.
28 The delay was due to a controversial provision on the interception of telecommunications.
29 Council recommendation for the establishment of Multinational Ad-Hoc Teams for Gathering and Exchanging Information on Terrorists, 25 April 2002, <http://www.consilium.europa.eu> (accessed 17 May 2006); Council 2003; Commission 2004: 27–8.
30 'Prokop: "Partnerschaft für die Sicherheit" zwischen EU und Drittstaaten beschlossen', *Austria Presse Agentur*, 5 May 2006.
31 For the text of the Convention see Council of the European Union 2005. It was hoped that this so-called Schengen III agreement among a vanguard of EU Member States would play a pioneering role and would later be incorporated under the legal umbrella of the European Union (Balzacq *et al.* 2006; Kietz and Maurer 2007).
32 'La coopération judiciaire franco-espagnole a contribué à la chute d'ETA', *AP French Worldstream*, 23 March 2006.
33 Lionel Jospin, in Conseil Européen extraordinaire de Tampere: conférence de presse conjointe du Président de la République, M. Jacques Chirac, et du Premier Ministre, M. Lionel Jospin, 16 October 1999, <http://www.doc.diplomatie.fr> (accessed 16 May 2006); French Ministry of Justice, in Bilan de la présidence française de l'Union européenne en matière de Justice: communiqué du Ministère de la Justice, Paris, 1 March 2001, <http://www.doc.diplomatie.fr> (accessed 16 May 2006).
34 Together with Britain, Spain, and Belgium.
35 Jacques Chirac, press conference with José Maria Aznar, Carcassone, 6 November 2003, <http://www.elysee.fr> (accessed 16 May 2006); 'Paris and Madrid in cross-border police deal', *The Guardian*, 7 November 2003; 'Le communiqué du Conseil des ministres du 14 avril 2004', *Agence France Presse*, 14 April 2004; 'La police nationale se redéploie à l'étranger', *Le Figaro*, 13 September 2004; 'M. de Villepin vise le patrimoine des trafiquants de drogue', *Le Monde*, 17 October 2004.
36 'JHA Council: Ministers agree to have common list of safe asylum countries', *European Report*, 4 October 2003.

37 Lionel Jospin, in Conseil Européen extraordinaire de Tampere: conférence de presse conjointe du Président de la République, M. Jacques Chirac, et du Premier Ministre, M. Lionel Jospin, 16 October 1999, <http://www.doc.diplomatie.fr> (accessed 16 May 2006).
38 Thanks are due to the Federal Criminal Police Office in Wiesbaden, Germany, which gave me the opportunity to study the documents concerning the Schengen negotiations on hot pursuit.
39 Home Office, 'EU framework decision on joint investigation teams', Circular 53/2002, 1 October 2002, p. 5.
40 Bob Ainsworth in the House of Commons Select Committee on European Scrutiny, 2 November 2001, Second Report of 2001.
41 Home Office, 'EU framework decision on joint investigation teams', Circular 53/2002, 1 October 2002, p. 5.
42 Bob Ainsworth in the House of Commons Select Committee on European Scrutiny, 26 March 2002, Twenty-First Report of 2002.
43 Bob Ainsworth in the House of Commons Select Committee on European Scrutiny, 17 December 2001, Tenth Report of 2001.
44 Home Office, 'Blunkett pledges EU crackdown on crack', press release, 13 February 2002; see also Home Office 2002b: 34.
45 Home Office, 'EU framework decision on joint investigation teams', Circular 53/2002, 1 October 2002, pp. 7, 11.
46 Bob Ainsworth in the House of Commons Select Committee on European Scrutiny, 26 March 2002, Twenty-First Report of 2002.
47 Home Office, 'Police Reform Act 2002', Circular 49/2002, 12 September 2002, p. 6. According to the Commission of the Communities (2005b: 25), this is not in compliance with the Framework Decision.
48 See Minister of State in the Home Office Hazel Blears in House of Lords 2005: E131.
49 See Griller *et al.* 1996: 111–121; see also Piepenschneider 1996 and the relevant contributions in Laursen 2002.
50 'Fischer: Tampere ein wichtiger Schritt zur Erweiterung der Union', *Allgemeiner Deutscher Nachrichtendienst*, 28 October 1999.
51 'Schily will EU-Fonds zur Entschädigung von Terroropfern', *Associated Press Worldstream German*, 25 April 2002.
52 'JHA Council: Ministers agree to have common list of safe asylum countries', *European Report*, 4 October 2003.
53 This case study benefits from three personal interviews in April 2004 at the Italian Foreign Ministry (DG European Integration) and at the Italian Ministry of the Interior (Service for International Relations; DG Preventive Policing).
54 Personal interview at the Italian Foreign Ministry (DG European Integration, April 2004).
55 Under-secretary of State Umberto Ranieri in Camera dei Deputati and Senato della Repubblica 2000: 76–7.
56 Council 2003; 'Pisanu: terrorismo bussa porte nostro continente' (sic!), *ANSA*, 2 December 2003; 'Europa: primo sì al mister antiterrorismo', *Il Sole 24 Ore*, 19 March 2004.
57 'Dove si rischia la collisione con la UE', *Il Sole 24 Ore*, 2 October 2001; 'Indagini UE: il Governo frena', *Il Sole 24 Ore*, 26 January 2002.
58 'Vigna: leggi sistematiche per criminalità di sistema', *ANSA*, 9 May 2006.
59 Minister of the Interior Giuseppe Pisanu in a hearing of the bicameral Schengen-Europol Committee (Comitato parlamentare Schengen, Europol e immigrazione),

24 July 2002, p. 4; 'Di Luca: rafforzato in UE ruolo Europol', *Agenzia Giornalistica Italia*, 28 November 2002.

60 'Terrorismo: nascono squadre miste europee per combatterlo', *Agenzia Giornalistica Italia*, 6 November 2003.

9 Results

1 N = 352. In a few carefully selected cases, some particularly important issues were counted twice to increase their weight. For the case studies on Terrorism/Legitimization/1970s (Chapter 3), 32 values on institutional depth are missing because no preferences were formulated.

2 N = 136. The general index (Ξ) is easily computed from the three sub-indices on scope, range, and depth. For the case studies on Terrorism/Legitimization/1970s (Chapter 3), eight values on institutional depth are missing because no preferences were formulated.

3 N = 384. The criteria for coding are discussed in Chapter 2 on pp. 28–30.

4 The full datasets are provided in the 'Downloads' section.

5 Statistical procedure: (1) establish the standard deviation of the four countries for each issue; (2) create a secondary dataset containing the standard deviations; and (3) compute the mean for the entire dataset or any sub-sample. Significance tests: T-test, ANOVA.

6 Mean standard deviation between 0.55 and 0.98.

7 Terrorism: 0.81. Drugs: 0.70. T-test: 0.123.

8 Drugs/1970s: 0.66; 2000s: 0.74. Terrorism/1970s: 0.82; 2000s: 0.80.

9 Drugs/Authorization: 0.55.

10 Terrorism/Authorization: 0.98.

11 Statistical procedure: (1) rank the four countries by the values of their indices for each of the 12 cases; (2) establish mean rank for the each of the four countries, either on the basis of the entire sample or of any sub-sample.

12 France/Drugs/1970s: 4.0; 2000s: 3.3. France/Terrorism/1970s: 2.3; 2000s: 2.5.

13 France/Scope: 2.9; Range: 2.5; Depth: 2.9. France/Legitimization: 3.5; Methods: 2.9; Authorization: 3.0.

14 France/All: 3.0; Germany: 2.8.

15 Germany/Terrorism: 3.2; France: 2.4. Germany/Drugs/1970s: 3.0; 2000s: 2.0.

16 Germany/Depth: 3.1; France: 2.9; Italy: 2.1; Britain: 2.0. Germany/Scope: 2.7; France: 2.9; Italy: 2.2; Britain: 2.2.

17 Britain/Legitimization: 1.3; Methods: 2.1; Authorization: 2.6.

18 Britain/Terrorism: 2.6; Drugs: 1.4.

19 Italy/Authorization: 1.6; Methods: 2.3; Legitimization: 2.5.

20 Italy/2000s/Terrorism: 2.0; Drugs: 3.0.

21 Logically it is not possible to observe three negative correlations in a set of three variables; nor is it possible to observe two positive correlations and one negative correlation.

22 For further details and a survey of the relevant literature see Friedrichs *et al.* 2005.

23 Statistical procedure: (1) rank the four countries by the values of their indices for each of the 12 cases; (2) conduct rank order correlation (Spearman's Rho) for the entire dataset or any sub-sample.

24 Scope∘Depth/1970s/Germany: –0.917 (0.029).

25 Scope∘Range/1970s: 0.475 (0.019); 2000s: 0.580 (0.003). Range∘Depth/1970s: 0.480 (0.032); 2000s: 0.664 (0.001). Scope∘Depth/1970s: 0.698 (0.001); 2000s: 0.759 (0.000).

26 It was necessary to consider two explanations for each dimension, since often the preferences of a state are the result of one explanation having a positive, and another explanation having a negative effect.
27 For the theoretical underpinnings of 'bureaucratic politics' see Allison 1999.
28 Cf. Aden 2001: 109–11.
29 First syllable: Dom = Domestic; Nat =National; Int = International. Second syllable: Int = Interests; Inst = Institutions; Id = Ideas. Third syllable: Pos = Positive impact; Neg = Negative impact.
30 On 'softer' versions of realism see Chapter 2, note 17.
31 Interestingly, there are three sub-samples of the dataset where national interests as often pose an impediment as an incentive to international cooperativeness: Terrorism, Britain, and Legitimization.
32 It should be recognized that this result is not quite as poor as orthodox realists or liberal intergovernmentalists would predict.
33 One should not forget, however, that international organizations also act as self-interested actors in a strategic environment (Barnett and Coleman 2005).
34 IntIntPos/1970s: 9.4; 2000s: 10.9; IntInstPos/1970s: 4.2; 2000s: 10.4; NatIntNeg/1970s: 17.7; 2000s: 10.9; NatInstNeg/1970s: 6.8; 2000s: 3.1.
35 {NatIntPos, IntIntPos, IntInstPos} ∪ {DomInstPos, DomInstNeg, NatInstPos, NatInstNeg, IntInstPos, IntInstNeg} = {NatIntPos, IntIntPos, DomInstPos, DomInstNeg, NatInstPos, NatInstNeg, IntInstPos, IntInstNeg}.
36 {NatIntPos, IntIntPos, IntInstPos} ∪ {DomInstNeg, NatInstNeg, IntInstPos} = {NatIntPos, IntIntPos, DomInstNeg, NatInstNeg, IntInstPos}.
37 {NatIntPos, IntIntPos} for Germany: 36.5; France: 44.8; Britain: 21.9; Italy: 30.3.
38 'International-positive' for Germany: 27.2; France: 29.2; Britain: 11.5; Italy: 16.7.
39 'Ideas-positive' for Germany: 18.8; France: 13.6; Britain: 5.2; Italy: 8.3.
40 'Ideas' for Germany: 26.1; France: 17.1; Britain: 9.4; Italy: 15.6. 'Domestic-negative' for Germany: 3.1; France: 7.3; Britain: 15.7; Italy: 24.0. NatIntNeg for Germany: 4.2; France: 12.5; Britain: 25.0; Italy: 15.6.
41 'International-positive' for Britain: 11.5; Italy: 16.7; Germany: 27.2; France: 29.2.
42 'National interests' for Britain: 44.8; Italy: 39.6; Germany: 29.2; France: 36.5. 'Ideas' for Britain: 9.4; Italy: 15.6; Germany: 26.1; France: 17.7.
43 NatIntNeg for Britain: 25.0; NatIntPos: 19.8. NatIntNeg for Italy: 15.6; NatIntPos: 24.0; NatIntNeg for Germany: 4.2; NatIntPos: 25.0; NatIntNeg for France: 12.5; NatIntPos: 24.0.
44 'Domestic-negative' for Italy: 24.0; Britain: 15.7; Germany: 3.1; France: 7.3.
45 On the Italian 'flight forward' towards Europeanization and internationalization see Mancini 2000.
46 In a completely different field, think of the adoption of the Euro.
47 NatIntNeg for Terrorism: 16.1; Drugs: 12.5.
48 NatIntPos for Terrorism: 17.2; NatIntNeg: 16.1.
49 NatIntPos for Drugs: 29.2; NatIntNeg: 12.5.
50 'Institutions' for Terrorism: 35.5; Drugs: 23.9.
51 'Interests' for 1970s: 57.8; 2000s: 48.3. 'Institutions' for 1970s: 27.1; 2000s: 32.4. Ideas for 1970s: 15.1; 2000s: 19.3.
52 'National' for 1970s: 60.9; 2000s: 46.9. 'International' for 1970s: 19.3; 2000s: 33.3.
53 'Ideas' for Authorization: 22.7; Legitimization: 18.8; Methods: 10.2. 'Interests' for Authorization: 46.9; Legitimization: 59.4; Methods: 53.0.
54 'Domestic institutions' for Methods: 24.2; Legitimization: 0.8, Authorization: 8.6.

55 'Domestic' for Legitimization: 6.3; Methods; 32.7; Authorization: 20.3.
56 'National institutions' for Legitimization: 0.0; Methods: 7.8; Authorization: 10.1.
57 'Interests' for Legitimization: 59.4; Methods: 53.0; Authorization: 46.9.
58 NatIntNeg for Legitimization: 20.3; NatIntPos: 18.8. NatIntNeg for Methods: 10.9; NatIntPos: 29.7. NatIntNeg for Authorization: 11.7; NatIntPos: 21.1.
59 NatIntPos for Mindset: 31.3; Scope: 22.9; Range: 21.9; Depth: 16.7.
60 NatIntNeg for Mindset: 12.5; Scope: 10.4; Range: 12.5; Depth: 21.9.
61 'Domestic' for Scope: 29.1; Mindset: 12.4; Range: 13.5; Depth: 24.1.
62 'Institutions' for Range: 38.5; Depth: 35.5; Mindset: 17.7; Scope: 27.1.

10 Postscript

1 The idea of a policy cycle was originally formulated in the fields of policy science and systems theory (see Lasswell 1956; Easton 1965, 29–33; for a more recent synthesis see Howlett and Ramesh 2003).
2 For an ambitious attempt to examine the policy cycle surrounding the Amsterdam Treaty see Laursen 2002.
3 It will be necessary to make due adaptations according to the research issue at hand.

Bibliography

Abellán Honrubia, V. (1975) 'El terrorismo internacional', *Revista Española de Derecho Internacional* 28: 33–56.

Aden, H. (1998) *Polizeipolitik in Europa: Eine interdisziplinäre Studie über die Polizeiarbeit in Europa am Beispiel Deutschlands, Frankreichs und der Niederlande*, Opladen: Westdeutscher Verlag.

—— (2001) 'Convergence of policing policies and transnational policing in Europe', *European Journal of Crime, Criminal Law and Criminal Justice* 9 (2): 99–112.

Adler, E. (1997) 'Seizing the middle ground: constructivism in world politics', *European Journal of International Relations* 3 (3): 319–63.

—— (2002) 'Constructivism in international relations: sources, contributions, debates, and future directions', in W. Carlsnaes, T. Risse and B.A. Simmons (eds) *Handbook of International Relations*, London: Sage, pp. 95–117.

Albrecht, H.-J. (2001) 'The international system of drug control: developments and trends', in J. Gerber and E.L. Jensen (eds) *Drug War, American Style: The Internationalization of Failed Policy and its Alternatives*, New York and London: Garland, pp. 49–60.

Alderson, K. (2001) 'Making sense of state socialization', *Review of International Studies* 27 (3): 415–33.

Alexander, Y. (ed.) (2002) *Combating Terrorism: Strategies of Ten Countries*, Ann Arbor: Michigan University Press.

—— (ed.) (2006) *Counterterrorism Strategies: Successes and Failures of Six Nations*, Washington, D.C.: Potomac Books.

Allison, G. (1999) *Essence of Decision: Explaining the Cuban Missile Crisis*, New York: Longman.

Anderson, M. (1989) *Policing the World: Interpol and the Politics of International Police Co-operation*, Oxford: Clarendon Press.

—— (1993a) 'The United Kingdom and Organised Crime: the international dimension', *European Journal of Crime, Criminal Law and Criminal Justice* 1 (4): 292–308.

—— (1993b) 'The British perspective on the internationalization of police cooperation in Western Europe', in C. Fijnaut (ed.) *The Internationalization of Police Cooperation in Western Europe*, Arnhem: Gouda Quint, pp. 19–39.

—— (2000) 'Counterterrorism as an objective of European police cooperation', in F. Reinares (ed.) *European Democracies against Terrorism: Governmental Policies and Intergovernmental Cooperation*, Aldershot: Ashgate, pp. 227–43.

Anderson, M. and Boer, M. den (eds) (1993) *Policing across National Boundaries*, London and New York: Pinter.

Anderson, M., Boer, M. den., Cullen, P.J., Gilmore, W., Raab, C. and Walker, N. (1995) *Policing the European Union: Theory, Law and Practice*, Oxford: Clarendon Press.

Andreas, P. and Nadelmann, E. (2006) *Policing the Globe: Criminalization and Crime Control in International Relations*, Oxford: Oxford University Press.

Andreassi, A. (2000) 'Dalla polizia politica alla polizia di sicurezza: un'evoluzione complessa', *Polizia Moderna*, supplement to no. 2, February.

Andreotti, G. (1981a) *Diari 1976–1979: Gli anni della solidarietà*, Milano: Rizzoli.

—— (1981b) 'Considerazioni sul terrorismo', in M. Galleni (ed.) *Rapporto sul terrorismo*, Milano: Rizzoli, pp. 545–53.

Apap, J. (ed.) (2004) *Justice and Home Affairs in the Eu: Liberty and Security Issues after Enlargement*, Cheltenham, Edward Elgar.

Aspinwall, M. (2002) 'Preferring Europe: ideology and national preferences on European integration', *European Union Politics* 3 (1): 81–111.

—— (2007) 'Government preferences on European integration: an empirical test of five theories', *British Journal of Political Studies* 37 (1): 89–114.

Avant, D.D. (2005) *The Market For Force: The Consequences of Privatizing Security*, Cambridge: Cambridge University Press.

Ball, K. and Webster, F. (eds) (2003) *The Intensification of Surveillance: Crime, Terrorism and Warfare in the Information Age*, London: Sterling.

Balzacq, T. and Carrera, S. (eds) (2006) *Security versus Freedom? A Challenge for Europe's Future*, Aldershot: Ashgate.

Balzacq, T., Bigo, D., Carrera, S. and Guild, E. (2006) 'The Treaty of Prüm and EC Treaty: two competing models for EU internal security', in T. Balzacq and S. Carrera (eds) *Security versus Freedom? A Challenge for Europe's Future*, Aldershot: Ashgate, pp. 115–36.

Bamford, J. (2002) *Body of Secrets: Anatomy of the Ultra-Secret National Security Agency*, New York: Anchor Books.

Barberini, R. (2002) 'Alcune osservazioni sul progetto di Convenzione globale contro il terrorismo', *La Comunità Internazionale* 2/2002, pp. 201–10.

Barnett, M. and Coleman, L. (2005) 'Designing police: Interpol and the study of change in international organizations', *International Studies Quarterly* 49 (4): 593–619.

Barr, A.M., Maybanks, E.F., Macmillan, J.R.A. and Sanchez Muñoz, P. (1979) *The Implications of the Increasing Sophistication and International Co-ordination of Terrorist Movements for the Organisation of Security Forces*, London: Seaford House Papers.

Barril, P. (1984) *Missions très spéciales*, Paris: Presses de la Cité.

Bean, P. (1974) *The Social Control of Drugs*, London: Martin Robertson.

—— (2001) 'American influence on British drug policy', in J. Gerber and E.L. Jensen (eds) *Drug War, American Style: The Internationalization of Failed Policy and its Alternatives*, New York: Garland, pp. 79–95.

Becker, K.-H. (1980) 'Competence and strategy concerning suppression of terrorism in the Federal Republic of Germany', paper presented at the conference of the Council of Europe on *Defence of Democracy against Terrorism in Europe: Tasks and Problems*, Strasbourg, 12–14 November 1980.

Beckwith, C.A. and Knox, D. (1983) *Delta Force*, San Diego: Harcourt Brace Jovanovich.

Bell, J.B. (1978) *A Time of Terror: How Democratic Societies Respond to Revolutionary Violence*, New York: Basic Books.

Benyon, J., Turnbull, L., Willis, A., Woodward, R. and Beck, A. (1993) *Police Co-operation in Europe: An Investigation*, Leicester: University of Leicester, Centre for the Study of Public Order.

Bergeron, H. (1999) *L'État et la toxicomanie: Histoire d'une singularité française*, Paris: PUF.

—— (2002) 'Policy paradigms, ideas, and interests: the case of the French public health policy towards drug abuse', *Annals of the American Academy of Political and Social Science* 582 (1): 37–48.

—— (2003) 'When describing is explaining: qualitative methods in the study of French drug addiction treatment policy', in R. Boudon, M. Cherkaoui and P. Demeulenaere (eds) *The European Tradition of Qualitative Research*, London: Sage, Vol. 2, pp. 40–62.

Bigo, D. (1996) *Polices en réseaux: L'expérience européenne*, Paris: Presses de la Fondation Nationale des Sciences Politiques.

Blekxtoon, R. and Ballegooij, W. van (eds) (2005) *Handbook on the European Arrest Warrant*, The Hague: Asser.

Blishchenko, I. and Zhdanov, N. (1984) *Terrorism and International Law*, Moscow: Progress Publishers.

Boekhout van Solinge, T. (2002) *Drugs and Decision-Making in the European Union*, Amsterdam: CEDRO.

—— (2004) *Dealing with Drugs in Europe – An Investigation of European Drug Control Experiences: France, the Netherlands, and Sweden*, The Hague: BJu Legal Publishers.

Boer, M. den (2003) 'The EU counter-terrorism wave: window of opportunity or profound policy transformation?', in M. van Leeuwen (ed.) *Confronting Terrorism: European Experiences, Threat Perceptions and Policies*, The Hague: Kluwer Law International, pp. 185–206.

Bonner, D. (1993) 'United Kingdom: the United Kingdom response to terrorism', in A.P. Schmid and R.D. Crelinsten (eds) *Western Responses to Terrorism*, London: Frank Cass, pp. 171–205.

—— (2000) 'The United Kingdom's response to terrorism: the impact of decisions of European judicial institutions and of the Northern Ireland "peace process"', in Fernando Reinares (ed.) *European Democracies against Terrorism: Governmental Policies and Intergovernmental Cooperation*, Aldershot: Ashgate, pp. 31–71.

Böse, M. (2004) 'Germany', in A. Moore and M. Chiavario (eds) *Police and Judicial Co-operation in the European Union*, Cambridge: Cambridge University Press, pp. 93–117.

Brana, P. (2001) *Mandat d'arrêt sans frontières? Rapport d'information déposé par la Délégation de l'Assemblée Nationale pour l'Union Européenne sur la proposition de décision-cadre relative au mandat d'arrêt européen et aux procédures de remise entre Etats*

membres (COM {2001} 522 final/E 1829), Paris: Assemblée Nationale (= rapport d'information 3506).
Bremer, L.P. III (1993) 'The West's counter-terrorist strategy', in A.P. Schmid and R.D. Crelinsten (eds) *Western Responses to Terrorism*, London: Frank Cass, pp. 255–62.
Bresler, F. (1992) *Interpol*, London: Sinclair-Stevenson.
Briesen, D. (2005) *Drogenkonsum und Drogenpolitik in Deutschland und den USA*, Frankfurt and New York: Campus.
Brodeur, J.-P. (1983) 'High policing and low policing: remarks about the policing of political activities', *Social Problems* 30 (5): 507–20.
Brodeur, J.-P. and Dupeyron, N. (2003) 'Democracy and secrecy: the French intelligence community', in J.-P. Brodeur, P. Gill and D. Töllborg (eds.) *Democracy, Law and Security: Internal Security Services in Contemporary Europe*, Aldershot: Ashgate, pp. 9–29.
Brogden, M. (1982) *The Police: Autonomy and Consent*, London: Academic Press.
Bruun, K., Pan, L. and Rexed, I. (1975) *The Gentlemen's Club: International Control of Drugs and Alcohol*, Chicago and London: University of Chicago Press.
Buckley, M. and Fawn, R. (eds) (2003) *Global Responses to Terrorism: 9/11, Afghanistan and Beyond*, London and New York: Routledge.
Bueno de Mesquita, B. (2001) *Principles of International Politics: People's Power, Preferences, and Perceptions*, Washington, D.C.: CQ Press.
Bundesminister des Innern (1978) *Leistungsbilanz Innere Sicherheit 1969 bis 1978*, Karlsruhe: C.F. Müller.
Bundesminister für Jugend, Familie und Gesundheit (1971) 'Stand der Bekämpfung des Missbrauchs von Rauschgiften und Drogen', in Deutscher Bundestag, 6. Wahlperiode, Drucksache VI/2474, 21 July.
—— (1972) 'Bekämpfung des Drogen- und Rauschmittelmissbrauchs', in Deutscher Bundestag, 6. Wahlperiode, Drucksache VI/3174, 21 February.
Bundesministerium für wirtschaftliche Zusammenarbeit und Entwicklung and Gesellschaft für Technische Zusammenarbeit (2004) *Entwicklungsorientierte Drogenkontrolle: Politik, Strategien, Erfahrungen und Intersektorale Lösungsansätze*, Bonn and Eschborn: Bundesministerium für Wirtschaftliche Zusammenarbeit und Entwicklung.
Bundesregierung (1970) 'Aktionsprogramm zur Bekämpfung des Mißbrauchs von Drogen und Rauschmitteln', *Bulletin des Presse- und Informationsamtes der Bundesregierung* 158, 14 November, pp. 1661–6.
—— (1977) *Dokumentation der Bundesregierung zur Entführung von Hanns Martin Schleyer: Ereignisse und Entscheidungen im Zusammenhang mit der Entführung von Hanns Martin Schleyer und der Lufthansa-Maschine 'Landshut'*, München: Goldmann.
Bunyan, T. (1976) *The History and Practice of the Political Police in Britain*, London: Julian Friedmann.
—— (ed.) (1993) *Statewatching the New Europe: A Handbook on the European State*, London: Statewatch, pp. 15–36.
—— (ed.) (1997) *Key Texts on Justice and Home Affairs in the European Union, Vol. 1 (1976–1993): From Trevi to Maastricht*, London: Statewatch.

Busch, H. (1995) *Grenzenlose Polizei? Neue Grenzen und polizeiliche Zusammenarbeit in Europa*, Münster: Westfälisches Dampfboot.

—— (1999) *Polizeiliche Drogenbekämpfung: Eine internationale Verstrickung*, Münster: Westfälisches Dampfboot.

Busch, H. and Funk, A. (1995) 'Undercover tactics as an element of preventive crime fighting in the Federal Republic of Germany', in C. Fijnaut and G.T. Marx (eds) *Undercover: Police Surveillance in Comparative Perspective*, The Hague: Kluwer, pp. 55–69.

Busch, H., Funk, A., Kauß, U., Narr, W.-D. and Werkentin, F. (1985) *Die Polizei in der Bundesrepublik*, Frankfurt and New York: Campus.

Cabinet Office (2002) *The United Kingdom and the Campaign against International Terrorism: Progress Report*, London: Cabinet Office. Online. Available HTTP: <http://www.fco.gov.uk> (accessed 2 July 2004).

—— (2005) *National Intelligence Machinery*, 3rd edn, London: Stationery Office.

Camera dei Deputati (1979) *Disegno di legge: Ratifica ed esecuzione della Convenzione europea per la repressione del terrorismo, aperta alla firma a Strasburgo il 27 gennaio 1977, presentato il 22 novembre 1979.*

—— (1980) *Disegno di legge: Ratifica ed esecuzione dell'Accordo relativo all'applicazione della Convenzione europea per la repressione del terrorismo tra gli Stati membri delle Comunità europee, firmato a Dublino il 4 dicembre 1979, presentato il 12 agosto 1980.*

—— (ed.) (1981) *Estradizione e reati politici: Il problema della Convenzione europea per la repressione del terrorismo*, Roma: Camera dei Deputati.

—— (1993) *Economia e criminalità: Come difendere l'economia dalla criminalità organizzata*, Roma: Camera dei Deputati.

—— (2002) *Relazione sull'attuazione della convenzione che istituisce l'ufficio europeo di polizia (Europol), presentata dal Ministro dell'Interno (Scajola)*, Roma: Tipografia del Senato.

—— (2003) *Relazione sull'attuazione della convenzione che istituisce l'ufficio europeo di polizia (Europol), presentata dal Ministro dell'Interno (Pisanu)*, Roma: Stabilimenti Tipografici Carlo Colombo.

—— (2004) *Relazione sull'attuazione della convenzione che istituisce l'ufficio europeo di polizia (Europol) (Anno 2003), presentata dal Ministro dell'Interno (Pisanu),* Roma: Tipografia del Senato.

—— (2006) *Relazione sull'attuazione della convenzione che istituisce l'ufficio europeo di polizia (Europol) (Anno 2004), presentata dal Ministro dell'Interno (Pisanu)*, Roma: Stabilimenti Tipografici Carlo Colombo.

Camera dei Deputati and Senato della Repubblica (2000) *Europol: Verso una FBI europea?* Roma: Camera dei Deputati.

Cancrini, L., Malagoli Togliatti, M. and Meucci, G.P. (1977) *Droga: Chi come perché e soprattutto che fare*, 2nd edn, Firenze: Nuova Biblioteca.

Carbonneau, T.E. (1977) 'The provisional arrest and subsequent release of Abu Daoud by French authorities', *Virginia Journal of International Law* 17 (3): 495–513.

Cardona, M. (1993) 'The European response to terrorism', in A.P. Schmid and R.D. Crelinsten (eds) *Western Responses to Terrorism*, London: Frank Cass, pp. 245–54.

Cassese, A. (1989) *Terrorism, Politics and Law: The Achille Lauro Affair*, Oxford: Polity Press.

Cerny, P.G. (1981) 'France: non-terrorism and the politics of repressive tolerance', in J. Lodge (ed.) *Terrorism: A Challenge to the State*, Oxford: Martin Robertson, pp. 91–118.

Cettina, N. (2003) 'The French approach: vigour and vigilance', in M. van Leeuwen (ed.) *Confronting Terrorism: European Experiences, Threat Perceptions and Policies*, The Hague: Kluwer Law International, pp. 71–94.

Chalk, P. (1996) *West European Terrorism and Counter-Terrorism: The Evolving Dynamic*, Basingstoke: Macmillan.

Chalk, P. and Rosenau, W. (2004) *Confronting the 'Enemy Within': Security Intelligence, the Police, and Counterterrorism in Four Democracies*, Santa Monica: RAND Corporation.

Chambliss, W.J. (2001) *Power, Politics, and Crime*, Boulder: Westview.

Chapman, B. (1970) *Police State*, London: Pall Mall.

Charters, D.A. (1991) 'Counterterrorism intelligence: sources, methods, process, and problems', in D.A. Charters (ed.) *Democratic Responses to International Terrorism*, New York: Transnational Publishers, pp. 227–66.

Chase, K.A. (2005) *Trading Blocs: States, Firms, and Regions in the World Economy*, Ann Arbor: University of Michigan Press.

Chauvin, L. (1990) 'French diplomacy and the hostage crisis', in B.M. Rubin (ed.) *The Politics of Counterterrorism: The Ordeal of Democratic States*, Washington: Foreign Policy Institute, pp. 91–104.

Chauvy, Y. (1981) *L'extradition*, Paris: Presses Universitaires de France.

Checkel, J.T. (1998) 'The constructivist turn in international relations theory', *World Politics* 50 (2): 324–48.

—— (ed.) (2005) 'International institutions and socialization in Europe', *International Organization* 59 (4): 801–1079 (= special issue).

Chiavario, M. (1986) 'La Convenzione europea contro il terrorismo al giro di boa della ratifica (con riserva)', *Legislazione Penale* 18 (3): 433–50.

Ciampicali, P.A. (1998) 'La nascita in Italia di una intelligence finanziaria: il ruolo dell'Ufficio Italiano Cambi', in F. Bruni and D. Masciandaro (eds) *Mercati finanziari e riciclaggio: L'Italia nello scenario internazionale*, Milano: EGEA, pp. 101–25.

Clark, W.R. (1998) 'Agents and structures: two views of preferences, two views of institutions', *International Studies Quarterly* 42 (2): 245–70.

Clutterbuck, R. (1975) *Living with Terrorism*, London: Faber & Faber.

—— (1990) *Terrorism, Drugs and Crime in Europe after 1992*, London and New York: Routledge.

—— (1993) 'Negotiating with terrorists', in A.P. Schmid and R.D. Crelinsten (eds) *Western Responses to Terrorism*, London: Frank Cass, pp. 263–87.

Coker, C. (2001) 'Outsourcing war', in D. Josselin and W. Wallace (eds) *Non-State Actors in World Politics*, Basingstoke: Palgrave, pp. 189–202.

Commission of the European Communities (2004) *Communication from the Commission to the European Parliament and the Council: Enhancing police and customs co-operation in the European Union*, COM(2004)376 final, 18 May.

—— (2005a) *Report from the Commission on National Measures Taken to Comply with the Council Framework Decision of 13 June 2002 on Joint Investigation Teams*, COM(2004)858 final, 7 January.

—— (2005b) *Annex to the Report from the Commission on National Measures Taken to Comply with the Council Framework Decision of 13 June 2002 on Joint Investigation Teams*, SEC(2004)1725, 7 January.

—— (2006a) *Report from the Commission based on Article 34 of the Council Framework Decision of 13 June 2002 on the European Arrest Warrant and the Surrender Procedures between Member States*, COM(2006)8 final, 24 January.

—— (2006b) *Commission Staff Working Document: Annex to the Report from the Commission based on Article 34 of the Council Framework Decision of 13 June 2002 on the European Arrest Warrant and the Surrender Procedures between Member States*, SEC(2006)79, 24 January.

Commissioner of Police of the Metropolis (1974) *Report to the Home Secretary on the Actions of Police Officers concerned with the Case of Kenneth Joseph Lennon*, London: Stationery Office.

Cornetta, M. (1996) 'Introduzione', in E. Palombi (ed.) *Il riciclaggio dei proventi illeciti: Tra politica criminale e diritto vigente*, Napoli: Edizioni Scientifiche Italiane, pp. 19–43.

Corradino, M. (2002) 'Strategie normative di contrasto al riciclaggio di denaro di provenienza illecita', in L. di Brina and M.L. Piccio Forlati (eds) *Normativa antiriciclaggio e contrasto della criminalità economica*, Milano: CEDAM, pp. 1–40.

Corves, E. (1978) 'International cooperation in the field of international political terrorism', *Terrorism: An International Journal* 1 (2): 199–210.

Council of Europe (1977) *Explanatory Report on the European Convention on the Suppression of Terrorism*, Strasbourg: Council of Europe.

Council of the European Communities (1978) 'Answer to Written Question No 346/77', *Official Journal of the European Communities* C 30, 6 February, p. 8.

Council of the European Union (2001a) *Initiative of the Kingdom of Belgium, the French Republic, the Kingdom of Spain and the United Kingdom for the adoption by the Council of a draft Framework Decision on Joint Investigation Teams*, Doc. 11990/01, 19 September.

—— (2001b) *Initiative of the Kingdom of Belgium, the French Republic, the Kingdom of Spain and the United Kingdom for the adoption by the Council of a draft Framework Decision on Joint Investigation Teams*, Doc. 11990/01 Add 1, 16 November.

—— (2002) 'Council Framework Decision of 13 June 2002 on Joint Investigation Teams (2002/465/JHA)', *Official Journal of the European Communities* L 162, 20 June, pp. 1–3.

—— (2003) *Justice and Home Affairs: 2529th Council Meeting on Multinational Ad Hoc Teams for Exchanging Information on Terrorists*, Doc. 12762/03 (Presse 278), provisional version, 2–3 October 2003.

—— (2005) *Prüm Convention*, Doc. 10900/05, 7 July.

Cusack, J.T. (1974) 'Response of the Government of France to the international heroin problem', in L.R.S. Simmons and A.A. Said (eds) *Drugs, Politics, and Diplomacy: The International Connection*, Beverly Hills and London: Sage, pp. 229–56.

Dalgaard-Nielsen, A. and Hamilton, D.S. (2006) *Transatlantic Homeland Security: Protecting Society in the Age of Catastrophic Terrorism*, London and New York: Routledge.

Davis, J.W. (2005) *Terms of Inquiry: On the Theory and Practice of Political Science*, Baltimore: Johns Hopkins University Press.

Deflem, M. (2002) *Policing World Society: Historical Foundations of International Police Cooperation*, Oxford: Oxford University Press.

Della Porta, D. (1993) 'Institutional responses to terrorism: the Italian case', in A.P. Schmid and R.D. Crelinsten (eds) *Western Responses to Terrorism*, London: Frank Cass, pp. 151–70.

Department of State (1973) 'U.S. votes against U.N. General Assembly resolution calling for study of terrorism', *Department of State Bulletin*, 22 January, pp. 81–94.

Dietl, W. (2004) *Die BKA Story*, 2nd edn, München: Knaur.

Dini, L. (1997) 'The problem and its diverse dimensions', in E.U. Savona (ed.) *Responding to Money Laundering: International Perspectives*, Amsterdam: Harwood, pp. 3–8.

Direzione Centrale per i Servizi Antidroga (2004) *Il contrasto al traffico illecito di sostanze stupefacenti: Annuale 2003*, Roma: Presidenza del Consiglio.

Dobson, C. and Payne, R. (1982) *Terror! The West Fights Back*, London and Basingstoke: Macmillan.

Dombrowski, P. (1998) 'Haute Finance and high theory: recent scholarship on global financial relations', *Mershon International Studies Review* 42 (1): 1–28.

Dorn, N., Murji, K. and South, N. (1992) *Traffickers: Drug Markets and Law Enforcement*, London and New York: Routledge.

Drake, R. (1982) 'The Red Brigades and the Italian political tradition', in Y. Alexander and K.A. Myers (eds) *Terrorism in Europe*, London and Canberra: Croom Helm, pp. 102–40.

Drogenbeauftragte der Bundesregierung (2003) *Aktionsplan Drogen und Sucht*, Bonn: Bundesregierung.

Dubin, M.D. (1991) *International Terrorism: Two League of Nations Conventions, 1934–1937*, Millwood: Kraus International Publications.

Dubois, J.-P. (1979) 'La défense des libertés en Europe: une tâche importante pour le Parlement européen', *Critique Politique*, no. 3.

Dugard, J. (1974) 'International terrorism: problems of definition', *International Affairs* 50 (1): 67–81.

—— (1982) 'International terrorism and the just war', in D.C. Rapoport and Y. Alexander (eds) *The Morality of Terrorism: Religious and Secular Justifications*, New York: Pergamon, pp. 77–97.

Easton, D. (1965) *A Systems Analysis of Political Life*, New York: John Wiley.

Ehrenberg, A. (1995) *L'individu incertain*, Paris: Calmann-Lévy.

—— (1996) 'Comment vivre avec les drogues? Questions de recherche et enjeux politiques', in A. Ehrenberg (ed.) *Vivre avec les drogues: Régulations, politiques, marchés, usages*, Paris: Seuil, pp. 5–25 (= *Communications* 62).

Elias, N. (2000 [1939]) *The Civilizing Process: Sociogenetic and Psychogenetic Investigations*, Malden: Blackwell.

Ellinger, H. (1972) 'Bekämpfung der Rauschmittelkriminalität: Hiltruper Seminare von Praktikern für Praktiker', *Kriminalistik* 26 (6): 265–7.

Elman, C. (2005) 'Explanatory typologies in qualitative studies of international politics', *International Organization* 59 (2): 293–326.

Elvins, M. (2003) *Anti-Drugs Policies of the European Union: Transnational Decision-Making and the Politics of Expertise*, Basingstoke: Palgrave-Macmillan.

Epstein, E.J. (1977) *Agency of Fear: Opiates and Political Power in America*, New York: G.P. Putnam's Sons.

Evans, E.N. (1978) 'American policy response to international terrorism: problems of deterrence', in M.H. Livingston (ed.) *International Terrorism in the Contemporary World*, Westport: Greenwood Press, pp. 376–85.

Evans, R.H. (1993) 'Terrorism and subversion of the state: Italian legal responses', in E. Moxon-Browne (ed.) *European Terrorism*, Aldershot: Dartmouth, pp. 467–95.

—— (1994) 'Italy and international terrorism', in D.A. Charters (ed.) *The Deadly Sin of Terrorism: Its Effect on Democracy and Civil Liberty in Six Countries*, Westport, CT: Greenwood Press, pp. 73–102.

Fauceglia, G. (1996) 'Il riciclaggio tra priapismo legislativo ed incontinenza regolamentare', in E. Palombi (ed.) *Il riciclaggio dei proventi illeciti: Tra politica criminale e diritto vigente*, Napoli: Edizioni Scientifiche Italiane, pp. 250–5.

Fazey, C.S.J. (2003) 'The Commission on Narcotic Drugs and the United Nations International Drug Control Programme: politics, policies and prospects for change', *International Journal of Drug Policy* 14: 155–69.

Fijnaut, C. (2004) 'Police co-operation and the Area of Freedom, Security and Justice', in N. Walker (ed.) *Europe's Area of Freedom, Security and Justice*, Oxford: Oxford University Press, pp. 241–82.

—— (ed.) (1993) *The Internationalization of Police Cooperation in Western Europe*, Arnhem: Gouda Quint.

Fijnaut, C. and Marx, G.T. (eds) (1995) *Undercover: Police Surveillance in Comparative Perspective*, The Hague: Kluwer.

Fijnaut, C. and Paoli, L. (eds) (2004) *Organised Crime in Europe: Concepts, Patterns and Control Policies in the European Union and Beyond*, Dordrecht: Springer.

Finnemore, M. (2003) *The Purpose of Intervention: Changing Beliefs about the Use of Force*, Ithaca: Cornell University Press.

Finnemore, M. and Sikkink, K. (1998) 'International norm dynamics and political change', *International Organization* 52 (4): 887–917.

Fischer, J. and Villepin, D. de (2002) *Joint Franco-German Proposals to the European Convention on an Area of Freedom, Security and Justice*, CONV 435/02, 28 November.

Foreign and Commonwealth Office (2003a) *The United Kingdom in the United Nations*, London: HMCO.

—— (2003b) 'UK's Approach to Tackling Drugs', paper submitted to the G8 Drug Trafficking Conference, 22 May 2003. Online. Available HTTP: <http://www.diplomatie.gouv.fr> (accessed 28 February 2006).

Franck, T.M. and Lockwood, B.B. (1974) 'Preliminary thoughts towards an international convention on terrorism', *American Journal of International Law* 68 (1): 69–90.

Frattini, F. (2001) 'La riforma dei servizi di informazione e sicurezza anche alla luce dei nuovi scenari di minaccia alla sicurezza del paese', in Istituto Alti Studi per la Difesa, *Quaderni* 53 (1): 1–5.

Freestone, D. (1981) 'Legal responses to terrorism: towards European cooperation?', in J. Lodge (ed.) *Terrorism: A Challenge to the State*, Oxford: Martin Robertson, pp. 195–224.

Freund, C. and Rittberger, V. (2001) 'Utilitarian-liberal foreign policy theory', in V. Rittberger (ed.) *German Foreign Policy since Unification: Theories and Case Studies*, Manchester: Manchester University Press, pp. 68–104.

Frieden, J.A. (1999) 'Actors and preferences in international relations', in D.A. Lake and R. Powell (eds) *Strategic Choice and International Relations*, Princeton: Princeton University Press, pp. 39–76.

Friedrichs, J. (2006a) 'Defining the international public enemy: the political struggle behind the legal debate on international terrorism', *Leiden Journal of International Law* 19 (1): 69–91.

—— (2006b) 'When push comes to shove: the territorial monopoly of force and the travails of neomedieval Europe', in M. Burgess and H. Vollaard (eds) *State Territoriality and European Integration*, London and New York: Routledge, pp. 228–51.

Friedrichs, J., Mihov, J. and Popova, M. (2005) 'Synergies and tradeoffs in international cooperation: broadening, widening, and deepening', *European Integration Online Papers* 13 (9). Online. Available HTTP: <http://eiop.or.at/eiop/texte/2005-013a.htm> (accessed 8 July 2007).

Friesendorf, C. (2001) *Der internationale Drogenhandel als sicherheitspolitisches Risiko*, Münster: LIT-Verlag.

—— (2007) *US Foreign Policy and the War on Drugs: Displacing the Cocaine and Heroine Industry*, London and New York: Routledge.

Friman, H.R. (1996) *NarcoDiplomacy: Exporting the U.S. War on Drugs*, Ithaca: Cornell University Press.

Fröhlich, S. (1985) 'Eröffnungsansprache', in Bundeskriminalamt Wiesbaden (ed.) *Internationale Verbrechensbekämpfung: Europäische Perspektiven. Arbeitstagung des Bundeskriminalamtes Wiesbaden vom 5.-8. November 1984*, Wiesbaden: Bundeskriminalamt, pp. 7–16.

Funk, A. (2000) 'Das deutsche System der Inneren Sicherheit im Prozeß der Europäisierung', in H.-J. Lange (ed.) *Staat, Demokratie und Innere Sicherheit in Deutschland*, Opladen: Leske+Budrich, pp. 291–309.

Gal-Or, N. (1985) *International Cooperation to Suppress Terrorism*, London and Sydney: Croom Helm.

Gardner, R.N. (1979) 'Drug abuse: the Italian response', *Drug Enforcement*, February, 13–15.

Garland, D. (2001) *The Culture of Control: Crime and Social Order in Contemporary Society*, Oxford: Oxford University Press.

Garrett, G. and Weingast, B.R. (1993) 'Ideas, interests, and institutions: constructing the European Community's internal market', in J. Goldstein and R.O. Keohane (eds) *Ideas and Foreign Policy: Beliefs, Institutions, and Political Change*, Ithaca: Cornell University Press, pp. 173–206.

Gennaro, G. de (2003) *La cooperazione di polizia nel quadro della nuova architettura europea*, Roma, 11 June 2003. Online. Available http: <http://www.poliziadistato.it> (accessed 22 November 2004).

Gennaro, G. di (1991) *La guerra della droga*, Milano: Mondadori.

Genova, R. (1985) *Missione antiterrorismo*, Milano: Sugarco.

George, A.L. and Bennett, A. (2005) *Case Studies and Theory Development in the Social Sciences*, Harvard, MA: MIT Press.

George, S. (1998) *An Awkward Partner: Britain in the European Community*, 3rd edn, Oxford: Oxford University Press.

Geraghty, T. (1993) *Who Dares Wins: The Story of the SAS 1950-1992*, London: Time Warner.

Gerber, E.R. and Jackson, J.E. (1993) 'Endogenous preferences and the study of institutions', *American Political Science Review* 87 (3): 639–56.

Gerber, J. and Jensen, E.L. (eds) (2001) *Drug War, American Style: The Internationalization of Failed Policy and its Alternatives*, New York: Garland.

Gerring, J. (2007) *Case Study Research: Principles and Practices*, Cambridge: Cambridge University Press.

Gévaudan, H. (1985) *La bataille de la 'French Connection': Récit*, Paris: Lattès.

Giddens, A. (1985) *The Nation-State and Violence*, Oxford: Polity Press.

Gilligan, G.P. (2004) 'Overview: markets, offshore sovereignty and onshore legitimacy', in D. Masciandaro (ed.) *Global Financial Crime: Terrorism, Money Laundering and Offshore Centres*, Aldershot: Ashgate, pp. 7–59.

Gilmore, D.C. (1999) *Dirty Money: The Evolution of Money Laundering Countermeasures*, 2nd edn, Strasbourg: Council of Europe Publishing.

Ginkel, B.T. van (2003) 'The United Nations: towards a comprehensive convention on combating terrorism', in M. van Leeuwen (ed.) *Confronting Terrorism: European Experiences, Threat Perceptions and Policies*, The Hague: Kluwer Law International, pp. 207–25.

Gioia, A. (2004) 'The definition of terrorism in international criminal law', in W.P. Heere (ed.) *From Government to Governance: The Growing Impact of Non-State Actors on the International and European Legal System*, The Hague: Asser, pp. 339–48.

—— (2006) 'The UN conventions on the prevention and suppression of international terrorism', in G. Nesi (ed.) *International Cooperation in Counter-terrorism: The United Nations and Regional Organizations in the Fight Against Terrorism*, Aldershot: Ashgate, pp. 3–23.

Glaeßner, G.-J. and Lorenz, A. (eds) (2005) *Europäisierung der Inneren Sicherheit: Eine vergleichende Untersuchung am Beispiel von organisierter Kriminalität und Terrorismus*, Wiesbaden: VS Verlag.

Glaser, B.G. and Strauss, A.L. (1967) *The Discovery of Grounded Theory: Strategies for Grounded Research*, New York: Aldine.

Goertz, G. (2005) *Social Science Concepts: A User's Guide*, Princeton: Princeton University Press.

Goldstein, J. and Keohane, R.O. (eds) (1993) *Ideas and Foreign Policy: Beliefs, Institutions, and Political Change*, Ithaca: Cornell University Press.

Greenfield, R. (1977) 'The Abu Daoud affair', *Journal of International Law and Economics* 11 (3): 539–82.

Gregory, F.E.C. (1991) 'Police cooperation and integration in the European Community: proposals, problems, and prospects', *Terrorism* 14 (3): 145–55.

Gregory, S. (2003) 'France and the war on terrorism', *Terrorism and Political Violence* 15 (1): 124–47.

Grevi, V. (2002) 'Il "Mandato d'arresto europeo" tra ambiguità politiche e attuazione legislativa', *Il Mulino* 51 (1): 119–29.

Griller, Droutsas, Falkner, Forgó, Klatzer, Mayer and Nentwich (1996) *Regierungskonferenz 1996: Ausgangspositionen*, Wien: Forschungsinstitut für Europafragen.

Grimm, D. (2003) 'The State Monopoly of Force', in W. Heitmeyer and J. Hagan (eds) *International Handbook of Violence Research*, Dordrecht: Kluwer Academic Publishers, pp. 1043–56.

Groom, A.J.R. and Taylor, P. (eds) (1975) *Functionalism: Theory and Practice in International Relations*, London: University of London Press.

Gross, N. (1972) 'Bilateral and multilateral efforts to intensify drug abuse control programs', *Department of State Bulletin*, 3 April, pp. 504–12.

Guillaume, G. (1993) 'France and the fight against terrorism', in A.P. Schmid and R.D. Crelinsten (eds) *Western Responses to Terrorism*, London: Frank Cass, pp. 131–5.

Haas, G. (2000) *Die Auslieferung in Frankreich und Deutschland*, Berlin: Berlin Verlag Arno Spitz.

Hafner, G. (2006) 'The definition of the crime of terrorism', in G. Nesi (ed.) *International Cooperation in Counter-terrorism: The United Nations and Regional Organizations in the Fight Against Terrorism*, Aldershot: Ashgate, pp. 33–4.

Haftendorn, H. (2001) *Deutsche Außenpolitik zwischen Selbstbeschränkung und Selbstbehauptung: 1945–2000*, Stuttgart and München: Deutsche Verlags-Anstalt.

Hain, P. (ed.) (1980) *Policing the Police*, Vol. 2, London: John Calder.

Hall, R.B. (1999) *National Collective Identity: Social Constructs and International Systems*, New York: Columbia University Press.

Hall, B. and Bhatt, A. (1999) *Policing Europe: EU Justice and Home Affairs Co-operation*, London: Centre for European Reform.

Hall, P.A. and Taylor, R.C.R. (1996) 'Political science and the three new institutionalisms', *Political Studies* 44 (4): 936–57.

Harrison, M.M. (1994) 'France and international terrorism: problem and response', in D.A. Charters (ed.) *The Deadly Sin of Terrorism: Its Effect on Democracy and Civil Liberty in Six Countries*, Westport: Greenwood Press, pp. 103–35.

Hebenton, B. and Thomas, T. (1995) *Policing Europe: Co-operation, Conflict and Control*, New York: St. Martin's Press.

Her Majesty's Inspectorate of Constabulary (2003) *A Need to Know: HMIC Thematic Inspection of Special Branch and Ports Policing*, London: Home Office Communication Directorate.

Hermant, D. and Bigo, D. (2000) 'Les Politiques de Lutte contre le Terrorisme: Enjeux Français', in F. Reinares (ed.) *European Democracies against Terrorism: Governmental Policies and Intergovernmental Cooperation*, Aldershot: Ashgate, pp. 73–118.

Herold, H. (1972) 'Gesellschaftlicher Wandel: Chance der Polizei', *Die Polizei* 63 (5): 133–7.

—— (1980) 'Perspektiven der internationalen Fahndung nach Terroristen: Möglichkeiten und Grenzen', *Kriminalistik* 34 (4): 165–71.

Hobbes, T. (1998 [1651]) *Leviathan*, Oxford: Oxford University Press.

Hoffacker, L. (1975) 'The U.S. Government response to terrorism: a global approach', in M.C. Bassiouni (ed.) *International Terrorism and Political Crimes*, Springfield: Charles C. Thomas, pp. 537–45.

Hollingsworth, M. and Fielding, N. (2003) *Defending the Realm: Inside MI5 and the War on Terrorism*, London: André Deutsch.

Home Office (2001) *Extradition: A Review*, London: Home Office.

—— (2002a) *Extradition Bill: Explanatory Notes*, London: Home Office.

—— (2002b) *Updated Drug Strategy 2002*, London: Home Office.

—— (2002c) *The Government's Drugs Policy: Is it Working? The Government Reply to the Third Report from the Home Affairs Committee*, London: Stationery Office.

—— (2004) *One Step Ahead: A 21st Century Strategy to Defeat Organised Crime*, London: Stationery Office.

Horchem, H.J. (1980) 'Terrorism and government response: the German experience', *Jerusalem Journal of International Relations* 4 (3): 43–55.

House of Commons European Scrutiny Committee (2002) *Thirty-Ninth Report of Session 2001–02*, London: Stationery Office.

—— (2004) *The EU's Justice and Home Affairs Work Programme for the Next Five Years*, London: Stationery Office.

House of Commons Home Affairs Committee (1989) *Drug Trafficking and Related Serious Crime. Volume II: Minutes of Evidence and Appendices*, London: Stationery Office.

—— (1990a) *Practical Police Co-operation in the European Community: Memoranda of Evidence*, London: Stationery Office.

—— (1990b) *Practical Police Co-operation in the European Community: Volume II*, London: Stationery Office.

—— (1991) *Practical Police Co-operation in the European Community: The Government Reply to the Seventh Report from the Home Affairs Committee*, London: Stationery Office.

—— (2003) *Extradition Bill: Government Response to the Committee's First Report,* London: Stationery Office.

House of Lords European Union Committee (2005) *After Madrid: The EU's Response to Terrorism. Report with Evidence*, London: Stationery Office.

—— (2006) *European Arrest Warrant: Recent Developments. Report with Evidence*, London: Stationery Office.

House of Lords Select Committee on the European Communities (1995) *Europol. With Evidence*, London: Stationery Office.

House of Lords Select Committee on the European Union (2001) *Counter Terrorism: The European Arrest Warrant*, London: Stationery Office.

—— (2003) *Government Responses: Review of Scrutiny; Europol's Role in Fighting Crime; and EU Russia Relations*, London: Stationery Office.

Hoveyda, F. (1977) 'The problem of international terrorism at the United Nations', *Terrorism: An International Journal* 1 (1): 71–83.

Howlett, M. and Ramesh, M. (2003) *Studying Public Policy: Policy Cycles and Policy Subsystems*, 2nd edn, Oxford and Toronto: Oxford University Press.

Hoyer, P. and Klos, J. (1998) *Regelungen zur Bekämpfung der Geldwäsche und ihre Anwendung in der Praxis: Geldwäschegesetz, Gesetz zur Verbesserung der Bekämpfung der Organisierten Kriminalität, Internationale Regelungen*, 2nd edn, Bielefeld: Erich Schmidt Verlag.

Hug, S. (2003) 'Endogenous preferences and delegation in the European Union', *Comparative Political Studies* 36 (1/2): 41–74.

Hug, S. and König, T. (2002) 'In view of ratification: governmental preferences and domestic constraints at the Amsterdam intergovernmental conference', *International Organization* 56 (2): 447–76.

Iezzi, M. (1990) *Agente provocatore e agente infiltrato nella lotta alla criminalità organizzata e al traffico di stupefacenti*, University of Genova: MA thesis.

Intelligence and Security Committee (2006) *Annual Report 2005–2006*, London: Stationery Office.

Istituto per la Documentazione e gli Studi Legislativi (ed.) (1976) *Nuova normativa sugli stupefacenti: Aspetti giuridici e sanitari*, Milano: Giuffrè.

Jachtenfuchs, M. (2002) *Die Konstruktion Europas: Verfassungsideen und institutionelle Entwicklung*, Baden-Baden: Nomos.

—— (2005) 'The monopoly of legitimate force: denationalization, or business as usual?', in S. Leibfried and M. Zürn (eds) *Transformations of the State?*, Cambridge: Cambridge University Press, pp. 37–52.

Jamieson, A. (1989) *The Heart Attacked: Terrorism and Conflict in the Italian State*, London and New York: Marion Boyars.

Jarach, A. (1979) *Terrorismo internazionale: Gruppi, collegamenti, lotta antiterroristica*, Firenze: Vallecchi.

Jelsma, M. (2003) 'Drugs in the UN system: the unwritten history of the 1998 United Nations General Assembly Special Session on drugs', *International Journal of Drug Policy* 14: 181–95.

Johansen, A. (2005) *Soldiers as Police: The French and Prussian Armies and the Policing of Popular Protest, 1889–1914*, Aldershot: Ashgate.

John, P.St. (1991) 'Counterterrorism policy-making: the case of aircraft hijacking, 1968-1988', in D.A. Charters (ed.) *Democratic Responses to International Terrorism*, New York: Transnational Publishers, pp. 67–121.

Johnston, A.I. (2001) 'Treating international institutions as social environments', *International Studies Quarterly* 45 (3): 487–515.

—— (2005) 'Conclusions and extensions: toward mid-range theorizing and beyond Europe', *International Organization* 59 (4): 1013–44.

Johnston, L. (2006) 'Transnational security governance', in J. Wood and B. Dupont (eds) *Democracy, Society and the Governance of Security*, Cambridge: Cambridge University Press, pp. 33–51.

Johnston, L. and Shearing, C. (2003) *Governing Security: Explorations in Policing and Justice*, London and New York: Routledge.

Jonge Oudraat, C. de (2004) 'The role of the Security Council', in J. Boulden and T.G. Weiss (eds) *Terrorism and the UN: Before and After September 11*, Bloomington and Indianapolis: Indiana University Press, pp. 151–72.

Josephson, J.R. (2000) 'Smart Inductive Generalizations are Abductions', in P.A. Flach and A. Kakas (eds) *Abduction and Induction: Essays on their Relation and Integration*, Dordrecht: Kluwer, pp. 31–44.

Joubert, C. (1995) 'National and international aspects of undercover policing', *The Police Journal* 68 (4): 305–18.

Joubert, C. and Bevers, H. (1996) *Schengen Investigated: A Comparative Interpretation of the Schengen Provisions on International Police Cooperation in the Light of the European Convention on Human Rights*, The Hague and London: Kluwer Law International.

Julien-Laferrière, F. (1979) 'La Convention européenne pour la répression du terrorisme', *Après-demain* 211 (February): 43–5.

Katzenstein, P.J. (1987) *Policy and Politics in West Germany: The Growth of a Semisovereign State*, Philadelphia: Temple University Press.

—— (1990) *West Germany's Internal Security Policy: State and Violence in the 1970s and 1980s*, Ithaca: Cornell University.

—— (1997) (ed.) *Tamed Power: Germany in Europe*, Ithaca: Cornell University Press.

—— (2003) 'Same war – different views: Germany, Japan, and counterterrorism', *International Organization* 57 (4): 731–60.

Keohane, R.O. (1982) 'The demand for international regimes', *International Organization* 36 (2): 325–55.

—— (1989) 'Neoliberal Institutionalism: a perspective in world politics', in R.O. Keohane (ed.) *International Institutions and State Power: Essays in International Relations Theory*, Boulder: Westview, pp. 1–20.

Keohane, R.O. and Martin, L.L. (1995) 'The promise of institutionalist theory', *International Security* 20 (1): 39–51.

Kerstetter, W.A. (1978) 'Practical problems of law enforcement', in A.E. Evans and J.F. Murphy (eds) *Legal Aspects of International Terrorism*, Lexington: Lexington Books, pp. 535–51.

—— (1979) 'Terrorism and intelligence', *Terrorism: An International Journal* 3 (1–2): 109–15.

Kietz, D. and Maurer, A. (2007) 'Fragmentierung und Entdemokratisierung der europäischen Justiz- und Innenpolitik: Folgen der Prümer Vertragsavantgarde', in M.H.W. Möllers and R.C. van Ooyen (eds) *Jahrbuch Öffentliche Sicherheit 2006/2007*, Frankfurt: Verlag für Polizeiwissenschaft, forthcoming.

King, G., Keohane, R.O. and Verba, S. (1994) *Designing Social Inquiry: Scientific Inference in Qualitative Research*, Princeton: Princeton University Press.

King, R. (1972) *The Drug Hang-Up: America's Fifty-Year Folly*, New York: Norton.

Klein, A. (2000) 'Misguided missiles: drugs war in Colombia', *Druglink* 15 (3): 16–17.

Kleine, M. (2004) *Die Reaktion der Europäischen Union auf den 11. September*, Münster: LIT-Verlag.

Knöbl, W. (1998) *Polizei und Herrschaft im Modernisierungsprozeß: Staatsbildung und Innere Sicherheit in Preußen, England und Amerika 1700–1914*, Frankfurt and New York: Campus.

Knopf, J.W. (1998) 'Domestic sources of preferences for arms cooperation: the impact of protest', *Journal of Peace Research* 35 (6): 677–95.

Koenig, D.J. and Das, D.K. (eds) (2001) *International Police Cooperation: A World Perspective*, Lanham: Lexington Books.

Koenig-Archibugi, M. (2004) 'Explaining government preferences for institutional change in EU Foreign and Security Policy', *International Organization* 58 (1): 137–74.

Koering-Joulin, R. and Labayle, H. (1988) 'Dix ans après: de la signature (1977) à la ratification (1987) de la Convention européenne pour la répression du terrorisme', *La Semaine Juridique* 62 (33–7), No. 3349.

Kolb, D.A. (1984) *Experiential Learning: Experience as the Source of Learning and Development*, Englewood-Cliffs: Prentice Hall.

Krüger, H. (1980) *The Great Heroin Coup: Drugs, Intelligence, and International Fascism*, Boston: South End Press.

Lacoste, I. (1982) *Die Europäische Terrorismus-Konvention: Eine Untersuchung des Europäischen Übereinkommens zur Bekämpfung des Terrorismus vom 27. Januar 1977 im Vergleich mit ähnlichen internationalen Abkommen und unter Berücksichtigung des schweizerischen Rechts*, Zürich: Schulthess Polygraphischer Verlag.

Lagoni, R. (1977) 'Die Vereinten Nationen und der internationale Terrorismus', in M. Funke (ed.) *Terrorismus: Untersuchungen zur Struktur und Strategie revolutionärer Gewaltpolitik*, Düsseldorf: Athenäum/Droste, pp. 259–71.

LaPierre, W. (2006) *The Global War on Your Guns: Inside the U.N. Plan to Destroy the Bill of Rights*, Nashville: Nelson Current.

Lasswell, H.D. (1936) *Politics: Who Gets What, When, How*, New York: McGraw-Hill.

—— (1956) *The Decision Process: Seven Categories of Functional Analysis*, College Park: University of Maryland.

Laursen, F. (ed.) (2002) *The Amsterdam Treaty: National Preference Formation, Interstate Bargaining and Outcome*, Odense: Odense University Press.

Lavenex, S. and Wagner, W. (2006) 'Which European public order? Sources of imbalance in the European Area of Freedom, Security and Justice', paper presented at the UACES Annual Conference, Limerick, 31 August–2 September.

Leander, A. (2005) 'Shifting political identities and global governance of the justified use of force', in M. Lederer and P.S. Müller (eds) *Criticizing Global Governance*, Basingstoke: Palgrave Macmillan, pp. 125–43.

Leeuwen, M. van (ed.) (2003) *Confronting Terrorism: European Experiences, Threat Perceptions and Policies*, The Hague: Kluwer Law International.

Legorjus, P. (1990) *La morale et l'action*, Paris: Fixot.

Legro, J.W. (1994) 'Military culture and inadvertent escalation in World War II', *International Security* 18 (4): 108–42.

—— (1996) 'Culture and preferences in the international cooperation two-step', *American Political Science Review* 90 (1): 118–37.

Legro, J.W. and Moravcsik, A. (1999) 'Is anybody still a realist?', *International Security* 24 (2): 5–55.

Leishman, F. and T. Wood (2000) 'Mood swings: debates and developments in drugs policing', in F. Leishman, B. Loveday and S.B. Savage (eds) *Core Issues in Policing*, Harlow: Longman, 2nd edn, pp. 140–55.

Levi, M. (1991) 'Regulating money laundering: the death of bank secrecy in the UK', *British Journal of Criminology* 31 (2): 109–25.

—— (1995) 'Covert policing and the investigation of "organized fraud:" the English experience in international context', in C. Fijnaut and G.T. Marx (eds) *Undercover: Police Surveillance in Comparative Perspective*, The Hague: Kluwer, pp. 195–212.

Levitt, G. (1986) 'Is "terrorism" worth defining?', *Ohio Northern University Law Review* 13: 97–115.

Lévy, R. (2002) 'Les livraisons surveillées de stupéfiants: légaliser pour mieux contrôler?', *Questions Pénales* 15 (5): 1–3.

Lieshout, R.H., Segers, M.L.L. and Vleuten, A.M. van der (2004) 'De Gaulle, Moravcsik, and The Choice for Europe: soft sources, weak evidence', *Journal of Cold War Studies* 6 (4): 89–139.

Loader, I. and Walker, N. (2006) 'Necessary virtues: the legitimate place of the state in the production of security', in J. Wood and B. Dupont (eds) *Democracy, Society and the Governance of Security*, Cambridge: Cambridge University Press, pp. 165–95.

—— (2007) *Civilizing Security*, Cambridge: Cambridge University Press.

Lodge, J. (1981) 'The European Community and terrorism: establishing the principle of "extradite or try"', in J. Lodge (ed.) *Terrorism: A Challenge to the State*, Oxford: Martin Robertson, pp. 164–94.

—— (1988) 'Terrorism and Europe: some general considerations', in J. Lodge (ed.) *The Threat of Terrorism*, Boulder: Westview, pp. 1–28.

—— (1989) 'Terrorism and the European Community: towards 1992', *Terrorism and Political Violence* 1 (1): 28–47.

Lodge, J. and Freestone, D. (1982) 'The European Community and terrorism: political and legal aspects', in Y. Alexander and K.A. Myers (eds) *Terrorism in Europe*, London and Canberra: Croom Helm, pp. 79–101.

Lutiis, G. de (1991) *Storia dei servizi segreti in Italia*, Roma: Editori Riuniti.

—— (2003) 'Terrorism in Italy: receding and emerging issues', in M. van Leeuwen (ed.) *Confronting Terrorism: European Experiences, Threat Perceptions and Policies*, The Hague: Kluwer Law International, pp. 95–109.

Lyman, M.D. (1989) *Practical Drug Enforcement: Procedures and Administration*, New York: Elsevier.

—— (2002) *Practical Drug Enforcement: Second Edition*, Boca Raton, Florida: CRC Press.

McAllister, W.B. (2000) *Drug Diplomacy in the Twentieth Century: An International History*, London and New York: Routledge.

McCoy, A.W. (2003) *The Politics of Heroin: CIA Complicity in the Global Drug Trade*, Chicago: Lawrence Hill.

McDonald, W.F. (1990) 'Politics, criminal prosecution, and the rationalization of justice: Italy and the United States', *International Journal of Comparative and Applied Criminal Justice* 14 (1): 15–24.

MacGregor, S. (1998) 'Pragmatism or principle? Continuity and change in the British approach to treatment and control', in R. Coomber (ed.) *The Control of Drugs and Drug Users: Reason or Reaction*, Amsterdam: Harwood, pp. 131–54.

Magnani, L. (2001) *Abduction, Reason, and Science: Processes of Discovery and Explanation*, New York: Kluwer Academic.

Mahoney, J. (2003) 'Strategies of causal assessment in comparative historical analysis', in J. Mahoney and D. Rueschemeyer (eds) *Comparative Historical Analysis in the Social Sciences*, Cambridge: Cambridge University Press, pp. 337–72.

Mahoney, J. and Goertz, G. (2006) 'A tale of two cultures: contrasting quantitative and qualitative research', *Political Analysis* 14 (3): 227–49.

Maihofer, W. (1975) 'Internationale Zusammenarbeit bei der Verbrechensbekämpfung', *Die Polizei* 66 (1): 24–5.

Malcolm, J.L. (2002) *Guns and Violence: The English Experience*, Cambridge, MA: Harvard University Press.

Mancini, G.F. (2000) 'The Italians in Europe', *Foreign Affairs* 79 (2): 122–34.

Mancusi, R. (1976) *Legislazione sugli stupefacenti: Raccolta sistematica di tutte le disposizioni legislative intervenute in materia*, Roma: Informazioni Parlamentari.

Mandel, R. (2002) *Armies without States: The Privatization of Security*, Boulder: Lynne Rienner.

Mani, R. (2004) 'The root causes of terrorism and conflict prevention', in J. Boulden and T.G. Weiss (eds) *Terrorism and the UN: Before and After September 11*, Bloomington and Indianapolis: Indiana University Press, pp. 219–41.

Mann, M. (1993) *The Sources of Social Power: The Rise of Classes and Nation-States, 1760-1914*, Cambridge: Cambridge University Press.

Manna, A. and Barone Ricciardelli, E. (1989) 'The limitations and formalities of criminal law provisions concerning narcotics: considerations on legislation in Italy', in H.-J. Albrecht and A. van Kalmthout (eds) *Drug Policies in Western Europe*, Freiburg: Max-Planck-Institut, pp. 195–234.

Mantelli Caraccia, C. (1973) *La politica della droga: Come è stato e come sarà amministrato in Italia il fenomeno-droga*, Roma: Napoleone.

March, J.G. and Olsen, J.P. (1989) *Rediscovering Institutions: The Organizational Basis of Politics*, New York: Free Press.

—— (1998) 'The institutional dynamics of international political orders', *International Organization* 52 (4): 943–69.

Mark, Sir R. (1977) *Policing a Perplexed Society*, London: Allen & Unwin.

Martini, F. (1999) *Nome in codice: Ulisse. Trent'anni di storia italiana nelle memorie di un protagonista dei Servizi segreti*, Milano: Rizzoli.

Marx, G.T. (1974) 'Thoughts on a neglected category of social movement participant: the agent provocateur and the informant', *American Journal of Sociology* 80 (2): 402–40.

—— (1988) *Undercover: Police Surveillance in America*, Berkeley: University of California Press.

Masciandaro, D. (ed.) (2004) *Global Financial Crime: Terrorism, Money Laundering and Offshore Centres*, Aldershot: Ashgate.

Massai, A. (1990) 'La cooperazione europea nella lotta al terrorismo', in N. Ronzitti (ed.) *Europa e terrorismo internazionale: Analisi giuridica del fenomeno e Convenzioni internazionali*, Milano: Franco Angeli, pp. 73–106.

May, T., Warburton, H., Turnbull, P.J. and Hough, M. (2002) *Times They Are A-Changing: Policing of Cannabis*, York: Joseph Rowntree Foundation.

Mearsheimer, J.J. (2001) *The Tragedy of Great Power Politics*, New York: Norton.

Mermet, F. (2001) 'Le renseignement: facteur d'union ou de discorde? Quel jeu pour la France entre l'Europe et l'Amérique?', in Démocraties (ed.) *Quel renseignement pour le XXIe siècle?*, Panazol: Lavauzelle, pp. 47–57.

Meyer, J. (2001) 'Umsetzung der Palermo-Konvention gegen das internationale Organisierte Verbrechen', in Fraktion der SPD im Deutschen Bundestag (ed.) *Transnationale Organisierte Kriminalität und Geldwäsche: Parasit der Weltwirtschaft, Konferenz der SPD-Bundestagsfraktion am 15. März 2001 in Berlin*, Berlin: Fraktion der SPD im Deutschen Bundestag, pp. 57–60 (= Dokumente 60/01).

Meyer, J.W., Boli, J., Thomas, G.M. and Ramirez, F.O. (1997) 'World society and the nation state', *American Journal of Sociology* 103 (1): 144–79.

Migliorino, L. (1976) 'International terrorism in the United Nations debates', in *Italian Yearbook of International Law*, Milano: Giuffre, Vol. 2, pp. 102–21.

—— (1979a) 'Il terrorismo internazionale nei dibattiti alle Nazioni Unite', in L. Bonanate (ed.) *Dimensioni del Terrorismo Politico: Aspetti Interni e Internazionali, Politici e Giuridici*, Milano: Franco Angeli, pp. 255–82.

—— (1979b) 'L'Italia e il terrorismo internazionale', in L. Bonanate (ed.) *Dimensioni del Terrorismo Politico: Aspetti Interni e Internazionali, Politici e Giuridici*, Milano: Franco Angeli, pp. 313–46.

Miller, A.H. (1980) *Terrorism and Hostage Negotiations*, Boulder: Westview.

Ministero del Lavoro e delle Politiche Sociali (2003) *Tossicodipendenze: Relazione annuale al parlamento sullo stato delle tossicodipendenze in Italia 2002*, Roma: Istituto Poligrafico e Zecca dello Stato.

Ministero dell'Interno (1992) *Schengen: Compendio sulle 'consegne controllate'*, Roma: Ministero dell'Interno.

—— (2001) *Rapporto sullo stato della sicurezza in Italia*, Roma: Ministero dell'Interno.

—— (2003) *Rapporto sullo stato della sicurezza in Italia*, Roma: Ministero dell'Interno.

Mission Interministérielle de la Lutte contre la Drogue et la Toxicomanie (1999) *Plan triennal de lutte contre la drogue et de prévention des dépendances, 1999–2001: Rapport officiel*, Paris: Documentation Française.

—— (2003) *Situation en France sur la consommation et le trafic d'Heroïne*. Online. Available HTTP: <http://www.diplomatie.gouv.fr> (accessed 19 January 2005).

—— (2004) *Plan gouvernemental de lutte contre les drogues illicites, le tabac et l'alcool, 2004–2008*, Paris: Documentation Française.

Mitrany, D. (1943) *A Working Peace System*, London: Royal Institute of International Affairs.

Mitsilegas, V. (2003) *Money Laundering Counter-Measures in the European Union: A New Paradigm of Security Governance versus Fundamental Legal Principles*, The Hague: Kluwer.

Mitsilegas, V., Monar, J. and Rees, W. (2003) *The European Union and Internal Security: Guardian of the People*, Basingstoke: Palgrave Macmillan.

Monar, J. (2006) 'Justice and Home Affairs', *Journal of Common Market Studies* 44 (S1): 101–17.

Monjardet, D. (1996) *Ce que fait la police: Sociologie de la force publique*, Paris: Éditions la Découverte.

Monjardet, D. and Lévy, R. (1995) 'Undercover policing in France: elements for description and analysis', in C. Fijnaut and G.T. Marx (eds.) *Undercover: Police Surveillance in Comparative Perspective*, The Hague: Kluwer, pp. 29–53.

Montebourg, A. (2001) *La Grande-Bretagne, Gibraltar et les dépendances de la Couronne*, Tome 1, Vol. 4 of A. Montebourg (ed.) *Rapport d'information déposé par la Mission d'Information Commune sur les obstacles au contrôle et à la répression de la délinquance financière et du blanchiment des capitaux en Europe*, Paris: Assemblée Nationale (= Rapport d'Information 2311).

—— (2002) *La lutte contre le blanchiment des capitaux en France: un combat à poursuivre*, Tome 2 of A. Montebourg (ed.) *Rapport d'information déposé par la Mission d'Information Commune sur les obstacles au contrôle et à la répression de la délinquance financière et du blanchiment des capitaux en Europe*, Paris: Assemblée Nationale (= Rapport d'Information 2311).

Moravcsik, A. (1993a) 'Preferences and power in the European Community: a liberal intergovernmentalist approach', *Journal of Common Market Studies* 31 (4): 473–523.

—— (1993b) 'Armaments among allies: European weapons collaboration, 1975–1985', in P.B. Evans, H.K. Jacobson, and R.D. Putnam (eds) *Double-Edged Diplomacy: International Bargaining and Domestic Politics*, Berkeley: University of California Press, pp. 128–67.

—— (1997) 'Taking preferences seriously: a liberal theory of international politics', *International Organization* 51 (4): 513–53.

—— (1998) *The Choice for Europe: Social Purpose and State Power from Messina to Maastricht*, Ithaca: Cornell University Press.

—— (2000) 'De Gaulle between grain and grandeur: the political economy of French EC policy, 1958–1970', *Journal of Cold War Studies* 2 (2): 3–43 and 2 (3): 4–68.

Moravcsik, A. and Nicolaïdis, K. (1999) 'Explaining the Treaty of Amsterdam: interests, influence, institutions', *Journal of Common Market Studies* 37 (1): 59–85.

Morgenthau, H.J. (1948) *Politics among Nations: The Struggle for Power and Peace*, New York: Alfred A. Knopf.

—— (1963) 'The political conditions for an international police force', *International Organization* 17 (2): 393–403.

Mott, J. and Bean, P. (1998) 'The development of drug control in Britain', in R. Coomber (ed.) *The Control of Drugs and Drug Users: Reason or Reaction?*, Amsterdam: Harwood, pp. 31–48.

Mouvement d'Action Judiciaire (1977) *L'affaire Croissant*, Paris: Maspero.

Müller, H. (2004) 'Arguing, bargaining and all that: communicative action, rationalist theory and the logic of appropriateness in international relations', *European Journal of International Relations* 10 (3): 395–435.

Münkler, H. (2005) *The New Wars*, Cambridge: Polity Press.

Murphy, J.F. (1975) 'United Nations proposals on the control and repression of terrorism', in M.C. Bassiouni (ed.) *International Terrorism and Political Crimes*, Springfield, IL: Charles C. Thomas, pp. 493–506.

—— (1989) 'Defining international terrorism: a way out of the quagmire', in *Israel Yearbook on Human Rights* 19, The Hague: Nijhoff, pp. 13–37.

Nadelmann, E.A. (1986) 'Unlaundering dirty money abroad: U.S. foreign policy and financial secrecy jurisdictions', *Inter-American Law Review* 18 (1): 33–81.

—— (1990) 'Global prohibition regimes: the evolution of norms in international society', *International Organization* 44 (4): 479–526.

—— (1993) *Cops across Borders: The Internationalization of U.S. Criminal Law Enforcement*, University Park: Pennsylvania State University Press.

Nakajima, C. (2004) 'Politics: offshore centres, transparency and integrity. The case of the UK territories', in D. Masciandaro (ed.) *Global Financial Crime: Terrorism, Money Laundering and Offshore Centres*, Aldershot: Ashgate, pp. 219–46.

Narr, W.-D. (2003) 'Die Technologisierung der Polizei und ihre dringliche Politisierung', *Bürgerrechte & Polizei/CILIP* 76 (3): 6–11.

Nixon, R. (1971) 'President calls for comprehensive drug control program: message from President Nixon to the Congress', transmitted on 17 June 1971, *Department of State Bulletin*, 12 July 1971: 58–66.

Nomikos, J.M. (2005) 'An EU intelligence service for confronting terrorism', in B.S. Sergi (ed.) *Ethical Implications of Post-Communist Transition Economics and Politics in Europe*, Bratislava: Iura, pp. 449–61.

Nuttall, S.J. (1992) *European Political Co-operation*, Oxford: Clarendon Press.

Occhipinti, J.D. (2003) *The Politics of EU Police Cooperation: Towards a European FBI?*, Boulder: Lynne Rienner.

Offenbach, D. and Dolan, K. (1978) 'Drug control: the failure of the law?', in D.J. West (ed.) *Problems of Drug Abuse in Britain: Papers presented to the Cropwood Round-Table Conference, December 1977*, Cambridge: University of Cambridge, Institute of Criminology, pp. 146–54.

Oliva, G. (1967) 'Il traffico degli stupefacenti', *Rivista della Guardia di Finanza* 15: 429–58.

Pantaleone, M. (1979) *Mafia e droga*, Torino: Einaudi.

Pastore, F. (2003) 'L'Europa della sicurezza interna', in G. Vacca (ed.) *L'unità dell'Europa: Rapporto 2003 sull'integrazione europea*, Bari: Dedalo, pp. 233–50.

—— (2004) 'Visas, borders, immigration: formation, structure, and current evolution of the EU entry control system', in N. Walker (ed.) *Europe's Area of Freedom, Security and Justice*, Oxford: Oxford University Press, pp. 89–142.

Peirce, C.S. (1998) *Collected Papers of Charles Sanders Peirce*, Bristol: Thoemmes (= reprint of the 1931–58 edn).

Pelletier, M. (1978) *Rapport de la Mission d'étude sur l'ensemble des problèmes de la drogue*, Paris: Documentation Française.

Pepino, L. (1991) *Droga e legge: Tossicodipendenza, prevenzione e repressione*, Milano: Franco Angeli.

Peterson, M.J. (2004) 'Using the General Assembly', in J. Boulden and T.G. Weiss (eds) *Terrorism and the UN: Before and After September 11*, Bloomington and Indianapolis: Indiana University Press, pp. 173–97.

Piepenschneider (1996) *Regierungskonferenz 1996: Synopse der Reformvorschläge zur Europäischen Union*, 2nd edn, working paper, Sankt Augustin: Kondrad-Adenauer Stiftung.

Pierson, P. (2004) *Politics in Time: History, Institutions, and Social Analysis*, Princeton: Princeton University Press.

Pizzorno, A. (1998) *Il potere dei giudici: Stato democratico e controllo della virtù*, Roma and Bari: Laterza.

Plachta, M. (2005) 'Joint investigation teams: a new form of international cooperation in criminal matters', *European Journal of Crime, Criminal Law and Criminal Justice* 13 (2): 284–302.

Plenel, E. (1986) 'La France et le terrorisme: la tentation du sanctuaire', *Politique Étrangère* 51 (4): 919–35.

Poggi, G. (1978) *The Development of the Modern State: A Sociological Introduction*, Stanford: Stanford University Press.

—— (1990) *The State: Its Nature, Development and Prospects*, Stanford: Stanford University Press.

—— (2000) *Forms of Power*, Cambridge: Polity Press.

Police College (1977) *Counter-Terrorism: A Comparative Study of Counter-Terrorism Arrangements in America, France, Sweden, Germany and Holland, with References to Particular Terrorist Incidents (Exercise Europa)*, Bramshill, UK: Police College (= Command Course, Part II, 1977).

Poncet, D. and Gully-Hart, P. (1986) 'The European model', in M.C. Bassiouni (ed.) *International Criminal Law, Vol. II: Procedure*, Dobbs Ferry: Transnational Publishers, pp. 461–543.

Popiz, H. (1992) *Phänomene der Macht*, 2nd edn, Tübingen: J.C.B. Mohr.

Porch, D. (1995) *The French Secret Services: From the Dreyfus Affair to the Gulf War*, New York: Farrar, Strauss and Giroux.

Powell, R. (1994) 'Anarchy in international relations theory', *International Organization* 48 (2): 313–44.

Pridham, G. (1981) 'Terrorism and the state in West German during the 1970s: a threat to stability or a case of political over-reaction?', in J. Lodge (ed.) *Terrorism: A Challenge to the State*, Oxford: Martin Robertson, pp. 11–56.

Pütter, N. (1998) *Der OK-Komplex: Organisierte Kriminalität und ihre Folgen für die Polizei in Deutschland*, Münster: Westfälisches Dampfboot.

Pütter, N. and Diederichs, O. (1994) 'V-Personen, Verdeckte Ermittler, NoePs, qualifizierte Scheinaufkäufer und andere', *Bürgerrechte & Polizei/CILIP* 49 (3): 24–37.

Ragin, C.C. (1987) *The Comparative Method: Moving beyond Qualitative and Quantitative Strategies*, Berkeley: University of California Press.

—— (2000) *Fuzzy-Set Social Science*, Chicago: University of Chicago Press.

—— (2004) 'Turning the tables: how case-oriented research challenges variable-oriented research', in H.E. Brady and D. Collier (eds) *Rethinking Social Inquiry: Diverse Tools, Shared Standards*, Lanham: Rowman and Littlefield, pp. 123–38.

Raimondi, G. (1990) 'Una corte penale europea?', in N. Ronzitti (ed.) *Europa e terrorismo internazionale: Analisi giuridica del fenomeno e convenzioni internazionali*, Milano: Franco Angeli, pp. 127–44.

Rebscher, E. (1981) 'Rechtliche und organisatorische Grundlagen der internationalen Zusammenarbeit bei der Drogenbekämpfung', in Bundeskriminalamt (ed.) *Polizeiliche Drogenbekämpfung*, Wiesbaden: Bundeskriminalamt, pp. 155–76.

Rees, W. (2006) *Transatlantic Counter-Terrorism Cooperation: The New Imperative*, London and New York: Routledge.

Reeve, S. (2000) *One Day in September*, London: Faber and Faber.

Reichertz, J. (2003) *Die Abduktion in der Qualitativen Sozialforschung*, Opladen: Leske und Budrich.

Reinares, F. (ed.) (2000) *European Democracies against Terrorism: Governmental Policies and Intergovernmental Cooperation*, Aldershot: Ashgate.

Reinhard, W. (2000) *Geschichte der Staatsgewalt: Eine vergleichende Verfassungsgeschichte Europas von den Anfängen bis zur Gegenwart*, München: C.H. Beck.

Risse, T. (2000) '"Let's argue": communicative action in world politics', *International Organization* 54 (1): 1–39.

Risse, T., Ropp, S.C. and Sikkink, K. (1999) *The Power of Human Rights: International Norms and Domestic Change*, Cambridge: Cambridge University Press.

Rixen, T. (2005) 'Internationale Kooperation im asymmetrischen Gefangenendilemma: das OECD Projekt gegen schädlichen Steuerwettbewerb', Discussion Paper 12 of Wirtschaftsuniversität Wien, SFB International Tax Coordination. Online. Available HTTP: <http://www2.wu-wien.ac.at/taxlaw/sfb/Working_Papers/workingpaper12.pdf> (accessed 4 June 2006).

Robertson, K.G. (1994) 'Practical police cooperation in Europe: the intelligence dimension', in M. Anderson and M. den Boer (eds) *Policing across National Boundaries*, London and New York: Pinter, pp. 106–18.

Rodotà, S. (1984) 'La risposta dello stato al terrorismo: gli apparati', in G. Pasquino (ed.) *La prova delle armi*, Bologna: il Mulino, pp. 77–91.

Rognoni, V. (1989) *Intervista sul terrorismo*, Roma and Bari: Laterza.

Rosen, S.J. and Frank, R. (1975) 'Measures against international terrorism', in D. Carlton and C. Schaerf (eds) *International Terrorism and World Society*, London: Croom Helm, pp. 60–8.

Rosenberg, J. (1994) *The Empire of Civil Society: A Critique of the Realist Theory of International Relations*, London: Verso.

Ruggie, J.G. (1998) *Constructing the World Polity: Essays on International Institutionalization*, London and New York: Routledge.

Rutherford, A. and Green, P. (1989) 'Illegal drugs and British criminal justice policy', in H.-J. Albrecht and A. van Kalmthout (eds) *Drug Policies in Western Europe*, Freiburg: Max Planck Institut, pp. 383–407.

Ryan, M., Mann, C. and Stilwell, A. (2003) *The Encyclopedia of the World's Special Forces: Tactics, History, Strategy, Weapons*, London: Amber Books.

Santino, U. (1997) 'Fighting the Mafia and organized crime: Italy and Europe', in W.F. McDonald (ed.) *Crime and Law Enforcement in the Global Village*, Highland Heights: ACJS/Anderson, pp. 151–66.

Sartori, G. (1970) 'Concept misformation in comparative politics', *American Political Science Review* 64 (4): 1033–53.

—— (ed.) (1984) *Social Science Concepts: A Systematic Analysis*, Beverly Hills: Sage.

Savona, E.U. (1997) *Responding to Money Laundering: International Perspectives*, Amsterdam: Harwood.

Schalken, T. and Pronk, M. (2002) 'On Joint Investigation Teams, Europol and supervision of their joint actions', *European Journal of Crime, Criminal Law and Criminal Justice* 10 (1): 70–82.

Scharpf, F.W. (1997) *Games Real Actors Play: Actor-Centered Institutionalism in Policy Research*, Boulder: Westview.

Schedler, A. (2007) 'Mapping contingency', in I. Shapiro and S. Bedi (eds) *Political Contingency: Studying the Unexpected, the Accidental, and the Unforeseen*, New York: New York University Press, forthcoming.

Schenk, D. (1968) 'Rauschgiftgefahren in der BRD', *Die Polizei* 59 (10): 298–304.

Schmitt, C. (1922) *Politische Theologie: Vier Kapitel zur Lehre von der Souveränität*, München and Leipzig: Duncker & Humblot; trans. G. Schwab (1986) *Political Theology: Four Chapters on the Concept of Sovereignty*, Cambridge, MA: MIT Press.

—— (1932) *Der Begriff des Politischen*, München and Leipzig: Duncker & Humblot; trans. G. Schwab (1995) *The Concept of the Political*, Chicago: University of Chicago Press.

Scholzen, R. and Froese, K. (2001) *GSG 9: Innenansichten eines Spezialverbandes des Bundesgrenzschutzes*, Stuttgart: Motorbuch Verlag.

Schorkopf, F. (ed.) (2006) *Der Europäische Haftbefehl vor dem Bundesverfassungsgericht*, Tübingen: Verlag Mohr Siebeck.

Schröm, O. (2005) *Gefährliche Mission: Die Geschichte des erfolgreichsten deutschen Terrorfahnders*, Frankfurt A. M.: Scherz.

Schur, E.M. (1962) *Narcotic Addiction in Britain and America: The Impact of Public Policy*, Bloomington: Indiana University Press.

Senato della Repubblica (1973) *Ratifica ed esecuzione della Convenzione Unica sugli stupefacenti, adottata a New York il 30 marzo 1961 e del Protocollo di emendamento, adottato a Ginevra il 25 marzo 1972: Disegno di legge comunicato alla presidenza il 10 aprile 1973 (N. 1046)*, Roma: Tipografia del Senato.

—— (1976) *Repressione e prevenzione dell'abuso di stupefacenti e sostanze psicotrope: Indagine conoscitiva*, Roma: Tipografia del Senato.

Senato della Repubblica and Camera dei Deputati (1999) *Bilanci e Prospettive della Lotta al Riciclaggio: Palermo, 9 e 10 luglio 1998*, Roma: Tipografia del Senato.

Shapiro, J. and Suzan, B. (2003) 'The French experience of counter-terrorism', *Survival* 45 (1): 67–98.

Shaw, J. (ed.) (1979) *Ten Years of Terrorism: Collected Views*, London: Royal United Services Institute for Defence Studies.

Shelley, L.I. and Picarelli, J.T. (2002) 'Methods not motives: implications of the convergence of international organized crime and terrorism', *Police Practice and Research* 3 (4): 305–18.

Sheptycki, J.W.E. (2000a) 'Policing the virtual launderette: money laundering and global governance', in J.W.E. Sheptycki (ed.) *Issues in Transnational Policing*, London and New York: Routledge, pp. 135–76.

—— (2000b) 'The "Drug War": learning from the paradigm example of transnational policing', in J.W.E. Sheptycki (ed.) *Issues in Transnational Policing*, London and New York: Routledge, pp. 201–28.

—— (2002a) *In Search of Transnational Policing: Towards a Sociology of Global Policing*, Aldershot: Ashgate.

—— (2002b) 'United Kingdom', in M. den Boer (ed.) *Organised Crime: A Catalyst in the Europeanisation of National Police and Prosecution Agencies*, Maastricht: European Institute of Public Administration, pp. 507–50.

Sievert, K.-G. (2004) *Kommandounternehmen: Spezialeinheiten im weltweiten Einsatz*, Hamburg: Verlag E.S. Mittler & Sohn.

Silj, A. (ed.) (1998) *L'alleato scomodo: I rapporti fra Roma e Washington nel Mediterraneo. Sigonella e Gheddafi*, Milano: Corbaccio.

Simmons, B.A. and Martin, L.L. (2004) 'International organizations and institutions', in W. Carlsnaes, T. Risse and B.A. Simmons (eds) *Handbook of International Relations*, London: Sage, pp. 192–211.

Singer, J.D. (1961) 'The levels-of-analysis problem in international relations', *World Politics* 14 (1): 77–92.

Singer, P.W. (2003) *Corporate Warriors: The Rise of the Privatized Military Industry*, Ithaca and London: Cornell University Press.

Sion, L. (2006) ' "Too sweet and innocent for war"? Dutch peacekeepers and the use of violence', *Armed Forces & Society* 32 (3): 454–74.

Siragusa, C. (1966) *The Trail of the Poppy: Behind the Mask of the Mafia*, Englewood Cliffs: Prentice-Hall.

Smith, T. (1987) 'Counter terrorism: administrative response in the United Kingdom', *Public Policy and Administration* 2 (1): 42–54.

Snow, P. and Phillips, D. (1970) *Leila's Hijack War: The True Story of 25 Days in September 1970*, London: Pan.

Sobiek, S.M. (1994) 'Democratic responses to international terrorism in Germany', in D.A. Charters (ed.) *The Deadly Sin of Terrorism: Its Effect on Democracy and Civil Liberty in Six Countries*, Westport, CT: Greenwood Press, pp. 43–72.

Spruyt, H. (1994) *The Sovereign State and its Competitors: An Analysis of Systems Change*, Princeton: Princeton University Press.

Stanbrook, I. and Stanbrook, C. (2000) *Extradition: Law and Practice*, Oxford: Oxford University Press.

Stessens, G. (2001) 'The FATF "black list" of non-cooperative countries or territories', *Leiden Journal of International Law* 14 (1): 199–208.

Stoessel, W.J. (1979) 'U.S.-German cooperation in narcotics control', *Drug Enforcement*, February 1979: 8–12.

Stortoni-Wortmann, L. (2000) 'The police response to terrorism in Italy from 1969 to 1983', in F. Reinares (ed.) *European Democracies against Terrorism: Governmental Policies and Intergovernmental Cooperation*, Aldershot: Ashgate, pp. 147–71.

Strauss, A. and Corbin, J. (1998) *Basics of Qualitative Research: Techniques and Procedures for Developing Grounded Theory*, 2nd edn, Thousand Oaks: Sage.

Taillon, J.P. de B. (2001) *The Evolution of Special Forces in Counter-Terrorism: The British and American Experiences*, Westport: Praeger.

Teschke, B. (2003) *The Myth of 1648: Class, Geopolitics, and the Making of Modern International Relations*, London and New York: Verso.

Thomas, C. (2003) 'Disciplining globalization: international law, illegal trade, and the case of narcotics', *Michigan Journal of International Law* 24 (2): 550–75.

Thomson, J.E. (1994) *Mercenaries, Pirates, and Sovereigns: State-Building and Extraterritorial Violence in Early Modern Europe*, Princeton: Princeton University Press.

—— (1995) 'State sovereignty in international relations: bridging the gap between theory and empirical research', *International Studies Quarterly* 39 (2): 213–33.

Tilly, C. (1984) *Big Structures, Large Processes, Huge Comparisons*, New York: Russel Sage Foundation.

—— (1985) 'War making and state making as organized crime', in P.B. Evans, D. Rueschemeyer and T. Skocpol (ed.) *Bringing the State Back In*, Cambridge: Cambridge University Press, pp. 169–91.

—— (1990) *Coercion, Capital, and European States, AD 990-1990*, Cambridge, MA: Basil Blackwell.

Toman, J. (1991) 'Developing an international policy against terrorism', in S. Flood (ed.) *International Terrorism: Policy Implications*, Chicago: Office of International Criminal Justice, pp. 111–29.

Tophoven, R. (1985) *GSG 9: Kommando gegen Terrorismus*, Koblenz: Bernard & Graefe Verlag.

Trebach, A.S. (1982) *The Heroin Solution*, New Haven and London: Yale University Press.

Tupman, B. and Tupman, A. (1999) *Policing in Europe: Uniform in Diversity*, Exeter: Intellect.

United Kingdom of Great Britain and Northern Ireland (1971) *Anglo-European Collaboration against Drug Abuse and Trafficking: Technical Committee on Enforcement*, London: HM Customs and Excise and Home Office.

United Nations (1964a) *United Nations Conference for the Adoption of a Single Convention on Narcotic Drugs, New York 24 January to 25 March 1961: Official Records Volume I*, New York: United Nations.

—— (1964b) *United Nations Conference for the Adoption of a Single Convention on Narcotic Drugs, New York 24 January to 25 March 1961: Official Records Volume II*, New York: United Nations.

—— (1968) *The Control of Psychotropic Substances not under International Control: Questionnaire to Governments and Replies Received by the Secretary-General*, UN Doc. E/CN.7/518 (13 August).

—— (1973a) *United Nations Conference for the Adoption of a Protocol on Psychotropic Substances, Vienna 11 January to 19 February 1971: Official Records Volume I,* New York: United Nations.

—— (1973b) *United Nations Conference for the Adoption of a Protocol on Psychotropic Substances, Vienna 11 January to 19 February 1971: Official Records Volume II,* New York: United Nations.

—— (1973c) *United Nations Conference to Consider Amendments to the Single Convention on Narcotic Drugs, 1961, Geneva 6 to 24 March 1972: Official Records Volume II*, New York: United Nations.

—— (1974) *United Nations Conference to Consider Amendments to the Single Convention on Narcotic Drugs, 1961, Geneva 6 to 24 March 1972: Official Records Volume I*, New York: United Nations.

United Nations Division of Narcotic Drugs (1973) *Information Letter No. 12*, December.

Van der Spuy, E. (1997) 'Regionalism in policing: from lessons in Europe to developments in Southern Africa', *African Security Review* 6 (6): 46–53.

Vannucci, M. (1973) *Le storie di droga del Commissario Cristaldi*, Firenze: Le Monnier.

Vercher, A. (1992) *Terrorism in Europe: An International Comparative Legal Analysis*, Oxford: Clarendon Press.

Vogel, J. (2001) 'Abschaffung oder Auslieferung? Kritische Anmerkungen zur Reform des Auslieferungsrechts in der Europäischen Union', *Juristenzeitung* 56 (19): 937–43.

Vogel, W. (2003) 'Frankreich, der 11. September 2001 und das Recht', in B. Rill (ed.) *Terrorismus und Recht: Der wehrhafte Rechtsstaat*, München: Hanns Seidel Stiftung, pp. 35–44.

Wagner, W. (2003) 'Building an international security community: the democratic peace and the politics of extradition in Western Europe', *Journal of Peace Research* 40 (6): 695–712.

Wagstaff, A. and Maynard, A. (1988) (eds) *Economic Aspects of the Illicit Drug Market and Drug Enforcement Policies in the United Kingdom*, London: Stationery Office (= Home Office Research Study No. 95).

Walker, C. (2003) 'Policy options and priorities: British perspectives', in M. van Leeuwen (ed.) *Confronting Terrorism: European Experiences, Threat Perceptions and Policies*, The Hague: Kluwer Law International, pp. 11–35.

Walker, N. (ed.) (2004) *Europe's Area of Freedom, Security and Justice*, Oxford: Oxford University Press.

Walsh, J.I. (2006) 'Intelligence-sharing in the European Union: institutions are not enough', *Journal of Common Market Studies* 44 (3): 625–643.

Walter, C. (2004) 'Defining terrorism in national and international law', in C. Walter, S. Vöneky, V. Röben, and F. Schorkopf (eds) *Terrorism As a Challenge for National and International Law: Security Versus Liberty?*, Berlin: Springer, pp. 23–43.

Waltz, K.N. (1959) *Man, the State and War: A Theoretical Analysis*, New York: Columbia University Press.

—— (1979) *Theory of International Politics*, Reading: Addison Wesley.

Warner, B.W. (1994) 'Great Britain and the response to international terrorism', in D.A. Charters (ed.) *The Deadly Sin of Terrorism: Its Effect on Democracy and Civil Liberty in Six Countries*, Westport, CT: Greenwood Press, pp. 13–42.

Weber, M. (1956) *Staatssoziologie*, Berlin: Duncker & Humblot.

—— (1968 [1922]) *Economy and Society: An Outline of Interpretive Sociology*, 3 vols, Berkeley: University of California Press.

—— (1992 [1919]) *Politik als Beruf*, Stuttgart: Reclam.

Weinberg, L. and Eubank, W.L. (1987) *The Rise and Fall of Italian Terrorism*, Boulder and London: Westview.

Wendt, A. (1999) *Social Theory of International Politics*, Cambridge: Cambridge University Press.

—— (2003) 'Why a world state is inevitable', *European Journal of International Relations* 9 (4): 491–542.

Wharton, P.J. (1981) *The Police Response to Terrorism in Britain and Western Germany Today*, London: Metropolitan Police, mimeo.

Whitehouse, A. (2003) 'A brave new world: the impact of domestic and international regulation on money laundering prevention in the UK', *Journal of Financial Regulation and Compliance* 11 (2): 138–45.

Wiesbrock, K. (2002) 'Wer ist Terrorist', *Vereinte Nationen* 50 (2): 72–3.

Wiesel, G. (1985) 'Die EDV-unterstützte internationale Zusammenarbeit: Stand und Perspektiven', in Bundeskriminalamt Wiesbaden (ed.) *Internationale Verbrechensbekämpfung: Europäische Perspektiven. Arbeitstagung des Bundeskriminalamtes Wiesbaden vom 5.-8. November 1984*, Wiesbaden: Bundeskriminalamt, pp. 211–80.

Wieviorka, M. (1990) 'French politics and strategy on terrorism', in B.M. Rubin (ed.) *The Politics of Counterterrorism: The Ordeal of Democratic States*, Washington: Foreign Policy Institute, pp. 61–90.

—— (1991) 'France faced with terrorism', *Terrorism* 14 (3): 157–70.

Wilkinson, P. (1974) *Political Terrorism*, Basingstoke: Macmillan.

—— (1981) 'Proposals for government and international responses to terrorism', in P. Wilkinson (ed.) *British Perspectives on Terrorism*, London: Allen & Unwin, pp. 161–93.

—— (1988) 'British policy on terrorism: an assessment', in J. Lodge (ed.) *The Threat of Terrorism*, Boulder: Westview Press, pp. 29–55.

—— (2000) *Terrorism versus Democracy: The Liberal State Response*, London: Frank Cass.

Williams, I. (2002) 'Abbringen, Verweigerung, Zusammenarbeit: der Ausschuss des Sicherheitsrats zur Bekämpfung des Terrorismus', *Vereinte Nationen* 50 (6): 213–16.

Wilson, J.Q. (1978) *The Investigators: Managing FBI and Narcotics Agents*, New York: Basic Books.

Wouters, J. and Naert, F. (2004) 'Of arrest warrants, terrorist offences and extradition deals: an appraisal of the EU's main criminal law measures against terrorism after "11 September" ', *Common Market Law Review* 41 (4): 909–35.

Wulf, H. (2005) *Internationalizing and Privatizing War and Peace*, Basingstoke: Palgrave Macmillan.

Zagaris, B. and Kingma, E. (1991) 'Asset forfeiture international and foreign law: an emerging regime', *Emory International Law Review* 5: 445–513.

Zürn, M. (1997) 'Assessing state preferences and explaining institutional choice: the case of intra-German trade', *International Studies Quarterly* 41 (2): 295–320.

Zürn, M. and Checkel, J.T. (2005) 'Getting socialized to build bridges: constructivism and rationalism, Europe and the nation-state', *International Organization* 59 (4): 1045–79.

Index

Note: Page numbers in **bold** denote text in tables or figures.

Lightning Source UK Ltd.
Milton Keynes UK
UKHW02f0609260818
327736UK00010B/223/P

9 780415 543514